W9-BAE-143

LEADING LADIES

II.

ALSO BY KAY BAILEY HUTCHISON

Nonfiction

Nine and Counting: The Women of the Senate (coauthor)
American Heroines: The Spirited Women Who Shaped Our Country

LEADING LADIES

American Trailblazers

KAY BAILEY HUTCHISON

HARPER

An Imprint of HarperCollins*Publishers*
www.harpercollins.com

FIRST EDITION

DESIGNED BY RENATO STANISIC

Library of Congress Cataloging-in-Publication Data is available upon request.

ISBN: 978–0–06–113824–9
ISBN–10: 0–06–113824–X

07 08 09 10 11   OV/RRD   10 9 8 7 6 5 4 3 2 1

To Bailey and Houston Hutchison, my beloved children.
When they begin to think of what their life's goals will be,
I hope this book will be one of their inspirations to always do
their best, contribute something to our great country,
and never give up when their dreams are distant
and seem beyond reach.

Copyright 2007 (handwritten)

IX. (handwritten)

Contents

Preface xi *to XII* .

Introduction xiii *to XV*

chpt. ONE: *The Good Fight: Women in the Military* 1 *to 38 =*

chpt. TWO: *First Ladies: The Hardest Unpaid Job in the World* 39 *to 126 =*

chpt. THREE: *If There's a Book You Want to Read:
Novelists and Journalists* 127 *to 165 = 39 pgs.*

chpt. FOUR: *A Dream of the Future: Women's Suffrage
and Civil Rights* 166 *to 206 =*

chpt. FIVE: *Everything I Discovered Was New: Women
in Medicine and Public Health* 207 *to 254 =*

chpt. SIX: *Lifting the Veil of Nature: The Nobel Prize in Science* 255 *to 292 =*

chpt. SEVEN: *Curing Social Misery: The Settlement House
and Peace Movements* 293 *to 334 =*

EIGHT: *Commitment Overcomes Adversity:*
The Making of Leaders 335 to 365 = 31 pgs

Acknowledgments 367 to only 1 pg. 367. = 1 pg.

Suggestions for Further Reading 369 to 378 = 10 pgs.

Index 379 to pg. 396... = 18 pgs.

Preface ⟩ goes to pg XII

When I wrote *American Heroines: The Spirited Women Who Shaped Our Country* in 2004, I was inspired by the first women to break barriers in business, aviation, sports, government, journalism, religion, and the arts. I have gotten so much pleasure from people telling me they read *American Heroines* and what they liked (or didn't); what they thought should be added (no one suggested deletions).

I was also touched by the letters and comments from friends and strangers suggesting women and professions that should have been included. Among the most common: Why not the military? What about science? Where are the suffragettes? The wheels started turning, and when the editor of *American Heroines* suggested I do another book, I gladly accepted the challenge. I reread the letters and e-mails I had received, and their ideas became the starting point for *Leading Ladies.*

I actually thought the military chapter would be pretty thin, since women were only allowed to officially enter the military in World War II. Was I wrong! Women fought in wars as far back as the American Revolution. Some in early wars were wives who wanted to be near their husbands; some just believed in the cause and dressed like men so they would not be recognized. Away from the battlefield, women have been among the most accomplished spies in every war. Women's desire to contribute to the war effort in more conventional ways, their courage, and the need for every man to be available for combat finally spurred the creation of the Women's Army Auxiliary Corps in the run-up to World War II. The Capitol was deluged with ten thousand letters per week from women wanting to join the effort. Congress passed the law to allow women to put on military uniforms in 1942.

My goal in writing the book is to inspire young women (and men) with the stories of women who have found their own path rather than following a conventional road. But it isn't just young people who can benefit from role models.

I think we all go through periods in our lives when we are in transition and our focus isn't clear. At these times, I find it best to step back and try to rejuvenate my spirit by rethinking and defining my goals. Reading biographies of people whose courage, brilliance, creativity, or perseverance has made a positive contribution to the world is one of the ways to get new ideas that might lead to a new direction.

Someday, I hope to read an interview with a woman who has just landed on Mars or discovered a cure for cancer and who was encouraged to pursue her goals by a book she read about an early pioneer who broke barriers to rise to the top of the military, be elected to Congress, or win the Nobel Prize.

End of Preface

Introduction

XIII.

goes to pg XV =.
(3 pgs.)

I have always believed that the United States is the greatest country on Earth because women have become full participants in our society. When 100 percent of a nation's brainpower is put to work, the result is exponentially improved.

But in every field, the opportunity has been won, not given. At first, even basic education was not considered necessary for girls. Innovators like Emma Willard and Catharine Beecher founded girls' schools and advocated access to public education in the early 1800s. Without their early effort, the course of this country could have been substantially altered. In 1821, Emma Willard also opened the Troy Female Seminary, the first institution to offer young women a curriculum comparable to that of a men's college.

Elizabeth Blackwell, the first woman to attend medical school, may have been admitted to Geneva Medical College in 1847 by a fluke, and her presence created an uproar when she entered the anatomy classroom, where a male cadaver was being dissected. "Some of the students blushed; some were hysterical," she wrote in her diary. Within a few years, several medical schools for women opened in Philadelphia and other cities, but another generation would pass before women were allowed to attend the men's medical colleges.

The first women who wanted to pursue scientific goals met the same resistance. They did not have the college preparation of their male counterparts, and if they did luck into graduate-degree programs, they could not get the appointments as professors that allowed them to do research. In fact, when Gerti Cori, the first American woman to win the Nobel Prize in science, did the work for which she was recognized in 1947, she was a mere research associate. She was finally made a full professor only in the year the award was bestowed.

Some of the women profiled in *Leading Ladies* were committed to a cause and excelled, always overcoming obstacles to achieve their goals, whether it was helping the poor, improving health care, or fighting for the nation's security.

The struggle for women's right to vote took seventy years. The leaders who initiated the effort in the 1840s died before their dream of universal suffrage came true. The Nineteenth Amendment was finally ratified in 1920, ushering in a new era of political participation by women and increasing their chances for election to public office.

Some in the book did not seek a national role, but when thrust into it, made significant contributions. First Ladies who married for love did not seek fame. But most turned their unrequested public role into an opportunity to make a positive impact on our country. Another chapter profiles women who responded to a personal crisis by rising to the occasion and becoming leaders in their own right.

Women authors have had profound influence on our nation's culture through literature. Harriet Beecher Stowe's *Uncle Tom's Cabin* aided the movement to abolish slavery. Pearl Buck cracked the window so Americans could begin to see the culture of China; Amy Tan opened the window wider. Liz Balmaseda did the same for the lives of Cuban refugees in the United States.

XV.

Two books I have written, *American Heroines: The Spirited Women Who Shaped Our Country* and *Leading Ladies,* are a tribute to women trailblazers. Without their spirit and perseverance, this country might not be the undisputed economic power of the world. The women in each generation of our young country have contributed enormously to our prosperity.

Thomas J. Rusk, who was Texas secretary of war in 1836, described the strength of the women when Texas fought to win its independence from Mexico. All the men had left the town of Nacogdoches to join the fight, and the women and children were left behind, not sure if the Mexican Army or the Indians might attack. "The men of Texas deserved much credit, but more was due the women," he wrote in his diary. "Armed men facing a foe could not but be brave; but the women, with their little children around them, without means of defense or power to resist, faced danger and death with unflinching courage." My own great-great-grandmother, Anna Mary Taylor, was one of those women. After losing all four of her children (ages seven and under) when she fled Nacogdoches during the war, she returned to help settle the new Republic of Texas and bore nine more children.

I could only tell the stories of a few of the incredible women who have contributed to the strength and progress of our nation. It is my firm belief that without the participation of women throughout our society, the United States would not be the world's greatest superpower. And the best is yet to come.

End of Intro.

XVI.

LEADING LADIES

XVIII

CHAPTER 1

The Good Fight

Women in the Military

CAPTAIN, I SHALL NOT GO INTO THAT CELLAR SHOULD
THE ENEMY COME. I WILL TAKE A SPEAR WHICH I CAN USE AS
WELL AS ANY MAN AND HELP DEFEND THE FORT.
–Mary Hagidorn (American, late eighteenth century)

In my time in the Senate, I have seen the role women play in the military transformed from limited support to full-fledged participation. Women throughout our history have shown great bravery–as spies for the American cause, as volunteers in hospitals, as ferry pilots–but full recognition has been slow to arrive. Women received general officer status for the first time in 1970, and there are still no women with four stars–the highest peacetime rank. Several of our top military leaders have daughters who have attended the prestigious military academies. Once while listening to a four-star general's briefing about women's roles in military conflict, I said to him, "I just want your daughter to be able to have enough experience to succeed you–if she earns the right." In other words, if we expect to attract the best women to military careers, they must know they have a chance of reaching the top. To do that, women must have enough time in combat zones to allow them to earn the credibility essential to leading a branch of the armed services.

There have been many issues to address, and we are addressing them. There were early concerns about fraternization between the sexes and about sexual harassment. There have been problems in this area, but there is zero tolerance for misconduct, and I believe the professionalism in our military is second to none in the world.

Women have proven themselves in our elite service academies and are gaining combat experience, flying fighter and carrier airplanes in war zones, and participating in many ground missions as well. This has been the traditional route to the top for men, and women are now in the pipeline. Though this is relatively new for the armed services, American women on the front lines in war is not. In the Revolutionary War, our first war for freedom, women participated when they could, sometimes even disguising themselves as men in order to join the battle.

SYBIL LUDINGTON

In many ways, Sybil Ludington was a typical child of colonial America. Born in Connecticut in 1761, Sybil had eleven brothers and sisters by the time she reached her early teens. For more than a decade, Henry and Abigail Ludington had been farming over two hundred acres of land in Fredericksburgh, now Putnam County, New York, where Henry Ludington became a prosperous farmer and mill owner, was involved in the political and religious life of his region, and served in local militias. He joined his first militia in 1756, when he was just seventeen, as a loyal British subject, but by the early 1770s he had transferred his allegiance to the independence movement. As colonel of a four-hundred-man regiment in Dutchess County, New York, Henry Ludington so effectively helped stymie British efforts to supply their troops that British General William Howe offered a reward of 300 English guineas to whoever captured or killed him.

One of the Ludington family's neighbors, Ichabod Prosser, thought he could surprise the colonel at home and collect the reward. He and a group of loyalists surrounded the Ludingtons' farmhouse one spring night, hoping to catch the colonel unawares. But Henry Ludington, who knew the rich reward would prove irresistible to someone, had drilled his children to keep watch over the house at night. When Sybil caught sight of Ichabod Prosser's men, she quickly roused four or five of her oldest brothers and sisters. The youngest was about six, but by lighting candles in the rooms visible to the Prosser band and marching back and forth in front of the windows, they gave the impression that a sizable armed guard was protecting the place from within. The Prosser group didn't dare storm the house. Instead, they hid until dawn and then withdrew.

By the time the American Revolution reached the Ludingtons' doorstep in 1777, Sybil was sixteen. On April 24, two thousand British troops, under General William Tryon's command, landed on the coast of Connecticut and headed for Danbury to seize the supplies the Continental Army stored there. A number of American soldiers were in the area, serving under Generals David Wooster, Benedict Arnold, and Gold Selleck Silliman, but they couldn't prevent the British from occupying Danbury. The British destroyed the supplies they found in town and burned nineteen houses, a meetinghouse, and twenty-two barns and storehouses, all of them belonging to people who sided with the revolutionaries.

On the farms around Fredericksburgh, seventeen miles from Danbury, the members of Colonel Ludington's militia were busy with spring planting. Colonel Ludington called on Sybil, an expert rider, to sound the alarm while he readied his regiment to pursue the British in Connecticut. Sybil rode all night in a hard rain, making a forty-mile circuit through the heart of Putnam County, from Carmel and Mahopac in the south as far north as Stormville, in Dutchess County. Early the next morning, the colonel led his four hundred men toward Connecticut to join forces with the twelve hundred troops already pursuing General Tryon's soldiers, who were hurrying back to their ships on Long Island Sound. Sybil's ride earned her the nickname "the female Paul Revere." In fact, her more famous predecessor rode only half as far as she did, on a clear, moonlit night–and he was forty years old, not sixteen.

Besides the lost supplies, the Americans suffered some casualties, among them General David Wooster, who was mortally wounded while attacking the British at North Salem, New York. But the Americans counted Danbury and its aftermath as a success. "The stores destroyed there have been purchased at a high price to the enemy," wrote Alexander Hamilton. "The spirit of the people on the occasion does them great honor–is a pleasing proof that they have lost nothing of that primitive zeal with which they began that contest, and will be a galling discouragement to the enemy of repeating attempts of the kind."

Lydia Darragh

Toward the end of 1777, the war entered a winter lull as both sides waited for better weather before resuming full-scale operations. The British general, William Howe, was in Philadelphia with many of his officers. The general was quartered in a mansion next door to the house of a Quaker couple, William and Lydia Darragh, and their children. The British wanted to take over the Darraghs' house to billet officers, but Lydia managed to resist them. She did agree, however, to allow them to use a large room in the house for meetings. The Darraghs were warned to stay away from the room whenever the officers met, but on December 2, Lydia listened behind a door as General Howe briefed his staff about plans to attack General Washington and the Continental troops who were encamped at Valley Forge and Whitemarsh, about twelve miles outside Philadelphia.

As Quakers, the Darraghs were pacifists, but they were loyal to the revolutionary cause, and one of their sons was even an officer in the Continental Army. This wasn't the first time that Lydia Darragh had learned secrets useful to General Washington. Previously, however, she had sent her fourteen-year-old son, on the pretext of visiting his older brother, to deliver the intelligence. This time she decided the news was so urgent that she would deliver it herself. She went next door to Howe's headquarters, explained that she needed to buy flour at a mill in nearby Frankford, and was granted a pass. She did buy some flour, but before heading home, she made her way through the snow toward Whitemarsh to alert Washington to Howe's intentions. She reported the intelligence either to Washington or to one of the general's cavalry officers and then quietly returned home. General Howe never discovered who the spy was, but Lydia Darragh's bravery denied him the element of surprise. When the British realized the Americans were expecting them, they abandoned their plans to attack before spring.

Of course, Lydia Darragh wasn't a spy, and Sybil Ludington's one-time exploit didn't make her a soldier, but the American Revolution was a war in which much of the fighting (and intelligence work) was done by volunteers. They were usually men, but not always. If all the able-bodied men in a community went off to join the fighting, women sometimes organized to defend themselves and aid the war effort. In one case, the women of Pepperell and Groton, Massachusetts, commanded by one of their own, guarded the local bridge over the Nashua River. They didn't try to disguise themselves, but they wore men's clothes and wielded whatever weapons they could find, expecting the British to attack. The assault didn't materialize, but when an area Tory, Captain Leonard Whiting, tried to cross the bridge, they searched him, found intelligence intended for the British hidden in his boots, and handed their prisoner and the captured evidence over to the local militia.

DEBORAH SAMPSON

There were, however, women who were determined to enlist in the Continental Army. Some of them, it's true, were seeking adventure, and others were enticed by the enlistment bonuses offered in an effort to attract men to serve. But as historian Linda DePauw has written, the overwhelming majority of the women "were not a bunch of eccentrics. These were the sort of good, solid, patriotic American females from whom the members of the DAR [Daughters of the American Revolution] are proud to claim descent." To enlist in the army, though, they had to pretend to be young men. The most famous of these military masqueraders was a young woman named Deborah Sampson.

Deborah was a great-great-granddaughter of William Bradford (1590–1657), author of *Of Plymouth Plantation* and governor of the colony nearly from its founding to his death. Her father, Henry Sampson, was a farmer in Middleborough, Massachusetts, but when Deborah was five, he abandoned his family, and Deborah's mother sent her to work as a servant, a common practice in indigent families, especially those with many young children (Deborah had six brothers and sisters). From 1770 to 1778, when Deborah turned eighteen, she lived and worked in the house of Jeremiah and Susannah Thomas, pious but not wealthy farmers in Middleborough. Whether or not she was formally an indentured servant is unclear, but her obligations to the Thomases ended when she reached her eighteenth birthday late in 1778. Her status made her a rarity in colonial America: an adult, controlled neither by her absent father nor by a husband (since she was unmarried), she was, in the legal parlance of the time, "masterless," subject to no authority but her own.

The Thomases must have treated Deborah well. She wasn't able to attend school, but she found the leisure to educate herself by borrowing books from the Thomas children. She also learned to spin and weave. These skills made it possible for her to earn a living; from 1779 to 1782, she taught in a one-room schoolhouse in Middleborough, and she found work as a weaver, a craft that was much in demand during the Revolution, when Americans boycotted British cloth.

Deborah actually enlisted in the Continental Army twice. The first time, in Middleborough, in early spring of 1782, she signed on as "Timothy Thayer." She apparently had a change of heart, because she failed to report for duty and immediately returned most of the enlistment bounty she had received. But a month later, on May 20, she went to a nearby town, enlisted under the name "Robert Shurtlief" (the spelling varies), received a bounty of 60 pounds, and three days later, at West Point, New York, was mustered into the Massachusetts Fourth Regiment.

In 1782, Deborah would have seemed an excellent prospect to army recruiters desperate to fill their quotas. Over five foot seven (taller than many full-grown men of the period), strong, physically fit, and able to read and write, she was even invited to join the regiment's elite light-infantry company. At this stage late in the war (a peace treaty was signed in November 1783), many of Deborah's companions would have been undersized and often underage adolescents who were assigned to duty as "waiters" (in contemporary terms, orderlies) and drummer boys. By contrast, Deborah was close to ideal—except for the fact that she was female.

Exactly what Deborah's duties were as a light infantryman is uncertain, but we do know that she was wounded at least twice. She almost certainly joined a number of small patrols in Westchester County, and saw most of her action during the second half of 1782. Although General Washington was worried about the possibility of a large attack by British regulars, the small scale of the fighting suggests that the enemy her regiment faced were Tory irregulars. After being wounded in the head, she wrote, "I considered this as a death wound, or as being equivalent to it; as it must, I thought, lead to the discovery of my sex." She somehow managed to avoid detection, probably by contriving to receive little or no medical attention.

It was actually after the fighting had ended, in 1783, that Deborah was finally "unmasked." By this time, she was a waiter on the staff of General John Paterson. She was part of the general's entourage in Philadelphia, where many of the new country's luminaries were gathered while the Continental Congress was in session. While in Philadelphia, Deborah fell ill and was hospitalized under the care of

Dr. Barnabas Binney, a kindly physician who discovered her identity and took pains to protect her secret–perhaps by transferring her first to the matron's quarters in the hospital and then to his own house for recuperation.

Back at West Point in October 1783, Deborah received an honorable discharge from General Henry Knox. While the war was going on, a woman who was found to have lied her way into the army would most likely have been fined and imprisoned. In Paterson's own regiment in 1777 (he was then a colonel), a woman named Ann Bailey who had enlisted by pretending to be a man was prosecuted. But in Deborah Sampson's case, things were different. The war had been won, and Deborah had played a small but real role in winning it. She had spent nearly eighteen months as a soldier and had shown courage in battle and chastity and sobriety in camp. During a war in which drunkenness, whoring, profanity, and desertion were common, she had proven herself an exemplary "Christian soldier" who just happened to be a woman. Paul Revere wrote after meeting her, "When I heard her spoken of as a soldier, I formed the idea of a tall, masculine female, who had a small share of understanding, without education, and one of the meanest of her sex–when I saw and discoursed with her I was agreeably surprised to find a small, effeminate, and conversable woman, whose education entitled her to a better situation in life."

Margaret Corbin

A small number of women accompanied their husbands when the men joined the Continental Army. Some may have been motivated by patriotic fervor, while others were women who preferred not to be separated from their spouses. These wives, who made no attempt to conceal their true identities, rarely if ever aroused suspicion. One of the most illustrious was Margaret Corbin. Margaret's life, before and after the Revolutionary War, had not been easy. Not much is known about her earliest years. She was born on the Pennsylvania frontier in 1751, and in 1756 she and a younger brother somehow escaped an Indian raid in which her father was killed and her mother captured. The children were raised by relatives, and when Margaret was twenty or twenty-one, she married John Corbin, who joined a Pennsylvania artillery regiment as a "matross"–what would now be called a gunner's assistant. Margaret followed her husband and probably expected to play the roles that women often filled in army camps and on the battlefield: washing, cooking, carrying water, and nursing wounded and sick soldiers. But when her husband's company, the First Pennsylvania Artillery, was surrounded by British and Hessian troops in the battle of Fort Washington in September 1776, Margaret assisted her husband in loading his cannon. He was killed early in the fighting, and she took over as cannoneer. Wounded during the battle, Margaret became a prisoner of the British when the Americans finally surrendered on November 16. She was soon released, but after being widowed at Fort Washington, losing the use of one arm as a result of her wounds, and spending time as a prisoner of war, Margaret's claim to being an American soldier was difficult to deny. When an Invalid Regiment was formed in 1777 to provide for wounded soldiers and employ them as guards, recruiters, and trainers, Margaret was made a member. In 1779, Congress granted her a military pension of half a soldier's pay for life, as well as rations. She thus became the first American woman to receive a military pension.

The members of Congress who voted Margaret Corbin her pension didn't necessarily consider her a true army veteran, however, and never explicitly referred to her as one. Their resolution stresses that she "was wounded and disabled . . . whilst she heroically filled the post of her husband who was killed by her side serving a piece of artillery." Even after she remarried, she continued to receive her pension. As one official letter noted, "her present husband is a poor crippled invalid who is of no service to her but rather adds to her trouble. . . ." In fact, when it was discovered that she hadn't received the daily allowance of liquor that was traditionally part of military rations (on the grounds that women weren't entitled to receive liquor), Colonel Tench Tilghman of West Point wrote, "It appears clearly to me that the order forbidding the issue of Rum to women does not extend to Mrs. Corbin." Somewhat prudishly he added, "Perhaps it would not be prudent to give them to her all in liquor." In fact, Margaret wasn't interested in the liquor at all, but in a lump-sum payment equal to the value of the withheld liquor allowance so that she could "procure sundry necessities that will render her present wretchedness a little more tolerable." When Margaret Corbin died, in about 1800, she was buried in a small cemetery on property a few miles south of West Point. The land was acquired in the nineteenth century by J. P. Morgan Sr. After his widow, Frances Tracy Morgan, died in 1925, the Morgan heirs feared that the property might be sold for development, so a DAR committee arranged for Margaret Corbin's remains to be re-interred in the West Point military cemetery. Her new headstone, erected April 26, 1926, bore a bronze plaque showing a large woman (Margaret was about five feet, eight inches) tending a cannon and an inscription that identifies her as "A Heroine of the Revolution."

Women played relatively small roles in the War of 1812 and the Mexican-American War (1846–1848), but the American Civil War was another story. Its toll of six hundred thousand dead on both sides makes it by far the costliest war, in human terms, in American history. As a result, the constant demand for new soldiers ensured that virtually anyone, male or female, who was determined to enlist could manage to elude the barriers of age, size, fitness, or sex that were intended to screen out unsuitable recruits. In the words of one scholar, "If a candidate was tall enough, wasn't lame, deaf or blind, had enough teeth to open powder cartridges, and a trigger finger with which to shoot, he (or she) was usually accepted." Historians today agree that the number of women who wore the uniforms of the Union or Confederacy at some time during the four-year-long conflict was probably close to a thousand, and the total may well have been higher.

As happened during the American Revolution, a few women went to war alongside their husbands without masquerading as men, while others pretended to be the brothers or comrades of their spouses and fiancés. One newlywed, Hattie Martin of Pennsylvania, donned men's clothing when she and her new husband enlisted, but revealed her identity to the examining physician, who let the couple join up. As often as not, women who enlisted with their husbands stayed at the front even after their men had been killed. When Amy Clarke's husband was mortally wounded at Shiloh, she stayed with her company until she herself was wounded and captured by Union troops, who sent her home—wearing a dress—after she had recovered. Some recruiting officers may have winked at the rules out of friendship with or sympathy for the protagonists, but that usually wasn't necessary. The women simply donned loose-fitting men's clothing, mimicked (as best they could) masculine hairstyles and mannerisms, and relied on the casualness of the physical exams to do the rest, just as sickly and underage enlistees did.

Too little is known about the women, Northerners or Southerners, who went to war—or dreamed of doing so—to speculate about how many acted out of patriotism, how many were seeking adventure, and how many saw a chance for independence and economic opportunity that was accessible to most men but very few women, especially those who lacked education.

Even women who accepted their traditional role as ladies sometimes chafed at the restrictions. Lucy Breckenridge confided in her journal, "I would gladly shoulder my pistol and shoot some Yankees if it were allowable." And there were others, like the twenty women in the Shenandoah Valley who wrote to Judah Benjamin, the Confederate secretary of war, proposing to form a volunteer regiment of women for local defense after all the men in the vicinity between age sixteen and sixty had been drafted. They gave up the idea after Benjamin declined their offer.

SARAH EMMA EDMONDS

We do know a great deal about the thinking of one "soldier girl," as women in the military were popularly known, whether passing as men or not. Sarah Emma Edmonds joined the Second Michigan Cavalry in 1861 under the alias "Frank Thompson" and served until 1863. Probably the best-known woman soldier in the Civil War, Sarah was born in New Brunswick, Canada, in 1841. At the age of seventeen, she left home disguised as a young man and found work in the United States as a traveling book salesman for a Hartford, Connecticut, company. She may have left Canada to escape from a tyrannical father or to avoid being pressured into marriage. She adopted her alias and male disguise because she assumed it would be easier to live independently if people believed she was a man.

When the Civil War started, Sarah was living in Michigan; less than six weeks later, she enlisted as Private Frank Thompson. An entry in her diary written during the early days of the war gives voice to her feelings: "It is true, I am not an American . . . not obliged to remain here during the terrible strife . . . But it is not my desire to seek personal ease and comfort while so much sorrow and distress fills the land."

Attached to a cavalry regiment, Sarah nevertheless started her army career as an infantryman, assigned to drill, picket, and guard duty. During the battle of Fredericksburg, she was General Orlando Poe's orderly, and then for six months a nurse in the regimental hospital and a general hospital in Georgetown, where she distinguished herself by the "care, kindness, and self-sacrificing devotion" she showed to patients. After the disastrous Union defeat in the first battle of Bull Run, on July 21, 1861, Sarah also served as a field nurse. "I had inherited from my mother a rare gift of nursing," she later wrote. In 1861 and 1862, she also carried the mail and troop orders, perhaps until the end of the year, when she was appointed General Poe's orderly. It was while working as a courier that she contracted malaria, but she enjoyed the freedom the work offered so much that she continued doing it despite the danger to her health.

The risk of discovery was greatest for women soldiers who required medical attention after being wounded or falling ill. A woman whose identity was discovered was almost always dismissed from service, so women often tried to conceal their conditions and refused medical help. Sarah suffered injuries three times, once in battle, but managed to avoid the doctors each time. In August 1862, while she was carrying mail between Manassas and Washington, she was thrown from her mule and suffered contusions to her leg and a lung hemorrhage (she coughed blood for a week and was lame for longer, but managed to camouflage the severity of her injuries). Another time, her horse bit her; again, she treated the wound herself. Finally, during a battle, the horse she was riding was shot, and Sarah broke a bone when she fell.

When the symptoms of her malaria returned in March 1863, Sarah refused, as usual, to go to the hospital, but she was afraid that if her condition worsened, she would be found out. So she applied for a leave of absence. When it was denied, she deserted near Lebanon, Kentucky, rather than risk discovery. "I never for a moment considered myself a deserter," she wrote. "I simply left because I could hold out no longer, and to . . . become a helpless patient in a hospital was sure discovery, which to me was far worse than death." More than thirty years later, when Sarah, who suffered from arthritis, requested supplementary benefits (she'd been granted a pension in 1884), the Pension Bureau refused on the grounds that the army had no medical record of her ever having been sick or injured during the war. In her rebuttal, Sarah struck the same note again: "Had I been what I represented myself to be, I should have gone to the hospital. . . . But being a woman I felt compelled to suffer in silence . . . in order to escape detection of my sex. *I would rather have been shot dead*, than to have been known to be a woman and sent away from the army."

From the scarce writings available, it appears that male

comrades of women who masqueraded as men usually liked and even admired the women with whom they served. This was true of single women as well as those who accompanied their husbands. Even pregnant women (who frequently succeeded in carrying their pregnancies to term without being detected) were described with affection. After one woman had given birth, another soldier described her as "a young and good-looking corporal, whose courtesy and military bearing . . . struck the officers very favorably, and who was a real soldierly, thoroughly military fellow."

Sarah Edmonds was no exception. The other soldiers liked her, and even those who knew—or suspected—her secret steadfastly kept it to themselves. She did take Jerome John Robbins into her confidence. He was an assistant surgeon in the Second Michigan Infantry, whom Sarah befriended at the regimental hospital in Alexandria, Virginia, where she was then a nurse. The otherwise circumspect Sarah's reasons for revealing to Robbins that she was a woman just two weeks or so after they'd met aren't clear (she may have taken a romantic interest in him), and her revelation strained their friendship for a time. Robbins apparently discouraged her interest—he insisted that he had a girlfriend back in Michigan—but he told no one about Sarah's identity. He recorded the fact in his diary on November 16, 1861, and then sealed the pages, which he marked with these words: "Please allow these leaves to be closed until the author's permission is given for their opening." Interestingly, Sarah did not tell Robbins what her real name was.

If romance was the reason for the temporary rift in Sarah's friendship with Robbins, the attachment probably wasn't her only military infatuation. Researchers have unearthed the diaries of two members of the Second Michigan Regiment, in which the soldiers hint that the cause of Sarah's decision to desert in April 1863 may have been not malaria (and her fear of being discovered were she sent to hospital) but a broken heart. Sarah's later testimony disputes that suggestion, but we will never be sure. We do know that in late 1862 she was attracted to Assistant Adjutant General James Reid, a lieutenant in the Seventy-ninth New York Infantry. There is no evidence that this relationship was any more substantial than the first, but Reid was married, so it is possible that this rejection left Sarah feeling trapped in an assumed identity she had outgrown. Just as important, these diaries confirm that at least two soldiers in the Second Michigan knew—or strongly suspected—that Frank Thompson was a woman, but they didn't consider betraying her, either.

After recuperating from her battle with malaria, Sarah surfaced again in Oberlin, Ohio, this time without her disguise. She served as a nurse under the auspices of the U.S. Sanitary Commission, the civilian corps of nurses headed by health-care reformer Dorothea Dix. In 1864, with the war still raging, she published a somewhat fictionalized memoir of her wartime experiences—originally under the sensational title *Unsexed; or, The Female Soldier*, but rechristened the next year *Memoirs of a Soldier, Nurse, and Spy*, a more demure title. The book (published by W. S. Williams, the Hartford firm that had formerly employed "Frank Thompson" as a salesman, and Jones Bros. in Philadelphia) was a popular success. It sold 175,000 copies.

Like many memoir writers of that time, Sarah borrowed liberally from fiction she had read and stories—fact or fancy—she had learned. The military experiences she wrote about were her own, although she omitted mentioning that she had done her soldiering as Frank Thompson. Her accounts of spying for the Union, though they are still repeated today as authentic, could have been invented or adapted from the exploits of other women. In her account of her espionage, she claimed to have impersonated a male slave, an Irish woman peddler, a female fugitive slave, and a Kentucky gentleman. Sarah never explicitly recanted her account, but when she applied for a federal pension in 1884, she danced around the question: "There is so much *mean* deception necessarily practiced by a spy that I much prefer that everyone should believe that I never was beyond the enemies lines rather than fasten upon me by oath a thing that I despise so much."

Whether her account was true or only partly true, Sarah did not publish *Memoirs of a Soldier, Nurse, and Spy* for personal profit. Despite the fact that she had little or no money at the time, she assigned almost all the royalties the book earned to the U.S. Sanitary Commission and the U.S. Christian Commission, two organizations dedicated to the soldiers' welfare.

Not long after the Civil War ended, Sarah returned to Michigan, where in 1867 she married Linus H. Seelye, another New Brunswick native and a carpenter. For the rest of her life, Sarah struggled with poverty and poor health. She lost three young children, born between 1869 and 1874 (the Seelyes also adopted two boys, who survived), and moved often, in search of a healthy climate and work for Linus. For years, the couple hopscotched over the American South, from La Teche, Louisiana, where Sarah ran a "colored orphanage" that was supported by the Freedman's Aid Society; to Missouri, whose climate agreed with her but where she lost Alice, her youngest child; to Fort Scott, Kansas, where a building boom promised carpentry work for Linus, and where Sarah dreamed of founding a rest home for Civil War veterans.

Poor health plagued Sarah for the rest of her life. In 1882 she decided to apply for a government pension for her military service, a challenge for someone who had been a soldier under an assumed name and gender. She wrote to her publisher and former employer, as well as to the Michiganders with whom she had served, requesting affidavits and testimonials to her army service and good character. To offer her old comrades visible proof that she and Frank Thompson were one and the same person, she attended a reunion of members of her former regiment held in Flint, Michigan, in 1884—this time, of course, as Sara Emma Edmonds Seelye.

The testimonials were many and glowing, and by 1886 Sarah had overcome the Pension Bureau's skepticism, been exonerated of the charge of desertion, and had her pension—$12 a month for life. Both the money and her old comrades' praises must have raised Sarah's spirits, but they weren't enough to restore her health or lift her and her husband out of poverty. Sometime after 1890, the Seelyes moved to La Porte, Texas, a little more than twenty miles up Galveston Bay. In 1897, Sarah became the first woman member of the Grand Army of the Republic (GAR), thanks to the efforts of the organization's McClellan Post in Houston. Three years after she died, in 1898, the McClellan Post had her remains re-interred in the GAR plot reserved for Civil War veterans in Houston's Washington Cemetery.

LORETA JANETA VELASQUEZ

In 1876, a remarkable volume of memoirs, *The Woman in Battle*, appeared. Its author was Loreta Janeta Velasquez. In the course of six hundred pages, her book narrates the details of her experience as a Confederate officer (disguised as "Lieutenant Henry Buford"), spy, secret service agent, blockade runner, and bon vivant. Despite the extravagant claims the author makes, many authorities have concluded that there is at least a kernel of truth in Loreta's memoir, though most people agree with the assessment of Confederate general Jubal Early (himself a hero of a number of the war's major battles): although Loreta may have seen action, "the book that is given to the public in her name cannot be the truthful narration of the adventures of any person." Among her claims: she recruited a battalion of soldiers in Arkansas in just four days; participated in major battles at Bull Run, Ball's Bluff, Shiloh, and other places; performed espionage in Washington, where she was in contact with President Lincoln and his generals, and throughout the North, all the while traveling nonstop, marrying, and being widowed. Most scholars believe that Loreta combined other accounts of Civil War experiences—such as those of Laura Williams, who fought under the nom de guerre Lieutenant Henry Benford—with her own exploits and those of literary works to fabricate an epic tale of warfare, intrigue, and romance.

Women like Sarah Emma Edmonds and Loreta Janeta

Velasquez, who embellished their own memoirs by weaving together borrowed episodes, invention, and autobiography, were often motivated by the desire to write popular books. Among their other reasons, women of the mid-nineteenth century often needed to earn their livings, and most lines of work open to men remained closed to them. The military, in fact, was one of them: a woman who had succeeded in masquerading as a man could earn her soldier's wages throughout the war. But once she was demobilized, she might not have a profession or trade by which to sustain herself.

ROSE GREENHOW

As difficult as postwar life sometimes was for women, surviving the war itself was the greater challenge. Rose O'Neal, born in Maryland in 1817, moved to Washington as a teenager, married Dr. Robert Greenhow, who worked in the State Department, and became an active member of Washington society. Related to James and Dolley Madison, close friend of presidents and other Washington luminaries, she never concealed her loyalty to the Southern cause. Invited to spy for the Confederacy, Rose used her access to prominent people and freedom of movement to gather information. Before the first battle of Bull Run, for example, she forwarded details of planned Federal troop movements that many experts believe helped the Confederates respond successfully to the attack. Arrested, she was imprisoned in Washington, but she continued to gather intelligence and transmitted coded information to her Confederate contacts by concealing it in woven tapestries and balls of yarn. She was finally deported to Richmond from Washington and later worked for the Confederate cause in England. In 1864 she attempted to return home aboard the British blockade runner *Condor*, but the ship ran aground near the mouth of the Cape Fear River in North Carolina while maneuvering to escape a pursuing Union ship. Rather than risk being captured and imprisoned again, Rose tried to reach shore in a lifeboat, but the boat capsized, and Rose, weighed down by $2,000 in gold coins that she was attempting to deliver to the Confederacy, drowned.

Elizabeth Van Lew

Elizabeth Van Lew, a Richmond native who spied for the Union, stayed close to home throughout the war and cultivated the persona of an eccentric, possibly even crazy, woman to conceal her activities. She smuggled information into and out of Libby Prison in Richmond, where captured Union agents and soldiers were incarcerated, by hiding coded messages in books when she visited prisoners to bring them food and help nurse the sick and wounded. A network of servants, relatives, farmers, factory workers, shopkeepers, and others carried intelligence concealed in food baskets, clothing, and floral bouquets. One of her agents was a seamstress, who worked messages into her dress patterns. Another was Mary Elizabeth Bowser, a former slave of Elizabeth Van Lew, who during the war worked as a house servant in President Jefferson Davis's Richmond home.

Elizabeth's network succeeded in hiding Northern agents and escaped prisoners of war. They intercepted Confederate plans to transfer thousands of prisoners and seized documents abandoned when Grant took Richmond. In fact, General Grant was the recipient of her "intelligence bouquets"; as the Union Army neared the city, she sent him flowers with messages hidden in them.

Grant never forgot his debt to Elizabeth Van Lew. After his troops had occupied the city, the general had guards posted outside her house. Some of her pro-Confederacy neighbors even took advantage of the added security; her diary revealed that before evacuating Richmond, some neighbors gave her their valuable items for safekeeping. Later, during Grant's presidency, he appointed Elizabeth postmistress of Richmond. Others she aided remembered how much they owed their benefactor as well. One of the Union officers imprisoned in the city was Major Paul Revere, grandson of the Revolutionary hero. Major Revere ultimately lost his life at Gettysburg, but the Revere family continued to help support Elizabeth until her own death in 1890. After she died, the

Reveres even purchased the flag she had raised over Richmond when the Union troops arrived, the first Union flag flown in Richmond since the war had started.

ENTERING THE MAINSTREAM ⌐

Despite the drama—and occasional scandal—of women on the battlefield or spying on the enemy, the major contribution by women on both sides of the Civil War was accomplished behind the lines, in nursing. Civil War nurses were still overwhelmingly male, but roughly four thousand women were hired by the Union and the Confederacy to act as nurses—usually in military hospitals distant from the front lines but, as the war dragged on, increasingly in field hospitals as well. Many others—a much higher number—served as volunteers under the aegis of the U.S. Sanitary Commission.

In every American war, women had been employed as nurses, but the pay was too low (rarely more than $6 a month, even in wartime) and their training and status negligible, so few signed up and fewer stayed on. In the Civil War, the shortage of able-bodied men left North and South with no other choice than to hire women for nursing. The need was acute. Of the roughly six hundred thousand Civil War casualties, 95 percent took place *after* the battles—as men died from wounds or, more frequently, infections and illnesses such as measles, smallpox, typhoid, and dysentery. It is estimated that for every man who died after being wounded, two died of illness.

Dorothea Dix, the noted social and prison reformer who was appointed superintendent of female nurses for the Union forces, required applicants to be "plain-looking" women over thirty and mandated that nurses wear drab brown or black outfits and no jewelry. Louisa May Alcott, who worked in Washington's Union Hospital in 1862, based her fictionalized *Hospital Sketches* (1863) on her experiences as one of Dix's nurses. In the South, the Confederate Congress conferred official status on the nurses it employed, specifying both job classifications and pay.

The only woman on either side to receive a commission as a *military* officer was Sally Tompkins, who set up a hospital in a Richmond house after the first battle of Bull Run and ran it so efficiently that her patients enjoyed a remarkably high rate of recovery. Jefferson Davis made her a cavalry captain in the Confederate Army. In the Union, Mary Edwards Walker, a physician, overcame opposition to be appointed an assistant surgeon; she worked as a field surgeon as well as in the U.S. Patent Office Hospital in Washington and was awarded the Congressional Medal of Honor in 1865, still the only woman to have received the country's highest military award. (Congress withdrew her medal in 1917, but Mary refused to surrender it, and it was restored, posthumously, in 1977.)

The Army Nurse Corps (ANC), the first institutional home for American women in the military, was created in 1901 in the aftermath of the Spanish-American War. Once the preoccupation with preparedness for war had ebbed, however, interest in developing the corps subsided as well and the number of nurses on active duty never rose much above four hundred. But during the intense period of American involvement in World War I, the ANC swelled to more than twenty-one thousand members. Of these, almost half saw duty in France, where the war's grimmest fighting took place, while smaller numbers were assigned to transatlantic transport ships or to Siberia. They and their colleagues who served at the stateside general, base, and camp hospitals established the ANC as a permanent element of the U.S. armed forces.

RUBY BRADLEY

During World War II, thousands of women served as army nurses. Ruby Bradley was a nurse on a base in the Philippines when the attack on Pearl Harbor occurred. Within minutes of hearing the news, she and her comrades heard Japanese planes overhead, raining bombs on the base. Captured and imprisoned with hundreds of other nurses, servicemen, and their families, Ruby was held at the Santo Tomas Internment Camp in Manila for three years.

Under extremely harsh conditions, with very little medical equipment and almost no access to supplies, materials, or medicines, Ruby herself participated in at least 230 operations and helped to deliver 13 babies. Her group of "Angels in Fatigues" (as she and the other nurses were called) sterilized hemp and pulled it into threads to make sutures, improvised bandages from pieces of cloth, and used cooking stoves to sterilize their instruments.

Ruby Bradley was a godsend to everyone at Santo Tomas, but the children were her special preoccupation. Not only did she make sure that every newborn's arrival was recorded on a birth certificate, she turned odds and ends of old bedding into stuffed animals for the infants to play with and stashed away some of her own meager rations every day to help take the edge off the children's constant hunger. "I'd save part of my food for the children, later in the day, when they started crying and being hungry," she told an interviewer. When the camp was liberated early in 1945, she weighed about eighty-five pounds.

Ruby tended to treat her heroics and the fact that she became the most decorated woman in American military history as if they were all in a day's work. She seems to have come naturally to her devotion to saving lives. One story often told about her happened just after the Santo Tomas bombardment on December 8, 1941. The base suffered heavy casualties, so she and the surgeon knew they would be working round the clock trying to save as many people as they could. The first casualty brought in was a little boy who had been out walking with his mother. He was in shock and had already started to turn blue. After failing to revive the child, the surgeon told her, "We've got to let him go." There were too many other gravely wounded people waiting for attention.

Ruby couldn't bear to give up on the child, so before the surgeon turned to the next case he handed her the six-inch needle that is sometimes used to inject a stimulant into a heart that has stopped beating. Ruby hesitated to use the needle, but suddenly she noticed a bottle of whiskey in the operating room. She poured a little bit of the whiskey onto a piece of gauze, added some sugar, and held it to the child's mouth. As soon as she did so, the little boy started to suck on the gauze and the whiskey did the trick. When the mother came into the operating room, crying, "Where's my baby? Where's my baby?" Ruby said simply, "Do you hear him? He's just fine."

Ruby refused to rest on her laurels. By the time American troops went to Korea in 1950, she was a major, and she went with the troops as a front-line chief army nurse for the 171st Evacuation Hospital. When the Americans began their retreat from the advancing hundred-thousand-strong Chinese army, she insisted on helping the last of the sick or wounded patients onto the waiting planes before she herself boarded. Before the plane carrying her had cleared the landing strip, her ambulance blew up on the ground behind the parting craft. "You get out in a hurry when you have somebody behind you with a gun," Ruby remarked coolly. She proudly proclaimed, "I was the last one out."

The army nurses who worked close to the front lines in World War II quickly learned that their hospital tents, despite the distinctive red crosses on their roofs, were anything but safe havens. In Anzio, Italy, where American and British troops established a shallow beachhead in January 1944, many soldiers considered the hospitals so dangerous that they tried to conceal minor wounds because they felt safer on the front lines. One reason was that the Allies' four evacuation hospitals were crowded into the slender shoreline literally next door to legitimate military targets: ammunition and supply depots, headquarters, and communications.

At Anzio, about two hundred U.S. Army Nurse Corps women, dressed not in scrubs but steel helmets and combat boots, ministered to patients and assisted surgeries knowing that they were as likely as the infantrymen to end up as casualties of war. If they ever forgot that fact, the sound of exploding bombs and artillery shells and the roar of the Luftwaffe planes overhead soon reminded them. When the German army threatened to overrun the tenuous Allied positions, General Mark Clark, who commanded American troops in Italy, decided to evacuate all the nurses to eliminate the risk of their being captured, but he changed his mind in order not to send a demoralizing signal to the soldiers who had to keep fighting.

Two weeks after the initial landing, a Luftwaffe bomber jettisoned its payload over the beach, and at least one of the bombs struck the hospital. Allied fighter planes were in pursuit of the Luftwaffe craft at the time, so the German pilot may only have been trying to lighten his plane in order to gain altitude and speed, but whatever his reasons, twenty-three people were killed in the explosions. Three of them were U.S. Army Nurse Corps members; the chief nurse, Lieutenant Colonel Blanche F. Sigman, was one of the victims. Among the others who died were a Red Cross representative, male medics, and patients.

Before the fighting at Anzio ended in February, three more women nurses were killed, and a total of sixteen wounded. All of them were awarded the Purple Heart, and four became the first American women to receive Silver Stars, the U.S. Army's decoration for valor.

VIRGINIA HALL

A special category for women who made extraordinary contributions was in the mainstream but clandestine world of underground operations. Women had been spies in every war, but became integrated into official missions in World Wars I and II.

THE WOMAN WHO LIMPS IS ONE OF THE MOST DANGEROUS ALLIED AGENTS IN FRANCE. WE MUST FIND AND DESTROY HER.

–From a Gestapo flier

The notices, bearing the likeness of a striking woman named Virginia Hall, were circulated throughout the French heartland, which was under German control. The Gestapo were pursuing an American spy, but the object of their manhunt looked nothing at all like a stereotypical secret agent. That's one of the reasons she was never unmasked during two tours of clandestine duty in France, first as a British special agent and then as an American spy.

A number of better-known American women acted as intelligence agents for the Allies during World War II. The singer and dancer Josephine Baker carried messages between France and England, written in invisible ink on her sheet music. The renowned chef Julia Child helped develop the recipe for a repellant used to keep sharks away from anti-submarine mines meant for German U-boats. But there was none more daring and valuable than Virginia Hall. The daughter of a Baltimore banker and cinema owner, Edwin Lee Hall, Virginia was born in 1906, attended a private secondary school in the city, studied modern languages at Radcliffe and Barnard, attended the Sorbonne in Paris and Vienna's Konsularakademie, and returned to the United States to prepare for a career in the Foreign Service by taking courses in economics and French at George Washington University. Fluent in French, German, and Italian, she took the Foreign Service examination, but did poorly, so she decided to get some experience by working as a clerk at the U.S. embassy in Warsaw. Throughout the 1930s, she hopscotched from one embassy to another–Izmir, Vienna, Venice, Talinn.

In 1933, while on a hunting trip in Turkey, she accidentally shot herself in the leg; she developed gangrene before reaching a doctor and as a result her left leg had to be amputated below the knee. After recuperating in Baltimore, Virginia was fitted with a wooden leg and returned to work in Europe. When she learned that a State Department regulation made it impossible for anyone with an "amputation of a portion of a limb" to work in the Foreign Service, she resigned in May 1939 and went to Paris, where she volunteered for the French Ambulance Service. When Germany invaded France in 1940, she left for England, where she discovered that the British

Special Operations Executive was happy to have someone with her background and talent.

The SOE had been formed in 1940 to sabotage and subvert German operations in Europe. Its mission encompassed both gathering intelligence and aiding the Resistance. Because Virginia could pass for a Frenchwoman, in August 1941 she was given the alias Marie Monin and sent to Vichy to help set up Resistance networks. She posed as a *New York Post* reporter. As long as Vichy France was nominally autonomous, she was able to work without having her identity discovered (although she regularly switched aliases) and even filed a number of stories for the *Post* about conditions in the unoccupied zone. For over a year, from an apartment in Lyon, she acted as liaison to the French Resistance in and around the city, aided pilots whose planes had been shot down, and kept the clandestine printers and forgers in ink and paper.

The Allied invasion of North Africa in November 1942 resulted in a flood of German soldiers in Vichy and made it unsafe for Virginia to remain in France. She escaped across the Pyrenees into Spain, where she was briefly jailed near the border until the local American consul intervened. The winter crossing of the mountains was difficult for a woman with a wooden leg, which had its own code name, Cuthbert. At one point, she cabled London, "Cuthbert is giving me trouble, but I can cope." The staff at headquarters evidently forgot what her cryptic phrase referred to and cabled back, "If Cuthbert is giving you trouble, have him eliminated."

In Madrid, she pretended to be a reporter for the *Chicago Times*, but found the absence of danger boring and asked to be allowed to return to France. Instead, she found herself back in England, briefing agents and officers before they crossed the Channel into the war zone and learning to be a radio operator. Communications experts would be essential in the coming Allied invasion of France, and Virginia wanted to get back to where the action was and where she could be more effective. Meanwhile, in recognition of what she had already achieved for the war effort in France, King George VI of England made her a Member of the Order of the British Empire.

By this time, the Americans had created an intelligence service of their own, the Office of Strategic Services, led by Major General William J. ("Wild Bill") Donovan. Patterned on the SOE, the OSS worked with the British service to support the activities of the Resistance. Virginia offered to transfer to the OSS on condition that she return to France. In March 1944, she appeared in the Haute-Loire region, not far south of Vichy and Lyon, where she had been in 1942. In an area where the Resistance was already exceptionally active, she passed as a local farmer named Marcelle Montagne, a slightly stooped older woman who sold her artisanal goat cheese in village markets. She concealed her slender figure under long skirts, padded her clothes to appear heavier, and altered her gait to hide her limp or rode an old bicycle.

The news that Virginia had resumed operations reached the German command, but no one detected the spy behind the cheesemonger, whose high cheekbones and sharp features gave her a striking resemblance to the Huguenots who had lived in the area for centuries. She eavesdropped on soldiers' conversations and activities as she went about her business in the villages, reported on troop movements, planned acts of sabotage, pinpointed drop zones for the Royal Air Force, sent messages by radio, or carried them by hand. When the Germans moved their staff headquarters from Lyon, where it had been since 1942, south to Le Puy, it was Virginia who reported the shift to London. Calm no matter how fraught the situation, she successfully ferreted out a double agent and engineered the escape of several French members of her network from a Gestapo jail.

In the summer of 1944, when Allied troops pushing northward from France's Mediterranean coast forced the German army to retreat, Virginia assisted a Jedburgh team: two Americans and a

Frenchman. Jedburgh teams–code-named for a town on the border between Scotland and England–were specially trained three-man guerilla units that worked with Resistance fighters and members of de Gaulle's Forces Françaises de l'Interieur. They carried out sabotage operations and harried the Germans from the rear. With Virginia's help, this group transmitted daily reports of German positions and troop strength, derailed trains headed to Germany, interrupted enemy communications, and killed or captured hundreds of soldiers.

Virginia remained in Europe through the end of the war, and even afterward. When the OSS disbanded in September 1945, she was attached to its successor, the Central Intelligence Group (CIG). After a five-year hiatus, she joined the still-young CIA as an analyst. She did have a few overseas postings during her years as a peacetime intelligence officer, but they couldn't match her wartime experience, when she risked her life–and was responsible for the lives of others–day in and day out.

Her reaction to being the only American civilian woman to receive a Distinguished Service Cross–the army's second-highest military honor–during the war attests to her modesty and seriousness. General Donovan thought that President Truman should present the award publicly, and he agreed, but Virginia sent a polite but terse refusal: "Still operational and most anxious to get busy." Instead, she accepted the medal privately, from General Donovan. A party might have blown her cover.

In 1950, Virginia married fellow OSS agent Paul Goillot, whom she met when he parachuted into France late in the war. They lived on a farm in Montgomery County, Maryland. She retired in 1966, as was then mandatory for agents when they reached sixty. Virginia died in 1982, and Paul in 1987. People who talked to them in later years, like Virginia's niece Lorna Catling, didn't hear many stories of intrigue. If she talked about the war at all, it was likely to be a tale of discovering a fully stocked wine cellar in an abandoned chateau, rather than a cache of explosives. Yet many of her colleagues in France agree with Resistance member Denis Rake's appraisal:

"From my point of view and that of many of my colleagues, Virginia Hall can be considered the greatest wartime agent."

This assessment is likely no exaggeration, a fact that has only recently come to light, more than a quarter century after Virginia's death, in part because of books like *The Wolves at the Door: The True Story of America's Greatest Female Spy*, Judith Pearson's 2005 biography. The French and British governments celebrated Virginia's intrepid service at a ceremony held in December 2006, after belatedly discovering that she never received the royal warrant—the certificate that is traditionally conferred along with the Order of the British Empire. At the ceremony President Jacques Chirac of France stated that "Virginia Hall is a true hero of the French Resistance. Her indomitable bravery, her exceptional selflessness, her staunch determination and her talents as a leader and organizer contributed greatly to the Liberation of France. On behalf of her comrades in the Resistance, on behalf of French combatants and on behalf of all of France, I want to tell her families and friends that France will never forget this American friend who risked her life to serve our country."

FINALLY . . . RECOGNITION

The lessons from Lyon, Santo Tomas, Anzio, and other places where American women's courage was tested and proven alongside their male comrades' might have established a beachhead for women within the military, but it didn't. Once the war had been won, the women who left the service weren't replaced. By 1950, when the Korean War began, the percentage of women in uniform had fallen far below the 2 percent provided by the Women's Armed Services Act. Only about 1 percent of the U.S. armed forces were women, and the only women who were allowed to go to combat zones in Korea were nurses. This was clearly a backward step: during World War II, women had served in every war zone.

It is hardly surprising, then, that campaigns to recruit women in the 1950s failed dismally: the military salaries promised were far below what the private sector paid, the women were sure of being shut out of their share of whatever adventure or glory the men might experience, and the WAC continued to require women to meet higher educational and mental standards than the regular army maintained for men. Despite the more rigorous requirements, women were eligible for fewer types of work than they had been during World War II; most could look forward to only two options if they signed up–secretarial or clerical work. As a result, few did.

Things started to change for women only in the late 1960s, when the army actively began to recruit women as it moved away from the draft and toward an all-volunteer force. To make a career in the military more attractive to women, the range of possible job assignments (military occupational specialties, or MOS) was restored to the level of World War II. And in a gesture that had great practical as well a symbolic significance, Congress and President Lyndon Johnson eliminated the ceilings on military rank for women in all branches of the armed forces. Before the legislation was passed, no woman could hold a rank higher than colonel in the army, air force, or marines, or captain in the navy.

When the draft was eliminated in 1973, the effort to recruit women accelerated. A part of that effort included opening all military occupational specialties to women, except those involving combat. Between 1972 and 1978, when the WAC was integrated into the regular army, the number of women in the armed services increased more than fourfold, to 52,900. Women were also encouraged to enroll in ROTC, and they were allowed to receive weapons training, even if combat itself remained off-limits.

ANNA MAE HAYS

Considering the crucial place of nurses in the history of women in the American military experience, it's fitting that the first woman promoted to general in the armed forces was a nurse, Anna Mae Hays. She was Army Nurse Corps chief from 1967 to 1971.

Born Anna Mae V. McCabe in Buffalo, New York, in 1920, to a pair of Salvation Army officers, Anna Mae and her four siblings got used to moving as they were growing up, since their parents' work often required them to relocate. She graduated from high school in Allentown, Pennsylvania, and earned her nursing degree at Allentown Hospital School of Nursing in 1941, a few months before Pearl Harbor. Anna joined the Army Nurse Corps out of a sense of patriotic duty, earned her commission in May 1942, and, in 1943, was posted to Assam, India, at the head of the Ledo Road that served as the Allies' route to the battlefields of Burma. She served in India until just before the war's end in 1945. Deeply religious, she often played the field pump organ at church services, drawing on the musical skills she had learned from her parents.

For the next five years, Anna held a number of supervisory and head nurse positions in stateside army hospitals, rising in rank to captain. In 1950, she and thirty other nurses staffed the Fourth Field Hospital, which supported the U.S. X Corps that landed at Inchon, South Korea, and drove deep into the north before being forced to retreat from a massive Chinese counterattack. Exhausting eighteen-hour days were typical for the nurses, who nevertheless earned high praise from army surgeons. Anna later remembered Korea as an even more brutal environment than the Ledo jungle. The weather was harsh, an overpowering stench filled the air, and the operating rooms lacked supplies or even heat. "It had nothing," she said. "We had some evacuation of combat casualties to our hospital via heli-copter but . . . most patients arrived by ambulance or train." Despite these conditions, she sometimes found time—and energy—to con-tinue playing the organ at church services.

After seven grueling months, Anna was rotated to Japan for a year, then back to the United States, where by the mid–1950s she was assigned to Walter Reed Hospital. At Walter Reed in 1956, she served as President Eisenhower's private nurse for a month and also got married. She was widowed in 1962. Anna later went back to Walter Reed as head nurse in the Nuclear Medicine and Radioisotope Clinic at Walter Reed Army Institute of Research (WRAIR). After relatively brief assignments in Korea, at Walter Reed, and as a special assistant to ANC chief Margaret Harper in the Surgeon General's office, she was named assistant chief to Colonel Mildred Irene Clark, the twelfth head of the ANC. In 1967, Anna succeeded Mildred Clark as chief. She was the first ANC head to hold the rank of colonel *before* being appointed as chief.

During her tenure as head of the ANC, which overlapped with a period of intense fighting during the Vietnam War, Anna coped with the difficult tasks of recruiting and retaining nurses to serve in a difficult war zone. To do so, she broadened opportunities for army nurses to improve their status and pursue education, practice, and research. General Hays, who didn't receive her own bachelor's degree until she was already a captain, encouraged ANC nurses to take courses and advanced degrees at civilian schools, sometimes by creating joint programs with universities. In 1970, a policy change made it possible for ANC officers to continue on active duty after they had given birth, and a year later husbands of army nurses were granted access to commissaries and PXs. To raise the nurses' profile and status, Anna appointed Major Susan Phillips the first female social aide at the White House. Similarly, she also persuaded the army to open more specialties to nurses, transformed hospital nursing sections into departments in order to give nurses more control and influence over decisions, expanded the number of ANC nurses who taught courses taken by medics, and enlarged or created pediatric care, midwifery, and ambulatory care as nursing specialties.

In 1967, when Congress passed the law that removed the restrictions on officer grades that women could hold, it was finally possible for a woman to be promoted to general. Many of the people around Anna hoped she would be the first. The Army Nurse Corps, considered the oldest women's branch of the military, had long been an integral part of the service.

The surprise of Anna's life came not through official channels but in a phone call from a reporter who asked whether she had a comment about her promotion to general. She remembers saying, "Oh, really?" She hadn't yet gotten the word, but on June 11, 1970, Anna became the first woman general in the U.S. armed forces. She was awarded her star by Army Chief of Staff General William C. Westmoreland and Surgeon General Hal B. Jennings, with the three living former ANC chiefs in attendance. The full impact of her new status may have been brought home to her as much by a chance encounter at the Fort Myers beauty parlor as by the ceremony itself. She told me that General Westmoreland's wife, Kitsy, was there and said to her, "Anna, I wish you would get married again." When Anna asked her why, Kitsy answered, "I want some man to learn what it's like to be married to a general."

Elizabeth Hoisington ⌒

A few minutes after Anna made military history, Colonel Elizabeth P. Hoisington became the second woman to receive her star. Elizabeth Hoisington is the daughter of Colonel Perry M. Hoisington, a pioneer in the National Guard in his native Michigan and in Kansas. A member of a proud military family—her father and three brothers were all West Point graduates—Elizabeth began her military career in 1942, when she enlisted in the Women's Auxiliary Army Corps (WAAC), after graduating from the College of Notre Dame of Maryland. Her two surviving brothers were serving in the army (the third had died in an automobile accident), and Elizabeth thought that she should contribute to the war effort as well. When she enlisted, the WAAC wasn't even considered part of the "real" army, but a month after completing Officer Candidate School, in May 1943, her rank metamorphosed from WAAC third officer into second lieutenant when her service was absorbed into the Women's

Army Corps. In September 1944, Elizabeth was one of the first six WACs to enter Paris after the city's liberation.

Elizabeth was director of the WAC from 1967 to 1971. Although her tenure overlapped with a key period of American involvement in Vietnam, her focus was on expanding opportunities for women in the military in general. She believed that the controversy over granting combat roles to women would impede their progress in other areas, and therefore opposed the idea. "In my whole lifetime," she said, "I have never known ten women who I thought could endure three months under actual combat conditions. We should listen to the men with the knowledge and experience in such matters. They alone know the endurance and the stamina required. They alone know the reaction to hand-to-hand combat, to bodies and minds being blown apart or crippled forever."

When I asked Elizabeth whether she thought that a woman could ever become army chief of staff, she replied that the chief had to have combat experience and she didn't believe the American people would approve of sending women into that sort of combat.

Elizabeth's brother, Major General Perry M. Hoisington II, who died in April 2006, was a highly decorated World War II pilot who later served in NATO and the Strategic Air Command, among other positions. When Elizabeth Hoisington received her star on June 11, 1970, the two of them became the only sister-and-brother team of generals in the history of the U.S. military, a distinction they still hold.

JEANNE HOLM

Jeanne Holm became the first woman general in the U.S. Air Force in 1971, a year after Anna and Elizabeth. Her perspective on the question of women in combat was different from that of her colleagues in the army, and she has been one of the most active people promoting women's service in the military. Jeanne notes that in the Persian Gulf War, thirty-five thousand women were deployed to war zones, yet none were officially engaged in combat duty. At the same time, some of those women were members of crews that operated long-range artillery and surface-to-surface missiles. Jeanne calls these "unisex weapons" and believes they blur the distinctions between combat missions and support assignments. Two of the women in the Persian Gulf were in fact the commanders of their missile battalions.

Planes, too, fell into the "unisex" category. In 1998, women navy pilots started flying combat missions in F-14s and F/A-18s, and an air force pilot flew on a long-range B-52 mission from Diego Garcia to Iraq.

Following these initial three promotions to star rank, other branches of the military followed suit with relatively little delay. First, in 1972, the navy promoted Alene B. Duerk to the rank of rear admiral. This was what is called a restricted line officer position, a designation for non–combat related specialties. She was head of the Navy Nurse Corps. The Air Force Nurse Corps made E. Ann Hoefly a brigadier general. Jeanne Holm became the first female air force major general in 1973, and in 1976 the navy named Fran McKee rear admiral, the first woman named to an unrestricted line officer rank. She was Director of Naval Education Development. Finally, in 1978, the U.S. Marines gave their first woman, Margaret A. Brewer, her star.

No one, least of all Jeanne Holm, would have predicted her rise to the upper reaches of the air force when she first enlisted in the WAAC in 1942. The diminutive Portland, Oregon, native, who was born in 1921, started out as a truck driver, but she was so short she had trouble reaching the brake and clutch pedals of her two-and-a-half-ton truck. She persevered, however, and ultimately became the leader of her class at motor transportation school. At the time, she wasn't thinking of the military as a career; she just wanted to help win the war and then get on with her life. In fact, when the war ended, she switched to reserve status and, like tens of thousands of veterans, attended college on the GI Bill. Part of the reason she left the army in 1946 was that she felt, as many women did, that the army wasn't really eager for them to stick around.

A few years later, however, when the cold war was looming and the U.S. military seemed a little less inhospitable to having women in its ranks again, she visited Fort Lewis in Washington State, where she met some old WAC friends who had reactivated. During the visit, she heard a bugle calling taps. "These beautiful bugle calls," she thought. "I just love this." It was a love affair that lasted until she retired twenty-five years later, though she traded her WAC uniform for air force blues in 1949, a year after her return, as soon as the law requiring the military to open all branches of the service to women took effect.

As director of women in the air force from 1965 to 1973, Jeanne concentrated on opening all military ranks to women, ending restrictions on job and duty station assignments for women, persuading ROTC programs and the service academies to accept women, and introducing policies that made it easier and more appealing for women to serve in the armed forces—including designing better-looking uniforms. In her eight years at the Pentagon, the number of women in the USAF doubled. Brigadier General Wilma L. Vaught has called Jeanne "the single driving force in achieving parity for military women and making them a viable part of the mainstream military."

Her retirement in 1973 didn't end her influence on women's roles in the military and, more broadly, in American society. We met when she was a special assistant on women to President Gerald Ford. At that time, Jeanne was one of the highest-ranking women in the Ford administration. She has believed for some time that the navy and the air force are the services that present women with the best chances of reaching four-star ranks because the physical constraints aren't as much of an obstacle as they are in the army and the marines. Women can fly airplanes and captain ships as skillfully as men can.

But until 1976, leadership opportunities were closed to women because they were not admitted to the military academies. That year, for the first time, over three hundred women entered the U.S. Military Academy, the U.S. Naval Academy, the U.S. Air Force Academy, and the U.S. Coast Guard Academy. They were still unable to serve in combat units or on ships or planes involved in combat, but their academic programs were identical to those of their male classmates. From the first co-ed commencement in 1980, women's graduation rates have been comparable to those of men, and the percentage of women who fail to finish for academic reasons has consistently been significantly lower. The academies are the training grounds par excellence for future officers; ever since women gained access to them, they have begun to rise through the ranks of the services as well. Kristin Baker, a member of the U.S. Military Academy's class of 1990, is the first female commander of the West Point Corps of Cadets, and Brigadier General Susan Y. Desjardins at the U.S. Air Force Academy became the first woman commandant at any of the four military academies in 2005. Since then, a second woman, Captain Margaret ("Peg") Klein, has assumed the same position at Annapolis. These key appointments hint at the changed status of women in the military.

In my conversations with Generals Hays, Hoisington, and Holm, I noticed a common thread: none of them had gone into the military with the expectation of making history. Reaching the general officer rank wasn't imaginable when they signed on. Each of them rose to the top through dedication and a sense of patriotism and duty. Each worked hard to increase opportunities for other women in the military, all the while working within what Jeanne Holm described as the "stovepipe system." That means that promotions are always from within and from the bottom up, so equality of training and education at the entry level is essential. In her own way, each of them strove to level the playing field.

Barriers to advancement continue to fall and women are emerging as leaders in the military. If there isn't yet a woman among the four-star officers, there are beginning to be enough at the three-star rank that it's only a matter of time. In the active ranks of today's military, there is the woman who will be the first to claim that final star. We can count on it.

Betty Ford > pg 39 85-
99-103
105-113

126..

First Ladies

The Hardest, Unpaid Job in the World

I HAD THOUGHT IT WOULD HATE BEING FIRST LADY . . . I LOVED IT.

—Betty Ford

When our founding fathers were constructing the new democracy for America, they took great care to differentiate between the egalitarian standards they sought and the trappings of royal society they eschewed. As the first president, George Washington set the tone avoiding an overly grand inauguration.

However, the president and First Lady have evolved, through the years, as representatives of the American people. Their every move is watched and chronicled. First Ladies attract attention in every respect, even though they are not elected. During campaigns, one of the factors the public seems to consider is this question: How will this family represent America? Will their conduct reflect what is best about our country?

First Ladies have left enormous legacies in history, from Jacqueline Kennedy's historic preservation, to Lady Bird Johnson's highway beautification, to Nancy Reagan's "Just Say No" to drugs, to

Barbara Bush's setting a goal of literacy for all. They can also be fashion trendsetters. If they wear hats, hats will be in fashion. If they have an attractive hairdo, it is copied. They can set the hemline length of the era. Jacqueline Kennedy and Nancy Reagan had to be the design world's dream. So even though we don't have royalty in the strict sense, Americans in the last fifty years have become more intrigued by First Families and especially First Ladies. And in recent times, most of them have used their influence to positive effect.

DOLLEY MADISON ⌒

I HAVE NEVER FELT THE ENTERTAINMENT OF COMPANY
OPPRESSIVE UNTIL NOW.

If George Washington set the tone for the presidency from the beginning, Dolley Madison began the evolution of meaningful First Lady. Neither a strict Quaker childhood nor a life marked by more than its share of tragedy was able to dampen the high spirits of the woman who shaped the role of presidential wives and set the tone for Washington social life more than anyone before or since. Dolley Payne was born in Virginia in 1768. Her family lived on plantations in eastern Virginia and North Carolina until 1783, when her father, John, freed his slaves and moved to Philadelphia, where he went into business as a starch manufacturer. Payne's business failed and he died in 1792. Dolley's mother, Mary, opened a boarding-house for a while in order to support herself and the children who remained at home, but by then Dolley was married to John Todd Jr., an attorney, and was the mother of an infant son, John Payne Todd.

In October 1793, Dolley's husband and three-month-old son, William Temple Todd, fell victim to the yellow fever epidemic that struck Philadelphia. Refusing to surrender to despair, the twenty-five-year-old widow soon resumed an active social life in the city, which from 1790 to 1800 (and earlier, for shorter periods) was the U.S. capital. Senator Aaron Burr introduced her to James Madison, then a Virginia congressman. Sometimes called "Great Little Madison," shy, scholarly, and slight, the forty-three-year-old bachelor had avoided romantic entanglements for at least a decade, after having been jilted by Catherine (Kitty) Floyd, the sixteen-year-old daughter of a Continental Congress colleague. But he courted Dolley assiduously and even helped her obtain a fair settlement from her late husband's estate. They were married in 1794.

At Montpelier, the Madison family estate in Virginia, Dolley abandoned her Quaker strictures on dress and behavior. She dressed in bright colors, turbans, and jewelry, took snuff, and started hosting large dinners and receptions on the estate. James Madison declined George Washington's invitation to be his secretary of state in 1794 and continued to represent his Virginia district in Congress. But when newly inaugurated president Thomas Jefferson asked his personal and political ally to serve in the post in 1801, Madison agreed, and the couple moved to Washington, D.C., for what proved to be a sixteen-year stay.

When Jefferson was sworn in as president, he had been a widower for nineteen years. At White House social occasions, Dolley sometimes acted as a stand-in for the First Lady. At other times, the president's oldest daughter, Martha Randolph, who was often in Washington, did the honors. In 1806, Martha–called Patsy–gave birth to her eighth child, James Madison Randolph. He was the first baby born in the White House. Dolley, besides acting as Jefferson's hostess, did a fair amount of entertaining at the Madisons' three-story brick house; by all accounts these were livelier affairs than the White House evenings.

Dolley's string of innovations began at her husband's inauguration in 1809. She was the first presidential wife to attend her husband's swearing-in, and that night she sponsored an inaugural ball that instantly became a Washington tradition. Four hundred guests attended the event at the hotel on Capitol Hill, where Dolley held court dressed in a velvet gown, pearls, and a plumed turban. At the formal dinner, Dolley was flanked by the French and British foreign ministers, General Louis-Marie Turreau de Garambouville and David Montagu Erskine.

Even before the inauguration, Dolley was firmly established as the doyenne of Washington social life. As First Lady, she greatly enlarged her role. A natural politician, she invited Washington wives to "dove parties," where the guests discussed politics and important events; held frequent political dinners; and orchestrated open houses. Her "drawing rooms" attracted crowds of several hundred friends, foes, and the merely curious. They were notable for innovative cuisine and were immensely popular with the politicians, diplomats, and local citizens who attended them. Although Martha Washington and Abigail Adams had hosted public gatherings (called levees), Dolley truly believed that political Washington was her milieu as well the president's, and the citizens were her responsibility as well. Shrewdly mixing entertainment and political discussion, Dolley emerged as her husband's most persuasive advocate, sometimes persuading a senator or diplomat, at other times directing her efforts to the official's wife. She was as hospitable to political opponents as to allies; one Washington figure claimed that at one of Dolley's parties it was impossible to distinguish Madison's supporters from his detractors. Her personality lent luster to her husband's reserve, and she often put her charm to work to recruit support for his political programs. After the 1812 presidential election, one of his political opponents even claimed that he would have been able to defeat James Madison alone, but was no match for the team of Dolley and James.

Her project of beautification of the building she referred to as the "President's Castle" was as important as her contributions to the capital's social life. The building had never been permanently furnished—Adams and Jefferson had brought their own furniture and taken it home with them when they left office—but she set about to beautify the interior, using funds allocated by Congress to augment the pieces brought up from Montpelier, striking a balance between elegance and simplicity, and taking pains not to seem too "European." She oversaw the choice of every settee and sideboard, carpet and china pattern, silver service and goblet. When the job was done, she hosted a huge party so that the nation could see the results.

Finding the right balance was even more of a challenge in early nineteenth-century Washington than it is two hundred years later. Dolley had to satisfy foreigners and natives, and try to please both Republican allies and Federalist enemies. Her friends praised her regal touch, but her opponents sometimes called her an innkeeper's daughter, a reference to the brief period when her mother had taken in boarders after John Payne's death. The importance of establishing social rules appropriate for the young nation was asserted by President Jefferson, who occasionally violated traditional rules of etiquette in order to make sure "that no man here would come to dinner where he was to be marked with inferiority to any other."

As well-deserved as Dolley's fame as the capital's most inspired hostess is, the occasion that earned her history's undying admiration wasn't social at all, but her courage in the face of the invading British troops during the War of 1812. On August 22, 1814, an unstoppable British force was marching on the city. The president had left to review the American troops under Brigadier General W. H. Winder at Bladensburg, Maryland. He intended to return in time to take his wife out of harm's way, but events didn't turn out as planned. Abandoning hope of saving any personal possessions, Dolley wrote to her sister Anna about her efforts to load as many Cabinet papers as possible into one carriage and filling a wagon with silver and other valuables that were spirited away to the Bank of Maryland.

With the sound of cannon fire in her ears and even the soldiers assigned to guard the executive mansion having withdrawn, Dolley refused to flee until Gilbert Stuart's large portrait of George Washington could be removed from the building. Because it would have taken too long to unscrew the frame from the wall where the portrait hung, "I have ordered the frame to be broken, and the canvas taken out. It is done! and the precious portrait placed in the hands of two gentlemen of New York, for safe keeping." The "gentlemen" were the Madisons' friends Jacob Barker and Robert DePeyster. Although some historians dispute the claim that Dolley wrote her letter during the tense hours when the events were unfolding, no one questions the accuracy of her version of what happened.

A day later, the British set fire to the White House and the entire interior was gutted by the flames. Even today, a few blocks of the building's original sandstone walls still bear the indelible stains from the two-centuries-old fire. After briefly occupying the city, the British withdrew, and the Madisons were able to return. For the rest of James Madison's second term, Dolley worked to restore what had been destroyed in a single night. Although she and James wouldn't be able to move back into the White House, she recommended entertaining as soon as possible, in order to revive spirits in the city. Dolley also devoted herself to the public good in other ways—among them, helping to found a home for orphaned girls in Washington and supporting the group of nuns who ran a Catholic school in the city. Dolley was the first presidential wife to assume a formal role in charity work of this kind.

When James Monroe was inaugurated in 1817, the Madisons returned to the family plantation, Montpelier. Although Dolley never complained that life was dull in their elegant but remote retreat, the rural atmosphere was in dramatic contrast to the excitement of the White House. Still, Dolley resumed the entertaining for which she had become known before Jefferson had recruited the Madisons to Washington, and Montpelier enjoyed its share of social life. Family members, American political figures, and foreign visitors were constant presences at Montpelier. But James Madison never returned to Washington; in fact, during the remaining nineteen years of his life, he never traveled farther than Richmond, where he went in 1829, to participate in the Virginia Constitutional Convention.

James and Dolley prospered until the 1830s, when falling agricultural prices reduced the income from their plantation. At the same time, Dolley's son, John Payne Todd, was a constant drain on the family's resources. Given to excessive drinking and gambling, he wandered back and forth between New York, Philadelphia, and Washington. He never made a career for himself and was continually given money by his mother and stepfather, but he was nevertheless imprisoned for debt in 1830. Dolley doted on her only son and implored him to come home, and James sold land and took out a mortgage on Montpelier in order to cover his stepson's debts. When James died in 1836, Dolley moved back to Washington, where she lived with her sister, Anna Cutts, and her brother-in-law, Richard. She left Montpelier in the care of John Payne Todd, who gradually ruined it. Finally, to resolve mounting debts, Dolley reluctantly sold Montpelier to Henry Moncure in 1844. As she wrote to the new owner, "No one, I think, can appreciate my feelings of grief and dismay at the necessity of transferring to another a beloved home."

Dolley's stature as a Washington personage had declined only slightly during her twenty-year absence. As the widow of the last founding father, her address was usually the second stop—after the White House itself—on the itinerary of important visitors to Washington. She was much more than a starchy symbol of American history who had personally known every president from Washington to Zachary Taylor. Still ebullient and colorful, she formed new friendships with the likes of Daniel Webster, Henry Clay, and William Seward.

In 1849, after a brief illness, Dolley died at the age of 81. She was given a state funeral, attended by a throng of mourners from every rank and station in Washington. It is said that President Taylor coined the phrase we use to refer to presidential wives when he said, in Dolley's eulogy, "She will never be forgotten, because she was truly our First Lady for a half-century."

HELEN "NELLIE" TAFT

I THINK YOU ARE THE ONE AMBITIOUS FOR THE PRESIDENCY.

—Theodore Roosevelt to Nellie Taft

Helen "Nellie" Herron visited the White House for the first time in 1878. Her father, John Herron, and President Rutherford B. Hayes, had been law partners in Cincinnati, and the Herrons were invited to be the guests of the president and Lucy Hayes. They stayed for two weeks, and Nellie decided that she'd like to return someday—as First Lady. A year later, when she met William Howard Taft, the ambitious, music-loving Nellie had found the man who would help her realize her ambition. Despite his ardent pursuit, however, Nellie refused to marry Will for several years, either because she was reluctant to surrender her independence or out of uncertainty about whether he had set his sights as high as she had.

The son of Alphonso Taft, a former secretary of war, attorney general, and ambassador (then called minister) to Austria-Hungary and Russia, Will had his heart set on a career in the law. Conscious of Nellie's driving ambition and intelligence, he teased her that if they made it to Washington, it would be when she was appointed Treasury secretary, though he hoped to become a Supreme Court justice. The Tafts in fact held very progressive views of women's rights; Will's high school commencement address in 1874 concerned women's suffrage.

Will and Nellie married in 1886. He was appointed to the Cincinnati Superior Court in 1887, and three years later became U.S. solicitor general, appointed by President Benjamin Harrison. Nellie was disappointed when, after two years in Washington, Will jumped at the chance to become a judge for the Sixth Circuit U.S. Court of Appeals, and they had to return to Ohio. She would have preferred to remain in the capital, but he saw the appeals court post as a stepping stone to the Supreme Court.

While in Washington, Will formed a friendship with Theodore Roosevelt, and promoted Roosevelt's interests with his fellow Ohioan, President William McKinley. In 1900, President McKinley offered Will the post of civil governor of the Philippines. Nellie was enthusiastic about the prospect of moving with her three young children (born between 1889 and 1897) to an exotic, distant land, and she probably also divined that preparing the islands for an eventual transformation—from one-time Spanish colony to democratic nation—would burnish Will's presidential credentials.

Her hunch was accurate. After four years in the Philippines, which included visits to China and Japan, the Tafts returned to Washington when Will became secretary of war in Theodore Roosevelt's second term and heir apparent. He continued thinking of the Supreme Court, and Roosevelt apparently broached the subject as late as 1906. According to one story, when a reporter asked whether Will would accept, nine-year-old Charlie Taft shot back, "Nope. Ma wants him to wait and be president." She got her wish, and on March 4, 1909, William Howard Taft took the oath of office as the nation's twenty-seventh president, in a ceremony driven indoors by a late-winter snowstorm that struck one day earlier. Despite the weather, Nellie rode back to the White House at her husband's side in an open carriage. Until that morning, the outgoing president always accompanied his successor, but the Roosevelts had already left Washington, so Nellie took advantage of the vacant seat in the carriage. In doing so, she set a precedent that has been followed at every subsequent inauguration.

The guiding force behind the creation of the Cincinnati Symphony Orchestra in 1895, Nellie had plans for using her position as First Lady to enrich the capital's cultural and social life. She would eventually realize them, but only after recovering from a serious stroke that occurred just two months after the inauguration. At first, Nellie's left side was paralyzed and she was unable to speak. For a year, she struggled to overcome difficulties speaking and walking, initially remaining out of sight on public occasions or making brief, highly orchestrated appearances designed to conceal from the public the seriousness of her condition. While Nellie was recovering, her sisters Jennie Anderson, Eleanor More, and Maria Herron spent time at the White House, and her daughter, Helen, took a year's leave of absence from Bryn Mawr College in order to help the First Lady and to act as her stand-in on social occasions. By early 1910, Nellie had resumed her full role as First Lady. She still had some trouble walking and spoke with a hesitation, but she succeeded in masking her debilities from all but the most discerning observers.

Nellie aimed for a degree of grandeur in her White House entertaining, and during the remaining three years of the Taft administration, she often achieved it. The glittering pinnacle of that period was the celebration of the Tafts' silver wedding anniversary on June 19, 1911. From evening until dawn, an overflow crowd of several thousand feasted, talked, and listened to orchestral music on a White House lawn illuminated by hundreds of Japanese lanterns strung around the mansion and its grounds.

Among Nellie's more enduring innovations in Washington were her efforts to create beautiful public spaces that would act as magnets to attract people to the area around the White House and other official buildings in the capital. To accomplish these ends, she drew upon her experiences in Asia, especially Japan and the Philippines. Remembering Manila's popular Luneta, a large half-moon-shaped park with a bandstand at each end, Nellie decided to create something like it in the swampy area that included the Speedway (today's Independence Avenue) that is now part of Potomac Park. She picked out the spot where a bandstand would be constructed and envisioned a row of cherry trees along both sides of the avenue.

At the time, public funds were rarely available for beautification projects like the one that Nellie had in mind (although Congress did appropriate some money later, for improvements), so Nellie depended on ingenuity and persuasion. She convinced the Department of Agriculture to dig up as many federally owned cherry trees as could be found, in order to replant them in the new park. Fortune smiled on Nellie, because when the Japanese consulate and some private Japanese citizens in Washington learned of her scheme for locating cherry trees, they persuaded the mayor of Tokyo to send two thousand trees as a gift to the American people. When the trees arrived in December 1909, they were found to be infested and had to be destroyed, so another shipment was sent–this time, three thousand pink and white cherry trees–and reached Washington in good condition in 1910.

Only a small crowd witnessed the ceremonial planting of the first two trees in March 1912, by Nellie and Viscountess Chinda, wife of the Japanese ambassador. But this small gesture ushered in what has become one of Washington's most beloved traditions, the annual cherry blossom festival. Cherry trees usually survive for only fifty to sixty years, so almost all of the first planting have long since been replaced, but the first two that Nellie and Viscountess Chinda planted ninety-five years ago can still be seen near the statue of John Paul Jones. Bronze plaques marking the trees recall the occasion. Every year, the National Park Service replaces aging specimens, and today the total has grown to nearly 3,800, spreading from the tidal basin to East Potomac Park and the Washington Monument.

Long before the park's landscaping was completed, the public was treated to the first of the semiweekly outdoor concerts that Nellie had planned. Six weeks into the Taft presidential term, on April 17, the Filipino Constabulary Band, which Nellie had been instrumental in organizing in Manila, played before an audience that numbered in the thousands. Their program of American and international music, led by Walter Loving, an African American composer and musician whom Nellie knew and had selected, thus struck a note of inclusion that the Tafts strongly believed in, as well as meeting a high standard of musical excellence. The out-door concerts continue to this day. Weather permitting, they are held near the Jefferson Memorial, not far from where the original bandstand stood.

Less well known than Nellie's role as a tastemaker and cultural innovator was her interest in improving conditions for workers and deserving groups who lacked effective advocates. Even before the Taft presidency began, she involved herself in the work of the National Civic Federation, which advocated cooperation between industry and labor to safeguard workers as well as improve productivity. She pledged to bring about reforms in the federal workplace, toured a number of sites, and lobbied Cabinet secretaries to create better conditions for their employees, many of whom were women. In 1912, the first executive order brought about through a First Lady's efforts was issued. It mandated inspections of the executive branch buildings and offices and set standards for sanitary and safe conditions that applied to areas such as lighting, plumbing, ventilation, heat, and running water. Other causes she supported included efforts to create public kindergartens in the South for African American children and federal pensions for the widows of Confederate veterans.

One question that will probably never be answered is what effect Nellie's stroke had on Taft's presidency. Before her illness, he depended greatly on her judgment about matters large and small, and it is generally acknowledged that she was blessed with a more sensitive political barometer than her husband. But after her stroke, Will tried to spare Nellie the stress of political decision making. He also lost the benefit of her talent for public relations, and as a result his popularity suffered. He was widely believed to be more pro-business than his predecessor, but it may have been simply that Roosevelt better understood how to make political capital out of his trust-busting efforts. More antitrust actions were initiated during Taft's tenure than had occurred under Roosevelt, but the public thought the opposite was the case.

How much difference this shift made to his policies and his subsequent failure to win reelection in 1912 is impossible to say. Nellie was more suspicious of Theodore Roosevelt than Will, who invariably excused his former ally's slights and took the defeat in the three-way contest with Roosevelt and Woodrow Wilson more philosophically than Nellie did. Nellie was passionately interested in the 1912 race, to the point of setting a double precedent by attending the Democratic Convention, held in Baltimore in July. No sitting president's wife had ever attended a nominating convention before, much less the opposing party's. By the time the Democrats met, Nellie knew that Roosevelt's third-party candidacy would split the Republican vote, and she was gratified that in Woodrow Wilson the opposition had nominated someone able to derail Roosevelt's plans.

Losing the White House was a bitter pill for Nellie, but it did free her to express support for some causes–like women's suffrage–that she had been more circumspect about before. The Tafts moved to New Haven, where Will lectured at Yale Law School and Nellie wrote a memoir–*Recollection of Full Years* (1914)–the first time a former president's wife had published an autobiography. Increasingly, she indulged her penchant for individuality, even after her husband was confirmed as chief justice of the Supreme Court in 1921, the only American ever to serve as both chief executive and chief judicial officer. Despite Will's position, she made no secret of the fact that she enjoyed drinking and argued with him over the prohibition laws. And she was an outspoken supporter of the League of Nations, despite broad Republican opposition to it. Nevertheless, she remained a lifelong Republican, and her son, Senator Robert Taft, narrowly missed making her the first woman since Abigail Adams to be both the wife and mother of an American president. Still, when her younger son, Charlie, was working for Franklin Roosevelt during FDR's first term, a reporter claimed that Nellie had told him she supported FDR's reelection. Older son Robert, who hoped to become president himself, quickly issued a denial.

Not even death could arrest Nellie's precedent-setting ways. When she died in 1943, she was the first presidential wife to be buried in Arlington National Cemetery. Jacqueline Kennedy Onassis would be the second.

EDITH WILSON

I AM NOT THINKING OF THE COUNTRY NOW, I AM THINKING
OF MY HUSBAND.

Edith Bolling was related to many of Virginia's most distinguished early settlers, and to Pocahontas, the daughter of the Algonquin chief Powhatan who married John Rolfe after converting to Christianity in 1614. Edith's father, William Holcombe Bolling, was a circuit court judge and attorney. Despite their distinguished lineage, Edith and her ten sisters and brothers grew up poor in Wytheville, Virginia, a small town in the foothills of the Blue Ridge Mountains. When she was fifteen, she enrolled in the first of two college-preparatory programs she attended between 1887 and 1890, but she never attended college. After leaving school, Edith spent much of her time in Washington, where her sister Gertrude lived after her marriage to Alexander Galt. In 1892, the tall, raven-haired young woman met Norman Galt, Alexander's cousin, whose family owned a prominent jewelry store. Four years later, Edith agreed to marry him, "overcome," as a biographer put it, "by his patience and persistence." They had a son in 1903, possibly born prematurely, who died when he was only a few days old, and complications of the birth made it impossible for Edith to have other children. Then in 1908 Norman died suddenly, leaving his wife a wealthy widow.

Edith, who spent much of her time traveling, had never desired to become part of Washington society, but late in 1914 she became friends with Helen Woodrow Bones, President Wilson's first cousin and social secretary to his wife Ellen until her death of Bright's disease in August 1914. Edith and Helen often took walks together, and in March 1915, as they returned to the White House after a long hike in Rock Creek Park, they ran into the president, who was coming home from a round of golf. Edith later wrote, "This was the accidental meeting which carried out the old adage of 'turn a corner and meet your fate.'"

President Wilson, age fifty-eight, who had been despondent for months, was immediately smitten, and the couple quickly became inseparable. On days when it was impossible for him to see Edith, he wrote to her, and she encouraged him to share his public thoughts as well as his feelings. "Much as I love your delicious love-letters, that would make any woman proud and happy," she wrote, "I believe I enjoy even more the ones in which you tell me (as you did this morning) of what you are working on—the things that fill your thoughts and demand your best effort, for then I feel I am sharing your work—and being taken into partnership as it were. . . ."

The president was happy to oblige her that summer, writing letters that alternated between declarations of his affection and deliberations about policy. Though Edith hesitated about whether to marry the president, she assured him that she relished his passion as well as his taking her into his confidence. "I am always with you and love the way you put one dear hand on mine, while with the other you turn the pages of history." The pages were truly momentous ones, and Edith was already starting to express her opinions about the matters of policy and politics that Wilson discussed with her: the American response to the German sinking of the *Lusitania* on May 7, 1915; the inexorable movement toward involvement in the war; and tactical questions about his campaign for reelection in 1916.

Insisting that Edith was the confidante, counselor, and wife he desired, President Wilson succeeded in vanquishing her resistance (or uncertainty) and brushed aside concerns that to remarry barely a year after Ellen Wilson's death might jeopardize his reelection (only two presidents, Tyler and Cleveland, had married while in office, and no one has done so since Wilson). They were married at Edith's home on December 18, 1915, and she betrayed no sign of displeasure at tailoring her life to accommodate the responsibilities of his office. They interrupted their honeymoon to return to Washington after another ship was sunk, the fifth since the beginning of the war. She immediately took charge, insisting that the entire staff adjust its schedule to suit the president's (she set an example by doing so herself), and she acted as gatekeeper to prevent even high-placed officials from exhausting her husband. Because of Edith's efforts, it was almost impossible to get in to see the president without an appointment.

The glare of attention didn't appeal to Edith; she preferred her roles of privileged confidante and protector of the president to public shows as First Lady. Doubts about the effect on his reelection of President Wilson's hasty second marriage proved unfounded; although his electoral vote total was lower in the two-way contest with Supreme Court Justice Charles Evans Hughes than it had been in 1912, he received over 9 million popular votes, as opposed to 6 million in his first election. The world political situation was much more on voters' minds, and the Wilsons responded by staging a subdued inauguration and canceling large-scale receptions and White House entertainments, especially after the country entered the war in 1917. Edith revealed a gift for inspired patriotic gestures by imposing various austerity measures in the executive mansion: meatless days, heatless days, and gasless Sundays that put an end to automobile outings. She also set an example by sewing pajamas for sick and wounded soldiers and stopped—despite her fondness for the latest fashions—buying new clothes until after the armistice. It was also Edith's idea to have a small flock of sheep graze the White House lawn to save the expense of mowing the grass. Every state was given a share of the wool they produced, which was auctioned off to raise money for the war effort. By this means, about $50,000 was brought in.

When the postwar Paris Peace Conference was held, the First Lady accompanied the president to France, where he and the prime ministers of the other three victorious great powers—England, France, and Italy—as well as representatives of a number of smaller countries met from January to June 1919. Edith, who joined her husband at many of the sessions, worried about her husband's health throughout the six intense months of negotiations.

When the Treaty of Versailles was drawn up, the president knew that the U.S. Senate opposed some of its provisions—especially the one calling for a League of Nations—and would refuse to ratify it. Despite being drained after months of eighteen-hour days of diplomatic deliberations, President Wilson decided to take his case directly to the American people. Over Edith's objections, he began his speech-making tour in September, but by the end of the month he was too exhausted to continue and returned to Washington. On October 2, 1919, Edith found her husband sitting on his bed, paralyzed on his left side.

Recognizing the symptoms of a stroke (she may also have known that Woodrow Wilson had suffered at least one minor stroke when he was thirty-nine), Edith's first reaction was to hide news of her husband's condition from the public. She summoned the president's personal physician, Cary T. Grayson, and other doctors to the family's quarters, and at the same time kept White House employees out. After confirming the diagnosis, the doctors told Edith that her husband needed calm. There was no question, at least for the time being, of his being able to handle his presidential responsibilities, so Edith and the doctors contrived to create the impression that the president's health crisis had affected his body but not his mind and that he simply needed time to mend. In fact, Wilson couldn't move his left arm, could walk only with great difficulty, couldn't sit at a desk or read more than a few sentences at a time, but one of his physicians told the press that "the President is able-minded and able-bodied, and that he is giving splendid attention to the affairs of state."

Thus the stage was set for a period that lasted into 1920. Edith, Dr. Grayson, and others successfully created the impression that Wilson was remaining out of sight in order to speed his convalescence from a condition that was nothing worse than exhaustion, but was in full control of the country's affairs. Her actions were sometimes called the "First Lady regency," and she resisted the efforts of Secretary of State Robert Lansing to have presidential powers transferred to Vice President Thomas Riley Marshall, at least temporarily, and to give cabinet members greater voice in executive decisions. Secretary Lansing, to whom the president had never given a free hand in his five years in the post, was asked to resign in February; whether at Edith's initiative or President Wilson's isn't certain. How much autonomous power over policy Edith exercised during these months is still the subject of disagreement. According to her, she consulted constantly with her husband, made no decisions on her own, but decided which issues demanded his direct involvement and acted as his intermediary solely to protect his health and speed his recovery and on the advice of his doctors.

When a suspicious Senate sent one of its members, Senator Albert Fall of New Mexico, to see the president's condition for himself, Edith propped Wilson up in bed so that his paralyzed side was hidden and only his profile was visible, and she remained in the room throughout the meeting. In the meantime, every question, memo, or issue meant for the president reached him, if it did, through the First Lady. She claimed that her extensive knowledge of the president's views qualified her to represent them authoritatively, and it is certainly true that he had been confiding in her and sharing even the most sensitive material with her almost since their first meeting. But whatever the nature of her role, it is likely that Edith Wilson exercised more direct executive power for at least several months in 1919–1920 than any First Lady in American history.

President Wilson had improved by the late spring of 1920 to the point of believing that he felt capable of serving a third term as president and hoped to be his party's nominee. Edith and Dr. Grayson were adamantly opposed to another election campaign; they feared that he would not survive. As matters turned out, the Democrats never seriously considered him as a candidate that year; his name wasn't even placed in nomination. It took forty-four ballots before Ohio governor and newspaper publisher James M. Cox was nominated (Franklin Delano Roosevelt, then assistant secretary of the navy, was his running mate). The Republican, Warren G.

Harding, won in November by the largest margin of any presidential election.

President Wilson never recovered fully from his debilitating stroke, and Edith continued to control access to her husband until his death in 1924. After he died, she kept an equally tight grip on his reputation, or tried to, by restricting access to the presidential papers to people she considered loyal. She even demanded–and received–editorial control of the biopic about her husband's life, *Wilson* (Geraldine Fitzgerald played Edith, and the relatively unknown Canadian actor Alexander Knox portrayed the president). She addressed the 1928 Democratic Convention, and there was even talk of nominating her for the vice presidency. Edith had no real political ambitions of her own, however, and devoted most of the time she spent in the public eye burnishing her late husband's image. She did maintain friendships with every First Lady after her, and was closest to Grace Coolidge, Eleanor Roosevelt, and Mamie Eisenhower. Her last public act was attending John Kennedy's inauguration in January 1961, eleven months before her death, at age eighty-nine.

ELEANOR ROOSEVELT

THERE ISN'T GOING TO BE ANY FIRST LADY. THERE IS JUST TO BE PLAIN, ORDINARY MRS. ROOSEVELT . . . I NEVER WANTED TO BE THE PRESIDENT'S WIFE, AND DON'T WANT IT NOW. YOU DON'T QUITE BELIEVE ME, DO YOU? VERY LIKELY NO ONE WOULD–EXCEPT POSSIBLY SOME WOMAN WHO HAD HAD THE JOB.

It's strange to think that the woman who made this statement in 1932 is also the person whose words and deeds set the stage for the most active First Lady, as measured by commitment to social causes, for at least half of the twentieth century. She was deeply involved in the issues affecting the country and the world, outspoken and independent, and at the same time an eloquent supporter of her husband's policies and presidency. But that wasn't how Eleanor Roosevelt saw herself, at least not until after she became First Lady.

Anna Eleanor Roosevelt was born in New York City in 1884, the first of Elliott and Anna Roosevelt's three children. Despite an illustrious pedigree, her childhood was difficult and filled with tragedy. Her mother, the former Anna Rebecca Livingston Ludlow Hall, a stunningly beautiful young woman, traced her ancestry to a signer of the Declaration of Independence and the person who administered the oath of office to George Washington. She thought that Eleanor was a homely child and was embarrassed by her. Eleanor's father, the younger brother of Theodore Roosevelt, was an enormously charming man whom his daughter called "the one great love of my life as a child." But he was also an alcoholic who spent long periods away from his children before he died of injuries from a fall in 1894. By then, Eleanor's mother and a young brother had died of diphtheria, in 1892 and 1893. Eleanor and her surviving brother, Hall, who was born in 1891, went to live with their maternal grandmother, Mary Livingston Ludlow Hall, a humorless, austerely religious woman, spending summers in Tivoli, New York.

Eleanor's early education was spotty. She didn't attend school at all until her mother was finally persuaded to hire teachers for her daughter and a few other young children. She was often too shy to speak when called on even in the tiny classroom, and grew up fearful of criticism, lonely, and uncomfortable around her peers. Her refuge was reading; she devoured the poems and novels of the great British and American poets and novelists of the mid- and late nineteenth century. When she was fifteen, Eleanor's aunts persuaded Mary Hall to send her granddaughter to Allenswood Academy in England, run by Marie Souvestre. They had been Mlle Souvestre's students at Les Ruches, near Fontainebleau, and foresaw that their niece would profit from a few years at boarding school.

Allenswood either transformed or liberated Eleanor—or both.

She found some of the rules ridiculous—students were permitted only three ten-minute baths a week and were expected to confess if they uttered even a single word in English (French was the language of instruction *and* conversation)—but the intellectual atmosphere was invigorating. Marie Souvestre also perceived that her new student was a diamond in the rough and encouraged—insisted is probably closer to the truth—Eleanor to go beyond the traditional finishing school curriculum of modern languages, literature, art, music, and dance to study history, geography, and philosophy as well. The young protégée lost her fearfulness and gained self-confidence; she told prospective students that she had been happier at Allenswood than anywhere else and hoped to stay on to teach at the school. Her classmates at the time later remembered Eleanor as a serious young woman, much more worldly and better informed than they were even when she first arrived at school, who had no trouble "chatting away" in French (which she had somehow managed to pick up) with Marie Souvestre at the dinner table.

Eleanor never joined the Allenswood faculty. In 1902, her family insisted that she come back to New York to make her debut into society later that year. She also did volunteer teaching at the College Settlement on Rivington Street, visited tenement houses, and joined the National Consumers League.

Franklin and Eleanor Roosevelt were fifth cousins once removed. They had known one another nearly their entire lives, but they did not become well acquainted until the summer of 1902, after Eleanor's return from England. They were engaged in November 1903, but Sara Delano Roosevelt, Franklin's mother, insisted that they were too young to marry (he was twenty-one and Eleanor was nineteen) and asked them to keep their plans secret for a year. In fact, Sara hoped to change her son's mind and attempted to cool his ardor by sending him on a five-week cruise. The couple kept their word but continued to see one another, and Franklin opted to attend Columbia Law School instead of Harvard in order to be closer to Eleanor. They announced their engagement in

December 1904 and were married the following March, two weeks after Uncle Theodore's second inauguration. At the wedding, held in the adjoining Manhattan townhouses of Eleanor's cousin, Susan "Susie" Ludlow Parish, and her daughter, more attention was paid to President Roosevelt, who stood in for his deceased brother to give the bride away, than to the newlyweds. Eleanor's cousin Alice Roosevelt, the president's daughter and maid of honor, notorious for her cruel wit, commented about her father, "He has to be the corpse at every funeral and the bride at every wedding."

Eleanor and Franklin divided their time between New York City and Franklin's ancestral estate at Hyde Park, where the matriarch, Sara Delano Roosevelt, was both a help and a hindrance. Between 1906 and 1916, they had a daughter and five sons. One, born in 1909 and named Franklin Delano Roosevelt Jr., did not survive infancy (their fifth child, born in 1914, was also Franklin Delano Roosevelt Jr.). Franklin won a seat in the New York State Senate in 1910, and the Roosevelts moved to Albany. There, Eleanor came out from under her mother-in-law's shadow, sat in on senate sessions, and started to develop her own points of view about politics.

When Franklin was appointed assistant secretary of the navy in 1913, he resigned from the New York State Senate and the Roosevelts relocated to Washington. He held that post until 1920, when he resigned just before the end of the ailing President Wilson's second term, to pursue the Democratic nomination for vice president. During the war years, Eleanor's work as a Red Cross volunteer had nudged her interests more in the direction of politics than had been the case before World War I. When the Cox-Roosevelt ticket lost the 1920 election to the Republican Warren Harding–Calvin Coolidge slate, Franklin was, politically speaking, temporarily sidelined, but Eleanor's support of the League of Nations and other international efforts held steady. The following summer, when Franklin contracted polio, it seemed that his career in public service might be at an end, but Eleanor, Franklin, and adviser Louis Howe labored to sustain FDR's public image. Franklin founded a rehabilitation center for polio victims in Warm Springs, Georgia, where he spent time in hopes of curing his own paralysis, and then slowly reinserted himself into Democratic politics. He nominated New York governor Al Smith for the presidency in 1924, and when Smith ran for president four years later, FDR succeeded him as governor.

Independently, Eleanor mapped out her own political program, one that at the same time supported her husband's political agenda, through activities in organizations like the National Consumers League, the Women's Division of the Democratic State Committee, and the League of Women Voters, whose legislative affairs committee she chaired. In that position, she reported regularly on federal and state legislative activity. She also edited the *Women's Democratic News*, her first foray into the journalism that she would later make integral to her public role. Just before Franklin's election as governor, Eleanor began teaching government and literature at a private girls' school in New York City headed by her friend Marion Dickerman. She continued teaching during his term, saying, "I teach because I love it. I cannot give it up," breathing life into her classes by visiting courtrooms, tenements, and markets with her students, so they could see social problems and what governments did about them firsthand. She maintained her political activities, too, though sometimes behind the scenes. She lobbied her husband to appoint more women to state jobs, spoke publicly about increasing women's stake in government, and lectured about the responsibilities of citizenship for men and women.

Eleanor probably contributed more to Franklin's 1932 campaign for the presidency than she did to any of his previous or later election efforts, even though his success meant a role for her—First Lady—that she did not covet. Among other things, she knew that as the president's wife she would be less free to speak her own mind about controversial matters. But she helped shape an image of the candidate that would attract voters across the political spectrum; mediated between the strong-willed campaign advisers James Farley and Louis Howe; discreetly aided Democratic National Committee efforts to encourage citizens, especially women, to register and vote for Franklin; traveled so that he could remain in Albany, but kept him abreast of the campaign's progress; and—once he won the presidential nomination—acted as his surrogate to help elect a Democratic gubernatorial successor, Herbert H. Lehman.

In characterizing Eleanor's tenure as First Lady, it's difficult to say which was more remarkable: what she did or what she didn't do. She didn't supervise the chef, worry about whether the household staff should be doing a better job, or re-landscape the White House grounds. Perhaps this was because the Roosevelts knew that Franklin owed his victory in part to the economic conditions brought on by the stock market crash and the Depression that followed. But regardless, Eleanor would have been more interested in civil rights for African Americans, doing something about poverty and housing shortages, and increasing women's political influence than in the menu for a state dinner or whether there were fresh flowers in the Diplomatic Reception Room. In fact, there were complaints about dusty furniture, and even Franklin expressed his displeasure about the food.

Eleanor simultaneously created a public persona that asserted her independence—as a woman and as a thinker—while it added luster to her husband's popularity as president. She traveled widely, spoke out on major issues in person and on her radio program, and published a number of her talks. She broke with tradition by deciding to hold her own press conferences—there were more than three hundred between 1933 and 1945—and allowed only women reporters into them, thus ensuring that every interested media outlet would have at least one woman on its staff. She wrote the first of four volumes of autobiography, a children's book about citizenship, and a daily syndicated column, *My Day*, which ran six days a week from the end of 1935 until two months before her death nearly twenty-seven years later. In every region of the country, Eleanor visited coal mines and migrant camps, fields and factories, and the homes of sharecroppers and slum dwellers. In addition, thousands of people wrote to her about their problems. Although she could read only a small fraction of this flood of mail (the others were all handled by her staff), she saw, read, and heard more about how the Depression affected Americans' lives than any member of the administration. What she learned became grist for her articles, talks, and newspaper column. She often proposed remedies to widespread ills or sent a letter she had received to the government office in a position to help, even, in some cases, to Franklin's office itself.

Eleanor had her own take on the First Lady's traditional activities as well. She received illustrious visitors to the White House, from King George VI and Queen Elizabeth of England, to Madame Chiang Kai-shek, Winston Churchill, and Amelia Earhart. When the Daughters of the American Revolution refused permission for Marian Anderson, the African American contralto, to perform at Constitution Hall, the organization's Washington, D.C., auditorium, Eleanor resigned her DAR membership and helped persuade the secretary of the interior to permit the singer to perform outdoors, at the Lincoln Memorial, on Easter Day, 1939. A few weeks later, she asked Marian to sing at the White House when the king and queen of England were visiting.

Eleanor didn't curtail her schedule after the United States entered World War II on December 8, 1941. There was no question of Franklin traveling, given his infirm state, as he began an unprecedented fourth term, so she went east to England and west to the Pacific theater, inspiring combat troops and comforting wounded soldiers, urging equal treatment of black servicemen, and worrying about her four sons, who were all in uniform. According to one estimate, during her tour of the Pacific, she saw approximately four hundred thousand soldiers, sailors, and marines. A number of servicemen became her pen pals, writing to her regularly about the conditions facing soldiers and sailors at home and overseas. She answered their letters and looked for ways to improve conditions on bases and in the field. Sometimes a small change, like giving enlisted men some of the choice seats at USO shows, instead of reserving them exclusively for officers, boosted morale as much as costlier initiatives could.

On the domestic front, Eleanor led the search for ways to make it easier for women to work outside the home, in order to support the war effort and expand economic opportunities for her sex. She proposed putting day care and kitchens in the places where women work, and she lobbied for equal pay for all.

And then, on April 12, 1945, the nation learned that Franklin had died in Warm Springs, Georgia.

"Plain, ordinary Mrs. Roosevelt" once more, Eleanor resumed her role as an advocate of the work of organizations with which she had long identified, among them the National Association for the Advancement of Colored People (NAACP) and the League of Women Voters. There was speculation that she would run for public office herself, and many friends urged her to, but she concluded that she could achieve more by remaining outside electoral politics and relished the freedom to speak without inhibition: "I am too old to want to be curtailed in any way in the expression of my own thinking," she wrote in an article in *Look* magazine, "Why I Do Not Choose to Run." She admitted that the prospect of holding high public office—governor, senator, or vice president—was attractive, but she believed that Americans weren't willing to elect women—yet. "Men and women both are not yet enough accustomed to following a woman and looking to her for leadership. If I were young enough it might be an interesting challenge, and we have some women in Congress who may carry on this fight."

Instead, Eleanor continued to choose her causes. She was a member of the American delegation to the United Nations until 1953, where as chair of the Human Rights Commission she guided the framing of the Universal Declaration of Human Rights. Her other achievements at the UN included assistance to refugees (a cause in which she had been active since the Spanish Civil War) and support for the creation of the state of Israel. An immensely popular speaker well into her seventies, she traveled widely in the United States and abroad, lecturing as often as twice a week and talking to international leaders in Europe, the Middle East, and the Soviet Union. She continued writing *My Day*, as well as many articles and books; hosted two radio programs; and even–for the last three years of her life–a television news program, *Prospects of Mankind*. She and Edith Wilson, both former First Ladies, were present at the inauguration of John Kennedy, who subsequently reappointed her to the American delegation to the United Nations. She died on November 7, 1962, and is buried in Hyde Park.

BESS TRUMAN ⌒

WE ARE ALL GOING TO HAVE TO DO A LOT OF THINGS WE HATE DOING IN THE NEXT FEW YEARS.

Elizabeth Virginia Wallace was born in 1885 in Independence, Missouri, a small town with a highly defined sense of social propriety. Bess's parents, David and Margaret Wallace, were part of the local elite, and she and her three brothers spent their early years in the protective, optimistic environment of their family and community. Bright, attractive, and athletic, blonde, blue-eyed Bess attended the local public schools until 1901, and enjoyed ice skating, horseback riding, tennis, baseball, and swimming. The eldest child and only daughter (her three brothers were born between 1887 and 1900), Bess was a tomboy when young, but grew into a proper young lady. She spent two years at Barstow, a private finishing school in Kansas City, Missouri. In 1903, David Wallace committed suicide, and Bess returned to Independence, where she provided emotional comfort and companionship to her mother and increasingly took on the role of head of the family.

Harry Truman was a year older than Bess, but they were classmates from fifth grade through high school after the Trumans moved into town from his grandparents' farm in nearby Grandview. By all accounts, Harry's interest in Bess was immediate, but he was too shy even to speak to her until five years after their first meeting. For their part, the Wallaces considered Harry, a Baptist from an undistinguished family, an unworthy suitor. A year after completing high school in 1901, Harry left Independence, first for Kansas City and then for the family farm in Grandview, returning only in 1910. He then began courting Bess in earnest, often traveling between Grandview and Independence via Kansas City, a complicated commute involving a combination of buggy, streetcar, and train. They announced their engagement before Harry left for the war in France, and they married in 1919, when he returned as a decorated artillery commander. His earlier dreams of attending West Point had been doomed by poor eyesight, but he proved a brave leader whose unit survived intact despite difficult battlefield experience. The Trumans' only child, Margaret, was born in 1924, after Bess had suffered several stillbirths and miscarriages.

After Truman & Jacobson, the Kansas City haberdashery business Harry opened with his army buddy Eddie Jacobson, failed in the recession of 1921, Harry entered politics. With the backing of Democratic boss Tom Pendergast (the uncle of another friend Harry had made during military training at Fort Sill, Oklahoma), he was elected to a Jackson County judgeship and served, except for two years, until 1934. Despite widespread corruption in the Pendergast machine, Harry maintained a reputation for scrupulous probity both on the bench and in the U.S. Senate, to which he was first elected in 1934.

Bess hadn't approved of her husband's decision to go into politics. She preferred to live as a private person rather than a public figure, and she was especially loath to leave Independence, and her aging mother, to live in Washington. She claimed that all the wife of a senator needed to do was "sit beside her husband, be silent, and be sure her hat is on straight." But in fact, she supported Harry's political efforts and was especially effective behind the scene in helping his career in the Senate and, later, during his vice presidency and presidency. He discussed the issues with Bess, and she kept herself informed; he depended on her help with his speeches and considered her a key member of his office staff. Still, when Margaret was young, Bess spent half the year in Independence so that her daughter could go to school there rather than in Washington.

Like other congressional wives at the time, Bess kept house in a small apartment and was active in social and service organizations like the Congressional Club, which attracted Washington spouses at the time. When World War II arrived, she volunteered at the H Street United Service Organization and for the Red Cross through the Senate Wives Club.

When President Franklin D. Roosevelt asked Harry to be his running mate in 1944, Bess reluctantly went along. At the nominating convention, after running the gauntlet of cheering, handshaking delegates, she reportedly asked, "Are we going to have to go through this for the rest of our lives?" During the campaign, she gamely played the role of candidate's wife, but except for one radio interview, she drew the line at speaking on behalf of the ticket. "I have nothing to say to the public," she told her husband.

Perhaps no First Lady has ever seemed more unlike her predecessor than Bess Truman when she stepped into Eleanor Roosevelt's shoes after FDR's death in April 1945. Rather than pay lip service to the public and political example Eleanor had set for twelve years, Bess took decisive steps to serve notice that things would be different during the Truman presidency. Eleanor had held weekly press conferences with women journalists. Bess announced, "You don't need to know me. I'm only the president's wife and the mother of his daughter," and never met with the press again, not even in one-on-one interviews. If reporters had questions for the First Lady, they would submit them in writing and wait for the replies, which might be composed by Bess's social secretary rather than herself. According to Margaret Truman Daniel, whose biography of her mother, *Bess W. Truman*, was based on family papers, Bess "felt more and more superfluous" as First Lady, because she hadn't wanted the role in the first place and resented being excluded from important presidential actions like the decision to use atomic weapons against Japan. Margaret characterized her mother's feelings as "a smoldering anger that was tantamount to an emotional separation."

If Bess was a reluctant First Lady, she was also a dutiful one who succeeded in masking her true feelings. With the return of peace, she brought back the social events—from state receptions to concerts—that had been suspended for four years, and she involved herself in all the details of preparation and execution. At the same time, she led a drive to voluntarily limit food consumption and donate the surplus to European countries whose people were short of food. She studied the history of the White House and her predecessors' roles as hostesses and entertainers. When asked, she often named Elizabeth Monroe as the First Lady she identified with most strongly, perhaps because she believed she had much in common with the charming but private woman who followed flamboyant Dolley Madison, just as she had succeeded Eleanor Roosevelt.

Inevitably, of course, Bess also found causes in which she believed strongly. Some fit the familiar pattern of long-held interests or newly emerging issues. They ranged from concern for returning veterans, support for the arts as the country emerged from the shadow of World War II, and funding medical research into cancer and other diseases that were starting to be understood. Like all modern presidential wives, she accepted honorary titles from many service organizations, including the Girl Scouts, the Women's National Democratic Club, the Washington Animal Rescue League, and the American Red Cross.

But Bess's signal achievement may have been her effort to save the White House from demolition. At the end of the war, the 150-year-old presidential mansion was in danger of collapsing, and some influential Americans advocated replacing the nineteenth-century structure with a modern building. The Trumans wanted to preserve the original White House by shoring it up from within with new steel supports. This was a costlier solution than razing the old building, but it prevailed, partly thanks to Bess's aggressive lobbying of Congress and the American people. Congress agreed to fund restoration, and the Trumans moved across Pennsylvania Avenue to Blair House, where they lived from 1948 to 1952 while the work went on.

President Truman always insisted that he considered Bess a trusted adviser and "full partner in all transactions–politically and otherwise." Particulars are difficult to pinpoint, but the president's respect and affection for his spouse are well known. According to Merle Miller, a Truman confidant and biographer, Bess's most valuable role was often to prevail on her husband to refrain "from doing what he shouldn't do." Elsewhere in Washington, however, Bess had her enemies, some of them quite vocal. One was Clare Booth Luce, writer, Republican congresswoman, and capital tastemaker. She tended to dismiss Bess as a provincial, so much so that when Bess became First Lady, she is said to have wondered out loud, "I wonder if Clare Booth Luce will think I'm real, now." Occasionally, she came under attack for failing to live up to Eleanor Roosevelt's examples, as happened when she agreed to be the guest of honor at a DAR tea in her honor. Eleanor had famously resigned from the DAR over their refusal to allow Marian Anderson to perform at Constitution Hall, but Bess defended her stance, declaring, "I deplore any action which denies artistic talent an opportunity to express itself because of prejudice against race origin," but refusing to dissociate herself from the organization because of its lapse.

Despite the occasional criticism, Bess was the sort of First Lady whom the American people came to like as well as admire. Down-to-earth and unpretentious, she could say, after her husband's victory in the 1948 election, "It looks like you're going to have to put up with us for another four years." She didn't shirk her duty to the nation, but she came across first and foremost as a wife and mother from Missouri, with an outgoing daughter who launched her own singing career during her father's presidency, including one 1947 concert in Constitution Hall.

When President Truman announced early in 1952 that he would

not seek reelection to the presidency, Bess was visibly pleased at the prospect of returning to private life in Independence. Her relief was mixed with sadness when in early December, just weeks before the Eisenhower inauguration, her beloved mother, Margaret Wallace, died at the age of ninety. She had lived with the Trumans from the time her son-in-law became president in 1945 until her death.

Right after Dwight Eisenhower's swearing-in on January 20, 1953, the Trumans took the train home to Independence. In the days before presidential pensions and Secret Service details for former presidents, they acted like just another middle-class retired couple. They bought Margaret Wallace's home on North Delaware Street from Bess's brothers and renovated it. It was a fourteen-room Victorian townhouse built by Margaret Wallace's father, George Porterfield Gates, who had made a fortune as co-owner of the Waggoner-Gates Milling Company. Margaret Wallace had moved into the house after her husband's suicide, and the Trumans had used it as their "summer White House" between 1945 and 1952. It was the first house she and Harry Truman had ever owned.

Margaret Truman Daniel, who wrote biographies of both her parents as well as memoirs of her own life as the Trumans' only child, called Bess "the least understood member of our family. She is a woman of tremendous character, which the public may sense, but in addition she is a warmhearted, kind lady, with a robust sense of humor, a merry, twinkling wit, and a tremendous capacity for enjoying life." Bess Truman died at home in Independence in October 1982. She was ninety-seven, the longest-living First Lady in our history.

MAMIE EISENHOWER ⌒

IKE RUNS THE COUNTRY, I TURN THE LAMB CHOPS.

The second of four daughters, Mamie Geneva Doud was born in Boone, Iowa, in 1896. Her parents were John Sheldon Doud, a meatpacker who in the process of amassing a fortune had followed the industry west from Rome, New York, to Chicago to Iowa, and Elvira Carlson Doud (known as "Minnie"). During Mamie's childhood, the family again moved several times, in search of a climate that agreed with their eldest child, Eleanor, who had a congenital heart condition. Between 1902 and 1905, they tried Pueblo and Colorado Springs, Colorado, before settling on Denver. The Colorado winters displeased Minnie Doud, however, so in 1910 the family started spending half of each year in San Antonio, Texas. Eleanor Doud died in 1912 at age sixteen, and another sister, Edna Mae, died in 1918, when she was seventeen. Only Mamie and her youngest sister, Mabel ("Mike") lived into old age.

Mamie attended high school in San Antonio during the winter and in Denver the rest of the year, so it's not surprising that she wasn't a standout student, but she displayed a gift for friendship and closeness to her family and was a talented pianist. Her only post–high school education was a year at a finishing school in Denver, where she was a student in 1914–1915. The following year, she married Dwight David Eisenhower, then a second lieutenant in the army. Mamie had met her future husband in San Antonio, when he was stationed at Fort Sam Houston, which became the first of the thirty-three places the Eisenhowers lived between their wedding day and Ike's (as he was always known) inauguration as president in 1953.

As soon as Mamie met Ike, she vastly preferred the handsome officer to the "lounge lizards with patent-leather hair" she knew from society gatherings, but it took Ike a month to get a date with her after they were introduced during a visit to the base. "What did he expect?" Mamie later said. "I was booked solid. It was my debutante year!" Their two sons were born in 1917 and 1922. The first, Doud Dwight ("Ikky"), died of scarlet fever when he was three, but John Sheldon Eisenhower had a distinguished career as an army officer and a diplomat, and served in the Eisenhower White House as well. Ikky's death left a permanent mark on his parents. For the rest of their lives they commemorated his birthday, but they could never bring themselves to mention the date of his demise. Mamie even claimed to have forgotten it.

Moving frequently, as military families often do, proved stressful for Mamie, especially during the early years of her marriage. The Eisenhowers lived in Panama, in Europe—where their apartment in 1920s Paris was a social gathering place nicknamed "Club Eisenhower"—and in the Far East. Mamie was even less prepared for the extended separations that are an inevitable part of military life. During peacetime as well as war, Ike was away from home for long periods, and Mamie's social world consisted mostly of other army wives. The women frequently engaged in projects to improve the conditions of the people living near the foreign army bases. In Panama, for example, they succeeded in creating a free hospital for the native population, who were excluded from U.S. Army hospitals on racial grounds.

The war years were particularly difficult for Mamie. Separated from Ike, whom she didn't see for the last three years of the war, and from her son, who graduated from West Point on D-day in 1944 and was promptly sent to join the fighting in Europe, she spent the entire time in Washington. She dutifully answered thousands of letters and questions from journalists, despite having no secretarial staff and being often in the dark about whether her own husband and son were safe. Close relatives and other army wives peopled her social life, which included volunteering at a D.C. army canteen, where one day she served coffee to Eleanor Roosevelt without being recognized by the First Lady. The mail from Europe, irregular as it was, reassured her, but it wasn't enough to lift the cloud of uncertainty and worry.

In the postwar period, Mamie rejoined Ike, especially after he stepped down as military governor of the U.S. occupation zone in Europe to become army chief of staff in Washington, president of Columbia University in New York City, and commander of NATO, which was then headquartered in Paris. When Ike campaigned for the presidency in 1952, the first election to target women voters as an identifiable group, Mamie accompanied him as he toured the country by train. Although she said little during the whistle stops and made only a handful of appearances in television interviews and commercials, she usually emerged from their car at the end of his speeches, after he asked the audience, "How'd you like to meet my Mamie?" Her behind-the-scenes role was more substantial: she helped him rephrase the language in his speeches to make them simpler and more comprehensible and acted as a buffer between the candidate and the crowds of people who wanted get to their car on the campaign train or their hotel suite when the entourage enjoyed an occasional layover during their seventy-seven-city marathon tour.

President Truman ordered the integration of the military in 1948, but it was the Eisenhowers who invited the first African American to participate in an inauguration: Marian Anderson sang the national anthem at Ike's second inauguration in 1957. Mamie also had a hand in other inaugural precedents. She favored having her husband compose and read a personal prayer at the January 20, 1953, ceremony, the day she also participated in the first presidential kiss bestowed in public by a newly installed chief executive on his wife. In other matters, she hewed to a more traditional line as First Lady, following the example of Bess Truman in projecting an image of a solidly middle-class homemaker, devoted to her family and entertaining in a style that blended dignity and informality. Behind her unpretentious demeanor was an efficient military officer's spouse who set high standards for White House domestic operations while also expressing genuine affection and concern for the people who made up the White House staff.

The Eisenhower years were marked by formal receptions for the many foreign heads of state who took advantage of a relatively peaceful world to travel. It was a rich period in American popular culture. A lover of musical theater, Mamie organized the first performances of selections from hit Broadway shows at the White House, but there were also occasions when she demonstrated discerning judgment about political symbolism as well. In 1953, she was instrumental in excluding Senator Joseph McCarthy from the invitation list of an annual dinner that traditionally included the entire Senate, in order to shield the president from the cloud of controversy surrounding McCarthy's witch-hunting tactics. She was also the hostess at the first state dinner for a head of state of African descent, when the president of Haiti visited the White House.

Like other First Ladies whose husbands suffered medical crises while in office, Mamie faced her most difficult test when the president had his first heart attack while the Eisenhowers were visiting Minnie Doud in Denver in 1955. After consulting the president's physician in Washington, she coordinated his transfer to Fitzsimmons Army Hospital (now Fitzsimmons Army Medical Center) in Aurora, Colorado. During Ike's weeks-long recuperation, she worked closely with his doctors to manage access to the president, limit his schedule of work and visitors, and oversee his medical regimen and diet. She would be called on to repeat her emergency role several more times, during Ike's bout of ileitis the following year, as well as after his mild stroke in 1957.

Although Mamie believed that married women shouldn't hold jobs, she thought that they should control the family finances, including making the decisions about investments and purchases. She imposed strict efficiencies on household expenses at the executive mansion, whether for the private residence or state receptions, favoring low-cost products over labor-intensive cuisine and even ordering the staff to stock up on supermarket specials. And she was an acknowledged expert at running a household, issuing orders, a former staffer said, "as if it were she who had been a five-star general."

Mamie generally avoided taking public positions about issues throughout her eight years as First Lady, and she tended to choose her friends on the basis of their personal virtues, not their partisan attachments. She once quipped, good-naturedly, "Ike runs the country, I turn the lamb chops," although in fact he was far and away the superior cook. On a few occasions, however, her personal values broke through the reserved veneer, as happened in 1957, when she privately defended the president's decision to send federal troops to Little Rock, Arkansas, to ensure that the schools there obeyed the Supreme Court's mandate to integrate. Similarly, when she revived the tradition of egg rolls on the White House lawn, she made sure that African American children were invited to take part. She also made a rare exception to her policy of not endorsing candidates for office in 1954, when Ellen Harris, an old friend in Denver, ran for Congress as a Republican. She toured the city's neighborhoods with the candidate, talking to voters and telling them, "Ladies, I hope you'll all vote for her. We women have to have a voice in things." Ellen Harris didn't succeed in her uphill battle as a woman and a Republican in a Democratic district, but Mamie's active effort on behalf of her good friend testifies to her loyalty and hints at a desire for women to have the greater voice in public affairs that she talked about.

Where public matters were concerned, Mamie generally kept her opinions to herself or discussed them privately with the president. Ike acknowledged that he valued her insights and claimed to consult her about policies and people. He characterized her as "my invaluable, my indispensable, but publicly inarticulate lifelong partner," and was known to respond to ideas by saying, "Let me try this out on Mamie. She's a pretty darn good judge of things." There are signs, however, that some members of Ike's staff may have stifled her plans to speak out more. After she held one press conference in March 1953, six weeks after the inauguration, White House press secretary James Hagerty overruled plans for repeat performances. Hagerty's hand can also be seen in the successful effort to prevent Mamie from giving vocal support for public television, claiming that it might seem that the government was sponsoring propaganda. When the First Lady proposed establishing a liaison to women's clubs, the president's chief of staff, Sherman Adams, put a stop to it.

Occasionally, when her views dovetailed with the official positions she was encouraged to speak out—in moments of military or foreign policy crisis, in favor of UN efforts to settle international differences peacefully, to promote citizen participation in blood drives, or to solicit women's support for civil defense. After the president's first heart attack, she became an articulate advocate for the American Heart Association and its sponsorship of research into the causes and possible cures for heart disease.

In every other case except one, Mamie put her personal opinions aside and went along, for the good of the administration. The exception was her efforts on behalf of the wives and widows of retired military veterans, many of whom were friends from her three dozen years as an army wife. These women often faced financial hardship when they were older, especially the widows, whose government benefits were meager. She led a drive to raise money to build retirement housing and provide health care for a group of overlooked women whose sacrifices for their country she knew to be as real as they were unrecognized. Knollwood, the first retirement home built for military widows, was completed in 1962. Amazingly, when shortly before her own death Mamie applied for a place at Knollwood, she was falsely accused of seeking preferential treatment and withdrew her application.

The Eisenhowers had bought a farm in Gettysburg, Pennsylvania, in 1950. When John F. Kennedy was sworn in as president in 1961, they chose it as their retirement home. Ike was healthy at the time, and the Eisenhowers traveled widely in Europe and the American South, where Ike enjoyed playing golf in the winters. She was cochair, with First Lady Jacqueline Kennedy, of the fundraising committee for the National Cultural Center in 1962, and she occasionally visited the White House. She persuaded her husband to respond to Harry Truman's overtures to resume a friendship that had faded when Ike entered politics.

Later in the decade, as the former president's heart condition deteriorated, she confided to Lady Bird Johnson that she worried about her vulnerability should she be widowed. Mamie Eisenhower expressed her fears of living alone and unprotected as a presidential widow. Prompted by concern about Jacqueline Kennedy and Mamie Eisenhower, President Johnson signed a bill extending Secret Service protection to presidential widows in 1965. President Eisenhower would live for several more years, much of it in worsening health. He was hospitalized for the last year of his life at Walter Reed Hospital, where Mamie lived in the room next door to his until his death in March 1969, at age seventy-eight, of congestive heart failure.

As a widow, Mamie maintained contact with a core group of close friends and family, including Richard and Pat Nixon, who became part of her family when their daughter Julie married her grandson David Eisenhower in 1968. At commemorations associated with President Eisenhower, she sometimes spoke in public, as she did at the dedication of a hospital wing named for her husband in Palm Desert, California, and at the first commencement of Eisenhower College in Seneca Falls, New York, a new college she had helped to found. She also taped a television endorsement of Richard Nixon during his 1972 reelection campaign, and she steadfastly maintained her friendship with Pat Nixon throughout the Watergate scandal and 1974 resignation. Mamie had a stroke on September 25, 1979, and died in Washington on November 1, at the age of eighty-two; she is buried on the grounds of the Eisenhower Library in Abilene, Kansas, next to her husband and young son, Ikky.

JACQUELINE KENNEDY

CAN ANYONE UNDERSTAND HOW IT IS TO HAVE LIVED IN THE WHITE HOUSE AND THEN, SUDDENLY, TO BE LIVING ALONE AS THE PRESIDENT'S WIDOW?

Jacqueline Bouvier Kennedy brought a sense of style to the role of First Lady that had not been seen before and may not be matched again. Born to John Vernou Bouvier III and Janet Lee Bouvier in

July 1929, Jackie spent her childhood in Southampton, Long Island, and New York City. Her mother taught her to ride horses, something she loved doing all her life, and she was also an avid reader and writer. Jackie's parents divorced in 1940. Her mother married Hugh D. Auchincloss II two years later, and Jackie moved with her to new homes in McLean, Virginia, and Newport, Rhode Island. Following boarding school in Connecticut and two years at Vassar College, Jackie spent a year studying abroad in Paris. Instead of returning to Vassar, she earned a bachelor's degree in French literature from George Washington University.

In her senior year at college, Jackie won a *Vogue* magazine essay contest on the topic of "People I Wish I Had Known." The prize was a year as a *Vogue* intern, split between the magazine's New York and Paris offices. Her parents, perhaps fearing that if Jackie returned to France she would join the community of American expatriates there, pressured her to turn the offer down. Instead, she became the "Inquiring Camera Girl" at the *Washington Times-Herald*, photographing people around the city and asking them questions about topics of interest. Her first interviewee was Pat Nixon; another was John Kennedy. Before long, however, it was the tall (five foot eight), striking Jackie who was being photographed, when she and the junior senator from Massachusetts, married in Newport, Rhode Island, in 1953. Three thousand star-struck spectators crowded around St. Mary's Church in tiny Newport for a look at the youthful, glamorous couple.

John Kennedy had been a Massachusetts congressman since 1947 and a senator since nine months before his marriage to Jackie. In January 1960, when Jackie was thirty, he declared himself a candidate for the presidency and immediately plunged into campaigning from coast to coast. After a few weeks of traveling with her husband, Jackie discovered that she was pregnant, and her doctors ordered her to stay at home. From their house in Georgetown, Jackie aided the effort by writing a newspaper column, "Campaign Wife," granting interviews, and being filmed for TV spots. Barely two weeks after John Kennedy's election, Jackie and John celebrated the birth of John Fitzgerald Kennedy Jr. He was their second child—Caroline Bouvier Kennedy had been born in 1957—and would be the first infant child of occupants of the White House since Frances Cleveland (the only First Lady to be married in the White House) gave birth to her second and third daughters, Esther (1893) and Marion (1895).

The first time Jackie saw the inside of the White House was in 1941, when her mother took her two daughters (Jackie's younger sister, Caroline Lee, usually known as Lee Radziwill). Only twelve at the time, she was, to put it mildly, disappointed by what she saw: very little of the furniture was historically significant or visually impressive, and visitors were given almost no information about the building's history. During the transitional period between the 1960 election and the inauguration in January, she paid another visit to what she afterward referred to as "that dreary Maison Blanche." What she envisioned as a museum of America's history showed visitors "practically nothing that dates back before 1948," she said in a 1961 interview. She resolved to fill it with things that, even if they weren't the furnishings and objects that former presidents had owned, at the very least were authentic representations of the periods and styles. "It looks like it's been furnished by discount stores," she said. "Everything in the White House must have a reason for being there. It would be sacrilege merely to 'redecorate' it—a word I hate. It must be restored—and that has nothing to do with decoration. That is a question of scholarship."

Jackie discovered that some old White House furnishings were in storage at various places around Washington, but other items had never belonged to the federal government. They were the personal property of the first families, who had taken them with them when their terms ended. Through the White House Fine Arts Committee, Jackie was able to locate many items of furniture and decoration that had once been in the White House—from the descendents of presidents and through old auction records—and often succeeded in getting the current owners to donate them to the nation. Among these were pieces of furniture that had been the property of Washington, Madison, and Lincoln during their presidencies. Other items were of nonpresidential provenance, but they exemplified the periods and styles of the building and its decoration.

To finance the ambitious restoration, Jackie conceived of a non-profit organization, the White House Historical Association, which would produce a guide to the executive mansion, the profits from which would cover the costs of purchase and restoration of historic objects. A new position, White House curator, was established. The curator worked with Jackie to oversee the text, choose the photographs, and design *The White House: An Historic Guide*, which was first published in 1962 and sold five hundred thousand copies within six months. It remains in print today and continues to fund the work of the White House Historical Association.

Featuring distinctive furniture like the Oval Office desk, constructed from a British sailing ship on the orders of Queen Victoria, who gave it to President Rutherford B. Hayes in 1878, Jackie led a television tour of the White House on Valentine's Day, 1962, walking through the restored spaces as she narrated the building's history and inviting Americans to visit in person.

Jackie's commitment to preservation embraced the White House grounds and the area surrounding the executive mansion as well. She persuaded her friend Rachel ("Bunny") Mellon, the art collector and horticulturist, to turn the Rose Garden, which is adjacent to the Oval Office, into a natural sanctuary and a place to welcome visitors to the White House. She saved the historic houses that face the White House on Lafayette Square from being razed in order to erect large government office buildings. At Jackie's urging, the buildings were preserved and the new offices were constructed behind them, using a red brick similar to that of the Federal-style townhouses in order to blend into the historic neighborhood. Extending her mission beyond the immediate environs of the executive mansion, she

initiated a plan to restore the section of Pennsylvania Avenue running from the White House to Capitol Hill.

Brief as the Kennedy presidency was, the president and Jackie
returned a sense of elegance to the White House, frequently using
official occasions to highlight American artistic and cultural accomplishments. A diplomatic ceremony in the Kennedy White House
might appear, to an inexperienced observer, more like a musical
performance than an affair of state. Guest lists were a heteroge-
neous mix of scientists and statesmen, performers and politicians,
artists and ambassadors. The evening's centerpiece was often a
recital, concert, or dramatic performance of work ranging from the
Renaissance to the Jazz Age by American talent. The twin messages
at such events were unmistakable: American cultural and intellectual achievement was on a par with that of any other country, and
the arts were central to our national life and identity.

Abroad, Jackie made as striking an impression as she did in
Washington or New York. Comfortable in foreign settings and fluent in languages–especially French–she found her hosts in other
countries eager to hear what she thought about her own society
and about theirs. She often traveled with the president on his trips
to Europe, Latin America, and southern Asia. The French greeted
her so enthusiastically in 1961 that John Kennedy, in a show of
witty self-deprecation, quipped, "I am the man who accompanied
Jacqueline Kennedy to Paris, and I have enjoyed it." On that trip,
Jackie met the French minister of culture, André Malraux. Not long
afterward, he approved the unprecedented loan of Leonardo da
Vinci's portrait of the *Mona Lisa*, the world's most famous painting,
to Washington's National Gallery. Malraux also gave her the ideas
that evolved into the National Endowments for the Humanities and
the Arts.

According to people who knew the Kennedys well, the image
of "lovely inconsequence" (in historian Arthur Schlesinger's phrase)
that Jackie projected was a mask that concealed deep interest in,

knowledge of, and concern about the urgent domestic and foreign issues with which the president dealt. But it is said that she believed she could communicate her opinions about policy to the president privately and would be more successful in advancing her historical and cultural agenda if she seemed uninvolved in politics. In less than three years, Jackie made more trips abroad than any First Lady before her, to at least fifteen countries, some of them more than once. Her friendships with foreign leaders continued after those visits. Even after John Kennedy's death she was able to write directly to the Soviet premier, Nikita Khrushchev, with whom her husband had entered into the 1963 Nuclear Test Ban Treaty, which she counted the high-water mark of the Kennedy foreign policy record, to urge him to move ahead with nuclear arms reduction and bring the smaller nations in the Soviet orbit along with him.

Sometimes, she found indirect and subtle ways to suggest her views without direct pronouncements, such as when she addressed, in Spanish, the Cuban refugees who had fought at the ill-fated 1962 Bay of Pigs invasion after their return to Miami; or released photographs of the racially integrated kindergarten she organized in the White House for her daughter, Caroline, and other children.

There were occasional darker moments, especially when the Kennedys' third child, Patrick Bouvier, was born prematurely in August 1963 and died two days later, with the entire country–and a good portion of the world–listening for news and praying. But of course, the moment that changed everything–for the nation, and for Jacqueline Kennedy–was November 22, 1963. At the age of thirty-four, she was a widow, the youngest presidential wife in American history to mourn her husband. Stoically, she supervised preparations for John Kennedy's state funeral and remained in Washington for several months to discuss with President Lyndon Johnson some legislative matters that she considered vital to her husband's vision. Then she moved to New York City with her two children and began planning the John F. Kennedy Library, which she decided to build on a spot overlooking Boston Harbor. She was also involved in planning the John F. Kennedy School of Government at Harvard University.

In 1968, Jackie married Aristotle Onassis, and until he died in 1975, she divided her time between the United States and her husband's houses in Paris, Athens, and Skorpios, an island he owned in the Ionian Sea. In the 1970s, she became an editor in New York City and was active in the effort to save the Beaux-Arts Grand Central Terminal, among other historically and architecturally significant buildings; protect and improve Central Park; and revive the Broadway theater district.

Jacqueline Bouvier Kennedy Onassis died at home in New York City, of non-Hodgkins lymphoma, on May 19, 1994. She was sixty-four years old. She was buried in Arlington National Cemetery, next to John Kennedy, the second presidential widow (after Nellie Taft) to be buried there.

LADY BIRD JOHNSON

THE FIRST LADY IS, AND ALWAYS HAS BEEN, AN UNPAID PUBLIC SERVANT ELECTED BY ONE PERSON, HER HUSBAND.

No American First Lady has ever assumed her role under more difficult circumstances than Lady Bird Johnson, not even her namesake Eliza Johnson, whose husband Andrew became president after Abraham Lincoln's assassination. It is also likely that few others were blessed with the tact and modesty to reassure a nation in shock after the assassination of President John F. Kennedy without ever appearing to upstage his grieving widow. She created a sense of continuity by adopting a number of Jacqueline Kennedy's projects, especially those that had to do with White House restoration and history. She consulted her predecessor frequently and followed her advice about displaying art in the executive mansion's public areas, receptions, and even the choice of china patterns. Moving into the White House on December 8, 1963, Lady Bird Johnson's first months as First Lady were overshadowed by the mourning for President Kennedy and a groundswell of sympathy for and interest in Jacqueline Kennedy. In consideration of this, Mrs. Johnson did not undertake a full-blown public role. President Johnson, for his part, issued an executive order to make the Committee for the Preservation of the White House a permanent entity. Jackie had formed the committee as an ad hoc group; the executive order publicly acknowledged that her vision would be carried forward into the future.

Nicknamed "Lady Bird" by her nanny when she was an infant, Claudia Alta Taylor was never called by her given name. She was born in Karnack, Texas, in December 1912, on her father's cotton farm. Her parents, Thomas Jefferson Taylor II and Minnie Pattillo Taylor, had moved to Texas from Alabama. Her father owned the general store in Karnack, farmed cotton on twelve thousand acres, and made his fortune by investing the profits from his businesses in local real estate. Minnie Taylor died in 1918, before Lady Bird reached her sixth birthday, and her sister, Effie Pattillo, took charge of raising the young girl and her two older brothers, Thomas Jefferson Jr. and Antonio ("Tony").

After high school and spending two years at a boarding school in Dallas, Lady Bird enrolled at the University of Texas at Austin, graduated with honors in history in 1933 and, a year later, earned a second degree in journalism. She was planning to work as a journalist, but barely two months after commencement, she met Lyndon Johnson, then an aide to Texas congressman Richard Kleberg. They married ten weeks later, on November 17, 1934. The Johnsons returned to Washington until 1935, when Lyndon was appointed head of the National Youth Administration, a New Deal organization, in Texas.

Although Lady Bird never had a career in journalism, she was a successful businesswoman whose ventures included broadcasting. She also urged all women to obtain a college education or more, and her advocacy was recognized by honorary degrees from thirteen colleges and universities, including her alma mater. Her attachment to the University of Texas, where she served a six-year term on the board of regents in the 1970s, was a factor in the Johnsons' choice of the Austin campus as the home of the Lyndon Baines Johnson Library and Museum. The first presidential library at a university, it draws more visitors than any other.

The Johnsons returned to Washington when Lyndon was elected to Congress in 1936. A man of modest means at the time (he bought Lady Bird's wedding ring from Sears for $2.50), his campaign was substantially underwritten by $10,000 Lady Bird inherited from her mother and her father's contribution of an additional $20,000. When Lyndon took his seat in the House of Representatives, Lady Bird formed friendships with a number of congressional wives, among them Pat Nixon and Betty Ford, as well as capital luminaries like Speaker of the House Sam Rayburn and Eleanor Roosevelt. At her first encounter with Mrs. Roosevelt, a Congressional Club benefit to raise money for a wheelchair for a disabled child, Lady Bird filmed the occasion with her own home-movie camera.

Rayburn, whose brief marriage had ended in divorce and who had no children, spent a great deal of time with the Johnsons. He and Sam Ealy Johnson, Lyndon's father, had served together in the Texas legislature, and Rayburn made the young congressman his protégé. His conversations about politics in the Johnsons' living room were a major element of Lady Bird's political education. When Lyndon was serving in the Pacific as a naval officer during World War II, Lady Bird had no trouble overseeing his office staff, keeping an eye on their district back home, welcoming visitors to Washington, and helping to solve constituents' problems. Their two daughters, Lynda Bird and Luci Baines Johnson, were born in 1944 and 1947, after Lyndon returned from military service.

With a further inheritance from her mother, Lady Bird bought a small radio station in Austin, KTBC, and took over all aspects of the operation. She hired staff, attracted sponsors, managed the finances, and starting paying off the money the station owed. Later,

Lyndon helped persuade the FCC to approve expanded operations for KTBC, which changed its call letters to KLBJ. The station ultimately became the flagship of a large media company, with diversified investments in ranching and other businesses. Lady Bird was the hands-on manager until the company was sold in the 1980s.

When Lyndon suffered a heart attack in 1954, he was already Senate majority leader, and Lady Bird moved into a room at Bethesda Naval Hospital in order to shield him from the pressures of his position. While she kept an eye on his medical condition, she conferred with his political aides to select the issues that she would take to her husband for decisions. After weeks as the one person—aside from the doctors and nurses—exposed to his irascible and sometimes overbearing temperament, Lady Bird emerged as one of the rare few who knew how to calm Lyndon and get him to refocus his attention.

By 1960, Lady Bird supported her husband's hopes of winning the presidency himself. When he lost the nomination to a younger John F. Kennedy, she is said to have advised him to refuse Senator Kennedy's invitation to be his running mate. After Lyndon accepted, Lady Bird became the loyal, energetic female face of the campaign. Logging thirty-five thousand miles in ten weeks, she made a difference in one of the most closely fought presidential elections in American history. One of Lady Bird's hopes was to preserve the South as a Democratic bastion—no small feat in a region split over integration, since she was ardently pro-integration (and was the only woman present when LBJ signed the Civil Rights Act in 1964). She won many crowds over by playing up her southern roots, and never lost her dignity or her temper, despite occasional protesters.

In 1964, LBJ, who had become president following the assassination of Kennedy, was running for election to a full term. Lady Bird again energetically spoke out for her husband. Bill Moyers, in his homily at the memorial for Lady Bird, who died on July 11, 2007, called this her finest hour. Against the advice of many in the campaign, she had insisted on focusing on the South, where integration continued to be an incendiary issue, and led a group of supporters on an old-fashioned tour by train–the "Lady Bird Special"–through a number of southern states. Everywhere the train stopped, Lady Bird delivered her stump speech from the caboose. She refused to wilt in the face of harsh signs and hostile words, winning the admiration of her entourage, including her Secret Service contingent, and the voters who heard her. Wherever she went, the First Lady telephoned Democratic leaders beforehand. Whether they agreed with her views on race or not, they felt they couldn't ignore an invitation from the wife of the president, so turnouts were large.

Her message was as simple as it was direct: "It would be a bottomless tragedy for our country to be racially divided." Except in five states in the Deep South and in Arizona, most voters agreed with her. LBJ enjoyed a landslide victory, with 61 percent of the popular vote. At the 1965 inauguration, Lady Bird set a precedent by holding the Bible on which her husband swore the oath of office, a practice that every presidential spouse since has followed.

Lady Bird often claimed that the First Lady's duty is to the president's agenda. Nearly twenty years after leaving Washington, she gave a brief statement of what might be called the job description for the First Lady: "She's not elected, he is elected, and they are there as a team. And it's much more appropriate for her to work on projects that are a part of his administration, a part of his aims and hopes for America." If so, Lady Bird met the test with flying colors: campaigning on Lyndon's behalf; befriending members of Congress from both sides of the aisle, and their spouses; mollifying cabinet members, staffers, and occasionally generals who'd felt the sting of his temper or demanding nature; and even learning about the history and society of the foreign countries she visited with the president, in order to act the part of respectful guest rather than dominating superpower.

However, there were also programs and causes that either grew out of Lady Bird's own interests or that she made her own. Head

Start was one. Originally designed to run for a mere eight weeks during the summer, the program gained immense visibility after she embraced it. Lady Bird appeared in a nationally broadcast film explaining Head Start's aims, visited a number of sites, and made sure its funding didn't fall victim to the political process. In her role as national chair, she called Head Start "the big breakthrough we have been seeking in education" for the children of the country's most deprived families. Forty years later, the successful program is now a cornerstone of early public education.

When we think about Lady Bird's accomplishments as First Lady, however, the one that is most intimately associated with her is "beautification." She claimed that the idea of devoting effort to conservation and restoration programs came to her while listening to Lyndon Johnson praise the country's landscape in a speech in Michigan in 1964, but if it originated with the president, it became her legacy. She knew from the start that her designs were ambitious. On January 27, 1965, a week before announcing her plans, she wrote this diary entry: "Getting on the subject of beautification is like picking up a tangled skein of wool. All the threads are interwoven–recreation and pollution and mental health, and the crime rate, and rapid transit, and highway beautification, and the war on poverty, and parks–national, state, and local. It is hard to hitch the conversation into one straight line, because everything leads to something else."

She had the vision to think big, and the good sense to start small, with the Committee for a More Beautiful Capital, a coalition of philanthropists, civic leaders, and government agencies, especially the National Park Service, under the direction of Interior Secretary Stewart Udall. While some thought attention should be focused on the areas that visitors to Washington saw–"masses of flowers where masses pass," in the phrase of one benefactor–others saw an opportunity to brighten the poorer areas of the city and involve the residents in the effort. Lady Bird, who was reviving a role created by Nellie Taft, encouraged a diversity of ideas, and added her own, to restore "the small triangles and squares with which Washington abounds, now quite barren except for a dispirited sprig of grass, and maybe a tottering bench, and put shrubs and flowers in them." Her vision included two new gardens on the White House grounds– one named for Jacqueline Kennedy and the other a Children's Garden–and helped to revitalize the Mall between the Capitol and the Washington Monument. She spurred the improvements along Pennsylvania Avenue that had started during the Kennedy presidency, and fostered dozens of landscaping, renovation, and cleanup projects in the capital's low-income neighborhoods. Much of the work was paid for by private donations.

Next, she set her sights on the entire country. Lady Bird launched a national effort in May 1965 with the White House Conference on Natural Beauty, a discussion of conservation and the environment with representatives of business, organized labor, the sciences, the public sector, and volunteer groups. The Keep America Beautiful campaign has enjoyed phenomenal success–public and private sites were cleaned up, and many cities emulated Washington's example. It also met with occasional opposition. When the Highway Beautification Act (known as "Lady Bird's Bill") proposed to limit billboards alongside roads, there was resistance from many congressman and the advertising industry. The persuasive Johnsons succeeded in gathering enough votes to get the measure passed, but afterward Congress refused to appropriate money for enforcement. There were more humorous moments, too, such as when the pork industry objected to an anti-litter campaign that described litterbugs as "pigs."

Although Lyndon Johnson was just sixty in November 1968, Lady Bird realized that an election campaign would imperil his health. The president had a serious heart condition, and his administration was beset by the Vietnam War abroad and racial and social upheaval at home. Whether she deserves the credit for persuading him not to run isn't known, but she did tell him of her concerns about his health and her doubts that he would be able to revive a sense of unity in the

American citizenry. We do know that it was her idea to include the words "I will not accept" in his announcement that he had decided not to seek his party's nomination, in order to close the door on any effort to draft him as the nominee at the convention.

When the Johnsons returned to Texas in 1969, Lady Bird's dedication to beautification and the environment continued. She joined the National Park Service's Advisory Board on National Parks, Historic Sites, Buildings, and Monuments, and was later praised by Interior Secretary Bruce Babbitt, who said in 1999, "Mrs. Johnson has been a 'shadow' secretary of the interior for much of her life." The Andrews Plantation house in Karnack, where she was born, is now a national historic landmark, the Lady Bird Johnson Home. The Johnsons also donated the LBJ ranch in Johnson City, Texas, as the Lyndon B. Johnson National Historic Park. In his will, Lyndon Johnson stipulated that it "remain a working ranch and not become a sterile relic of the past."

Lady Bird published *A White House Diary* in 1971, a selection of the hundreds of hours of reflections that she recorded daily throughout her time as First Lady. This passage from it appears in the program for her July 14 memorial service: "As I look back on those five years of turmoil and achievement, I feel amazement that it happened to me, and gratitude that I had the opportunity to live them, and strongest of all–out of all the trips that I made and all the people that I met–a deep roaring faith in and love for this country."

Attending the private gathering in Austin were Lady Bird's family, closest friends and former staff, First Lady Laura Bush, former presidents Clinton and Carter, former First Ladies Clinton, Bush, Reagan, and Carter, as well as Susan Ford Bales and Caroline Kennedy Schlossberg. Her daughters Lynda and Luci spoke, as did many of her grandchildren. It was a beautiful tribute that highlighted her legacies–among them, highway beautification, wildflower preservation, and Head Start. The service ended with the playing of "The Eyes of Texas" by the University of Texas Longhorn Band, and most of us–myself included–tearfully joining in the singing.

PAT NIXON ⌒

BEING FIRST LADY IS THE HARDEST UNPAID JOB IN THE WORLD.

Thelma Catherine Ryan took the name "Pat" after her father, William Ryan Sr., died in 1930. He was descended from Irish stock, and when she was born on March 16, 1912, in Ely, Nevada, where he worked as a copper miner, he called her "St. Patrick's babe in the morn." Her mother, Kate Halberstadt Bender, was a widow with two young children when she married William Ryan. Pat was the youngest of their three children, all born in quick succession; William "Bill" Jr. arrived in 1910, and Thomas the following year.

Probably no modern First Lady worked as much or as hard as Pat Ryan did during her childhood and young adulthood. In Artesia, California, southwest of Los Angeles, William Ryan bought a ten-acre "truck farm" in 1913, and by the time Pat started school she was accustomed to the cycles of planting and harvesting the vegetables that her family sold from a truck that made the rounds of area towns and cities. The land is now Pat Nixon Park, in Cerritos. When her mother fell ill in 1924, Pat took charge of household chores for her family and the seasonal farm workers they hired. Kate Ryan died of cancer in 1925, and three years later William Ryan's tuberculosis incapacitated him as well. To pay her father's medical bills until his death in 1930, Pat worked at a local bank, as a cleaner in the early morning and a bookkeeper in the afternoon, before and after attending classes at Excelsior High School in Norwalk, California. She somehow also found time to play leading roles in school drama productions and take an active role in the debating team and student government.

Pat took courses at a local business college after graduating from high school and continued working. In 1931, a year after her father's death, she enrolled at Fullerton Community College, where she spent one year and resumed her stage acting. Then she left school, drove an elderly couple who were family friends cross-country to

New York in exchange for a return ticket to California, and took a job at the Seton Hospital for Incurables in New York City, founded by the Catholic Sisters of Charity. From 1932 to 1934, she lived at the hospital with the nuns while working as a laboratory assistant, typist, pharmacy manager, and X-ray technician. She completed one course in radiology at Columbia University, perhaps because she was considering a career in the medical field, but the next year she returned to California to pursue a business degree at the University of Southern California.

Pat had been awarded a research scholarship to USC that paid her tuition and a living stipend in exchange for grading papers and doing library work for a psychology professor. From 1934 to 1937, she attended school full-time, and held down clerical jobs at the university, waitressing, and testing beauty products. She may have continued to nurse hopes of an acting career as well, since she was an occasional extra for film shoots. Despite her demanding schedule, in three years Pat graduated from USC with honors, receiving both a B.S. in merchandising and a certificate in teaching that was the equivalent of a master's degree. She thus became the first future First Lady to earn a graduate degree. At Whittier Union High School, she taught business courses during the day and typing classes for adults at night, also planned student field trips and rallies, attended the sports teams' games and meets, and directed school plays.

While acting in the Whittier Community Players production of the George S. Kaufman–Alexander Woolcott play *The Dark Tower*, Pat met a young lawyer and Whittier College graduate, Richard Nixon, who also had a part in the play. According to some accounts, he proposed after the first rehearsal; they married two years later, in 1940, and Pat resigned from teaching at Whittier Union High School in the summer of 1941. With war approaching, she went to work for the Red Cross. When Richard won his naval commission, she followed him to Iowa. After he was posted to the South Pacific, she returned to California and found employment in San Francisco as an economist for the Office of Price Administration.

The first of the Nixons' two daughters, Patricia ("Tricia"), was born in 1946, the same year that Richard was elected to the U.S. Congress. Julie was born in 1948, two years before his election to the Senate. Like many spouses of politicians, Pat wasn't drawn to politics before marrying Richard, but she took an unusually vigorous role in every one of her husband's campaigns. Later, she said, "I have sacrificed everything in my life that I consider precious in order to advance the political career of my husband." And advance it she did. When he first ran for Congress in 1946, she learned everything possible about the record of his opponent, incumbent Jerry Voorhis, and then managed every detail of Richard's campaign literature, from writing and editing to handing out fliers on street corners.

In later campaigns, her role was less central but no less crucial. She attended opponents' campaign events and used her secretarial skills to record their speeches in shorthand, then helped Richard devise the most effective presentations. She was an indefatigable presence at rallies, fundraisers, and smaller meetings, with an enthusiastic personal manner that counterbalanced her husband's somewhat standoffish demeanor. Although Pat resented the no-holds-barred nature of politics and its tendency to intrude on family and personal life, she never shrank from supporting her husband's career and often counseled him to meet opposition head-on. For example, it was she who urged Richard to refute the charges made against him about campaign contributions when he was running for vice president, telling him, "If you do not fight back but simply crawl away, you will destroy yourself." His response was his now-legendary Checkers speech, where he praised Pat's "fighting Irish spirit," her indifference to luxury, and her probity.

President Eisenhower valued Pat's effectiveness as a standard-bearer and goodwill ambassador for his administration and put her talents to good use. When Mamie Eisenhower was unavailable for an event, he sometimes called on Pat to pinch-hit for the First Lady.

The president almost always asked her to accompany the vice president on his many foreign trips, where she never limited herself to official functions but made a point of meeting ordinary citizens at schools and hospitals, orphanages and old-age homes.

While raising their daughters, who were twelve and fourteen when Richard's two terms as vice president ended in 1960, Pat helped her husband with speeches and other writing, oversaw his schedule, and helped him strategize about how to turn the vice presidency into a stepping-stone to further opportunities and not the political dead end it often was. It has been suggested that Pat transformed the role of vice president's wife from understudy to "second lady."

In the 1960 presidential race, the Nixons attempted to turn Pat's appeal to their advantage. Just as there had been "I Like Mamie Too" buttons in 1952, this campaign paraded the slogan "Pat for First Lady," the first time the role had been mentioned so prominently in an effort to win votes. Pat rarely suggested that women should run for office on their own (though a few had successfully done so), but she did propose that women get involved in politics as volunteers. The tactic failed, both in the presidential race, which Richard narrowly lost to John Kennedy, and in the 1962 California gubernatorial election, which also ended in defeat and seemed to mark the end of his career in politics.

Instead of remaining in California, the Nixons moved to New York City, where Richard joined a prominent law firm and seemed to be putting his old career behind him. When he made a comeback in 1968 and won the Republican presidential nomination, Pat seemed at first reluctant to reprise her on-stage role as campaigner, but by the reelection campaign of 1972, she had regained her zeal and took on a more visible and outspoken role. Her address to that year's Republican National Convention was the first by a First Lady of her party. Even on the 1968 campaign trail, she displayed tenaciousness, as Richard Nixon noted in 1971: Pat "was the one that always insisted on shaking that last hand, not simply because she was thinking of that vote, but because she simply could not turn down that last child or that last person."

Whatever reluctance she may have felt during the preliminaries to the Nixon presidency, Pat had a number of surprises in store for anyone who expected her to act the part of a passive, demure First Lady. Conscious, perhaps, of the changes in women's roles that were part of the 1960s, she spoke in favor of the equal rights amendment. She announced that she thought it was time to appoint a woman to the U.S. Supreme Court and pressured her husband to do so (but that wouldn't happen until President Ronald Reagan named Sandra Day O'Connor to the Court in 1981). In 1973, after the Supreme Court ruled in *Roe v. Wade* that women had a constitutional right to abortion, she revealed to reporters that she was pro-choice. She also made a fashion statement by appearing in slacks in a national magazine. Despite such independent moves, Pat unfailingly projected the image of a middle-class wife and stay-at-home mom, the antithesis of the liberated woman.

Pat traveled the world more than any First Lady before Hillary Clinton in the 1990s, sometimes with the president but often on her own. Not long after an earthquake in Peru claimed eighty thousand lives and left an equal number homeless, she decided to kick off an international effort to aid the victims by flying to Lima with tons of food, clothing, and medical supplies that had been donated to the Peruvian people. Her action bolstered the relief effort and may have led to improved relations between the United States and its neighbor. In gratitude, Peru conferred on Pat the Grand Cross of the Order of the Sun, the Western Hemisphere's oldest decoration. When she visited West Africa in 1972, her discussions with Liberian, Ghanaian, and Ivory Coast leaders covered U.S. African policy and human rights, and was not mere symbolism and photo ops. As usual, she made a point of meeting the local people, not just top officials. In 1974 she attended the installation of Venezuela's new president, Carlos Andres Perez, despite the fact that in the 1950s she and her husband, who was then vice president, had been attacked by anti-American protestors when they visited the country.

Pat also made headlines when she and Richard traveled abroad. In Yugoslavia, she said that women should run for public office and thought that the Yugoslav and American legislative branches would be better off if they elected more women members. She said that she would even consider voting for a woman who wasn't a Republican—if she were qualified. On visits to the Soviet Union and the People's Republic of China, Pat maintained a more discreet silence, but in Moscow she toured the city with Victoria Brezhnev, making a point of meeting as many ordinary people as possible—laborers, students, and artists, among others. She made such a strong impression on Zhou Enlai that he personally made her a gift of two giant pandas, which became the most popular members of the Washington Zoo's menagerie. In South Vietnam in 1969, she set a precedent for First Ladies by going into a combat zone, flying eighteen miles from Saigon in an open helicopter—surrounded by heavily armed Secret Service agents. On that trip, she also visited an orphanage and a military hospital, to cheer up wounded American servicemen.

One stance that contributed to her traditional image was her enthusiastic promotion of volunteer activities as the solution to many social problems, which she characterized as "the spirit of people helping people." Early in the Nixon presidency, Pat asked people to commit time as volunteers to help deliver community services and praised programs that successfully addressed problems without relying on government funds or legislation. Exemplary groups were often invited to the White House, which guaranteed a shower of publicity for their work and for volunteerism in general. She praised the National Center for Voluntary Action, which did receive some federal funding, participated in their annual award presentations, and helped attract publicity to the organization's goals. She also toured privately run summer camps for underprivileged children and attracted helpful publicity to the programs by inviting some of the campers for an afternoon sail on the presidential yacht.

In subtle ways, Pat often boosted Nixon administration programs merely by showing interest in them. After President Nixon established the Environmental Protection Agency in 1970, he might attend a meeting where pollution was on the agenda while Pat visited nearby conservation and reclamation projects. If there was a conference on law enforcement, Pat might show up at an education center for troubled teenagers. She showed her concern for at-risk youth in more overt ways as well, by initiating free concerts, called Evenings in the Park, in Washington, D.C., one of them on the White House lawn. To create opportunities for recreation for urban dwellers who lacked the opportunity to spend time in remote national parks, Pat promoted the Legacy of the Parks program, which transferred control of fifty thousand acres of federal land to states and municipalities for the purpose of developing outdoor spaces in or near cities.

Pat's attitude toward the White House reveals her concern for the average citizen. Remembering her own long workdays, perhaps, she scheduled evening Candlelight Tours of the executive mansion, especially when it was decorated for Christmas, to give working people the chance to visit. In spring and fall, she opened the White House grounds to visitors as well, the first time the public had been allowed into the gardens since the late nineteenth century. On Thanksgiving 1969, she invited over two hundred residents in local nursing homes to dinner at the White House. She hosted an eclectic performance series, Evenings at the White House, that showcased every American musical art form, from classic to folk. She invited ordinary citizens to join the official attendees for the nondenominational Sunday services in the East Room and made the building accessible to the handicapped.

To make it possible for the visually and hearing impaired, as well as the physically handicapped, to enjoy White House tours, the rules were changed to allow the blind to handle the antiques on display, tour guides were told to speak more slowly to accommodate lip-readers, and ramps were built to facilitate wheelchair access. Pat frequently circulated among the people waiting in line for the tours, talking to them, signing autographs, and posing for snapshots. For the first time, the illustrated pamphlets visitors received were made available in languages other than English. She expanded the acquisition of historically significant items introduced by Jacqueline Kennedy, adding more works of art and furniture than any other First Lady. At her direction, the north portico of the White House was illuminated at night, to make it visible to tourists and even travelers landing at or taking off from nearby National airport.

Pat supported President Nixon's decision to run for reelection in 1972 and was a staunch supporter of his Vietnam policy even as it overshadowed nearly everything else about his presidency. At the same time, while supporting the troops who were risking their lives, she thought that war resisters who had fled the United States should be granted amnesty. She also criticized the shooting deaths of antiwar protesters by National Guardsmen at Ohio's Kent State University in 1970. When the Watergate scandal erupted several years later, she counseled her husband not to resign, but she supported his decision to do so and return to California in 1974. Their estate in San Clemente was his main bulwark in a storm of legal, physical, and emotional problems that included questions about the resignation, a near-fatal bout of phlebitis, and a deep depression.

In July 1976, the woman who had come through her parents' early deaths and the vicissitudes of Richard Nixon's political fortunes unscathed had a stroke that left her unable to speak or use her left side. After a long regimen of physical therapy, she recovered her motor and speaking skills, but was never again as strong as she had been for nearly sixty years. After the Nixons began spending most of their time on the East Coast and her husband's reputation and spirits rebounded, Pat increasingly devoted herself to her family and her garden.

Occasionally, she would get involved in a project like the overhaul of the Smithsonian Institution's First Ladies exhibit or a Carter

Center conference on women and the U.S. Constitution, but she spent more time with her four grandchildren (born to her daughter Julie and David Eisenhower, Dwight and Mamie Eisenhower's grandson, and to Tricia and Edward Cox) than in the public eye, especially after suffering a second stroke in 1983. She did attend the dedication of the Pat Nixon School in Cerritos, California, in 1975; the dedication of the Richard Nixon Birthplace and Museum in Yorba Linda in 1990, and the 1991 dedication of the Ronald Reagan Library and Museum. When Richard Nixon made his first return trip to China as a former president, Pat accompanied him, but she never set foot in the White House after August 1974. She died in June 1993 in New Jersey, at the age of eighty-one, ten months before her husband's death in April 1994. They are buried side by side at the Richard Nixon Birthplace and Museum in Yorba Linda.

BETTY FORD   *died July 8 - 2011 (at age 93 yr. old)*

NOT MY POWER, BUT THE POWER OF THE POSITION, A POWER
WHICH COULD BE USED TO HELP.

The physical grace that Americans have long associated with Betty Ford came naturally, a dancer's gift. But the social grace under pressure that we also admire was something she learned from difficult experiences during her early life. Born Elizabeth Ann Bloomer in 1918, to William Bloomer Sr., a traveling salesman, and his wife, Hortense, Betty (as she has always been called) was the youngest of three children and the only daughter. The family settled in Grand Rapids, Michigan, where Betty attended public schools and discovered a talent for and love of dancing. She not only attended dance school from the age of eight, but when the Depression arrived, twelve-year-old Betty also taught the waltz, fox-trot, and other popular dances to local children.

In 1934, William Bloomer, who had struggled with alcoholism, died. Betty was still in high school. After graduating from Central

High School, she wanted to study dance in New York, but Hortense Bloomer wouldn't agree to the plan. Betty did manage to attend the Bennington School of Dance in Vermont for two summers, where she studied with several choreographers, including Martha Graham. Graham was impressed enough to invite Betty to join the auxiliary troupe of her company. She accepted, moved to New York City, and continued to study and perform with Graham. Many years later, when Betty was First Lady, she would pay tribute to her mentor when she helped influence the choice of Martha Graham as one of the recipients of the Presidential Medal of Freedom in 1976.

Hortense Bloomer, who had remarried, continued to pressure Betty to give up her dreams of a career in dance and return to Grand Rapids. In 1941, she finally gave in and went to work at a Grand Rapids department store. For a while, however, she taught dance to children, including some with physical handicaps, and formed her own small company, which gave recitals around the city. After she'd been back in Michigan for a year, she married William G. Warren, a salesman she had known since junior high school. They had no children and divorced five years later, in 1947.

Just before the national elections of 1948, Betty married Gerald Ford Jr., who was running for a seat in the U.S. Congress. The wedding, on October 15, was less than three weeks before election day. They had waited until the last minute, a newspaper reported, because "Jerry was running for Congress and wasn't sure how voters might feel about his marrying a divorced ex-dancer." He won the election, and the couple settled in a Washington suburb; they had four children between 1950 and 1957, and Gerald Ford eventually rose to become the House's highest-ranking Republican. He served thirteen consecutive terms in Congress, until 1973, when he was appointed vice president after the resignation of Spiro Agnew. When Richard Nixon resigned as president in August 1974, Gerald Ford became the nation's thirty-eighth president.

For a nation unsettled by the Watergate scandals and an unwinnable war in Vietnam, Betty proved to be a reassuring, immensely likable First Lady. She took the country into her confidence, speaking sensibly and candidly about her continuing fondness for dance and the abiding love the Fords shared after more than twenty-five years of marriage. She could be refreshingly frank about subjects that troubled many Americans at the time but had previously been off-limits in interviews with her predecessors: experimenting with drugs, premarital sex, abortion (*Roe v. Wade* had been decided in 1973, but the public debate was far from settled), and medical treatment for mental and emotional conditions. Although she was criticized in some circles for her openness, her overall popularity was extraordinarily high.

As brave as Betty's candor about contemporary social issues was, her willingness to talk openly about her own medical problems helped bring about a sea-change in American attitudes toward topics like cancer and substance abuse. After Betty's September 1974 breast cancer surgery, she chose not to keep the facts about her mastectomy a secret from the public. Doctors perform cancer surgery every day, but as she told an interviewer, "that I was the wife of the president put it in headlines and brought before the public this particular experience I was going through." Realizing that she could turn her illness into a way to make women more conscious of the risk of breast cancer, she decided that going public would help save lives. "I'm sure I've saved at least one person—maybe more." Characteristically, Betty decided that one life would more than compensate for the awkwardness and loss of privacy the revelation and press attention would cost her. I'll never forget the impression of her tossing a football in her bathrobe just a couple of days after the mastectomy. That photograph said it all.

If it took courage to let the world know about her experience as a breast cancer patient, Betty's decision in the early 1980s to share the details of the time she spent in drug rehabilitation to treat her dependency on alcohol and the opiates that she started taking in the 1960s to manage the pain from a pinched nerve and arthritis was many times more courageous. Her addictions were something that she had denied for years, until members of her family confronted her in 1978. As she wrote in *Betty: A Glad Awakening*, her 1987 memoir about her rehabilitation, "I liked alcohol . . . And I loved pills. They took away my tension and my pain." She went through detox at Long Beach Naval Hospital, and since then has learned to treat pain medications warily. A quadruple-bypass operation in 1987 required pain medication, but this time Betty made sure that she remained in control. "There were a lot of sleepless nights where I just walked the floor," she recalled about the postoperative period when she endured discomfort rather than risk another addiction.

Betty didn't stop with her own recovery. As she had done when she had her cancer surgery, she transformed addiction into a medical condition people could talk about in public. In 1982, after her successful treatment, she cofounded the Betty Ford Center with former ambassador Harvey Firestone on the campus of the Eisenhower Medical Center near the Fords' own home in Rancho Mirage, California. The hundred-bed center treats men and women with alcohol and drug dependencies and conducts a five-day program for families to augment the core therapy. Her willingness to talk about her own experience with dependency and therapy helped lift the veil over the topic and made it more likely that others would find it easier to admit—to themselves and their families—that they had drug or alcohol problems and to seek therapy.

This shift in attitudes is even more crucial for women than for men, because women more frequently keep their alcoholism a secret, are more susceptible to liver damage, and are more likely to get help once they have talked to a physician or other health-care professional. Her talent for turning her own, often difficult, experiences into ways of improving the lives of others is one reason John Robert Greene, a biographer, has said, "Betty Ford did things that public women hadn't done before, not just First Ladies."

Betty served as chair of the center's board of directors until 2005, when at the age of eighty-seven, she passed the reins to her daughter, Susan Ford Bales. While she was actively involved in the center, she wrote a second book, *Healing and Hope* (2003), about six women who recovered from chemical dependencies at the Betty Ford Center.

ROSALYNN CARTER

ONCE YOU GET INVOLVED, THE NEEDS ARE SO GREAT.

Rosalynn Carter learned the lessons of hard work and responsibility from her mother, Frances Allethea ("Allie") Smith, when Wilburn Smith, Rosalynn's father, died in 1940. Left a widow with four young children—Rosalynn, the eldest, was thirteen—Allie worked at a series of humble jobs in Plains, Georgia, in order to provide for her children. When Allie's own mother died the next year, she looked after her aging father as well. To help her mother, Rosalynn pitched in with housekeeping and child care and worked part-time while attending the local public high school, yet she still managed to graduate as class valedictorian in 1944. She then attended Georgia Southwestern College (now Georgia Southwestern State University), before marrying her insistent suitor, the young Annapolis graduate Jimmy Carter, in 1946. The two were neighbors and had been introduced by Jimmy's sister, Ruth, who was a friend of Rosalynn's, when Jimmy was still a midshipman.

For the first seven years of their marriage, the Carters moved around the country, to naval bases on both coasts, as well as in Hawaii. Their first three children—all boys—were born in this period: John William "Jack" (1947), James Earl "Chip" (1950), and Donnel Jeffrey "Jeff" (1952). In 1953, Jimmy's father, James Earl Sr., died, and Jimmy moved back to Plains to manage the family's peanut farming business. Despite her reluctance to return to their small hometown, Rosalynn became the company's business manager, although she was never on the payroll, and somehow managed to raise her children at the same time. When Jimmy ran unsuccessfully for the state senate and governorship in 1962 and 1966, Rosalynn pitched in to help with his campaigns. She did the same again in 1970, when he ran for governor a second time, even though she was tending to three-year-old Amy at the time. This time, Jimmy won the election, and served one term, until January 1975.

As Georgia's First Lady, Rosalynn took charge of financial management at the governor's mansion in Atlanta, wrote a book about the building's history, and took responsibility for the financial accounting of the operations there. But her chief interest was in doing something about the state's services for the mentally ill and handicapped. In 1971, she sat on the Governor's Commission to Improve Services to the Mentally and Emotionally Handicapped, and thereafter kept watch on reforms introduced to streamline and improve Georgia's aid to those in need. Throughout Jimmy's term as governor, she was honorary chairperson of the Georgia Special Olympics. Her successes in Georgia emboldened her in 1976 to make a campaign promise of her own on the campaign trail: if Jimmy Carter was elected, she would take responsibility for reforming the country's mental health services and policies.

Well-informed about the issues and Jimmy Carter's positions, Rosalynn was an indefatigable campaigner for her husband in both of his presidential races. In 1975 and 1976, she visited more than forty states to speak to voters. When Jimmy was elected, she had an influence on both the style and substance of the Carter presidency. She almost certainly had a role in the decision to lend a populist touch to the inauguration by walking back to the White House after the swearing-in ceremony, as only Thomas Jefferson had done in 1801, and setting a low price on tickets to the inaugural ball so that ordinary citizens could attend as well as celebrities and the politically connected.

Rosalynn made no secret of the fact that she and the president discussed foreign and domestic policy issues. Her office was in the East Wing of the White House, but she often attended cabinet meetings, spoke to the public about the president's positions, and reported back to him about how citizens reacted to the White House's directions. Due to her highly visible role, it was during the Carter administration that Congress acknowledged that a First Lady assisted the president in critical ways and appropriated funds to pay for her staff. Once a week Rosalynn and her husband met formally to go over policy matters in which she had a particular interest or planned to discuss with the public. She also spent a good deal of time with the cabinet secretaries whose purview included the areas in which she was active: Patricia Harris, secretary of housing and urban development, and Joseph Califano, secretary of health, education and welfare. When she disagreed with the president about substance or timing, she invariably told him what she thought. To complaints that she was enlarging the First Lady's role too much, she replied, "I don't think that any man who would be President of the United States would have a wife with no ambition, who'd just sit and do nothing."

Just as she had reshaped the First Lady's role along more active lines, Rosalynn advocated greater equality for women in all walks of life. As Pat Nixon and Betty Ford had done when they were First Ladies, she supported the equal rights amendment and visited states that hadn't yet ratified it in an effort to persuade their legislatures to do so. Together with Lady Bird Johnson and Betty Ford, she opened the 1977 Women's Conference held in Houston, Texas. In Washington, she convinced the Pentagon to appoint more servicewomen to the White House honor guard. Throughout her husband's term, she supplied him with lists of women capable of serving in positions the president filled by appointment, and when Jimmy Carter was planning his 1980 reelection campaign, she lobbied for more minority women in high staff positions. She also recruited the attorney general to join her in asserting that it was time to appoint a woman to the Supreme Court and suggested qualified women for other federal court appointments. In 1988, almost a decade after leaving Washington, Rosalynn and the wives of three other former presidents presided over a conference on "Women and the Constitution" at the Carter Center, an exploration of how the U.S. Constitution has affected women's lives, carrying on a tradition that started with early suffragists like Elizabeth Cady Stanton.

As she had promised during the campaign, Rosalynn devoted special attention to the area of mental health. Less than a month after Jimmy Carter's inauguration, she plunged in as active honorary chair of the President's Commission on Mental Health. After conducting a series of public hearings and consulting health-care experts, practitioners, activists, and former patients, the commission recommended dramatic changes in how mental health care is carried out and paid for and what facilities—from housing to institutionalization for chronic cases—were provided. In addition, a bill of rights for the mentally ill that outlawed discrimination against them because of their medical condition was proposed. The president made it part of federal policy by proclamation, and it was included in the Mental Health Systems Act, which became law in 1980. Even before Congress voted on the bill, Rosalynn succeeded in raising the amounts of federal money available for research into mental health issues. During deliberations, she testified to Congress in support of the bill. The last First Lady to give congressional testimony had been Eleanor Roosevelt, in 1945. Rosalynn also signaled by supporting Green Door, a Washington, D.C., organization that helps people with serious mental illness hold jobs and live independently, that people should not simply wait for government to step in.

Another vulnerable group whose cause Rosalynn adopted as her own were senior citizens, especially those with limited resources. In her methodical way, she formed a task force to study existing federal programs and consulted with White House staff, interested members of Congress, and community groups. The effort yielded a number of initiatives, including the Age Discrimination Act, which eliminated the mandatory retirement age for federal employees and raised it in the private sector; the Older American Act, broad legislation whose aim is to help the elderly preserve their autonomy and dignity; more federal money for services for seniors; the Rural Clinics Act, which targets areas where medical services are lacking; and Social Security reform earmarked for seniors. When the White House Conference on Aging was held in 1981, Rosalynn chaired it, even though she was no longer First Lady.

Rosalynn departed from tradition by visiting a number of countries in the Caribbean and Latin America on Jimmy Carter's behalf. At every stop, she exchanged views about issues ranging from defense to the drug trade, alternative energy sources, human rights, and international commerce. To facilitate face-to-face talks with Latin American leaders, she studied Spanish before making the trip. She also played a role in humanitarian crises, notably in November 1979, when she rushed to Cambodia to see for herself the plight of its millions of refugees. Her testimony helped persuade the United Nations to coordinate relief efforts for the region. Rosalynn herself helped to raise tens of millions in private humanitarian aid in the United States and lobbied the president to allow more refugees from Cambodia to come to this country and let the Peace Corps to send volunteers.

Rosalynn's passionate concern for victims of war, injustice, and prejudice sometimes overshadowed her lighter side, but that was in evidence in the roles she played in bringing the first poetry and jazz festivals to the White House. To make it possible for people throughout the country to enjoy the music being played for a relatively small live audience, the jazz performances were broadcast live, as were a classical music series, called *In Performance at the White House*. To bring Washington's legislative community together at Christmastime, she staged a winter festival for the families of members of Congress on the White House lawn, with a skating rink as the centerpiece.

After Jimmy Carter lost his bid for reelection and the Carters left the White House, Rosalynn continued to devote herself to the causes that engaged her as First Lady of Georgia and the United

States. She was vice chair of the Carter Center's board of trustees until May 2005, and she continues to head the center's Mental Health Task Force, which proposes and advocates reforms in mental health treatment and services. Each year, the Rosalynn Carter Symposium on Mental Health Policy assembles leaders in the field for discussions of the impact of mental illness on all demographic groups, the best ways to pay for mental health services and research, new approaches to treatment, and efforts to discourage discrimination against the mentally ill.

For more than ten years, the Rosalynn Carter Fellowships for Mental Health Journalism have been awarded to writers whose work deals with these issues. They have helped journalists who raise public awareness and understanding and combat stereotypes by reporting more accurately and widely about mental illness. The International Committee of Women Leaders for Mental Health, which she also chairs, is a worldwide network of current and former First Ladies, royalty, and heads of state that educates people around the world about mental health. She also presides over the Rosalynn Carter Institute for Caregiving at Georgia Southwestern State University, her alma mater. This organization creates research, education, and training programs that aim to improve the care of the mentally ill and handicapped and proposes policies that encourage a more humane social environment. In addition, she is associated with Habitat for Humanity, a volunteer home-building program for the needy, and Project Interconnections, a public-private partnership that targets housing the mentally ill homeless population.

Rosalynn published her autobiography, *First Lady from Plains*, in 1984; wrote *Everything to Gain . . . Making the Most of the Rest of Your Life* (1987) with her husband; and authored two books about caregiving, *Helping Yourself Help Others: A Book for Caregivers* (1994) and *Helping Someone with Mental Illness: A Compassionate Guide for Family, Friends, and Caregivers* (1998), written with Susan Golant.

NANCY REAGAN ⌒

FIRST LADIES AREN'T ELECTED, AND THEY DON'T RECEIVE A SALARY.
THEY HAVE MOSTLY BEEN PRIVATE PERSONS FORCED TO LIVE PUBLIC
LIVES, AND IN MY BOOK THEY'VE ALL BEEN HEROES. ABIGAIL ADAMS
HELPED INVENT AMERICA. DOLLEY MADISON HELPED PROTECT IT.
ELEANOR ROOSEVELT WAS FDR'S EYES AND EARS. NANCY REAGAN
IS MY EVERYTHING.

–Ronald Reagan

Nancy Reagan has often described her life as if it were a two-act
play: before she met and married Ronald Reagan and after their
marriage in 1952. The first act had more than its share of problems. Her parents, Edith Luckett, an actress, and Kenneth Robbins,
a salesman, divorced in 1928, when Nancy was seven. Her mother,
who returned to the stage even before her marriage ended, sent her
daughter to live with an aunt and uncle in Bethesda, Maryland, for
several years. During this time, mother and daughter visited irregu-
larly. In 1928, Edith married Loyal Davis, a neurosurgeon and professor of surgery at Northwestern University Medical School, gave
up acting, and took Nancy with her to Chicago. Loyal Davis–who
also had a son by his first marriage–legally adopted Nancy in 1935,
and she considered him her true father.

Nancy attended private schools in Washington, D.C., and Chicago, and graduated from Smith College, in Northampton, Massachusetts, with a degree in dramatic arts in 1943. Through theater
friends of her mother's, she got a small role in a touring production that later had a run on Broadway. Other New York stage successes followed, notably the 1946 musical *Lute Song*, which starred
Mary Martin, Yul Brynner, and Mildred Dunnock. She appeared in
her first film in 1948, one year before signing a seven-year contract
with Metro-Goldwyn-Mayer. All told, Nancy made a dozen films,
always billed as Nancy Davis, even when she starred opposite her

husband in the 1957 release *Hellcats of the Navy*. After 1958, however, she stopped accepting film roles, at about the time her second child, Ronald Prescott Reagan, was born, but she had occasional parts in television series as late as 1962.

Nancy first met Ronald Reagan in 1949, when he was acting in movies and television and serving as president of the Screen Actors Guild. They married in 1952 and continued their acting careers. Their first child, Patricia Ann, was born late in that same year, and Nancy increasingly shifted her attention away from the movie business and toward life as wife, mother, and homemaker for her husband, their children, and Maureen and Michael Reagan, Ronald's daughter and son from his previous marriage to actress Jane Wyman. One of the Reagans' homes during the 1950s was a model house built for them in the Pacific Palisades suburb of Los Angeles by General Electric. Ronald Reagan was the company's media spokesman, and the house was chock-full of the latest GE appliances and gadgetry.

Ronald Reagan had also been a staunch Democrat his entire life. He continued to be a registered Democrat through the 1950s, even as he supported the presidential candidacies of Dwight Eisenhower and Richard Nixon. After the national elections of 1960, however, he switched party affiliations, explaining, in a famous phrase, "I didn't leave the Democratic Party, the party left me." In 1964, he campaigned for Barry Goldwater and caught the attention of California's Republican leadership with a speech in which he said, "The Founding Fathers knew a government can't control the economy without controlling people. And they knew when a government set out to do that, it must use force and coercion to achieve its purpose. So we have come to a time for choosing."

Ronald Reagan served two terms as governor of California, beginning in 1967, and started exploring the possibility of a presidential bid as early as 1968. While her husband was governor, Nancy embraced the causes of Vietnam War veterans, especially those who had been wounded or encountered problems readapting to civilian

life (symptoms of post-traumatic stress disorder were not yet recognized). She was even more closely identified with the plight of
missing and captured servicemen and donated her income from a
syndicated newspaper column to the National League of Families
of American Prisoners & Missing in Southeast Asia. A third group
whose plight she took up were elderly people and handicapped
children who were being cared for in state facilities. After she advocated for the Foster Grandparent Program, designed around visits
by the children to the aged shut-ins, the program spread to the
entire state and, in time, the country.

When Nancy became First Lady in 1981, she initially gave
her attention to restoring the faded splendor of the White House.
Undertaking major renovations that included redecorating public spaces, replenishing the china service, and taking other steps
to recapture the traditional elegance of official entertainment, she
made a point of raising private funds instead of dipping into public monies for the work. In the second year of the Reagans' tenure in Washington, Nancy once again took up social programs of
the kinds that she had embraced in California. This time her focus
was on making young people aware of the dangers of drugs and
drawing attention to the prevention and rehabilitation programs
that were available throughout the country. She visited schools and
centers in the United States and abroad, talking to students and
teens, while attracting the media attention that inevitably follows
the president's wife. During a visit to a school in California, according to some accounts, when Nancy asked a group of children what
they should do if someone offered them drugs, a number of them
shouted, "Just say no!" She turned the phrase into the rallying cry
for her campaign against experimentation with drugs. To plug the
campaign, she appeared—as herself—in the sitcom *Diff'rent Strokes* in
1983. A large number of clinics bearing the slogan "Just Say No" still
exist around the country.

Throughout the decade, she carried her message around the
world, speaking about the dangers of drugs wherever she traveled

and enlisting international cooperation by inviting the wives of foreign heads of state and ministries to meet at the White House when they visited this country. Many observers saw her hand in the 1986 National Crusade for a Drug-Free America anti–drug abuse law. She celebrated its passage with a rare joint address with President Reagan to discuss the problems posed by drug use. Not long afterward, in October 1988, she spoke to the UN General Assembly about international efforts to end drug trafficking. She was only the second First Lady–after Eleanor Roosevelt–to address that body.

Some believe that Nancy may have helped nudge the United States toward improved relations with the Soviet Union when she encouraged President Reagan to explore the possibility of dialogue with President Mikhail Gorbachev shortly after he came to power in 1985. The two men became friends. One outcome of the friendship was the signing of the Intermediate-Range Nuclear Forces (INF) Treaty in 1987, an agreement between the two superpowers that did away with an entire class of missiles.

When the Reagans left the White House in January 1989, Nancy began dividing her time between what their friend Charlton Heston has called "the greatest love affair in the history of the American Presidency" and her abiding commitment to drug abuse prevention. She published a memoir, *My Turn*, in 1989 and set up the Nancy Reagan Foundation (since merged with the Best Foundation for a Drug-Free Tomorrow). The fruit of that effort is the still-active Nancy Reagan Afterschool Program, which emphasizes drug prevention and life skills.

In my view, many of Nancy Reagan's finest moments have come after her years as First Lady. The strength, courage, and patience she displayed during her long goodbye to the love of her life have encouraged thousands of families dealing with the impact of Alzheimer's disease. It was she who decided in 1994 to announce publicly that President Reagan suffered from the disease. She no doubt felt a need to explain why he would no longer accept public engagements and further wished to protect him from harm or embarrassment. I also believe that she intended to focus attention on this disease, as Betty Ford had done through her own personal revelations about her breast cancer and drug addiction. Her promotion of education and research into the treatment and understanding of Alzheimer's has increased awareness, research, and treatment, while helping families cope, as she did, with extended caregiving for loved ones.

In the years after the 1994 announcement of President Reagan's affliction, Nancy resolutely insisted on looking after him herself. In order to be near her husband as much as possible, from then until his death in 2004, she rarely left the area near their Los Angeles home, so her public appearances were largely restricted to the city. When the 1996 Republican Convention was held in San Diego, however, she did agree to speak—only the second time a former First Lady had addressed a national convention (again, Eleanor Roosevelt had set the precedent). She took on the cause of promoting research, establishing the Ronald and Nancy Reagan Research Institute in Chicago, Illinois, associated with the National Alzheimer's Association, to foster research in the disease. And even though she rarely expressed public disagreement with her husband, she endorsed stem call research as a promising avenue in finding a cure for the condition that now afflicts at least 5 million people in the United States alone.

Nancy personally called me and other members of Congress to ask for our support of legislation to allow the use of embryonic stem cells in federally funded research when those cells would otherwise be discarded. The research seeks to advance treatment for people with degenerative brain, nerve, and muscle diseases and blood disorders. Her efforts made a big impact. At a benefit for the Juvenile Diabetes Research Foundation in May 2004, less than a month before Ronald Reagan's death, she told the audience, "Science has presented us with a hope called stem-cell research, which may provide our scientists with answers that have so long been beyond our grasp. I just don't see how we can turn our backs on this—there are just so many diseases that can be cured, or at least helped. We have lost so much time already, and I just really can't bear to lose any more."

BARBARA BUSH

GIVING FREES US FROM THE FAMILIAR TERRITORY OF OUR OWN NEEDS BY OPENING OUR MIND TO THE UNEXPLAINED WORLDS OCCUPIED BY THE NEEDS OF OTHERS.

Barbara Bush is only the second woman in history to achieve the remarkable distinction of being the wife of one president and the mother of another. She is distantly related to Abigail Adams, the other woman to have done so. Barbara Bush grew up in Rye, New York, where she was born in 1925, to Marvin Pierce, a magazine publisher, and Pauline Robinson Pierce, conservation chair of the Garden Club of America. Athletic and outgoing, she met George H. W. Bush at a Christmas dance in 1941, when she was a sixteen-year-old student at Ashley Hall, a girls' boarding school in Charleston, South Carolina; and George was a senior at Phillips Academy, in Andover, Massachusetts. They immediately began an exchange of letters that continued even after he enlisted in the navy in 1942 and went through an intensive training course in aviation. In June 1943, just short of his nineteenth birthday, George H. W. Bush became the youngest pilot in the navy at the time.

That same year, Barbara completed high school and entered Smith College, but she withdrew from college after a year and a half, when George returned from the war in the Pacific, a highly decorated torpedo bomber pilot. They were married in January 1945 and spent nine months moving from Michigan to Maine to Virginia, where George trained new pilots at naval air bases. In September, the couple moved to New Haven, where George was a freshman at Yale; the first of their children, George W., was born in

July 1946. The nearly constant motion of the Bush family's first year hinted at what lay ahead for Barbara, who guided at least twenty-nine moves during her marriage. George went into the oil business after graduating from Yale, and during the early years they lived in a number of cities in Texas and southern California.

By the time the 1950s drew to a close, the Bushes, now with five young children (their first daughter, Robin, had died of leukemia in 1953, at the age of four), were in Texas, where Barbara emerged as a behind-the-scenes stalwart of her husband's political career, starting with an unsuccessful Senate bid in 1964 and continuing for nearly thirty years, until the end of George's term as the country's forty-first president. In the intervening years, George won a U.S. congressional seat but two years later lost another bid for the Senate; served as Richard Nixon's ambassador to the United Nations; led the Republican National Committee; went to China as head of the U.S. Liaison Office in Beijing in 1974, a pivotal moment in East-West relations; and returned as director of the Central Intelligence Agency for several years before entering the 1980 presidential race and ultimately becoming Ronald Reagan's vice president from 1981 to 1988.

As the vice president's wife, Barbara deferred to the Reagan White House, but also cultivated interests in pressing social issues, adult and child illiteracy, in particular, and developed into a polished public speaker known for flashes of sharp wit. At the 1988 Republican Convention that nominated her husband for president, she became the first candidate's spouse to address the nominating convention, with a speech that celebrated George's roles as husband, father, and grandfather to their twelve grandchildren. Many observers at the time believed that Barbara influenced her husband's platform and policies, but she shrewdly perfected an unthreatening, apolitical image, calling herself "everybody's grandmother" and insisting that any influence on policy was merely the result of "osmosis." There may have been an element of calculation in Barbara's self-deprecation, but she also stressed that "everyone has something to give," some through their professions and others through volunteer efforts.

Whatever Barbara's political role, she did influence the tone of the Bush presidency. From a precedent set by Jimmy and Rosalynn Carter, the Bushes adopted the popular gesture of walking back from the swearing-in ceremony to the White House. And the next morning, in an echo of Nellie Taft's years as First Lady, she opened the White House to thousands of ordinary citizens. People had stood in line all night for the chance to meet the new first couple and visit the executive mansion. These light touches helped the public see the Bushes as accessible, but they didn't obscure Barbara's serious side, which could be seen in her concerted efforts to use her new position to marshal resources to bring universal literacy to the American people. In the previous eight years, she had gotten to know everyone—in publishing, politics, education, social reform, and philanthropy—with a stake in combating illiteracy. Now she created the Barbara Bush Foundation for Family Literacy to raise the money needed for effective literacy programs. With 10 percent of the adult population reading at a fourth-grade level or lower, she took her cause to the public through radio and television, labeling it "the most important issue we have." Barbara didn't want to make English the country's official language—"when you say 'official,' that becomes a racial slur"—but she wanted to drive home the message that people who can't read well pay a price in school, at work, in health and safety, raising families, and many other critical areas of life. Behind the scenes, she is known to have pushed for passage of the National Literacy Act, legislation that made it possible for libraries and other public venues to serve as adult literacy centers during after-work hours.

Barbara also raised the profile of social problems that may best be seen as part of the fallout of illiteracy, like homelessness, HIV/AIDS, and teenage pregnancy. She visited homeless shelters and soup kitchens and highlighted the plight of single mothers, many of them teenagers, whose partners had left them to provide for the children on their own. During an AIDS memorial vigil, she lit candles in the windows of the executive mansion and invited relatives of AIDS victims to bring sections of the AIDS quilt to the White House. It was widely speculated that Barbara had a hand in the successful passage of the Hate Crimes Statistics Act. She had openly opposed discrimination since the early 1950s, when she refused to stay in hotels that would not give accommodations to the African American housekeepers who were traveling with the family.

While in the White House, Barbara hired an African American press secretary, made a point of appearing at Martin Luther King Jr. Day school programs in Washington, was an advocate of the traditionally black colleges and had been a trustee of Morehouse College. In 1989, the first year of the Bush presidency, Barbara pointedly chose to deliver the commencement address at Bennett College, a little-known black women's school in Greensboro, North Carolina. The following year, she made a subtler but equally bold point at Wellesley College, where the invitation to speak elicited objections from students who felt that Barbara was President Bush's wife rather than her own person. Instead of answering the protests, she took them in stride, saying simply, "I was twenty myself." At the Massachusetts campus, she won her audience over by including Raisa Gorbachev, First Lady of the Soviet Union, in the program and talking about women's desires to enjoy careers and families, growing social diversity, and the changing contemporary world. Saving her best surprise for last, she predicted, "Somewhere out in this audience may even be someone who will one day follow my footsteps, and preside over the White House as the president's spouse. I wish him well!"

Barbara Bush was a First Lady Americans saw as feisty and funny as well as down-to-earth. Though descended from old New England stock, she could relate to people of all backgrounds. She was a beloved First Lady and an asset to both her husband and son during their presidential campaigns.

HILLARY CLINTON

DON'T CONFUSE HAVING A CAREER WITH HAVING A LIFE.

In January 2007, Hillary Rodham Clinton did something that no former First Lady had ever done when she announced that she would seek her party's presidential nomination in 2008. "I'm in to win" read an item on her website. Already the only presidential wife ever elected to the U.S. Senate (from New York), her announcement fueled discussions in many quarters about whether the day was rapidly approaching when a woman would be elected president of the United States.

For Hillary Clinton, the road to Washington ran from Chicago, where she was born in 1947, through Arkansas, where she moved to Fayetteville, joined the faculty of the University of Arkansas Law School, and married fellow Yale Law graduate Bill Clinton, also a law professor at Arkansas. In addition to teaching, Hillary directed a law clinic for poor people where the cases often involved family issues like foster care and child abuse. Her interests in children's health and legal rights had taken shape while she was a law student; she worked on child-abuse cases involving patients at the Yale–New Haven Hospital, and her thesis addressed the issue of children's legal rights. Before Hillary moved to Arkansas, she spent two years in the nation's capital, working as a staff attorney for the Children's Defense Fund and as a member of the House Judiciary Committee's Impeachment Inquiry staff during the Watergate Impeachment hearings. Hillary's concern about the problems of young children stemmed in part from listening to her own mother, Dorothy Howell, talk about what she faced when she was a child. Dorothy was the daughter of a young fireman and his wife. When she was eight years old, her parents decided they weren't able to look after her and her three-year-old sister, so they sent the two girls to live with strict grandparents in Los Angeles.

Dorothy married Hugh Rodham, and together they raised Hillary and her two brothers. Hugh started a small business and moved his family to suburban Park Ridge, where Dorothy taught Sunday school and Hillary was active in her church's youth group. Hillary then attended Wellesley College, where she graduated with honors in 1969; her peers selected her to be the first student speaker at a Wellesley commencement.

When Bill decided to run for the U.S. Congress in 1976, Hillary continued to espouse children's causes and also joined an Arkansas law firm. Her husband's first election campaign was unsuccessful, but in 1978 he ran a successful race for Arkansas attorney general, and two years later he was elected governor–the same year their daughter, Chelsea, was born. Bill held the governor's post, except for the 1982–1984 term, until he made his presidential run in 1992. In the late 1970s, President Jimmy Carter appointed Hillary to the board of the U.S. Legal Services Corporation, a federally funded program that supports legal assistance to the poor. While she was the governor's wife she took on additional advocacy roles, including heading a task force that looked for ways to raise Arkansas's educational standards, serving on the Arkansas Children's Hospital board and the national boards of the Children's Defense Fund and the Child Care Action Campaign.

As head of the American Bar Association's Commission on Women in the Profession, which highlighted the presence of sexual harassment and discriminatory patterns of earnings in the legal profession, Hillary was active in the area of fair treatment for women even before the Clintons moved into the White House. As First Lady, she broadened her concerns to include cases of abuse of women globally as well as domestically. She and Attorney General Janet Reno joined forces to establish a Justice Department Office on Violence Against Women. More broadly, she also supported efforts aimed at improving the situations of families, by enlarging early-learning and child-care programs, leading a national effort to combat teen pregnancy, and advocating for provisions in the Adoption and Safe Families Act of 1997 that streamline the process of adopting children who are in foster care. Other initiatives on behalf of children included promoting a national immunization program and a campaign to provide medical insurance to children whose parents lacked coverage.

No First Lady had played as direct a role in shaping policy as Hillary. She had an office in a part of the West Wing normally occupied only by senior presidential staff, and when issues she was working on were discussed she often attended the staff meetings. Outside the White House, she became one of the country's most outspoken figures on women's rights, at forums like the World Conference on Women, held in Beijing in 1995, where she criticized the host country's own record in this sensitive area. Her broad agenda included equal rights and opportunity for women in areas of economics, employment, health care, and education. The area where her efforts were not as successful was the Task Force on National Health Care Reform. She headed the commission that attempted to overhaul health-care coverage, but it met strong resistance from Congress and the public. Some people felt that the First Lady shouldn't be directly involved in shaping policy, although Bill Clinton had explicitly promised that voters would get "two for the price of one" if they elected him.

In Hillary, the nation also got a First Lady who turned a deep interest in American history into an effort to preserve and restore artifacts and places that are part of the country's heritage, including the flag that Francis Scott Key immortalized in "The Star-Spangled Banner" and the National First Ladies Historic Library in Ida McKinley's house in Canton, Ohio. She arranged to borrow contemporary American sculpture from museums for the Jacqueline Kennedy Garden, displayed donated handicrafts inside the executive mansion, and oversaw restoration and redecoration of several areas, including the Blue Room and the Treaty Room. To commemorate the 200th anniversary of the White House's completion in November 2000, Hillary created an evening of living history by bringing more former presidents and First

Ladies back to the mansion than had ever assembled there at one time.

She became a bestselling author in 1996 with her book *It Takes a Village*, and won an Emmy for the audiobook version, the first First Lady so honored. Her memoir, published in 2003, became one of the leading sellers in publishing history.

Hillary was one of the most watched freshman senators in the history of that body. Senators are often described as workhorses or show horses, and there was intense interest in which variety she would turn out to be. The answer is both. As a former First Lady, she of course commands press attention. But she has been careful to do her homework, attend committee hearings, wait her turn to question witnesses, and earn her spurs. She regularly joins with Republicans on bills and amendments. She and I teamed with other women colleagues—Barbara Mikulski, a Maryland Democrat, and Susan Collins, a Republican from Maine—to introduce legislation to expressly allow public school systems to offer single-sex classes and schools. Barbara and I have had tried for years to open this option for public schools, but we met resistance from the American Association of University Women, among other groups. We finally prevailed in allowing—not mandating—single-sex schools and classes so that parents would have more options available to them in their search for the best possible public education for their children. Every woman senator supported this option, and a school in New York City—the Young Women's Leadership School of East Harlem—was our role model. Hillary and I both visited the school, and I took the secretary of education, Rod Paige, with me, to learn more about the successes this excellent school was producing.

Since being elected to the U.S. Senate in 2000, Hillary has continued to press for measures designed to improve the viability of families and the lives of children. Hillary is a member of the Armed Services Committee, where her efforts include improvements in health care for active service members and veterans, including National Guardsmen and reservists. I served on the Armed Services

Committee during my first years in the Senate, until I transferred to the Appropriations Committee, where I chose the Defense and Military Construction Subcommittees. Quality of life issues for our military have been one of my highest priorities. Hillary and I cosponsored legislation to allow widows of military retirees to remarry after the age of fifty-five without losing their spousal benefits.

There are now sixteen women in the Senate. We are all friends, though we are as diverse in philosophy as the Senate as a whole. From the time that I came to the Senate (when we were seven), we have met for monthly dinners, where we commiserate, laugh a lot, and never discuss issues. When there were nine of us, we wrote *Nine and Counting,* about our experiences in politics and gave the proceeds to the Girl Scouts.

Hillary Clinton, at this writing, is the most serious woman candidate for president in our nation's history.

LAURA BUSH

SINCE SEPTEMBER 11, I'VE HAD THE OPPORTUNITY, OR MAYBE
I SHOULD SAY THE RESPONSIBILITY, TO BE STEADY FOR OUR
COUNTRY, AND FOR MY HUSBAND, CERTAINLY . . .

If there ever was a woman who did not want to be in the spotlight, it was Laura Welch Bush. When her alma mater, Southern Methodist University, named her its Outstanding Alumna, she said, "I am outstanding by marriage." Still water runs deep would be my description of Laura, and every poll of Americans puts her at the top of the most popular lists. Her quiet grace and self-effacing manner have endeared her to the American people.

For almost as long as she can remember, Laura Bush has been concerned about educating young people and encouraging them to read. One of her earliest role models was her second-grade teacher in Midland, Texas, and when Laura enrolled at Southern Methodist

University in 1964, she knew she would major in education. After graduation, she taught second grade in Houston, before returning to school for a master of library science degree in 1972. From that time until she met and married George W. Bush in 1977, she was an elementary school librarian.

Laura says that she extracted one promise from George W. Bush before she agreed to marry him: that she would never have to make a speech. He kept his word . . . for a few weeks, anyway! Shortly after their marriage, he entered the race for the U.S. Congress from the west Texas district that included Midland, their hometown. Though unaccustomed to politics, she gamely campaigned for him. He lost that race to a Democrat, Kent Hance, who is now chancellor of Texas Tech University.

After the election, she did volunteer work in Midland, Texas, and then joined the effort to win the Republican presidential nomination for her father-in-law, George H. W. Bush, in 1980. The elder Bush ultimately became Ronald Reagan's running mate and vice president that year, and Laura put politics temporarily aside when her twin daughters, Jenna and Barbara (named for their two grandmothers), were born in 1981. She concentrated on raising her children and acting as a steadying influence in her husband's life while he devoted himself to the oil business.

In 1988, Laura and her family moved briefly to Washington, D.C., in order to assist in George H. W. Bush's successful run for the White House. After the campaign, she returned to Texas and put thoughts of active engagement in politics largely out of her mind. In fact, when George W. Bush first discussed running for the governorship in Texas in 1994, Laura initially opposed the idea. He ran against the incumbent, Ann Richards, and Laura was a big asset in the successful campaign. A very popular First Lady of Texas, she made use of her public position to call for increased state support for causes close to her heart: early reading, literacy, and early childhood development programs, which became the social issues on which she focused. Through highly publicized events like an early childhood development conference, Laura put a spotlight on the effectiveness of starting educational initiatives when children are young. One of her most significant legacies to our state is the annual Texas Book Festival, which she founded. It continues to raise significant funds for book acquisitions throughout the state's public library system. It is also one of the capital's most festive events. National and Texas authors give presentations and read from their current releases. The meeting rooms in the capital are filled with avid readers who seize the chance to ask questions of some of their favorite writers. Each author spends time autographing books after the readings. Throughout an entire Saturday and Sunday, thousands of Texans descend on Austin for this annual enclave. The author appearances are free to all, and the gala dinner that follows raises funds for libraries.

Laura hosted the festival every year, attending the events for the entire two days and listening to many of the author presentations. Truth be told, she was probably more fulfilled doing this than many of her other duties as First Lady of the state. As we all know, reading is her favorite pastime.

Laura may have begun as a reluctant public figure, but she quickly proved a remarkably effective one. When she addressed the Republican National Convention in 2000, she wowed her audience. Her initial themes were reading and education, child development and health care, human rights and opportunities for women. But the emphasis changed dramatically after September 11. She began to speak about what adults could do to help children traumatized by the attacks, a much-appreciated gesture. She has also promoted women's rights throughout the world, especially where there is oppression or abuse. In the fall of 2001, after meetings with a number of Afghan women who had suffered under Taliban rule, she preempted one of the president's weekly radio broadcasts to make their situation more widely known. This year, 2007, she also attended a meeting of women senators Dianne Feinstein and I hosted to highlight the plight of Aung San Suu Kyi, who in 1990 was elected Prime Minister of Burma. However, the military refused to hand over power and she has been under house arrest most of the time since.

Education and the central role of reading are often interwoven with this First Lady's other concerns. At George W. Bush's 2001 inauguration, she included a homage to American authors in the program. Later that year she joined forces with the Library of Congress to hold a National Book Festival in Washington, D.C., patterned after the Texas Book Festival she created in Austin. It is now a popular annual event, held on the outdoor Mall, under tents, near the Capitol. Thousands of people hear authors reading and answering questions, while they sip coffee. She has also continued the White House Salute to America's Authors series, initiated by Lady Bird Johnson, in which well-known writers are invited to discuss the work of their distinguished predecessors. In one program, for example, Elizabeth Spencer, author of the novel *Light in the Piazza* and other works, presented the fiction of Eudora Welty.

As a former librarian, Laura has also identified closely with the work of the Institute of Museum and Library Services, which funds various programs for the country's museums and libraries. Grants are helping to recruit new librarians, educate current and future members of the profession, and carry on research, to give librarians, in Laura's words, "the training they need to keep libraries and education at the center of community life."

To improve the lot of the nation's teachers, Laura has been particularly vocal about the need to enhance teacher training and raise salaries in the field of education in order to attract and retain talented people. I worked on a program with her called Transition to Teaching, for people in other professions who want to switch to education; another program, Troops to Teachers, is designed to attract former servicemen and women. These programs encourage alternative certification to teach subjects for which the professionals are qualified by virtue of their experience and college majors, even if they haven't taught or been accredited as teachers. Certain technical fields and foreign languages can be offered by these participants, in places where schools would not be able to offer these courses to their students.

A lover of American history and landscape, Laura helped to shape and serves as honorary chair of Preserve America, an effort to promote and protect the nation's natural and physical heritage. Through this program, historic properties owned by the government are preserved and put to practical use; the federal government encourages states and localities to make better use of the man-made and natural resources they oversee. Far more than just a building preservation program, Preserve America is dedicated to protecting historic streets, town squares, and public parks; promoting tourism and education activities that increase public awareness and appreciation of our heritage; and encouraging efforts to maintain or restore the natural environment by protecting and replanting native species.

Laura Bush has blossomed as First Lady and is universally respected for her beautiful manners. And she is likely the most well-read First Lady our country has ever had.

Fri, September 10/2010

DOLLAR TREE STORES, INC.

Store# 631
16719 Torrence Ave
Lansing IL 60438

(708) 474-0849

DESCRIPTION	QTY	PRICE	TOTAL
FIRST AID KIT	1	1.00	1.00T
AJAX DISH LIQUID	1	1.00	1.00T
APRICOT JAM	1	1.00	1.00T
APRICOT JAM	1	1.00	1.00T
PUFFY CRISP COOKIE	1	1.00	1.00T
PUFFY CRISP COOKIE	1	1.00	1.00T
BOARD BOOK	1	1.00	1.00T
BOOK NOVEL ASTD	1	1.00	1.00T

Sub Total	$8.00
FOOD TAX	$0.09
SALES TAX	$0.36
Total	$8.45
Cash	$20.00
CHANGE ====>	$ 11.55

005150 0531 02 00012 34884   9/10/10 11:42
Sales Associate: Latora

You could INSTANTLY

WIN

an **iPod®! PLUS** receive **10**
CHANCES to **WIN $1,000** by
completing our Customer Satisfaction Survey at
www.dollartreefeedback.com
CASH & iPod PRIZES available to be
WON DAILY!

OR receive 1 chance to win $1,000 by calling
1-866-514-1935.
To see PREVIOUS WINNERS & complete rules
please visit www.dollartreefeedback.com

Apple iPod® prize value of $200 per day. iPod® is a registered trademark
of Apple Inc. All rights reserved. Apple is neither a participant in nor a
sponsor of this promotion.

So that we may continue to provide you extreme value, we
reserve the right to limit quantities, do not offer refunds and
consider all sales final. We will gladly exchange any unopened item
with original receipt. Sorry no exchanges on seasonal merchandise.

Cht. 3) goes to pg. 165

CHAPTER 3

If There's a Book You Want to Read

Novelists and Journalists

IF THERE'S A BOOK YOU REALLY WANT TO READ BUT IT HASN'T
BEEN WRITTEN YET, THEN YOU MUST WRITE IT.
—Toni Morrison

HARRIET BEECHER STOWE

I WROTE WHAT I DID BECAUSE AS A WOMAN, AS A MOTHER I WAS
OPPRESSED AND BROKENHEARTED, WITH THE SORROWS AND
INJUSTICE I SAW, BECAUSE AS A CHRISTIAN I FELT THE DISHONOR
TO CHRISTIANITY, BECAUSE AS A LOVER OF MY COUNTRY I
TREMBLED AT THE COMING DAY OF WRATH.

If not for *Uncle Tom's Cabin*, most of us might not even recognize
Harriet Beecher Stowe's name today. But she was certainly not a
one-book phenomenon. She was, in fact, a celebrated and popular author who published thirty books over half a century of an

extremely busy life as a wife, mother, and political and religious activist. She was the daughter of Lyman Beecher (1775–1863), a famous Presbyterian minister. Lyman Beecher's thirteen children included seven sons who followed him into the ministry–the abolitionist Henry Ward Beecher (1813–1887) was the best known– and three daughters who lived into adulthood. Catharine Beecher founded the Hartford Female Seminary in 1824, one of the earliest schools for young women on a par with men's colleges, and Isabella Beecher Hooker became one of the leading champions of women's suffrage.

When Harriet was born in 1811, Lyman was a minister in Litchfield, Connecticut. While in his first pulpit on Long Island in 1806, he had achieved fame with the publication of a sermon condemning dueling after Aaron Burr's fatal shooting of Alexander Hamilton. Lyman changed positions several times during his career, usually in search of better salaries in order to support his large family and pay for his children's educations. Harriet's mother, Roxana, died of tuberculosis when Harriet was five. Isabella, born in 1822, was a half-sister.

Lyman, who was a central figure in the Second Great Awakening, the early-nineteenth-century religious revival, hewed to a strict interpretation of Christianity strongly influenced by evangelical strains of Calvinism. His children later espoused more benevolent doctrines. He also spoke out strongly against slavery during the debates over whether to permit slaves in the western territories and the new state of Missouri. In 1826, he left Litchfield to become pastor of Boston's Hanover Church.

As a primary school student at Litchfield Female Academy, Harriet's writing was already attracting attention. The earliest of her essays that survives, written when she was twelve, hints at her precocious seriousness. It is called "Can the Immortality of the Soul Be Proved by the Light of Nature?" When she was twelve or thirteen, she enrolled at her sister Catharine's Hartford Female Seminary; after graduating she stayed on to teach rhetoric and composition until 1832. In that year, Lyman Beecher was appointed president of Lane Theological Seminary, in Cincinnati, Ohio, and Harriet moved west to be with him. Cincinnati was a large, bustling city, and a stop on the Underground Railroad for slaves heading north from neighboring Kentucky. Harriet taught at the Western Female Institute, a new school that Catharine established in Cincinnati; she also joined the Semi-Colon Club, a literary salon, and started publishing her stories and reviews in the *Western Monthly Magazine*, a journal edited by one of the members, Judge James Hall.

Two of the other regulars at the Semi-Colon Club were a Lane theology professor, Calvin Ellis Stowe, and his wife, Eliza Tyler Stowe. A close friendship formed between Harriet and Eliza, who died of cholera in 1834. In January 1836, the plump, balding, scholarly widower and Harriet were married. At the end of September, Harriet gave birth to the first of her seven children, the twins Eliza Tyler and Harriet Beecher Stowe. Five more children were born over the next fourteen years; only three, the twins and one son, Charles Edward, outlived their parents. Throughout the Stowes' "lean and stormy years" in Cincinnati and thereafter, Harriet managed to continue writing and publishing while also running her household and raising her children. Her first book, *Primary Geography for Children*, written with her sister Catharine, became a widely adopted textbook, notable for its liberal views on racial and religious diversity.

Situated in the southwest corner of the state, Cincinnati is just across the Ohio River from Kentucky, then a slave state. In the years leading up to the Civil War, slaves often escaped into Ohio. Most continued on to Canada, but some stayed, at least for a while. With the exception of one brief visit to a former student in Kentucky, Harriet had no direct contact with slavery, but she had grown up listening to her father's sermons and remembered his "prayers offered with strong crying and tears which indelibly impressed my heart and made me what I am from my very soul, the enemy of all slavery." While she and her family lived in Cincinnati, "we have never shrunk from the fugitives, and we have helped them with all we had to give." The children of former slaves were welcomed as students in Harriet and Catharine's school, where they studied alongside the Stowes' own children.

Harriet's first book of fiction, a collection of tales called *The May-flower; or, Sketches of Scenes and Characters Among the Descendents of the Puritans*, was published in 1843. When the Fugitive Slave Law was passed in 1850, requiring escaped slaves apprehended in free states to be returned to their owners, Harriet's sister-in-law, Isabella Beecher, wrote to her. "If I could use a pen as you can, I would write something that would make this whole nation feel what an accursed thing slavery is." By this time, the Stowes were living in Brunswick, Maine, where Calvin was a professor at Bowdoin College. According to her son and biographer, Charles Edward, in February 1851, Harriet imagined the scene of Uncle Tom's death while sitting in church, wrote the vision out as soon as she returned home, and read the passage to her family that day. Years later, in a letter, she recalled what it was like to write *Uncle Tom's Cabin*: "My heart was bursting with the anguish excited by the cruelty and injustice our nation was showing to the slave, and praying God to let me do a little, and to cause my cry to be heard. I remember many a night weeping over you as you lay sleeping beside me, and I thought of the slave mothers whose babes were torn from them." Memories of the death of her own infant son, Samuel Charles ("Charley"), from cholera in 1849, sharpened the pain of her maternal vision.

Harriet's cry was heard around the world. First serialized in 1851 and 1852 in the *National Era*, a Washington, D.C., weekly, it attracted so much interest that it came out in book form even before the last installment had been published. The first printing of five thousand copies sold out in two days, and by the end of the year *Uncle Tom's Cabin* had sold three hundred thousand copies in a country with a population of 31 million. Widely condemned in the South—and even by some reviewers in the North—as inaccurate and sensationalizing, the novel nevertheless touched a nerve in the

American people and is acknowledged to have influenced public opinion on the subject of American slavery more than anything else, written or spoken. It was also highly successful in England, and was translated into so many languages that Oliver Wendell Holmes playfully mentioned sixteen of them in a poem he wrote in celebration of Harriet's seventieth birthday. According to Charles Edward Stowe, when Harriet visited the White House in 1862, President Lincoln greeted her by saying, "So this is the little lady who made this big war?"

Uncle Tom's Cabin attracted attention because it portrayed slavery with a human face and connected the slaves' experiences with those of the readers. The famous scene of Eliza's desperate flight across the frozen river was based on scene witnessed by a Cincinnati friend of Harriet's one winter night of a woman making her way across the Ohio River by just that means. Harriet also recast her own maternal feelings of attachment and loss to imagine what a slave mother might feel when she anticipated having her child taken from her and sold. The result was the section called "A Mother's Struggle."

> If it were your Harry, mother, or your Willie, that were going to be torn from you by a brutal trader, tomorrow morning,—if you had seen the man, and heard that the papers were signed and delivered, and you had only from twelve o'clock till morning to make good your escape,—how fast could you walk? How many miles could you make in those few brief hours, with the darling at your bosom,—the little sleepy head on your shoulder,—the small, soft arms trustingly holding on to your neck?

Harriet's fame led to invitations to visit the British Isles and Europe, where she met and developed friendships with prominent writers, including George Eliot and Elizabeth Barrett Browning. In the course of several trips during the 1850s, she took an even more public role in the debate over slavery. She wrote a regular column in a New York newspaper, in which she exhorted readers to pressure their political leaders and educate the public. In 1853, the Stowes left Bowdoin for Andover, Massachusetts, where Calvin spent a decade as professor of theology at Andover Theological Seminary. Harriet continued writing, of course, and in 1856 issued a second antislavery novel, *Dred: A Tale of the Great Dismal Swamp*. Similar in structure to *Uncle Tom's Cabin*, this book is more pessimistic about the possibility of resolving the North-South schism peacefully.

The war years also brought personal tragedy to Harriet. In 1863, Lyman Beecher died. He had been in failing health for years and had been living in Brooklyn with his son Henry Ward Beecher. In that same year, Harriet and Calvin's son Frederick, a Union soldier, was wounded at Gettysburg. Once an aspiring medical student, Frederick battled alcohol addiction for many years. At the end of the war, he drifted out to California, where he is presumed to have died in about 1870.

Closer to home, there were also happier times. When Calvin retired in 1864, the couple built what Harriet called her "dream house" in Hartford, Connecticut, and spent the rest of their lives in the city. One of their neighbors was Samuel Clemens (Mark Twain), then a young writer just a year older than the Stowe twins, whose own great novels still lay in the future. As Calvin had earlier encouraged Harriet to write, she now inspired him to write a book of his own. The *Origin and History of the Books of the Bible* (1867), which was a popular as well as critical success, is one of the first scholarly analyses of scripture from a historical perspective.

After the Civil War ended, Harriet and Calvin bought land in Mandarin, Florida, a town on the St. John's River, where they began spending the winters. They built a house, hired former slaves to operate a plantation they established, helped establish schools for African American children, and were associated with a church that welcomed all denominations and races. Harriet had a simple explanation for her deeds: "It's a matter of taking the side of the weak

against the strong, something the best people have always done."
One of Harriet's later books, *Palmetto-Leaves* (1873), is a collection
of short pieces about the Florida estate and her life there.

Harriet's mental faculties began to decline not long after Calvin's
death in 1886. Her son, Charles Edward Stowe, compiled her biography, the *Life of Harriet Beecher Stowe*, from letters and diaries she
had written earlier; it was published in1889. Cared for mostly by her
twin daughters, who never married, Harriet lived in Hartford until
1896. Two years after she died, Annie Fields, a long-time friend,
published the *Life and Letters of Harriet Beecher Stowe*, the second
record of her life composed by someone who knew Harriet well.

Eliza Jane Poitevent

SOME OF YOU MAY NOT WANT TO WORK FOR A WOMAN.

Of the few occupations open to respectable American women in the
second half of the nineteenth century, teaching was almost certainly
the most common. Writing, however, offered important advantages.
It could often be done in the privacy of one's own home, a more
dignified alternative to working outside the home and one that also
allowed women, if they were sufficiently adept, to juggle work and
household management at the same time. This was the course followed by Harriet Beecher Stowe, among many others.

In the South, where ladies were expected not to work, a career in
a field such as daily journalism was unthinkable—at least until Eliza
Jane Poitevent came along. She was born in 1849 into a genteel
Mississippi family; her father, J. M. Poitevent, served as a captain
in the Confederate cavalry. Eliza Jane's childhood in Pearlington,
Mississippi, was exceptional only in that she spent part of it living
with an aunt and uncle in neighboring Hobolochitto because her
mother was too ill to care for her large family. She began writing
poems—mostly conventional verses about nature—while she was an
adolescent, and after she graduated from the Female Seminary of

Amite, Louisiana, in 1867, some of her work was published in periodicals.

At the time, a proper southern lady might share her poetry with close friends or family, but she would not publish what she had written. To violate this taboo required a pseudonym; Eliza Jane chose "Pearl Rivers," after the river that flowed along the border with Louisiana, near her home and not far from Mississippi's Gulf Coast. One of her poems, "A Chirp from Mother Robin," appeared in the *New Orleans Daily Picayune* in 1868, when Eliza Jane was eighteen or nineteen. Colonel Alva Morris Holbrook, the paper's editor and part owner, hired her as literary editor.

As Eliza was learning the newspaper business, Colonel Holbrook acquired a larger share of the *Picayune*, divorced his wife, and, in 1872, married the diminutive Eliza, who was then twenty-three and about forty years his junior. If the scanty available information is reliable, his divorce must have been acrimonious, since his first wife is said to have threatened Eliza with a gun, hit her with a bottle, and then taken an ax to some furniture. The colonel died in 1876, and after some soul-searching, Eliza decided to try to turn the debt-ridden daily into a going concern.

"I never felt so lonely and little and weak in my life as on the first day when I took my seat in Mr. Holbrook's big editorial chair," Eliza recalled after making her decision. As she knew, no woman had ever been editor or publisher of a major daily newspaper, and in the Deep South no woman had headed a daily of any size. Two of her key employees, business manager George Nicholson and José Agustín Quintero, the Cuban-born editorial writer, had pledged to support her, but she wasn't sure about the rest. Calling the staff together, she announced boldly, "I am a woman. Some of you may not want to work for a woman. If so, you are free to go, and no hard feelings. But you who stay—will you give me your undivided loyalty, and will you advise me truly and honestly?"

One or two of the men cheered her words, and most of the others assented. Quintero volunteered to represent the *Picayune* whenever it was challenged to a duel. The handful who expressed discontent Eliza fired, and to those who stuck with her, she said, "Nowhere are there men so true and chivalrous." George Nicholson, whom Eliza married in 1878, offered to provide operating funds for the paper in return for a minority interest. Through a combination of bold editorial and staffing innovations, the new publisher set about making journalistic history.

Over time, Eliza transformed the *Picayune* into a better publication by turning it into a family newspaper. Circulation tripled. The style grew livelier, but shunned lurid or sensational touches, and news reporting increased. She introduced political commentary and cartoons, including those drawn by Thomas Nast, and used illustrations—including the "Society Bee" and "Weather Frog"—to enliven the visual layout. Sports coverage was introduced, especially of local teams like the New Orleans Pelicans of the Southern Association. A society page was added, reporting on the city's upper crust. At first, the public considered this sort of journalism a scandal, but the society page quickly became the Sunday edition's largest section.

New features proliferated: comic strips and other items aimed at young readers, household hints, medical columns, reports on fashion, and even a complaint department. Eliza was as bold about staffing as about content and journalistic style. When the local Reconstructionist paper, the *New Orleans Republican,* ceased publishing in 1877, Eliza was criticized for offering jobs on her paper to some of her rival's staff who had been Union officers. Her strategy of inclusiveness prevailed, however, as it did when she added more women writers to the *Picayune*'s staff.

As an extension of its status as a family-oriented paper, the *Picayune* evolved into a publication that served as an advocate for the community and also as its conscience. Articles and editorials appeared that favored development of local businesses, supported prison reform, and advocated cultural undertakings—for example, the erection of monuments to Confederate heroes and the founding of the Southern Historical Society. Equally distinctive and civilizing were the *Picayune*'s stances on humane treatment of people and animals. Editorials condemning the beating of draft horses and mules and the sport of dog-fighting appeared with some frequency (George Nicholson was active in the local SPCA chapter), and the paper campaigned to outlaw boxing, with no concrete success.

Eliza's greatest coup was her discovery of Elizabeth M. Gilmer (1870–1951), a native of Tennessee whom she met in 1895. Elizabeth was recovering in Bay St. Louis, Mississippi, from stress brought on when she realized that her new husband, George Gilmer, a cousin of her stepmother, was mentally unstable and incapable of supporting them. Eliza liked an informal essay Elizabeth showed her, "How Chloe Saved the Silver," bought it for $3, and told the *Picayune*'s editor, Nathaniel Burbank, to hire her. Elizabeth never divorced Gilmer, but from then on she was the breadwinner. Starting out as a general reporter, she began writing a weekly column for women, *Sunday Salad*, in 1896, under the pseudonym "Dorothy Dix."

Written with witty, yet compassionate insight, *Sunday Salad*, like her later, syndicated *Dorothy Dix Talks*, captured the essence of the rapidly changing times to which women were struggling to adapt. One column about marriage counseled women not to wait passively to attract husbands, cautioning that a woman who does so risks turning into "the sour and disgruntled old maid, eating the bitter bread of dependence, the fringe on some family that doesn't want her. Or else she has to take any sort of poor stick of a man as a prop to lean on." Her characteristically practical advice: "Learn a trade, girls. Being able to make a living sets you free. Economic independence is the only independence in the world."

Women resonated to Dorothy Dix's bracing, self-reliant take on experience and started writing to her at the paper. Thus was born the women's advice column. Five years later, William Randolph Hearst hired Elizabeth as a reporter for his *New York Journal*, where she reported on temperance movement leader Carry Nation, as well as on so many sensational murder trials that a running joke took shape in New York journalistic circles: "Dorothy Dix has arrived. The trial may now proceed." Her popularity, however, was no joke. By 1908, her column appeared daily in newspapers all over the United States, and in 1926, she moved back to New Orleans, where she concentrated full-time on her syndicated advice column.

Although Eliza's marriage to George Nicholson was relatively short—less than eighteen years—it was a happy one of shared beliefs and efforts. The Nicholsons had two sons, Leonard Kimball and Yorke Poitevent, born in 1881 and 1883. Early in 1896, George and Eliza both caught influenza and died in February, within days of one another. He was seventy-six, but she was just forty-seven. By this time, Eliza had transformed the *Picayune* into a newspaper that we would recognize today as a modern publication, at a time when most newspapers, especially in the South, had changed little in half a century. It earned bragging rights as "the South's leading newspaper." Her sons and grandchildren continued as the daily's editors and publishers until 1962, when the *Times-Picayune*, as it was called after acquiring its main rival in 1914, was sold to Advance Publications, the Newhouse family chain. Two Pulitzer Prizes in the past decade, both for public service reporting, testify to the fact that the paper's stature is undiminished. In 1997, it won the prize for a series of reports on threats to the world's fishing supply. In 2006, coverage of Hurricane Katrina under difficult conditions that affected the *Times-Picayune*'s own facilities, brought a second Pulitzer.

PEARL BUCK

NONE WHO HAVE ALWAYS BEEN FREE CAN UNDERSTAND THE
TERRIBLE FASCINATING POWER OF THE HOPE OF FREEDOM TO
THOSE WHO ARE NOT FREE.

Pearl Buck was born in her maternal grandparents' twelve-room farmhouse in Hillsboro, West Virginia, in June 1892. Her parents, Absalom and Caroline Sydenstricker, Presbyterian missionaries who spent most of their adult lives in China, were on home leave, but three months later, they took their infant daughter, named Pearl Comfort, back to Zhenjiang, China. Absalom, who had grown up in a log house on a farm forty miles from Hillsboro, traveled a great deal as a missionary, but Caroline stayed in Zhenjiang, where she treated Chinese women in a medical dispensary she had set up there. When the Boxer Rebellion erupted in 1900, Caroline and her children took refuge in Shanghai, while the Boxers targeted missions, missionaries, and Chinese converts, first in the countryside and later in cities as well. For several months they did not know whether Absalom was alive. When he finally returned, the Sydenstrickers went back to the United States for another period of home leave.

Pearl's first language was Chinese, and her first teachers were her mother and native tutors. When she was fifteen, she was sent to boarding school in Shanghai for two years, and in 1909 returned to Hillsboro for a year of study in an American school before entering Randolph-Macon Woman's College, in Lynchburg, Virginia. She planned to remain in the United States after graduating in 1914, but returned to China when the news that her mother was seriously ill reached her. In 1915, she met John Lossing Buck, a Cornell-educated agronomist, and married him—over her parents' objections—in 1917. The Sydenstrickers' reasons for disapproving of Pearl's fiancé, Caroline told her, were that he wasn't an intellectual. Pearl pointed out that John had graduated from an American college, but her mother "retorted that it was an agricultural college and that is not what our family considers education."

As soon as they were married, the Bucks moved to rural Nanxuzhou, where John taught agricultural techniques to the provincial farmers who, Pearl later wrote, weren't especially interested in adopting western farming methods. As Pearl traveled through the countryside with her husband, which she often did, she seized the opportunity to get to know the local people. Her experiences were transformed into the material on which she based the trilogy of novels that later established her international reputation (*The Good*

Earth, *Sons*, and *A House Divided*), as well as other stories and essays set in China.

In 1920, John was appointed professor of agricultural economics at Nanjing University, and the couple lived in that city until 1934. Pearl also taught English and American literature at the university, but her marriage was unhappy, especially after the Bucks' daughter, Carol, was born in 1921. Although Carol at first appeared normal, she soon showed signs of impaired development. The Bucks traveled frequently between China and the United States, and throughout the decade Pearl had her daughter examined by many doctors. It was a while before she was able to admit that Carol was mentally impaired, and through much of this time she concealed the girl's condition—and even her existence—as much as she could. In 1930, when Carol was nine, Pearl placed her in a home for the retarded in New Jersey, where Carol lived until her death in 1973. When she was an adult, she was finally diagnosed with phenylketonuria (PKU), a genetically transmitted metabolic disorder that causes severe mental retardation. Pearl later wrote about her relationship with her daughter in a memoir, *The Child Who Never Grew* (1950).

During Carol's delivery, Pearl's doctors discovered a uterine tumor. To remove the tumor, they performed a hysterectomy, which ended Pearl's chances of having other biological children; the Bucks adopted a daughter in 1925, an American girl whom they named Janice. Caroline Sydenstricker died in 1921, and soon afterward, strict, narrow-minded Absalom (Pearl later wrote that "he would have burned witches") moved in with the Bucks in Nanjing, until his death in 1931. There was political unrest as well, especially in 1927, when a confrontation in Nanjing between Chiang Kaishek's Nationalists and Chinese Communists imperiled the lives of westerners in the city. After being rescued, Pearl and her family were forced to leave the region temporarily. Despite the continual personal, emotional, and military crises, and the frequent travel they necessitated, the 1920s in China were enormously productive for Pearl. Except for the year that she and John spent at Cornell

University in 1925–1926, when she earned a master's in literature, Pearl spent her time writing. Out of this period came a number of stories and essays, as well as her first novel, *East Wind, West Wind* (1930); her best-known book, *The Good Earth* (1931); and a number of other books that followed in quick succession, including her twin biographies of her parents, *The Exile* and *Fighting Angel* (both 1936).

In *East Wind, West Wind*, readers took notice of Pearl's familiarity with Chinese culture, about which most westerners knew next to nothing, as well as her stylistic device of using stilted English to suggest the rhythms of spoken Chinese. As the title suggests, the novel represents the disturbing effects of western values and attitudes on traditional Chinese through events in the life of a single Chinese family. In the first section, Kwei-lan, a young woman from a provincial village, is unhappy after her arranged marriage to a man with progressive western ideas. The second section is also narrated by Kwei-lan. In it, her older brother, who has gone to the United States to study, returns with his pregnant American wife. Kwei-lan's mother is horrified, because she will not accept a "half-white" grandson as a member of her family.

The novel, which was rejected by at least twenty publishers before Richard Walsh of the John Day Company agreed to publish it, was modestly successful, but *The Good Earth* (1931) became an instant publishing phenomenon. After the influential Book-of-the-Month Club made it a unanimous selection, John Day moved its own publication date up to early March, and the novel established itself as the bestselling book in each of the next two years. The story grew out of the lives that Pearl observed among the farmers of Anwhei (now Anhui) province early in her marriage. It concerns Wang-lung, descended from generations of poor farmers inured to the meager existence their harsh region provides and unable to imagine life anywhere else. When it is time for him to marry, his father urges him to buy a homely slave from the house of Hwang, the richest family in the province, because she will cost less than a more desirable bride. O-lan, the woman he marries, emerges as a remarkable presence: stoical, dutiful, courageous, and resourceful, and thoroughly devoted to Wang-lung and their family.

For a while, Wang-lung enjoys an almost unbroken string of good fortune, thanks to his industry and O-lan's support. With his farming profits, he buys more and more land, to his mind the only valuable commodity, that the house of Hwang is forced to sell to raise cash to support vices like opium and slave girls. He and O-lan have two sons, an auspicious sign in a culture that values sons over daughters. The one ominous note is their third child, a girl, who is later revealed to be retarded. Besides prefiguring reversals for Wang-lung, the daughter is also a clear allusion to Pearl's own child, Carol, whom she always felt she had abandoned.

Bad times follow. Wang-lung's corrupt, indolent uncle manipulates his nephew into supporting him, and then a prolonged drought impoverishes the family. When O-lan gives birth to a second daughter, she strangles the newborn rather than let it starve. Rather than sell some of his land, as the uncle insists, however, Wang-lung takes his family to a southern city, where they build a makeshift hut and survive by begging and doing menial labor until it is possible for them to return home. When an invading army forces the wealthy city dwellers to flee, Wang-lung joins a group of looters, extorts money from a wealthy man, and takes his wife and children home.

The family rebuild their farmhouse, plant new crops, and enjoy a period of contentment and increasing prosperity. When Wang-lung discovers that O-lan had found a cache of jewels in the southern city, he buys yet more land from the house of Hwang. O-lan has twins, a boy and a girl, and the couple start to marry off their older children. After seven years of good harvests, they withstand another round of flood, famine, and extortion at the hands of the uncle and his son; Wang-lung even takes over the sprawling villa the formerly powerful Hwang family had once occupied in town. Meanwhile, O-lan has died, and Wang-lung, now an old man, abandons the town to spend his remaining days in the small mud hut on his ancestral farm. There, he overhears his sons planning to sell the land that he has spent his life acquiring. When he warns them that losing the land will mean the end of the family, they promise not to sell, but the story ends with the clear signal that the wheel of fortune has come nearly full circle.

The reception *The Good Earth* received set in motion a series of events that led to the Pulitzer Prize for the novel in 1932, unleashed a flood of works from Pearl (sixteen titles in the eight remaining years of the decade), and culminated in the Nobel Prize for Literature in 1938. It was the fourth time a woman had won the Literature prize, but only the second time an American woman had been recognized in any field (Jane Addams had been the first, for Peace, seven years earlier). To be honest, there was quibbling about the choice of Pearl as the country's first literature laureate, when major figures like Henry James, Theodore Dreiser, and Mark Twain had been overlooked. Pearl herself is reported to have said, when she first heard the news, "That's ridiculous. It should have gone to Dreiser." But in his presentation speech, Per Hallström, permanent secretary of the Swedish Academy, hinted at the nerve Pearl's writing had touched.

Of the many problems in this novel, *The Good Earth*, the most serious and sombre one is the position of the Chinese woman. From the very beginning it is on this point that the writer's pathos emerges most strongly, and amid the calm of the epic work it constantly makes itself felt. An early episode in the work gives the most poignant expression of what a Chinese woman has been worth since time immemorial. It is given with impressive emphasis, and also with a touch of humour, which is naturally rare in this book. In a moment of happiness, with his little first-born son dressed in fine clothes on his arm, and seeing the future bright before him, Wang Lung is on the point of breaking into boastful words but restrains himself in sudden terror. There, under the open sky, he had almost challenged the invisible spirits and drawn

their evil glances upon himself. He tries to avert the menace
by hiding his son under his coat and saying in a loud voice,
"What a pity that our child is a girl, which no one wants,
and is pitted with smallpox into the bargain! Let us pray
that it may die!" And O'Lan joins in the comedy and acqui-
esces—probably without thinking at all.

The lesson was not lost on readers of the novel, who were, at this
period, American and European, not Asian.

In 1934, Pearl returned to the United States permanently. The
political situation in China had deteriorated, she had decided to get
a divorce from her husband, and she wanted to be closer to Carol.
She bought a farmhouse in Bucks County, Pennsylvania, and in
1935 married Richard Walsh, her publisher, who had also recently
divorced his first wife. A natural storyteller, she continued writing
and publishing, of course—her list of publications ultimately grew
to over seventy—and she also turned her attention to a number of
social and political causes. Over a period of years, Pearl and Richard
adopted six children, and Pearl focused her attention on overcoming resistance to the adoption of mixed-race children. In 1949, she
founded the Welcome House Adoption Program, and later set up
the Pearl S. Buck Foundation to help support Amerasian (a term
she coined) children in the Far East.

More broadly, she and Richard Walsh founded the East and
West Association, to foster cultural exchange with Asia, but, two
years after the People's Republic of China in 1949 closed the mainland to the West, the organization folded. Pearl was also a trustee
of Howard University for twenty years, and she frequently spoke
and wrote about the ways in which women had been swept to the
margins of history. As early as 1941, she argued that women were
partly to blame because they were too often "ignorant of their own
past and ignorant of their own importance in that past. In curiosity a few months ago I asked a haphazard score of women of my
acquaintance if they had heard of Elizabeth Cady Stanton. Only

one had even heard her name, and she had no recollection of more. Yet only a generation ago Elizabeth Cady Stanton was called the greatest woman in the United States, and by some the greatest in the world." If women have forgotten, she said, they can't blame men for doing the same.

When she died in 1973, at the age of eighty, Pearl was working on a sequel to *The Good Earth* that was to have brought the story of Wang-lung and O-lan's descendants up to the period following the Cultural Revolution that began in 1966. She herself had not been back to China since the 1930s, although she had applied for a visa in 1972, the year before her death. The application had been refused by Zhou Enlai himself, reportedly because of critical remarks Pearl had made about Mao Zedong in the 1950s.

TONI MORRISON

Toni Morrison, the second of George and Ramah Willis Wofford's four children, was born Chloe Anthony in 1931. Her parents had moved north to Lorain, Ohio, an industrial center on Lake Erie midway between Cleveland and Sandusky, in search of economic opportunity and a better environment to raise children. George Wofford took great pride in his success in supporting his family and in his work as a shipyard welder. He sometimes "signed" his work by putting his name alongside the seams he welded and held three jobs at once in order to make sure that his wife and children wouldn't have to go to work. From her father, the young Chloe heard stories of the Deep South, and from her mother, a deeply religious woman who sang in the church choir, she absorbed African American songs and musical traditions and the talk of women's family relationships and daily lives. She would later weave these threads–African American folklore, religious and secular songs, and women's gossip–into all of her major work.

Lorain, with a population composed of central and eastern European immigrants and their children, Mexicans, and blacks who had migrated north, enjoyed relatively harmonious race relations. The schools were integrated, though not every neighborhood was. Chloe was the only student in her first-grade class who knew how to read when the school year started, and she was also the only African American. But the students formed friendships without regard to race or ethnicity, and she detected no racial tension until high school, when students started dating.

In high school, Chloe discovered the great European novelists of the nineteenth century, including the Russian writers Leo Tolstoy and Feodor Dostoyevsky, the French writer Gustave Flaubert, and the English novelist Jane Austen. She later told an interviewer, "Those books were not written for a little black girl in Lorain, Ohio, but they were so magnificently done that I got them anyway." She also read Pearl Buck's work and once joked that the author of *The Good Earth* had given her a false impression of fiction. Pearl Buck "made me feel that all writers wrote sympathetically, empathetically, honestly and forthrightly about other cultures."

After graduating with honors from Lorain High School in 1949, Chloe went south for the first time, to Howard University in Washington, D.C. It was at Howard that she started calling herself Toni—she said people had trouble pronouncing her given name—and it was also during her college years that she observed the lives of southern blacks at first hand, especially when she and other members of the Howard University Players toured in the segregated South.

Armed with a B.A. in English from Howard, from which she graduated in 1953, and a master's degree in American literature from Cornell in 1955, Toni was hired to teach freshman English at Texas Southern University in Houston. At Texas Southern, Toni encountered African Americans who regarded their culture and history as objects of study, not merely individual and family identity. Thus when she returned to Howard University as a faculty member in 1957, she was better prepared for the self- and race-consciousness of figures who would soon become leaders in the civil rights and black nationalist movements who were at the university in the late 1950s: people like Leroi Jones (who took the name Amiri Baraka in 1965, after Malcolm X was assassinated); Andrew Young, associate of Martin Luther King Jr., Georgia congressman, U.S. representative to the United Nations, and mayor of Atlanta, Georgia; and Stokely Carmichael, one of the leaders of the Student Nonviolent Coordinating Committee (SNCC). Another student, Claude Brown, published the autobiographical *Manchild in the Promised Land* in 1965, a book that redefined the image of the black urban ghetto.

In Washington, Toni also met Harold Morrison, a Jamaica-born architect. They were married in 1958 and had two sons, Harold Ford and Slade Kevin. Their marriage didn't work out, however, and they divorced in 1964. In fact, to get some relief from her impossible domestic predicament, she started writing and joined a local writer's group. "I had no will, no judgment, no perspective, no power, no authority, no self–just this brutal sense of irony, melancholy and a trembling respect for words. I wrote like someone with a dirty habit." Finally, while Toni was pregnant with Slade, she resigned from her teaching job and went to Europe with young Harold in tow. When she returned, she initiated divorce proceedings and went home to Lorain with the two boys.

Toni got into publishing when she found a job as an editor for the textbook division of Random House, located in Syracuse, New York. She spent her days at the office and the early evenings with her two sons. After she had put the boys to bed, she went back to a story she had dashed off for the Washington writer's group a few years earlier, about Pecola Breedlove, a young black girl in the 1940s who believes she's ugly because she doesn't look like the white children she envies. Pecola's dreams of having her eyes magically turn blue and the violence that swirls around her are narrated by her friend, Claudia McTeer. The character of Claudia was loosely based on Toni herself, and many of the other figures in the novel, which became *The Bluest Eye*, were drawn from Toni's recollections of people she had known.

After moving to New York in 1967, where she edited trade books at Random House, Toni also found a publisher for her first novel. Though it wasn't a commercial success, a number of critics praised *The Bluest Eye* for its harsh beauty. The *New York Times* reviewer, for example, observed that "it is one thing to state that we have institutionalized waste, that children suffocate under mountains of merchandised lies. It is another thing to demonstrate that waste, to recreate those children, to live and die by it. Miss Morrison's angry sadness overwhelms." To write her novels while working full-time meant "leaving my children to child-minders and the public school in the fall and winter, to my parents in the summer," all the while so short of money that "every rent payment was an event; every shopping trip a triumph of caution over the reckless purchase of a staple. The best news was that this was the condition of every other single/separated female parent I knew. The things we traded! Time, food, money, clothes, laughter, memory—and daring."

The attention generated by her first novel sparked an invitation to Toni to return to teaching, which she did while continuing to work at Random House and to write. In 1971, she joined the faculty of the State University of New York at Purchase and completed her second novel, *Sula*, an exploration of the friendship of two adult women that is also a meditation on the dichotomy of good and evil. When *Sula* was published in 1973, it attracted widespread attention, including selection as a Book-of-the-Month Club alternate and nomination for the National Book Award in fiction.

Visiting appointments at Yale University and other institutions followed, as did, every few years or so, a new book, and an increasing shower of awards. President Jimmy Carter appointed Toni to the National Council on the Arts, a post she held for six years. Toni's accomplishments are even more remarkable in light of the fact that she continued as a senior editor at Random House until 1983, nearly twenty years. Then she moved to Albany, as Albert Schweitzer Professor of the Humanities at the State University of

New York in Albany. It was there that she wrote the remarkable
Beloved, about an escaped slave who attempts to kill her children
after they are captured rather than have her daughters returned to
slavery. It was based on the true story of Margaret Garner, who
escaped to Ohio from Kentucky in 1856 and tried to slit her four
children's throats when they were apprehended. Only one of the
children died; the rest of the family were taken back to Kentucky,
under the terms of the Fugitive Slave Act. *Beloved*, published in
1987, won the Pulitzer Prize for fiction the following year.

In 1989, Toni went to Princeton University as the Robert F.
Goheen professor in the Council of Humanities. She taught mainly
creative writing courses, but was also involved in the university's
African American, American, and women's studies programs. In
1993, the news arrived that Toni Morrison had been awarded the
Nobel Prize in Literature. Seven women had been Nobel laureates in literature before her, but only one American woman (Pearl
Buck), and no black woman of any nationality. In presenting the
award, Professor Sture Allén of the Swedish Academy said that in
depicting "the world of the black people, in life as in legend, Toni
Morrison has given the Afro-American people their history back,
piece by piece."

A year ago, Toni announced she was retiring from her post at
Princeton, at the age of seventy-five. At about the same time, the
New York Times Book Review selected *Beloved* as the best novel published in the United States since 1981. Far from curtailing her writing, she has continued to enlarge its scope to embrace other genres,
especially in a series of books for children that she had written with
her son, Slade, now a painter and musician, that take their points
of departure from the stories he made up as a child. So far, six have
been published, *The Big Box*, *The Book of Mean People*, and the *Who's
Got Game?* series, adaptations of Aesop's fables that include *The Ant
or the Grasshopper*, *The Lion or the Mouse*, *Poppy or the Snake*, and *The
Mirror or the Glass*.

149.

Oprah Winfrey ~ (to pg. 153)

THOUGH I AM GRATEFUL FOR THE BLESSINGS OF WEALTH, IT HASN'T
CHANGED WHO I AM. MY FEET ARE STILL ON THE GROUND. I'M JUST
WEARING BETTER SHOES.

Performing must have been in Oprah Winfrey's genes, because even
as a preschooler on her grandmother's farm in Kosciusko, Mississippi, where she was born in 1954, she learned to read before she
was three and began doing recitations in church. "They'd put me up
on the program, and say, 'Little Mistress Winfrey will render a reci-
tation,' and I would do 'Jesus rose on Easter Day, Hallelujah, Hallelujah, all the angels did proclaim.'" Her mother and father, Vernita
Lee and Vernon Winfrey, never married and separated soon after
their daughter was born, so until she was six, Oprah lived with her
maternal grandmother, Zelmah Winfrey, a woman without education who nevertheless inspired her granddaughter to love reading,
in part by telling her stories from the Bible. When Oprah was six,
she went to live with her mother in Milwaukee, where she suffered
through years of sexual abuse at the hands of a teenaged cousin and
other relatives and their friends.

After enduring seven years of mistreatment and continual
conflict with her mother, the thirteen-year-old bolted, but was
caught, judged a delinquent and remanded to a juvenile detention
home. Because there was a shortage of space in the detention home,
Oprah's mother decided to send her to live with her father, Vernon
Winfrey, a barber, in Nashville. His regimen of discipline was exactly
what she needed, and she later gave him credit for saving her life.
She had to be home before midnight, read a book a week and write
a book report on it, and wouldn't get dinner until she had mastered
her five daily vocabulary words. "As strict as he was," she reflected
years later, "he had some concerns about me making the best of
my life, and would not accept anything less than what he thought
was my best." In 1971, when she graduated from East Nashville

High School, her classmates voted her most popular member of the senior class. She had acted in school theater productions, won prizes in oratory competitions, including a $1,000 college scholarship for a speech on "The Negro, the Constitution, and the United States," and even won a couple of local beauty contests.

The combination of broadcasting ambition and parental discipline soon paid off. Kept close to home, Oprah discovered educational and career possibilities right in Nashville. When she was only seventeen, she went to work at WVOL, a local radio station, and within two years, at nineteen, was a reporter at WTVF-TV and the first black woman co-anchor in Nashville. By then she was also a student at Tennessee State University, the historically black land-grant school, majoring in Speech Communications and Performing Arts. When Oprah graduated in 1976, WJZ-TV in Baltimore took her on as a news reporter and co-anchor. Two years later, she assumed the identity we recognize as Oprah's natural self, talk-show host: with Richard Sher, she cohosted WJZ-TV's new weekly program, *People Are Talking*, a stint that continued for five years.

The move wasn't entirely a promotion, however. As an on-air reporter and anchor, Oprah sometimes lost the detachment essential to journalism. "I would cry for the people in the stories, which really wasn't very effective as a news reporter to be covering a fire and crying because the people lost their house." But from her first day as a talk-show host in 1978, she felt at home. "And so, I took what had been a mistake, what had been perceived as a failure with my career as an anchor woman in the news business and turned it into a talk-show career that's done OK for me!"

In Chicago, the local ABC affiliate station, WLS-TV, had a half-hour morning talk show, *AM Chicago*, that was in trouble. Oprah was hired away from WLS's sister station in Baltimore to rescue *AM Chicago*; by the end of 1984, her first year, it was the city's most popular program. Soon *AM Chicago* was made a one-hour talk show, with Oprah as solo host. The next step, in September

1985, was rechristening it *The Oprah Winfrey Show,* the name it bore when it was nationally syndicated on September 8, 1986.

Within a year, *The Oprah Winfrey Show* was the country's most widely watched talk show. The program won numerous broadcasting awards, and in 1988, Oprah became the youngest person (and the first woman) to be recognized as "Broadcaster of the Year" by the International Radio and Television Society. Ten years later, after receiving the National Academy of Television Arts and Sciences' Lifetime Achievement Award, she announced that she was withdrawing from the competition for any future daytime Emmys. She explained her decision by saying, "After you've achieved it for a lifetime, what else is there?"

Oprah has appeared in a number of television shows, but she has been selective about films. In 1985, she played Sofia in *The Color Purple,* the Steven Spielberg adaptation of Alice Walker's 1982 novel. For her performance, Oprah was nominated Best Supporting Actress in both the Academy Awards and the Golden Globes. She was praised as well when she portrayed Mrs. Thomas in the film adaptation of *Native Son,* based on Richard Wright's 1940 novel, and for her role as Sethe, the protagonist of the film based on Toni Morrison's *Beloved,* in 1998.

Oprah once said, "Some women have a weakness for shoes . . . I can go barefoot if necessary. I have a weakness for books." Since 1996, she has been urging others to share her "weakness" by selecting books for the on-air Oprah Book Club. Every book that makes the list sells widely and, as a result, is widely read and discussed. One of her first year's choices was Toni Morrison's 1977 novel *Song of Solomon.* Three of Toni's other novels have been Oprah selections since then, and in 2004 Pearl Buck's *The Good Earth* was chosen as well.

In recognition of Oprah's service to books and authors, the National Book Foundation presented her with its fiftieth-anniversary gold medal in 1999. "Doing this book club has given me the courage to pursue the things I care about," she told one interviewer.

Time magazine included Oprah as one of its 100 Most Influential People of the twentieth century, a compilation published in 1998, and she has used her on-air influence to inspire others to act.

True to her philosophy that "the essential question is not, 'How busy are you?' but 'What are you busy at? Are you doing what fulfills you?'" in 1999 she began bestowing $100,000 Use Your Life awards on organizations whose members invest their time in improving the lives of others. She has given considerable support to A Better Chance, a program based in Boston that underwrites the cost of sending promising inner-city students to college preparatory schools. She has contributed millions to the Oprah Winfrey Academy for Girls in South Africa; it will grow over several years to its target of 450 students in grades 7 through 12. The school opened early this year, "and it will be one of the great days of my life to see 450 girls, most of them orphans who would not have had the opportunity for education in their lives, come to school."

One of the great traits of Americans is generosity, the belief that if you are fortunate, you should share; and if you have suffered, you want to do something to protect others from the pain that you have experienced. I have seen this as a community volunteer and as a U.S. senator. I have seen more than one committed American move mountains. Oprah is such a person. The abuse she suffered as a child must be part of her motivation to give hope to South African girls and create self-esteem and leadership for a generation of young women who would otherwise have no prospects for success.

In 1991, after a four-year-old girl in Chicago was molested and murdered, Oprah created a campaign to set up a national database of convicted child abusers that law enforcement agencies and other legitimate parties could share. During the debate on the National Child Protection Act, she testified at a hearing of the Senate Judiciary Committee on behalf of what came to be known as the "Oprah Bill." It became law in 1993.

I do not know Oprah Winfrey, but my friends who do are uniformly crazy about her. They say that she is down-to-earth, fun, easy to be with, and–if she trusts you–very open. If she thinks you are using her, you are history–not an uncommon trait for famous people. One of the wealthiest women in the United States, Oprah has been generous with her money, giving a hand to those with whom she shares a troubled background. Through her example, she has encouraged many young women to realize that being dealt a bad hand doesn't mean you can't win. She is an American phenomenon.

Amy Tan

Amy Tan was born in Oakland, California, in 1952. Both of her parents had fled the upheaval in mainland China. Their high hopes for their new life is suggested by their daughter's Chinese name, An-mei, which means "blessing from America." Her father, John Tan, was an electrical engineer who worked for the United States Information Service in China after World War II. Also a Baptist minister, he immigrated to the United States in 1947. Her mother, Daisy, the victim of an abusive first marriage, divorced her husband and managed to board the last ship leaving Shanghai before the Communists took control in 1949, but had to leave her three daughters behind, in the custody of their father.

The Tans eventually made their home in Santa Clara, after trying several other communities in the area. Besides Amy, they also had two sons. A precocious student who took naturally to English, she won a local essay contest for grade-schoolers, on the topic "What the Library Means to Me," which was published in a local newspaper. Her parents dreamt of great things for their daughter, a distinguished career as a neurosurgeon who moonlighted as a concert pianist. At the same time, they unwittingly inspired her storytelling impulse, her father by reciting the sermons he was readying for the coming Sunday as if they were bedtime stories, and her mother by telling tales of their family while she and Amy's aunts prepared food around the kitchen table. Years later, Amy also discovered that one of her grandfathers in China had been an editor.

After John Tan and his oldest son, Peter, died of brain tumors within a year of one another, in 1968 Daisy Tan took her surviving children to live in Montreux, Switzerland. Amy, who was fifteen when her father died, graduated from a Swiss high school, and the family returned to the United States so that Amy could attend Linfield College, a Baptist school in Oregon that her mother had chosen for her. There Amy met Louis DeMattei on a blind date; later they would marry. When Louis left to study in San Jose, California, Amy defied her mother twice: she switched to San Jose City College in order to be with her boyfriend, and then changed majors, from the pre-med program that Daisy wanted her to pursue to English and linguistics.

This double rebellion resulted in the first serious break between mother and daughter. Daisy stopped speaking to Amy for about six months, but the daughter excelled in her studies, matriculated at San Jose State University, and completed the requirements for the bachelor's and master's degrees. As an undergraduate, she was a President's Scholar and received her degree cum laude. Before beginning graduate studies, she spent a summer on scholarship in Santa Cruz at the University of California's Summer Linguistics Institute. Amy and Louis married in 1974, and she began studying for a Ph.D. in linguistics at Santa Cruz, but soon transferred to Berkeley, where Louis was starting a practice as a tax lawyer. After two years, jolted by the brutal robbery and murder of their best friend, Amy dropped her plans for an academic career, deciding instead to work with the developmentally disabled. The Alameda County Association for Retarded Citizens hired her as a language development consultant, and she later ran a training program for developmentally disabled infants and children through their fifth year.

Amy started writing in the late 1970s. Her first efforts weren't as a novelist, however, but as a consultant to business: speeches for corporate executives and brochures and books like one she did for IBM: *Telecommunications and You.* Her other clients included Apple

Computer, AT&T, and Pac Bell. Using her business profits, she was soon able to buy a house for her mother, with whom she had reconciled and who had returned to California to live. Despite her success, however, Amy felt discontented and started looking for an avocation to fill the void. She tried jazz piano, returning to music, an art she had practiced—and abandoned—as a child. And she started to write stories.

Her earliest efforts attracted attention. She submitted a draft of her first story, "Endgame," to the Squaw Valley writer's workshop, was invited to attend, and continued writing and meeting in an informal workshop setting with some of the people she had met there. In 1986, "Endgame" became her first published work, in a small literary journal, *FM Five*. It later appeared a second time, in *Seventeen*. Her next story, "Waiting Between the Trees," brought a suggestion from a literary agent that she compile a book of short stories. At about the same time, however, Daisy Tan became seriously ill, and Amy decided that when her mother was well, they would travel to China together, to see Daisy's three daughters from her first, ill-fated marriage. It was 1987 before they were able to make the trip, which made it possible for Amy to see her mother in an entirely new light and helped her understand Daisy's driven, dictatorial attitude during her daughter's formative years.

Amy noticed that in China her mother's relationships with people were as prone to misunderstandings as they had been in the United States, and realized that the cause wasn't Daisy's poor skills in English, as she had formerly believed. With her Chinese daughters, "I saw her interact with my sisters and that she was the same with them, that she was both motherly and oppressive and loving and irritating." Then mother and daughter began talking, and Amy was able to see things from Daisy's perspective for the first time. The experience also gave Amy the idea for what became *The Joy Luck Club*, a novel loosely based on her own mother-daughter relationship and the voyage back in time represented by their visit to China.

The Joy Luck Club concerns four Chinese American women who socialize together over games of mah-jong. Each of the women has an intense, often stressful relationship with her own daughter, and one of them, June, also has twin sisters her mother was forced to abandon in China. As Daisy herself had done, June witnesses the suicide of her mother, Suyuan, a widow who was forced to become a powerful man's fourth wife and who sank into despair when the son she bore was given to the man's higher-ranking wife. The key events of the novel occur after the twins are located, and June's three Joy Luck Club friends pool their resources to send her to reunite with them. In the novel, which takes place after the death of Suyuan, June comes to understand her mother and feels reconciled with her after meeting the two long-lost sisters. When she gets her first glimpse of them at the airport, she at first feels that she is seeing two visions of her own mother. Later, when she watches a Polaroid image of the three of them take shape, she realizes they all resemble their mother.

Back in San Francisco, it took Amy just four months to complete the novel, which was published in 1989. It was an immense critical and commercial success, spending forty weeks on the New York Times bestseller list, and was widely translated—into Chinese as well as more than thirty other languages. In 1993, Amy collaborated with Ronald Bass to adapt *The Joy Luck Club* to the screen.

Her second novel, *The Kitchen God's Wife*, appeared just two years later, in 1991. It, too, was successful, and the events it recounts also took their inspiration from Daisy's family history, relating some of her mother's journey. This time, Tan traces the life of Jiang Weili, from the time she is a young girl in China until many years later, when she is a widow with a sprawling extended family based in San Francisco. Abandoned by her own mother when she was six, Jiang Weili endures a tragic marriage and the loss of three children in China, and further trials despite a happier second marriage that takes her to the United States.

Although Amy and her husband decided not to have children

of their own, she has published two books for young readers, *The Moon Lady* and *The Chinese Siamese Cat*. Her novels written since *The Kitchen God's Wife* include *The Hundred Secret Senses* (1995) and *The Bonesetter's Daughter* (2001). The latter is a meditation on memory—"the things we remember and the things that should be remembered"—that Amy began after Daisy was diagnosed with Alzheimer's disease in 1995 but which she was able to complete only following her mother's death in 1999. The novel ends with the protagonist, LuLing, telling her daughter, "I'm worried that I did terrible things to you when you were a child, that I hurt you very much. But I can't remember what I did . . . I just wanted to say that I hope you can forget, just as I've forgotten."

Amy's most recent novel is *Saving Fish from Drowning* (2005). It represents a departure for Amy, since this novel is set, in part, in Myanmar, rather than China. She has also collected a number of her essays, in *The Opposite of Fate: A Book of Musings* (2003).

Amy hasn't entirely given up music, either. She makes occasional appearances in a "literary garage band," whose members include novelists Stephen King and Scott Turow, cartoonist Matt Groening, and humor writer Dave Barry. The band performs concerts to benefit literacy and First Amendment rights groups. Despite what Amy's agent calls the group's "dubious" talent, their performances have raised more than $1 million for their chosen causes. Proceeds from sales of the group's album, *Stranger than Fiction*, go to the PEN Writers Fund.

LIZ BALMASEDA

Liz Balmaseda was born January 17, 1959, in Puerto Padre, an industrial city on Cuba's eastern end. The 1959 revolution had occurred just two weeks earlier. When Liz was ten months old, her parents emigrated to Florida and settled in Miami, joining the area's rapidly growing community of Cuban émigrés. Her father found work in a Miami hotel, and by the time Liz started school, the

Balmasedas had moved from an apartment in the city to houses in the suburbs, first in Sweetwater and then in East Hialeah. Her mother kept house and had two more children, a boy and a girl.

Liz's parents had little education, but they encouraged their precocious daughter, who even as a preschooler preferred adult talk shows to television's programming for children, to do well in school. While still in first grade, she won a spelling bee sponsored by the *Miami Herald*. In high school, she joined the staff of the Notre Dame Academy's newspaper, but she considered music her first love. Liz had never taken music lessons, but she had picked up the guitar on her own. At Miami Dade Community College, she planned to concentrate on music, but she also enrolled in an intro-ductory journalism class, taught by José Quevedo.

Like Liz, José was originally from Puerto Padre. He demanded the best of his students, and they delivered: the *Falcon Times*, the school paper that he advised, consistently won awards for regional community college publications. Liz was initially reluctant to join the paper's staff, but her teacher persuaded her to cover performing arts and review records. Before long, she was editor-in-chief and the winner of a fellowship to the Modern Media Institute (now the Poynter Institute), in St. Petersburg, Florida. Thanks to that experi-ence, two of Liz's stories appeared in the *St. Petersburg Times*, and Liz envisioned a future as a freelance journalist.

José Quevedo, whose students called him "Q," encouraged Liz to attend Florida International University instead of striking out on her own. FIU had a journalism program that proved to be perfect for her. Liz, who referred to Q as "my angel," later told an interviewer, "You can't learn journalism from a book, and one of the things you get from a program like FIU's is the element of real life. You get the possibility for jobs and internships—you get the street that goes into the classroom. . . . The program lends itself to that and to be collaborative with local press." She also learned to treat every story as if she were writing it for a major paper. José died in 1992, shortly before his star student won journalism's top award.

Before receiving a B.S. in communications from FIU in 1981, Liz was an intern at the *Miami Herald*, where one of her first assignments was covering the arrival of refugees in the Mariel boatlift in 1980. When she graduated, the paper hired her for their Spanish-language edition, *El Herald*, but soon shifted her to reporting for the *Herald* itself. After four years in Miami, Liz went to Central America as *Newsweek*'s bureau chief and later joined NBC as a news producer based in Honduras. She rejoined the *Miami Herald* in 1987 and wrote features for the daily edition and the Sunday magazine until 1991, when she started writing her own column.

Liz had been attracting attention for her writing from her earliest days as a reporter, but it was her features and commentary that first brought major recognition. In 1989, her feature, "Natives: The Heirs Apparent," won the Guillermo Martinez-Marquez Award from the National Association of Hispanic Journalists. In the early 1990s, her commentary received numerous citations, culminating in the 1993 Pulitzer Prize for commentary for her columns about the Cuban Americans in Miami and social and political conditions in Haiti. She was the first Latina journalist to win a Pulitzer Prize. About that first award, Liz said, "It was a shock to win. Nobody was writing about Cuban-American stuff then, though many are now. There wasn't really that kind of writing back then, that kind of voice"–emotionally engaged and open to shades of gray that often angered doctrinaire members of Miami's Cuban community–"especially from someone young. Nobody had the access, I guess."

Eight years later, Liz shared in a second Pulitzer, this time for breaking-news reporting of the story of Elián González, the six-year-old boy who fled Cuba with his mother and other refugees in November 1999 and became the center of months of legal and diplomatic maneuvering. Elián's mother perished during the voyage across the Straits of Florida. The boy was rescued by fishermen and cared for by relatives in Miami until he was seized by Immigration and Naturalization Service agents in April 2000, reunited with his father, and, after a protracted legal battle, returned to Cuba. Liz was part of a team of six *Herald* reporters, five FIU graduates, and one FIU student who was an intern at the time, who reported on the story. As usual, Liz's commentary captured the emotional tension in both camps, as well as the uncertainty about Elián's fate that would linger for months after the crisis had passed.

Liz left the *Miami Herald* in 2003, but she continues to write for the *Palm Beach Post* and other publications. She has also written screenplays and collaborated on several books. One of those is *I Am My Father's Daughter*, on which she worked with María Elena Salinas.

María Elena Salinas

María Elena Salinas, the syndicated newspaper columnist and longtime Noticiero Univisión news anchor, is one of the most widely recognized personalities on Spanish-language television in the United States. In her memoir *I Am My Father's Daughter: Living a Life Without Secrets*, María turns her investigative skills on her own life. After her father died in 1985, a friend of his gave her a box that her father had entrusted to him years before. Inside, she discovered a secret that she had never suspected: at one time, before leaving Mexico for a new life in the United States, her father had been a Roman Catholic priest. This incredible discovery became the inspiration for her to write about her life and family.

María was born in Los Angeles in 1954. Her parents, José and Luz Salinas, had immigrated from Mexico in the 1940s, but returned to Mexico City shortly after she was born. They also had two older daughters, all born in the United States. The family returned to southern California when María was eight, but by then her father had lost his residency status. María remembers that they were always struggling to make ends meet. The family's deep ties of affection and sense of responsibility for each other, however, compensated for their material difficulties. Her mother, from a small town near the Pacific Coast city of Mazatlan, worked as a seamstress in the Los Angeles garment industry, and her father held a number of jobs—as a real estate agent, an accountant, a manager of a bowling alley, and a professor. María's overwhelming impression of him was that he wasn't interested in money, but in good works, "by a sense," as she later put it, "of mission and charity." She knew that he came from a respectable Mexican family of opera singers, artists, priests, and lawyers, but little else about him.

When she was still quite young, María noticed the dramatic differences between her parents, without understanding what they meant. Her mother spoke only Spanish, while her father was fluent in at least six languages, though he insisted on Spanish at home. It was her mother, Luz, she took as her role model, constantly working "with a pin cushion around her wrist," yet also "loving, patient, kind, witty, strong, and comforting." As a child, she remembered one glimpse behind the mask when the family went out to dinner at a German restaurant, where she had never been before, but where the regulars all knew José, addressed him as "Professor," and conversed in German.

At school, María mastered English and soon became comfortably bilingual and bicultural. She attended a parochial high school, and from the time she was fourteen worked—in garment factories, as her mother did—to earn money to help her family make ends meet. After high school, she studied marketing at East Los Angeles Community College and continued working at various jobs, including one where she advertised cosmetics on the air at a local Spanish-language radio station.

The on-air spots led to María's first journalism job; the station manager noticed her talent and invited her to work as a DJ and news reader. She was a radio reporter for two years before switching to television news in 1981, at KMEX-34, the first Spanish-language TV station in Los Angeles and the local affiliate station of Univisión. At the time, Channel 34 was a bare-bones operation with just two reporters who did everything, digging up the stories and then presenting them on the air. Still, María was self-conscious about her lack of training—"I only had a background in marketing and radio. I had no experience in journalism or broadcasting"— and was the only woman journalist. She took some journalism courses at UCLA while she worked at Channel 34, and before long she was also hosting a daily public affairs show, *Los Angeles Ahora*, and a weekend music program, *Domingos Alegres*, while continuing to report the news. There were only 14 million Hispanics in the United States at the time, but a quarter of the people in Los Angeles were Spanish-speaking, with virtually no political voice.

Her first story at Channel 34 came just before local elections for city council, the board of education, and the Los Angeles County Board of Supervisors. Redistricting had created opportunities for Hispanics to be elected to public offices, but when María conducted man-on-the-street interviews about the elections, she discovered that almost no one knew the city was in the midst of an election campaign. "I thought, you know, our people are never going to be empowered, our people are never going to have representation. They're never going to have political clout unless we educate them."

As a result, María recast her role. She decided she needed to do more than just report the news. At Channel 34, María became "a social services provider, teaching members of the community how to defend themselves, how to find out about their rights, how to take advantage of available services, telling them how to start a business, what tools are needed to be successful." Sometimes the information viewers found most useful was basic—about education programs, vaccination, immigration laws, or voting. It may not have been news, strictly speaking, but for the immigrant community it was invaluable.

María's gift for informing southern California's Latino viewers about breaking news and how it affected their lives attracted viewers. Her father lived long enough to take pride in the fact that she was starting to make a name for herself in journalism and to counsel her to learn the story behind the story, not just settle for reading the copy that came off the teletype machine. Her work also caught the attention of executives at Noticiero Univisión. In 1987, she began to enter more mainstream news positions. She moved up to the network's national programming and has been there ever since, first as a news reader, then as nightly co-anchor. In more than a quarter of a century on Hispanic television, she has been called "the most recognized and trusted Hispanic newswoman in America." Her programs are telecast throughout most of the Western Hemisphere, where she is widely considered "The Voice of Hispanic America."

In recent years, María has increased her presence on and off the air. She is cohost of the weekly TV news magazine *Aqui y Ahora*. Her weekly newspaper column, concerning domestic and Latin American issues, is one of just a handful of syndicated features by an Hispanic journalist. She has also added a daily commentary on radio, Radio Unica, and a weekly column on www.univision.com. Her analyses can also be heard on National Public Radio, where the host of *Latino USA*, María Hinojosa, regularly solicits her observations.

As Noticiero Univisión's most visible woman journalist, María has enjoyed unrivalled access to the world's leading figures in politics, religion, and culture. She covered many of the international trips of the globe-trotting Pope John Paul II, including his visit to Cuba in 1998. She has met with nearly every American president of the past three decades and interviewed every important figure in Latin American politics, including Mexican presidents Carlos Salinas de Gortari, Ernesto Zedillo, and Vicente Fox; Argentina's Carlos Ménem; Nicaragua's Daniel Ortega, Violeta Chamorro, and Enrique Bolaños; Colombia's Cesar Gaviria, Andres Pastrana and Alvaro Uribe; Peru's Alberto Fujimori and Alejandro Toledo; and the Zapatista leader Sub-Comandante Marcos. When she interviewed General Augusto Pinochet, former Chilean president, she asked about human rights violations during his years in power, and she confronted the deposed Panamanian dictator

Manuel Antonio Noriega about his questionable policies and tactics. But her interests in Latin America, as in the United States, always go beyond the countries' leaders, to the ordinary citizens and their concerns.

The breadth and quality of María's journalistic work has brought prestige and recognition to her network. Univisión won two national Emmy Awards in 2000 for its reporting on Hurricane Mitch, thanks in part to Maria's broadcasts. That was the first time a Spanish-language network received an Emmy. When she moderated a town hall meeting for Univisión with Mexican president Vicente Fox in Los Angeles, she was honored with another Emmy. There have been other prizes as well, including an Edward R. Murrow Award for Univisión's coverage of the bombings at the Atlanta Olympics in 1996, which Maria reported on along with other members of the network's news team.

María now traces many of her interests and accomplishments in her career to her father. The realization surprised her at first: "I always wanted to take after my mother and ended up being like my father." But she acknowledges that her devotion to the cause of the American Hispanic community reflects José Salinas's values. Unabashedly practicing "advocacy journalism," she often brings attention to efforts to convince Hispanic students to stay in school, promotes voter education, and highlights for government agencies the issues important to her audience. She has covered the national debate about immigration reform. In areas of health and education, she is often able to reach her audience with messages about the importance of immunization for young children, reducing heart disease risks, and how parents can encourage their children in school more effectively than Washington can.

María sees the growing size and economic power of the Latino community in the United States as a good thing. With a population that now exceeds 40 million, "we are demonstrating our presence in a very positive way because we are integrating ourselves with the cultural life of this country." Annual spending now hovers between

$600 billion and $700 billion, a figure that has attracted the attention of every industry. María thinks the trend toward acceptance of immigrants in the United States continues to improve. "I have been around long enough to understand the issues that affect us. I believe there are many misconceptions about immigrants, both legal and illegal."

María, who has worked out of Univisión's Miami studios for some years, met Elliott Rodriguez, an anchorman for WFOR, the CBS affiliate station in Miami, after Hurricane Andrew struck the area in 1992. Elliott "helped me clean out the debris from my house and move into a temporary apartment. He helped with my insurance nightmares." Early in 1993, the couple married in Mexico. They now have two daughters, Julia Alejandra and Gabriela María, as well as Erica and Bianca, Elliott's children from his previous marriage, whom Maria considers her own children as well.

María isn't sure that she would encourage her daughters to follow in her professional footsteps. "If they decide they want to become journalists, I will tell them about the downside of the profession, and that it is not all about fame and travel. If they still want to, I will support them." She may be influenced by the recent experience of writing a book on a subject that proved at times uncomfortably close: her own family. "I didn't know whether I had the right to reveal my family secrets, there's nothing more intimate than that. . . . In this book, I discuss that close relationship that exists between father and daughter. Everything is there: my career, professional anecdotes, my social conscience and political ideas, and how the past influences the person I am today."

María does hope that talented young Hispanics will go into journalism. To help make that possible, she has established the María Elena Salinas Excellence of Journalism in Spanish Scholarship, administered by the National Association of Hispanic Journalists. Outstanding students receive grants of $10,000 and spend a year as interns in the Univisión network.

End of Cht. 3

chpt. 4 > goes to pg. 206.,

CHAPTER 4

A Dream of the Future

Women's Suffrage and Civil Rights

THE TRUE WOMAN IS AS YET A DREAM OF THE FUTURE.
–Elizabeth Cady Stanton

SUSAN B. ANTHONY

Susan Brownell Anthony's father, Daniel, was a strict Quaker who firmly believed that education was as essential for his daughters as for his sons. Although his wife, Lucy Read Anthony, was from a Baptist family, the eight Anthony children were taught the tenets of Quaker beliefs, one of which was that women were equal before God. At Quaker meetings, women had the same right to speak as men did, and their views were given equal weight. Susan, a brilliant child born in 1820 in Adams, Massachusetts, thrived in this high-minded atmosphere, where there were no children's games or toys, but boundless respect for the worth of the individual and for self-reliance.

By the time Susan was three, she was reading and writing on her own, and in 1826 she entered the district school in Battenville, New

York, where her father, a cotton miller, had moved to operate a larger mill. Soon afterwards, however, Susan's teacher refused to teach long division to girls, so Daniel Anthony established a school for his children and the children of his neighbors and hired Mary Perkins—more enlightened and better educated than the district school's staff. She taught classical languages, mathematics, and science in addition to the elementary subjects.

Women teachers were rare through much of the nineteenth century in the United States. Even primary school teachers were overwhelmingly male, except during the summer, when able-bodied men were busy with farmwork and women took their places in the classroom, which only children too young to help in the fields and stables attended. In most cases, women lacked the requisite education to teach anything beyond the rudimentary subjects. When Susan was born, there wasn't a single American school offering a serious secondary education or college-level courses to young women. The first to do so, Emma Willard's Troy Female Seminary, opened a year later, in 1821. Mary Perkins, independent and knowledgeable, presented Susan and her sisters with an unprecedented role model.

When she was fifteen, Susan was the schoolmistress during the summer term for children who met in her parents' home. Two years later, in 1837, she left Battenville to attend Deborah Moulson's Friends' Seminary near Philadelphia. Guelma, the eldest of the Anthony children, was already attending Miss Moulson's school, and the family expected their second daughter to excel as well. She quickly proved herself academically, and found her studies in science and mathematics exciting, but she chafed at Miss Moulson's continual disapproval and criticism. It isn't known whether the schoolmistress recognized Susan's intellectual gifts and meant to spur her to work even harder at her studies and on her character, but it's clear from her diary that the effect on Susan was devastating. Stung by one unspecified tongue-lashing by Miss Moulson, she wrote, "If I am such a vile sinner, I would that I might feel it myself."

Susan lasted barely one academic year at Miss Moulson's, probably because her father suffered severe financial losses in the panic of 1837, one of the country's worst economic depressions. She and Guelma returned to Battenville in May 1838, and the Anthony family moved to Hardscrabble, a town just two miles from their former home, settling into a building that had once been a hotel. To Daniel, the town's name was painfully emblematic of his failure. Some years later when he was appointed postmaster of Hardscrabble he had it renamed Center Falls.

As soon as the family had settled into their new surroundings, Susan went to work teaching school, and for the next five years she handed all of her earnings over to her parents. In the middle of the decade, her mother, Lucy, came into an inheritance, which she and Daniel used to buy a farm in western New York, near Rochester. Instead of joining her family, Susan struck out on her own; in 1846, she was hired as headmistress at Canajoharie Academy, a boarding school in the center of the state. During her three years in Canajoharie, Susan tasted true independence for the first time. The money she earned was her own, and free of Quakerism's aesthetic of simple severity, she invested some of it in new outfits.

Susan objected to the fact that women teachers were almost always paid less than their male counterparts, even when they did exactly the same work (in fact, one of the arguments in favor of hiring women as teachers was that since they weren't supporting families they would accept lower salaries), but she also didn't really enjoy being a schoolmistress. When her father branched out into insurance in 1849, Susan moved back to Rochester to run the family farm. In contrast to Canajoharie, where the only reform activity was temperance, Rochester was abuzz with political debate and activity—about temperance, women's rights, and abolition—and Daniel and Lucy's home was at the center of it. Their visitors included such luminaries as Frederick Douglass, William Lloyd Garrison, and Wendell Phillips, the plainspoken orator so persuasive that he was known as "abolition's golden trumpet."

Susan had still been in Canajoharie in 1848, when the first women's rights convention was held in Seneca Falls, New York, but both her parents and her sister Mary had been among the participants. They told her about one of the convention's organizers, Elizabeth Cady Stanton, author of the Declaration of Sentiments, which was modeled on the American Declaration of Independence and included a demand for voting rights for women. Even after Susan met Elizabeth through their mutual friend Amelia Bloomer, she didn't immediately take up the cause of women's suffrage, but continued to focus her reform efforts on temperance. A temperance rally in Albany, New York, in 1852, changed all that. She wasn't allowed to speak at the event–solely because she was a woman. Susan and Elizabeth immediately formed the Woman's State Temperance Society to give women a public voice, and Susan rapidly realized that until women were able to own property and vote, they would not be able to wield real political influence.

The Woman's State Temperance Society lasted less than two years, but it launched a lifelong partnership between the two women whose names became synonymous with the American woman suffrage movement. Their talents complemented each other perfectly. Susan, endlessly energetic and relatively unencumbered by family obligations, was the organizer: she scheduled lectures, raised money, organized women's rights conventions, collected signatures on petitions that put pressure on legislatures to pass women's suffrage and property laws. Elizabeth, who had seven children between 1842 and 1859, was not as free to travel as Susan, but she was more outgoing and a brilliant writer and speaker. In her account, Susan was "slow and analytical in composition, I am rapid and synthetic. I am the better writer, she the better critic. She supplied the facts and statistics, I the philosophy and rhetoric." Furthermore, Elizabeth relished public attention, while Susan, who suffered from a slight squint (which is partly responsible for the intimidating impression she makes in most photographs), looked severe and tended to speak in an expressionless monotone; she didn't enjoy being in the public eye, though she was in fact a forceful, persuasive personality. Although she generally preferred working away from the limelight and recognized that the division of labor that she and Elizabeth had worked out was the most productive for their cause, she sometimes got tired of playing second fiddle to the affable, eloquent Elizabeth. In the early 1860s, when she went to Oregon alone, after the two of them had made a political tour through California together, she wrote, "I miss Miss Stanton, but I cannot but enjoy the feeling that the people call on *me*. . . . There is no alternative—whoever goes into a parlor or before an audience with that woman does it at the cost of a fearful overshadowing, a price which I have paid for the last ten years, and that cheerfully."

Political successes were few and far between in the suffrage movement's early years, but there were occasional glimmers of progress: in 1860, for example, when New York enacted legislation that guaranteed married women the right to keep money they earned (formerly, it became their husbands' property) and to sue in court. The decade was also in many ways a solitary period for Susan, whose stern appearance masked a warmhearted, loyal person with a gift for friendship. She saw much less of her family, who approved of her commitment to social causes, but she stayed close to her parents and sisters through letters. Her circle of friendship, however, became increasingly her comrades-in-arms in the temperance, abolition, and suffrage movements. Elizabeth's marriage to Henry Stanton was far from harmonious, but she remained committed to her large family.

Susan, already thirty years old by the time she met most of the people who would become her political collaborators, would no longer have been considered "marriageable" by mid-nineteenth-century standards, and she may have felt a twinge of regret when some of the younger reformers married—especially Lucy Stone (who was two years older than Susan) and Antoinette Brown, who married two brothers, Henry and Samuel Blackwell, in 1855 and 1856. According to several of her biographers, Susan wasn't the humorless figure she appears to be from her portraits, but a friendly woman who had a number of suitors but chose not to marry because she was convinced that a family would interfere with her work for social and political reform. "I never felt I could give up my life of freedom to become a man's housekeeper," she later explained. "When I was young, if a girl married poor, she became a housekeeper and a drudge. If she married wealthy, she became a pet and a doll." Neither drudge nor doll, as she approached forty, Susan confided to fellow suffragist Lucretia Mott that she believed that marriage–"spiritual or legal"–would inevitably limit one's freedom of action.

In the decade leading up to the Civil War, the public roles that Susan took shaped her life and her place in history. She participated in the Underground Railroad network that sheltered escaped slaves as they traveled north to avoid capture, arranged for abolitionist lecturers who toured western New York State, and conducted a campaign to lobby for emancipation through the Woman's Loyal National League (founded by the Stanton-Anthony team) until the slaves were finally freed at war's end.

Ironically, the postwar successes of antislavery advocates desirous of conferring full rights of citizenship on the masses of freedmen blunted the women's suffrage movement. When the language of the Fourteenth Amendment was written to mandate full voting rights for all men, but not for women, Susan felt shocked and betrayed. She had expected Northern politicians to repay women for their strong support of the war and their allegiance to the abolition movement. She couldn't have been more mistaken. It would be another half-century before the winds of national sentiment would shift and women would win the right to vote.

Susan and many of her suffrage colleagues had allied their movement with a strategy that combined the drive to enfranchise blacks with the women's suffrage effort. She was present at the birth of the American Equal Rights Association in 1866; the group's president was Lucretia Mott. Susan herself was corresponding secretary, and many of her longtime allies, including Elizabeth Cady Stanton, were active in its work. The group petitioned state and national legislatures and constitutional conventions and campaigned in states where referenda were being held on the questions of enfranchising blacks and women. They were unsuccessful on every front.

In Kansas, where Susan and Elizabeth campaigned on behalf of the twin suffrage referendums, they encountered George Francis Train, who opposed voting rights for women but was in the state to support the referendum on behalf of blacks. An eccentric man who made a fortune from real estate and railroads, George also set several records for round-the-world travel; the first, in 1870, was probably the basis of Jules Verne's classic, *Around the World in Eighty Days*. George Train, who may have wanted to take advantage of Elizabeth and Susan's reputations as traveling lecturers, offered to underwrite a speaking tour for the three of them and to pay the costs of publishing a newspaper, *The Revolution*, that first appeared in 1868. Its slogan was "Men, their rights and nothing more; women, their rights and nothing less," and the paper primarily espoused the causes to which Susan and Elizabeth were dedicated: the right to vote without restrictions based on race or gender, education for girls that would prepare them for careers as well as for marriage, greater access to jobs for women, and more liberal divorce laws. The paper also promoted a number of Train's ideas, including bans on imports, liberal immigration policies, and replacing "hard" currency (currency backed by gold or silver) with "greenback" (paper) currency supported only by the "full faith and credit" of the federal government. (Train was the short-lived Greenback Party's presidential candidate in 1872.)

The "Train cloud," as it was called, damaged the images of Susan and Elizabeth in the eyes of many of their fellow social reformers, so it is probably fortunate that their mercurial benefactor's interest flagged after a few months, and he stopped paying the bills. It took Susan eight years to pay the debts that had accrued; she did it by lecturing tirelessly all over the country, about voting rights

and other social issues. At the same time, she kept the woman suffrage issue alive in other ways. The first of a series of woman suffrage conventions took place in Washington, D.C., in 1869, and that
year she founded the National Woman Suffrage Association. The
NWSA lobbied for other reforms, like equal pay, as well as voting
rights, and the stigma of having accepted George Train's money
was still fresh. As a result, some suffragists formed a rival group, the
American Woman Suffrage Association, whose focus was solely on
the right to vote. Lucy Stone was the first AWSA president, and the
two groups did not set aside their differences until 1890, when they
acknowledged that they would advance their cause more effectively
if they were unified, and merged to form the National American
Woman Suffrage Association.

Some women, including Victoria Woodhull, a flamboyant figure
who was a minority party candidate for the presidency in 1872,
began to argue that the Fourteenth Amendment *did* give women
the right to vote. Acting on this assumption, Susan, three of her
sisters, and several other women successfully registered and voted
in Rochester in that year's national election. Although they were
allowed to vote, they were arrested some days later. Susan played
the events to the limit, refusing to go to U.S. Commissioner Anthony
Storrs' office to discuss the matter, saying, "I sent word to him that
I had no social acquaintance with him and didn't wish to call on
him." She described Storrs' office as the "dingy little room where,
in the olden days, fugitive slaves were examined and returned to
their masters." She didn't even want to post bail. Her lawyer, Henry
Selden, finally decided to post her bail himself, although he knew
that she was hoping to use her detention as a means of pressuring
the U.S. Supreme Court to hear the case. But, Henry explained, "I
could not see a lady I respected put in jail."

Concerned that a Rochester jury would be sympathetic to the
defendants, the U.S. attorney had the trial moved to Canandaigua,
thirty miles south of the city, where the federal district court judge
instructed the jury to find Susan and her codefendants guilty and

fined them each $100. Susan refused to pay, hoping to appeal the verdict to the Supreme Court. She told the judge, "May it please your honor, I will never pay a dollar of your unjust penalty." Because no effort was made to compel her to pay the fine, there were no grounds for appeal. The experiment with voting convinced Susan that legislative action, not court tests, was the best route to winning the vote for women, but the publicity her case generated did increase public sympathy for the cause. As one New York newspaper quipped, "She has voted and the American Constitution has survived the shock."

The Declaration of Rights for Women, presented at the United States Centennial Exposition in Philadelphia's Independence Hall on July 4, 1876, was one of the NWSA's most dramatic stratagems for drawing attention to women's demands for equal political and civil rights. Denied permission to present the declaration at the Centennial celebration itself, the women then began distributing copies of their declaration, and a commotion ensued as people in the hall eagerly reached for them.

Susan had no intention of leaving Philadelphia without reading the Declaration of Rights for Women herself, however. When the women left Independence Hall, she mounted a platform outside that had been built for the musicians who performed at the exposition and read the demand for relief for American women, who "still suffer the degradation of disfranchisement." Quoting Abigail Adams, she said, "We will not hold ourselves bound to obey laws in which we have no voice or representation," and concluded, "We ask of our rulers, at this hour, no special favors, no special privileges, no special legislation. We ask justice, we ask equality, we ask that all the civil and political rights that belong to citizens of the United States be guaranteed to us and our daughters forever."

Susan was busy throughout the decade. She began to compile the history of the women's suffrage movement. Working mainly with Elizabeth and Matilda Joslyn Gage, a founding member of NWSA and editor of its newspaper, the *National Citizen and Ballot*

Box, she co-authored the first six volumes of the *History of Woman Suffrage* between 1881 and her death in 1906. Two more volumes appeared under Ida Husted Harper's editorial supervision, the last in 1922.

Indefatigable and single-minded, Susan's persistence was largely responsible for the introduction of a women's suffrage amendment in Congress, for the first time in 1878, and then again every year until it finally passed forty-one years later. Long before the Nineteenth Amendment was ratified, it became known as the Susan B. Anthony amendment. Her driving temperament and tendency to demand equivalent dedication from her colleagues sometimes made her difficult to work with. She earned the nickname, not always affectionate, of "General." But to most of her fellow suffragists, she was a loyal friend. Unlike many founders, who cannot tolerate the idea of being replaced by a younger person, she actively cultivated women she thought might be able to carry on the work, although she sometimes distanced herself from protégées whose enthusiasm flagged or who married and had families. Carrie Chapman Catt, who became Susan's chief lieutenant, eventually succeeded her when she retired as president of NWSA in 1900.

In 1889 Wyoming became the first state to enact a women's suffrage law (a few territories, including Wyoming, allowed women to vote earlier). It was also that year that Susan began to cut back on her national activities. She returned to live in Rochester year-round, after spending most of the previous twenty-five years in Washington, D.C., or New York City. She threw herself into local causes, among them raising an endowment to make it possible for women to attend the University of Rochester.

With age came recognition and, fortunately, some support for the woman who hadn't received a salary since she resigned her teaching post in Canajoharie in 1849. She was affectionately referred to as "Aunt Susan" by a generation of women who identified with the struggle for voting rights. At the age of seventy-five, in 1895, she received an annuity of $800 a year, and three years later, Ida Husted Harper published the first two volumes of *The Life of Susan B. Anthony* (she brought out a final volume in 1908, two years after Susan's death). She was anything but retired, however. Despite what was probably a mild stroke in 1895 (Susan described it as a fainting spell), she kept up a busy schedule of lectures and campaigning. Even after a second, much graver stroke in 1900, she didn't stop. As late as 1904, she went to Berlin to help found—and accept the honorary presidency of—the International Woman Suffrage Association.

In failing health, she braved a blizzard to go to Baltimore for her last woman suffrage convention in February 1906. Once there, however, she was well enough to attend just one of the sessions. But the agenda in Baltimore included a birthday tribute, where Susan proclaimed that "failure is impossible." Dozens of birthday greetings were read at her celebration, but when Susan spoke she asked, "When will the men do something besides extend congratulations? I would rather have President Roosevelt say one word to Congress in favor of amending the Constitution to give women the suffrage than to praise me endlessly!" (In fact, in 1912, Roosevelt, running for president as the Progressive Party candidate, was the first major-party candidate to include a pro-women's suffrage plank in his platform.) She returned to Rochester, where Anna Howard Shaw, then NWSA president, stayed with her until her death a month later. One piece of advice Anna later remembered hearing from Susan at the time might well serve as her credo: "Take your stand and hold it: then let come what will, and receive the blows like a good soldier."

After Susan's death, even many of those who opposed her in life acknowledged her importance and strength of character. Lucy Stone's husband, Henry Blackwell, had criticized her alliance with George Francis Train in the harshest terms, but forty years later, he acknowledged that she possessed "qualities of leadership such as are possessed by few women or men. . . . Her name will always be identified with this greatest of all political reforms."

_177._

None of the women who began the struggle for women's suffrage lived long enough to applaud the ratification of the Nineteenth Amendment. But their influence certainly turned the tide. After the amendment passed in Congress in May 1919, it made the long circuit of the state legislatures for ratification. The deciding state, in July 1920, was Tennessee; the legislature was thought to be one vote short of ratification until a young representative, twenty-four-year-old Harry Burn, announced his support for the amendment. Burn had a letter from his mother in his pocket that day. "Don't forget to be a good boy," it said. "Vote for suffrage."

Elizabeth Cady Stanton and Lucretia Mott

"Oh, my daughter, I wish you were a boy!" Elizabeth Cady recalled her father saying shortly after her only brother, Eleazer, died in 1826. Her reply, as she remembered it in her autobiography, was, "I will try to be all my brother was." The precocious ten-year-old studied Greek, Latin, and mathematics and eventually learned law and its history, became a skilled horsewoman, and mastered chess. One thing she could not do, however, was matriculate at Union College, the men's college her brother had attended in Schenectady, New York. Instead, she enrolled at Troy Female Seminary, the school Emma Willard founded to offer young women a liberal arts education on a par with the best men's colleges. Elizabeth graduated in 1832.

Elizabeth never succeeded in convincing her lawyer father, Daniel Cady, that she was a man's intellectual equal, but the experience spurred her to devote her life to claiming equal status for herself and other women. As a young adult in the 1830s, Elizabeth discovered the temperance and abolition movements on visits to her maternal cousin Gerrit Smith, in Peterboro, New York. A wealthy landowner, antislavery and temperance activist, and congressman, Gerrit's friends included Frederick Douglass and John Brown. In 1839, Elizabeth met journalist Henry Brewster Stanton at an abolition meeting in Peterboro. They married the next year, after Elizabeth struggled to overcome her parents' objections to Henry's politics and her own reservations about the conventions of marriage (she insisted that "obey" be cut from her wedding vow).

The Stantons honeymooned at the World Anti-Slavery Convention in London, to which Henry, a member of the American Anti-Slavery Society, was a delegate. At the convention, Elizabeth met Lucretia Coffin Mott, the only American woman delegate. She shared her new friend's anger when the meeting organizers refused to allow the women delegates to sit with the men, and the two of them became friends and allies in a collective effort that flowered into the Seneca Falls Convention of 1848.

Lucretia became Elizabeth's mentor in political tactics in the struggle for women's rights, and the Seneca Falls Convention they conceived is usually described as the opening act in the dramatic campaign waged by American women in pursuit of their political and economic rights. Elizabeth later traced the genesis of the Seneca Falls Convention to the conversations she and Lucretia had when they first met in London in 1840, where they and the five other American women at the World Anti-Slavery Convention were forced to sit behind a curtain in the balcony while the men conducted the conventions business on the main floor below.

A generation older than Elizabeth, Lucretia was the daughter of prominent Quakers descended from the original settlers of Nantucket, Massachusetts. She later credited the equal status of Quaker women for the ease with which she asserted herself in public life. She understood and was empowered by this inheritance. In 1869, in a letter to the British reformer Josephine Butler, she reflected, "In the executive department of the Society, the right conceded to woman to act conjointly with man has had its influence, not only in making her familiar with the routine of business relating to our 'Discipline,' but in giving her self-reliance in mingling with the various reformatory societies in the great movements of the age." It is no coincidence that the largest single group signing the 1848

Declaration of Sentiments at Seneca Falls were Quakers or former Quakers.

Like many of the islanders, Lucretia's father, Thomas Coffin, was in the China trade, and his seven children grew up in what was largely a society of women. The men's whaling and trading voyages kept them absent from home for months or years at a time, so religion, education, and social life were very much in the hands of the women, including her mother, Anna Folger Coffin, who also owned a shop that sold items from the East India trade. As a result, Lucretia said of herself, "I grew up so thoroughly imbued with women's rights that it was the most important question of my life from a very early day."

In 1804, Thomas Coffin left shipping and moved his family to Boston, where he became a merchant. At first, Lucretia attended a private school in the city, but her parents soon decided that the "democratic" thing to do was to enroll their children in the local public schools. From the age of thirteen or fourteen, Lucretia attended a Friends boarding school at Nine Partners in New York's Dutchess County. After two years as a student, she joined the staff of the school as an unpaid assistant teacher. Lucretia, dedicated to social service, didn't object to working without a salary (in return, a younger sister was allowed to attend the school tuition-free), but her discovery that the full-fledged women teachers at the school were paid just half of what the men received transformed her into a lifelong advocate of equal pay for equal work.

One of the other teachers at Nine Partners was James Mott. When Lucretia's family moved to Philadelphia in 1809, James followed them, went to work for Thomas Coffin, and married Lucretia at the Pine Street Meetinghouse on April 10, 1811. The Motts had six children between 1812 and 1828 (one son died in 1817, at the age of five), but after Lucretia's father died in 1815, she returned to teaching while her husband established himself in business. By 1820, she recognized a calling to the Quaker ministry and began speaking about social issues at Friends meetings, a step that undoubtedly led to her emergence as a noted speaker outside the meetinghouse as well.

One of the causes Lucretia and James embraced during the 1820s, along with most members of the Hicksite branch of the Society of Friends, was abolition. In her speeches, Lucretia advocated using only "free produce," products that were obtained without slave labor, and she herself stopped wearing cotton or using cane sugar. By the end of the decade, James, who had built a prosperous cotton-trading firm, switched his operations to the wool commission business at considerable personal cost. Because organizations like William Lloyd Garrison's American Anti-Slavery Society were closed to women, Lucretia helped found the Philadelphia Female Anti-Slavery Society in 1833 and organized an Anti-Slavery Convention of American Women in that city in 1838. Her resolve and courage in the face of danger became legendary after anti-abolitionists burned down the meeting hall and threatened to set fire to the Motts' house. Two years later, she was on a speaking tour in Delaware when a pro-slavery mob tarred and feathered Daniel Neall, who was traveling with her. Lucretia tried to convince them to seize her instead, since she was the one who was speaking out against slavery, but they refused because she was a woman. Her reply: "I ask no courtesy at your hands on account of my sex."

When Lucretia, her sister Martha Coffin Wright, and Elizabeth Cady Stanton organized the first annual women's rights convention in Seneca Falls, New York, in 1848, the idea of women speaking for themselves was still so novel that they asked a man—Lucretia's husband, James—to preside over the meeting. Despite this nod to propriety, Lucretia was the central figure; her speeches opened and closed the convention. The highlight of the event was the Declaration of Sentiments, patterned on the Declaration of Independence, that declared that "all men and women are created equal," condemned the social, religious, and political disenfranchisement of women, and demanded "immediate admission to all the rights and privileges which belong to them as citizens of these United States."

At the convention, a dozen resolutions were passed by the delegates. About the right to vote, however, Lucretia and Elizabeth disagreed. Elizabeth considered it the key to equal rights for women, while Lucretia gave it less weight. In "Discourse on Woman," a speech about gender inequality Lucretia wrote not long after the convention, she emphasized a number of other factors, including inferior education, lower wages and exclusion from the professions, as well as the absence of the right to vote.

After emancipation, Lucretia redoubled her efforts to improve economic opportunities for former slaves, open more schools, and secure the franchise for black men and all women. When the American Equal Rights Association came into being in 1866, Elizabeth insisted that Lucretia be its first president. Three years later, the group split into rival factions over the question of whether women should defer their own efforts to gain the vote until black men were enfranchised. Lucretia, who personally agreed with antislavery activist Wendell Phillips' assertion that "This is the Negro's hour" (and, like many Quakers, was committed on principle to refusing the vote as long as slavery was the law of the land), struggled to avert a schism in the women's movement, but she wasn't able to prevent Elizabeth and Susan from forming a new organization, the National Woman Suffrage Association.

If Lucretia was, as Elizabeth described her, "an entirely new revelation of womanhood" and the symbol of the movement, Elizabeth Cady Stanton increasingly emerged as its voice. It was from Lucretia that Elizabeth discovered the English writer Mary Wollstonecraft's *A Vindication of the Rights of Woman* (1792), but it was Elizabeth who composed most of the Declaration of Sentiments and Resolutions that was presented in Seneca Falls in 1848. And much of the organizational energy and direction can be credited to Susan, who became Elizabeth's closest collaborator once they met in 1851. Unlike Lucretia, they both felt that woman suffrage shouldn't be sacrificed or postponed until after the voting rights of freed male slaves were secured.

Unlike Susan, however, for whom woman suffrage was the cause par excellence, Elizabeth Cady Stanton busied herself in a number of areas that were important to women. Among these were efforts to make it possible for married women to own property independent of their husbands, to enjoy parental rights, and to obtain divorces from husbands who were abusive, endangered the children, and imperiled the family's economic well-being.

Elizabeth's long marriage to Henry Stanton, who died in 1887, was not without its strains. The legal restrictions that marriage imposed on a woman undoubtedly played a part in Elizabeth's interest in expanding the legal prerogatives of married women, but the Stantons' forty-seven years together were, on balance, personally contenting to her. She and her husband often disagreed about politics, but they and their seven children (born between 1842 and 1859) enjoyed a placid home life in Boston and New York State. Concurrently, Elizabeth petitioned and lobbied for reforms such as a New York State law that permitted married women to own property (it passed the legislature in 1848). Seneca Falls became the venue of the first women's convention because the Stantons had moved there in 1847. About three hundred men and women attended the convention, July 19–20, 1848.

The continuing disapproval and resistance to her ideas and her work that both her father and her husband expressed very likely spurred Elizabeth to stress the importance of physical and economic independence even to women who were neither oppressed nor mistreated. After visiting her family in 1855, she wrote to Susan, "I never felt more keenly the degradation of my sex. To think that all in me of which my father would have felt a proper pride had I been a man, is deeply mortifying to him because I am a woman." The disapproval—whether of family or friends—only strengthened her determination "to speak as soon as I can do myself credit."

More than any other nineteenth-century figure in the struggle for women's rights in the United States, Elizabeth made good on her promise to speak out and write. From her pen flowed many of the movement's eloquent pronouncements, from the first Declaration of Sentiments; through the multivolume history of the suffrage movement; her more idiosyncratic *The Woman's Bible*, which criticized control of women in the name of religion; and her autobiography *Eighty Years and More*. Many of the speeches Susan delivered were actually written for her by Elizabeth. They were integral to the intimate collaboration of these two extraordinary women, and most of the time Elizabeth did her part enthusiastically. But occasionally the strain of turning out yet another speech or pamphlet showed, as when she confided to her diary late in her life (1896), "One would think that I were a machine; that all I had to do was turn a crank and thoughts on any theme would bubble up like water."

Far from being a machine, Elizabeth was an infectious public presence: short and stout, but a natural orator who laced her lectures with humor, spontaneity, and an air of friendliness and fearlessness. Unafraid of staking out controversial positions, she declared, "It is a settled maxim with me that the existing public sentiment on any subject is wrong" with such good nature that audiences listened even when they didn't immediately concur. In 1866, more than half a century before women were allowed to vote in New York, Elizabeth ran for Congress from that state, to test whether a woman had the right to seek elective office. She received only twenty-four votes.

As had been the case with the earliest women trailblazers in the eighteenth and nineteenth centuries, the three leaders died before their dream of women's suffrage was realized. Passage and ratification of the Nineteenth Amendment to the Constitution finally granted women the right to vote in 1920. Lucretia passed away first, in 1880, followed by Elizabeth in 1902, and Susan in 1906.

Seventy-seven years later they gained the most coveted recognition, a memorial in the U.S. Capitol. The Elizabeth Cady Stanton, Susan B. Anthony, and Lucretia Mott statue sits in the crypt under the Rotunda.

The Sewell-Belmont House in Washington, D.C., where many of

the historic papers documenting the struggle for women's suffrage are preserved today, sits one block from the Capitol. It contains archives, scrapbooks, and original newspaper accounts of the drive to achieve voting rights for women. The second floor is a museum furnished with period pieces—Susan B. Anthony's desk and Elizabeth Cady Stanton's chair. Senator Barbara Mikulski and I have helped the preservation project. In 1997, we hosted a historic dinner of the women senators and the two women justices on the U.S. Supreme Court, Sandra Day O'Connor and Ruth Bader Ginsberg, in the dining room of this historic building, surrounded by treasured mementoes of the determined women who laid the foundation for us to become participants and leaders in the political process.

ROSA PARKS

A century after Lucretia Mott, Elizabeth Cady Stanton, Susan B. Anthony, and a handful of other intrepid women launched the campaign to secure the vote for American women, the modern civil rights movement took its first steps in the United States. The story of Rosa Parks, a Montgomery, Alabama, seamstress who refused to surrender her seat on a city bus so that a white commuter could have it, is familiar to most American schoolchildren. But the woman behind the story and her life before and after December 1, 1955, are not as well known.

Born in Tuskegee, Alabama, in 1913, to James and Leona Edwards McCauley, Rosa grew up mostly on her grandparents' farm in tiny Pine Level, about fifty miles from her birthplace. Her mother, a schoolteacher with two young children, two-year-old Rosa and Sylvester, an infant, took her family back to Pine Level in 1915. James, a skilled carpenter, often worked in other parts of the state, and he soon abandoned the family. Rosa wrote that her father left Pine Level to find work, and "I did not see him again until I was five years old and my brother was three. He stayed several days and left again. I did not see my father any more until I was an adult and married."

Throughout her early childhood, Rosa was cared for by her grandparents, Sylvester and Rosie Edwards, while her mother taught school in a nearby town. She was educated in the local one-room schoolhouse until she was eleven.

Rosa's memories of life in the close-knit Edwards-McCauley family were happy ones, but far from idyllic. When she was just six years old, she joined her relatives picking cotton on the eighteen-acre farm, a small slice of a former plantation that Sylvester Edwards had purchased during Reconstruction. Whereas white children attended school from September through June, the primary schools black children attended were in session just five months a year, from after the harvest until planting time in early spring. Black farm children, Rosa recalled, "were needed by their families to plow and plant in the spring and harvest in the fall. Their families were share-croppers like my grandparents' neighbors."

It was probably Grandfather Edwards who inspired Rosa to refuse to accept the racist attitudes and treatment that were com-monplace in the South in the early part of the last century. Light-skinned, Sylvester Edwards was sometimes taken for a white man, and he exploited the ambiguity by insisting on calling himself "Edwards" despite the unwritten customs that required blacks to identify themselves only by their first names while addressing their betters as "Mister" or "Miss." He would shake hands with whites, even though Jim Crow conventions prohibited physical contact between the races. "My grandfather," she remembered, "had a somewhat belligerent attitude toward whites in general, and he liked to laugh at whites behind their backs."

It was not a good time to be a proud black man in the South, however. The Ku Klux Klan grew rapidly in numbers and influ-ence after World War I. "By the time I was six, I was old enough to realize that we were not actually free." Church burnings, beat-ings, and killings were a constant threat, directed against immi-grants and ethnic minorities as well as African Americans. Rosa's grandfather kept a loaded shotgun with him and told his family to sleep in their clothes, the better to flee if Klansmen attacked the house. "I don't know how long I would last if they came breaking in here," he would say, "but I'm getting the first one who comes through the door."

Somehow, the prospect of lawless vigilantes failed to terrify the child. Instead, the threat excited her, and when her grandfather settled into his rocking chair near the front door at night, Rosa often went to sleep on the floor next to him. "I remember thinking that whatever happened, I wanted to see it. I wanted to see him shoot that gun." The showdown never came, but her grandfather's lesson—not to answer racism with meek acceptance—stayed with Rosa. Rosa got used to living with fear—of Klan mayhem, of lynchings, and house burnings. That may be why, nearly forty years later, when the time came to face down the hostility of segregationists on Montgomery's buses, she said, "I didn't have any special fear. It was more of a relief to know that I wasn't alone."

When Rosa was eleven, she went to live with an aunt in Montgomery, where she attended the Montgomery Industrial School for Girls. Staffed by white teachers and supported by benefactors in the North, the private school was a bold experiment at a time when there were no public schools in the region beyond the primary grades for African American girls. The girls who attended "Miss White's School," as it was known (for Alice White, the principal, who founded it with Margaret Beard in the late 1880s), were ridiculed by the local white children, who pelted them with trash and insults as the girls walked to and from classes. In many ways, Rosa found segregation as it was practiced in a small city like Montgomery harsher than daily experience in her small town. The whites-only water fountains embittered her, as did her awareness as she grew older that the downtown restaurants refused to serve African Americans.

In 1928, just after Rosa completed the eighth grade, Miss White's School was forced to close. For the next two years, she attended the high school run by the Alabama State Teachers College in Montgomery, but dropped out when she was sixteen to help take care of her grandmother, who was dying. Rosa originally planned to return to school, but not long after her grandmother's death, her mother fell ill as well, so she stayed in Pine Level to nurse her back to health. About these crucial years, Rosa later wrote in her matter-of-fact manner, "I was not happy about dropping out of school either time, but it was my responsibility to help with my grandmother and later to take care of my mother. I did not complain; it was just something that had to be done." She would not actually complete high school until she was twenty-one. Raymond Parks, whom Rosa married in 1932, when she was nineteen, urged her to get her diploma.

Ten years older than Rosa, Raymond almost certainly encouraged Rosa's interest in civil rights as well. They both joined the Montgomery chapter of the NAACP, where Raymond worked on behalf of the Scottsboro boys, nine African Americans between the ages of twelve and nineteen who were accused of raping two white girls and who were subjected to numerous trials between 1931 and 1938. Rosa became adviser to the NAACP Youth Council in the local chapter.

In the early 1940s, Rosa was active in an NAACP-sponsored voter registration drive. In the course of the drive, Rosa got to know Edgar Daniel "E. D." Nixon, the president of the NAACP in Alabama, a connection that would bear fruit some ten years later. Rosa was no stranger to the obstacles southern blacks faced when they tried to register to vote. She herself attempted to register three times before she succeeded in getting her name on the voters' rolls.

Working with the NAACP taught Rosa how long the wait for justice can sometimes be. As she later wrote, "I worked on numerous cases with the NAACP, but we did not get the publicity. There were cases of flogging, peonage, murder, and rape. We didn't seem to have too many successes. It was more a matter of trying to challenge the powers that be, and to let it be known that we did not wish to continue being second-class citizens."

Rosa had a glimpse of a more egalitarian society when she was employed at Maxwell Air Force Base sometime after the integration of the military in 1948. Interestingly, when she talked to biographer

Douglas Brinkley about her experience, she singled out the issue of public transportation: "I could ride on an integrated trolley bus on the base, but when I left the base, I had to ride home on a segregated bus. . . . You might just say Maxwell opened my eyes up."

In fact, Rosa's eyes had been open to segregation's indignities for years, and like many others in the South, she avoided using the drinking fountains, elevators, and other public facilities marked "Colored." Rather than ride the segregated elevator in a department store or office building, she preferred to take the stairs, and she often walked instead of riding Montgomery's buses. "I did a lot of walking in Montgomery," she said.

Black passengers, who made up roughly two-thirds of the ridership in the city, were restricted to the rear section of the bus. The first four rows of seats were reserved for white passengers; no matter how crowded a bus might be, blacks were not permitted to sit in the front even if not a single white passenger was aboard. In the middle of the vehicle were several rows where blacks were allowed to sit only if no white passengers wanted the seats. But if even one white rider wanted to sit in the "buffer zone," the blacks were required to vacate the entire section. As one observer wrote, "This was, as you can see, pure madness, and it caused no end of trouble and hard feeling." It's difficult to say whether the resentment was greater when blacks were forced to give up seats to accommodate white riders or when they were forced to stand in the crowded rear of the coach when the front was nearly empty.

To make matters even worse, black riders had to climb aboard the bus through the front door, deposit their fares in the fare box, then get off the bus and scurry to the back door to board the bus a second time, from the rear. Sometimes drivers pulled away from the bus stop before a black passenger, who had already paid the ten-cent fare, had time to get to the back door and reboard. When this happened, there was nothing the aggrieved passenger could do about it except hope for better luck when the next bus arrived. Rosa herself was once forced off a Montgomery bus because she refused to pay, exit, and reboard through the back door. "I didn't want to pay my fare and then go around to the back door, because many times, even if you did that, you might not get on the bus at all. They'd probably shut the door, drive off, and leave you standing there."

Black riders grumbled in the early 1950s, and a handful of women were arrested for not surrendering their seats to white men who wanted to sit down, but Montgomery's segregated buses kept rolling. Rosa was working as a seamstress at Montgomery Fair, the city's finest department store (affectionately known as the Fair), and part-time for Virginia and Clifford Durr. As a Wellesley College sophomore in 1922, Virginia had objected to a custom called "rotating tables," whereby students were expected to get acquainted by having meals and conversation together in the dining hall, because doing so would have required her to sit at the same table with African Americans. Given the choice between "rotating tables" and withdrawing from college, she decided to stay. The outcome for this daughter of a Presbyterian minister from Birmingham was a lifelong commitment to achieving racial equality. Looking back when she was in her eighties (she died in 1999, at the age of ninety-six), she wrote, "The problem is, once you open a gate, there's another and another gate beyond each one. It makes you think you want to live forever to continue the work."

The Durrs were much more to Rosa than employers. They, too, were ardent civil rights activists (Clifford, an attorney, had spent sixteen years in Washington during the Roosevelt and Truman administrations, chiefly at the FCC). Their efforts as private citizens were directed in particular at helping minorities and women gain their political and legal rights, improving labor conditions, and abolishing the poll tax that was employed for generations in the South to deny the poor in general and African Americans in particular their voting rights. Besides encouraging Rosa's involvement in the work of the NAACP, they encouraged her to attend an important training workshop on racial desegregation at the Highlander Folk School (now the Highlander Research and Education Center) in Tennessee during the summer of 1955.

Rosa always insisted that when she left work on the evening of December 1, 1955, "I did not get on the bus to get arrested. I got on the bus to go home." She wasn't, as she has sometimes been portrayed, a leg-weary older woman, but a resilient forty-two-year-old committed to the principles of patient, piecemeal progress through legal means. At the same time, when she and four other black passengers were told to clear out a row of seats so that a single white rider could sit in one of them, she was impelled to resist because "our mistreatment was just not right, and I was tired of it. I kept thinking about my mother and my grandparents, and how strong they were. I knew there was a possibility of being mistreated, but an opportunity was being given to me to do what I had asked of others." Maybe the fact that the driver, James Blake, was the same man who had thrown Rosa off his bus in 1943, when she objected to reboarding through the rear door, had something to do with it. According to Rosa, "He was still mean-looking."

As secretary of Montgomery's NAACP chapter, however, Rosa certainly knew that the organization was planning to challenge the constitutionality of segregation in public transportation. Throughout much of 1955, each time a black bus passenger was arrested for violating the segregation laws by refusing to yield her seat to a white rider, the NAACP leadership considered whether she would be a good candidate on which the build a test case—able to stand up under the pressure and scrutiny of the press, the judicial process, and the community. Several—like Claudette Colvin, a pregnant teenager, and Mary Louise Smith—were considered too risky. They were found guilty, paid their fines, and nobody protested.

All of that changed when Rosa was arrested for refusing to yield her seat in the fourth-row buffer zone. By all accounts, when she was threatened with arrest if she didn't give up her seat, Rosa remained calm and polite. She said, "I had decided that I would have to know once and for all what rights I had as a human being and a citizen, even in Montgomery, Alabama."

E. D. Nixon, the local civil rights leader and NAACP official, was ecstatic. When he heard that the secretary of the Montgomery NAACP had been arrested, he cried, "My God, look what segregation has put in my hands!" Rosa, who had worked with E. D. for years, would make the perfect plaintiff in the effort to overturn the segregation laws: married, mature, educated, courteous, soft-spoken and serious, law-abiding, industrious, employed at the city's premier department store, and volunteer worker with young people. "I had to be sure that I had somebody I could win with," was Nixon's explanation for waiting for a model citizen like Rosa.

Planning for the response to Rosa's arrest was under way before she was released from jail that evening. Her bail was posted by Clifford Durr, although because the Durrs didn't own property in Montgomery, E. D. Nixon actually signed the bail bond. Nixon asked Rosa whether she was prepared to act as the plaintiff in the NAACP's test case of Montgomery's segregation laws. "With your permission," he told her, "we can break down segregation on the bus with your case." The next morning, after talking the matter over with her mother and her husband, Rosa committed to the role in what turned out to be one of the U.S. Supreme Court's major constitutional decisions in the area of civil rights.

While those discussions were going on, members of Montgomery's Women's Political Council were handing out the first of thirty-five thousand fliers bearing this message: "We are . . . asking every Negro to stay off the buses Monday in protest of the arrest and trial . . . You can afford to stay out of school for one day. If you work, take a cab, or walk. But please, children and grown-ups, don't ride the bus at all on Monday. Please stay off the buses Monday." The WPC was headed by Alabama State professor Jo Ann Robinson, who in 1949 endured verbal abuse from a Montgomery bus driver for taking a seat in the white section of an otherwise empty bus.

The city's black ministers supported the boycott, and many of them publicly endorsed the plan from their pulpits on the morning of Sunday, December 4. The *Montgomery Advertiser,* the city's black newspaper, ran a front-page story about the boycott plans, and the heads of Montgomery's eighteen minority-owned cab companies pledged to pick up passengers at bus stops for ten cents a head–the same fare the bus charged–no matter how far a passenger was traveling. People who owned their own cars organized car pools, and those without cars geared up to walk to work. Monday morning, December 5, it rained in Montgomery, but the city's black residents shunned the buses, while the taxis and car pools filled the gap as well as possible, no easy task with some forty thousand black commuters going to and from work and school. Some of them had to make trips as long as twenty miles in order to get to their jobs.

There was also a large crowd waiting at the municipal courthouse when Rosa arrived for her scheduled trial. She wore a black dress trimmed in white and a gray coat, which she accented with a small black hat and white gloves. Someone in the throng of supporters called out, "Oh, she's so sweet. They've messed with the wrong one now!"

In 1946 the Supreme Court ruled–in a case argued by future Justice Thurgood Marshall–that segregation was unconstitutional in interstate transportation. Also, city buses had been integrated in Baton Rouge, Louisiana, and Columbia, South Carolina. Nevertheless, the verdict in Rosa's trial came as no surprise. In less than half an hour, she was found guilty and fined–$10, plus $4 in court costs. Rosa refused to pay the fine. Instead, her lawyer, Ed Gray, announced that he would appeal the verdict.

That same evening, Rosa attended the meeting of the newly formed Montgomery Improvement Association (MIA). She didn't speak, but one of those who did made a powerful impression on the crowd. He was a relative newcomer who had been selected to head the new association, the minister of the Dexter Avenue Baptist Church: twenty-six year-old Martin Luther King Jr. He sounded one of the themes in the struggle for equality: "There comes a time that people get tired. We are here this evening to say to those who have mistreated us so long that we are tired–tired of being segregated and humiliated, tired of being kicked about by the brutal feet of oppression. When the history books are written in the future generation, the historians will pause and say, 'There lived a great people–a black people–who injected new meaning and dignity into the veins of civilization.'"

As Dr. King watched bus after empty bus wind through Montgomery's black neighborhoods, he later wrote that "a miracle had taken place. The once dormant and quiescent Negro community was now fully awake." The MIA next had to decide whether to continue the boycott or declare it a one-day symbolic success and end it. This was a measure of how risky a tactic even a peaceful–and legal–protest like the bus boycott was in 1955. After considerable wrangling, and prodded by a tongue-lashing from E. D. Nixon, the MIA leadership decided to put the question to a vote of the community that night. The vote was unanimous, in favor of continuing the boycott.

Still, no one, neither Montgomery's black activists nor the city officials, expected the boycott to last for 382 days. On December 8, just four days into the boycott, in fact, the MIA proposed a compromise plan: most rows in each bus would have integrated seating, but small sections in the front and rear would be restricted all-white and all-black areas. The proposal was modeled on a plan adopted in Baton Rouge, which had staged the longest boycott–seven days–in 1953, and several other cities in the South, including Mobile. The bus company immediately rejected the idea, and the city commissioners added to the pressure by threatening to prosecute any cab driver who charged a passenger less than the minimum: forty-five cents.

To replace the black-owned taxicabs that had been running along the city's bus routes, the MIA created its own fleet of "private taxis" that ran between specified pickup and drop-off points. A mixture of privately owned vehicles and station wagons purchased by local churches, the taxis ran with "military precision" until a number of owners discovered that they couldn't get automobile insurance. That problem was solved through a black insurance agent in Atlanta, who had Lloyd's of London underwrite the policies, whereupon the Montgomery police began arresting drivers for minor traffic violations. Dr. King himself, who was driving one of the private taxis, was arrested for speeding–driving thirty miles per hour in a twenty-five-mile-an-hour zone.

When harassment on relatively minor grounds failed to break the resolve of the boycotters, their opponents escalated their efforts. Both King's and Nixon's houses were bombed in late January and early February 1956. No one was charged with these crimes; instead, the city prosecutors charged eighty-nine blacks under a forgotten law that outlawed boycotting. As the movement's most visible and most eloquent figure, Dr. King was the first defendant to stand trial. He was found guilty and fined $500 plus $500 in court costs, which the MIA appealed as the antisegregation suit made its slow way through the federal courts.

Claiborne Carson, professor of history and director of the King Institute at Stanford University, has said, "We wouldn't be talking about Martin Luther King if it weren't for Rosa Parks." There is no question that the role King played in the Montgomery bus boycott conferred great credibility on the young minister as the civil rights struggle outgrew the Montgomery city limits and Alabama's borders. Dr. King himself acknowledged Rosa's importance to the effort, writing in *Stride Toward Freedom* that she was "ideal for the role assigned to her by history. She was a charming person with a radiant personality, soft-spoken and calm in all situations. Her character was impeccable and her dedication deep-rooted. All of these traits together made her one of the most respected people in the Negro community."

Rosa modestly resisted the title "mother of the civil rights movement" that had been bestowed on her, preferring to give credit to the collective effort made by the entire community, including thousands whose names will never be known: "I was not the only person involved. I was just one of many who fought for freedom." However, by bearing up under the constant media attention, political pressure, and threats from diehard segregationists with patience, calm, and dignity, she played a major part in opening a new chapter in race relations in the United States.

The appeal of Rosa's conviction stalled in the state courts, but in a similar case, *Browder v. Gayle,* decided by the U.S. district court in the Montgomery jurisdiction, the three-judge panel ruled in June 1956 that segregated seating on public buses was unconstitutional. On November 13, the U.S. Supreme Court upheld the district court's decision. The boycott itself wasn't actually ended until December 21, however, the day after the Supreme Court's order arrived in Montgomery.

The boycott was over, but worse things lay ahead. There were snipings—gunfire aimed at the buses and Dr. King's house—and churches and other ministers' homes were bombed. Rosa and her family were threatened as well, on the streets, by mail, and in anonymous telephone calls. Because of her role in the boycott, Rosa was unable to find work, and Raymond Parks—despite his long experience as a civil rights activist—suffered a nervous breakdown. In 1957, Rosa, Raymond, and Rosa's mother, Leona, moved twice. Hoping to stay in the South, they briefly tried Hampton, Virginia, but later in the year, they joined Rosa's brother Sylvester in Detroit, Michigan.

Rosa and her family couldn't completely escape from her fame—and notoriety—in Detroit, either, but she was able to find work there as a seamstress and, in 1965, as a member of John Conyers' congressional office staff in Detroit. Congressman Conyers, now the second most senior member of the House, remembers Rosa as someone who never lost her temper or got into an argument. "I never heard her raise her voice in my life. I never heard her speak in angry tones or negatively about anybody. It wasn't in her." He later said about Rosa, "There are very few people who can say their actions and conduct changed the face of the nation, and Rosa Parks is one of those individuals."

Rosa's stature as a symbol and spokesperson of the nonviolent civil rights movement increased with the passing years. She traveled frequently on behalf of the NAACP and other organizations, while her husband, Raymond, who had introduced Rosa to political activism, usually remained in Detroit to look after Rosa's aging mother until the end of her life. Raymond, ten years older than his wife, was also in declining health, but his support for Rosa's public role was unwavering.

After the death of her husband in 1977, she founded the Rosa and Raymond Parks Institute for Self-Development, in collaboration with Elaine Eason Steele, whom Rosa met when they were working in a Detroit sewing plant. The institute's activities emphasize the education of young people about their history through the summer Pathways to Freedom tours, oral history training and projects, and tutoring and mentoring programs.

The dozens of awards that Rosa herself received during the last quarter century of her life were tributes to the crucial role she played in the struggle for racial equality. But perhaps none speaks as eloquently for her contributions as an award she never received, but is named in her honor. The Rosa Parks Freedom Award is given annually by the Southern Christian Leadership Conference. When President Clinton presented her with the Presidential Medal of Freedom in 1996, he summed up the significance of the act that brought Rosa national and worldwide attention in 1955: "When she sat down on the bus, she stood up for the American ideals of equality and justice and demanded that the rest of us do the same."

Despite her fame, the modest, quiet woman didn't always attend the anniversary celebrations of the movement she had helped to start. But to many people who knew firsthand what it meant to struggle for freedom, she was impossible to overlook. When Nelson Mandela visited the United States in 1990, Rosa was added only at the last moment to the list of people who would greet him at Detroit's Metro Airport. But when the South African president spotted her as he stepped off the plane, "tears filled his eyes as he walked up to the small, old woman with her hair in two silver braids crossed atop her head, and, in a low, melodious tone, Mandela began to chant 'Rosa, Rosa Parks. Rosa Parks.'" He told her that remembering her deeds had kept his hope alive while he was imprisoned on Robbins Island. In one speech, Mandela described Rosa as "the David who challenged Goliath. . . . Before King there was Rosa Parks. She is who inspired us, who taught us to sit down for our rights, to be fearless when facing our oppressors."

By the time of her death at ninety-two in October 2005, a civil rights monument and interactive learning center was being planned for Detroit's Belle Isle Park. Her home in Montgomery had been on the National Register of Historic Places for several years. And before her funeral and burial in Detroit, her casket lay in state in the rotunda of the U.S. Capitol for two days, where tens of thousands of mourners paid their respects. It is rare that anyone other than a former president is memorialized in this way, and Rosa was the first woman. The honor was bestowed by a unanimous vote of Congress.

Barbara Jordan

Like Rosa Parks, Barbara Jordan credited her maternal grandfather with instilling in her a sense of pride in herself while growing up in the segregated South. Unlike Rosa, however, Barbara accepted the racial status quo in Houston, Texas, where she was born in 1936 and where she grew up in the city's Fifth Ward. As a child in a large city, she was used to seeing whites of all ages sitting at lunch counters, but she didn't dream of joining them. "That was part of some other world," she commented years later. It wasn't until the movement Rosa helped ignite forced the issue of civil rights onto the nation's agenda that Barbara, then a college senior, started to think about it.

The example Barbara's grandfather, John Ed Patten, set for her seemed to the young girl to have nothing to do with race. What impressed her was his air of being "a little cut above the ordinary man, black or white." His independent spirit rubbed off on his grand-daughter. "You just trot your own horse and don't get into the same rut as everyone else."

Barbara took his advice to heart, distinguished herself in school both as a scholar and orator, but always within the confines of the segregated world she tacitly accepted. "I decided that if I was going to be outstanding or different, it was going to have to be in relation to other black people. There was nothing you saw to indicate that a black person and a white person could be together on a friendly basis." As a student at Phillis Wheatley High School, named for the first African American (born in about 1754, died 1784) to publish poetry in the New World, Barbara emerged as a brilliant orator and debater. In 1952, her senior year, she won the Texas State Ushers Oratorical Contest. By winning, she qualified for the national championships in Chicago, where she came in first again.

Traveling outside the South for the first time, Barbara was as delighted by the fact that she could enter a restaurant through the front door as by the recognition of her gift for public speaking. She returned to Houston to be named Phillis Wheatley's Girl of the Year. To mark the occasion, Barbara's mother borrowed money from a relative so that her daughter would have a new dress—bought at a Houston department store—to wear to the award ceremony.

At Texas Southern University, in her hometown, Barbara majored in political science. She graduated magna cum laude in 1956, but her accomplishments as a member of the school's debate team eclipsed even her academic record. The debate coach, Tom Freeman, prodded Barbara to hone her debating skills. She delivered, and she also employed her talents on the coach himself. The only woman on the debating team, Barbara chafed at having to stay behind when the men traveled to tournaments out of state. Texas Southern had adopted the policy because of the restrictions the black students faced when they traveled through segregated areas; they usually couldn't stay in hotels, eat in restaurants, or even use public restrooms. To get around these restrictions, instead of taking the shortest routes, the students and their coach mapped out itineraries that took them through places where friends and relatives could put them up for the night. Taking a young woman on these trips was thought to be too much of a logistical hurdle.

If the debate team's northern road trips gave Barbara a taste of the obstacles that segregation continued to place in the way of black people, it was Texas Southern's match against a visiting team from Harvard University that opened her eyes to brighter possibilities, for herself and other gifted African Americans. The debate ended in a draw, which Barbara interpreted as a win for Texas Southern. She later said the debate taught her two things: that "some black people could make it in this white man's world, and that those who could had to do it."

Following her graduation from the Houston college, Barbara went north to Boston University's law school. Tom Freeman, Barbara's mentor at Texas Southern, was instrumental in convincing her to explore life outside the only region she knew well. She found herself one of just six black students in the class of 1959, and only one other was a woman. Besides the radical social shift for a young woman who had spent sixteen years in segregated schools, Barbara was also forced to acknowledge the educational cost. "I realized that my deprivation had been stark. The best training available in an all-black university was not equal to the best training one developed as a white university student. Separate was not equal, it just wasn't."

Barbara passed the bar exams in both Massachusetts and Texas soon after completing law school, and she was offered a chance to practice law in Boston. Instead of law, however, she decided to teach at Tuskegee Institute (since 1985, Tuskegee University) in Alabama. The next year, she returned to Houston and started practicing law. She was only the third African American woman licensed to practice law in the state. Her first "office" was in her parents' home.

It took Barbara three years to build a lucrative enough practice to permit her to rent office space outside the house, but it didn't take more than a few months before people started to recognize that she was a force to reckon with. During the Kennedy-Johnson election campaign in 1960, Barbara volunteered for the Harris County Democratic Party. Despite her law degree, she was assigned to routine office work. "One night we went out to a church to enlist Negro voters, and the woman who was supposed to speak didn't show up. I volunteered to speak in her place and right after that, they took me off licking and addressing."

Although she wasn't a candidate for office in 1960, Barbara Jordan the politician emerged in the course of the Kennedy-Johnson campaign. People in the city and state Democratic leadership took notice of Barbara and her talents of persuasion and organization. In her own words, "By the time the Kennedy-Johnson campaign ended successfully, I had really been bitten by the political bug."

She soon discovered that it was one thing to convince black citizens to vote and another to persuade them to vote for her. For one thing, many black civic leaders disapproved of her affiliation with the Democratic Party, since the Democrats had kept African Americans out of political office since Reconstruction. But Barbara recognized that it was the dominant party in Texas politics at the time.

In 1962, she declared her candidacy for a seat in the Texas House of Representatives, despite the fact that she lacked sufficient financial backing for the campaign (she even had to borrow the $500 filing fee). Barbara lost to Willis Whatley, whose campaign got a boost from a series of paid ads. Two years later, she ran and lost again, but in 1966, thanks in part to redistricting, she became the first black woman ever elected to the Texas Senate in the newly created Eleventh District. This time, she won the primary by a 20 percent margin over her opponent and triumphed easily in the general election.

Rather than attempting to stand out because she was different, Barbara shrewdly went about fitting into a political culture that was overwhelming white and male (she was the only woman and the only African American). She sought out the body's most powerful members, men like Dorsey Hardeman, a senator from San Angelo whose family boasted long, distinguished ties to Texas political and military history. Senator Hardeman made no secret of the fact that he didn't welcome her to the senate, but he soon adopted her as a protégée. In Barbara's words, "I was coming to be a senator, and I wasn't coming to lead any charge. I was not coming carrying the flag and singing 'We Shall Overcome.' I was coming to work and I wanted to get that message communicated personally."

She succeeded admirably, especially with Dorsey Hardeman. "She conducted herself in a most commendable manner from the start," he later remembered. "Not forward in any respect. She didn't press her race or color." By the time Barbara's first term ended, Dorsey had cosponsored a resolution naming her Outstanding Freshman Senator.

As a news reporter for KPRC, the NBC-TV affiliate in Houston, I was able to watch Barbara operate in the state senate. I had graduated from law school in 1967, but when I moved to Houston, I learned, as she had, that the doors of the major law firms were not open to women. I decided to use my legal degree as a news reporter covering the legislature. What impressed me about her was that she played by the traditional rules of the senate. Though her male colleagues were wary that she wouldn't fit in, their concerns were short-lived. She was effective, she did her homework, and she kept her word. Once I heard her response to a colleague who asked for her support on a bill that she fully intended to support. She said no, she could not at that time because she had given her word not to vote for that measure until another unrelated but more important bill had passed. She kept her word and did not support the measure even though she was philosophically in favor of it. I learned a lesson that day that proved valuable to me later, when I became a state representative (elected the same year Barbara won her seat in the U.S. Congress). There are many times I have kept my word once I gave it, even when circumstances made it difficult. In public service, a reputation for keeping your word is one of the keys to success.

I've heard disparaging references to people who are described thus: "He will vote with the last person who talked to him about a bill." In other words, when he makes a promise, he may not keep it. Barbara was respected in the state senate and one of the few who have served there whose portrait hangs in the chamber.

Throughout her two terms in the senate, Barbara worked on legislation to improve the lives of the poor, women, and minorities in Texas. She did so without concealing her passion and power as a speaker. As one of her senate colleagues described it, "That voice had a certain whip to it." Among her notable successes were a minimum wage law and better environmental laws. As chair of the Labor and Management Relations Committee, she also helped enact legislation prohibiting discrimination in business contracts.

Midway through her second term, she declared her candidacy for a seat in Congress. Her election in 1972 made her the first black woman ever elected to the U.S. House of Representatives from a southern state and—with Andrew Young, who was elected a U.S. representative from Georgia that year—one of the first two African Americans from the South in Congress since 1901. As a congresswoman, she was an outspoken advocate of civil rights, supported extending Social Security benefits to homemakers, focused on legislation to aid American cities, and sponsored an extension of the deadline for state ratification of the equal rights amendment.

It was as an orator rather than legislator that Barbara made her most lasting impression on the nation and the world. She was a member of the House Judiciary Committee in 1974 and was active in the hearings investigating the Watergate break-in. "Now she had a message that matched her voice," one of her biographers wrote, describing her evolution from an effective practical politician to inspirational leader. In what many have judged the high point of the hearings, Barbara electrified her audience when she said that despite the fact that Gouverneur Morris, Alexander Hamilton, James Madison, and others at the Constitutional Convention of 1787 didn't have people like her in mind when they wrote the phrase "We the people" in the preamble to the Constitution, "My faith in the Constitution is whole, it is complete, it is total. I am not going to sit here and be an idle spectator to the diminution, the subversion, the destruction of the Constitution."

The impact of Barbara's bearing during the Judiciary Committee hearings enhanced her stature in her party as well as in Congress. When the time came to select the keynote speaker for the 1976 Democratic National Convention, Barbara received the call: the first woman so honored by the Democratic Party. Her speech was an impassioned plea to Americans to act out of a shared sense of national community. Doing so, she explained, depended on the will—and the goodwill—of the American people; no law was capable of compelling people to form a community. "This we must do as individuals, and if we do it as individuals, there is no president of the United States who can veto that decision."

That year, Barbara's star seemed to grow brighter by the day, and there was speculation that she might be nominated for the vice presidency. The talk brought the practical politician in Barbara to the fore. No African American could be elected vice president in 1976, she declared, let alone a black woman. The speculation stopped.

Always a private person, in 1979, just three years after it seemed that her own political horizon might be limitless, Barbara unexpectedly gave up her House seat to teach at the University of Texas Lyndon B. Johnson School of Public Affairs. She had served three terms. It would be years before the public learned that she suffered from multiple sclerosis, but Barbara had known about her condition for some time, and health may have played a part in her decision to leave politics for the comparatively serene environment of the university. But in 1977, when she announced that she would not be a candidate for reelection in the following year, the announcement concealed as much as it revealed. Barbara said only that her departure from politics was "predicated totally on my internal compass directing me to divert my energy to something different and to move away from demands which are all-consuming."

As the Lyndon Baines Johnson Public Service Professor, Barbara lectured on intergovernmental relations, political values, and ethics. To her new vocation of professor, she brought the same passionate perfectionism she had practiced in politics, and her students responded with a combination of devotion and awe. "A conscientious student would never consider walking into her class unprepared," one of them later remembered. "If you have to go without food, go without sleep, you go without in any way you can, but you don't take a gamble that this particular time you will be overlooked."

Barbara's students might have been intimidated by her teaching style, but they weren't. Instead, they were enthralled by her insights and by her conviction that they were capable of bringing about change for the better. In fact, so many students applied for a place in her classes that admissions were by lottery.

After she left Congress, Barbara published her autobiography, *Barbara Jordan: A Self Portrait*, but she kept largely out of the public eye through most of the next decade. Once her health had deteriorated to the point that she was forced to use a wheelchair, Barbara actually took on a more public role. In the early 1990s, she was Governor Ann Richards' ethics adviser, and at the 1992 Democratic National Convention she accepted Bill Clinton's invitation to deliver a second keynote address. After the election, President Clinton appointed Barbara chairwoman of the U.S. Commission on Immigration Reform.

Bill Hobby, who knew Barbara well as a Democratic Party leader in Texas, is also from Houston and was one of her strong supporters. He was lieutenant governor of Texas (1973–1990), and they were also colleagues at the LBJ School of Public Affairs. He captured Barbara's genius as a speaker in a few words: "She didn't speak unless she had something to say. When she had something to say, she said it without a wasted word."

In her 1992 speech, she exhorted the country to live up to its ideals by including African Americans and women as full participants in political and economic life. "We are one, we Americans, and we reject any intruder who seeks to divide us by race or class. We honor cultural identity. However, separatism is not allowed. Separatism is not the American way." Despite opposition and the frustratingly slow pace of progress, she looked forward to an era where society no longer struggled to function "using less than half of its human resources, brain power and kinetic energy." She saw signs of change, among them women in greater numbers "challenging the councils of political power dominated by white-male policy makers. That horizon is limitless. What we see today is simply a dress rehearsal for the day and time we meet in convention to nominate . . . Madame President."

Despite making frequent pronouncements about the position of women and African Americans in American society, Barbara resisted being cast as a symbol or spokesperson for her race or her sex. When she addressed the Texas Daily Newspaper Association, she asked, "Who speaks for the Negro?" and responded in classic Jordan manner: "Well, I'll answer that question: No one. No one can." She also turned down a group who wanted to nominate her for the vice presidency in 1976, in order to use the nomination as a pretext for bringing issues affecting blacks to the convention floor. Barbara, who always ran to win, dismissed the proposal by saying, "I really do not have much interest in being a symbol."

Barbara's talents and achievements guaranteed that she didn't need to be a symbol. She gave her native state much of the credit for her confidence that despite the long odds, she would succeed in doing great things. In one interview, she told a reporter, "I get from the soil and spirit of Texas the feeling that I, as an individual, can accomplish whatever I want to, and that there are no limits, that you can just keep going, just keep soaring. I like that spirit."

Her own rise from poverty to prominence set an example for many others who came after her. One is Ruth Simmons, the youngest of twelve children whose parents had started out as share-croppers in Grapeland, Texas. In Houston, her father worked in a factory and her mother cleaned houses, but they made sure their daughter got the best education available to her. Every day, as she walked past Barbara Jordan's old house in the Fifth Ward on her way to Phillis Wheatley High School, Ruth said to herself, "If Barbara Jordan can make it out of here, so can I." And she did, too. In 1995 she became the first African American woman to head a major American college when she was chosen to lead Smith; and she has been the president of Brown University since 2001.

Barbara's spirit never stopped soaring, but her body continued to weaken. Throughout the early 1990s, her multiple sclerosis worsened, and in 1994 she contracted leukemia as well. Less than two years later, in January 1996, she died at the age of fifty-nine.

In tribute to what she had done for the people of Texas and the United States, Barbara was interred in the Texas State Cemetery in Austin. She was the first African American to be buried there.

Deborah Sampson (1760–1827) joined the Continental Army under an assumed name in 1782, the first American woman known to have served as a soldier. *Courtesy American Antiquarian Society*

Virginia Hall (1906–82) spied for Britain and the U.S. in France throughout World War II. Maj. Gen. William J. Donovan, founder of the OSS, awarded her the Distinguished Service Cross in 1945. *Courtesy CIA Museum*

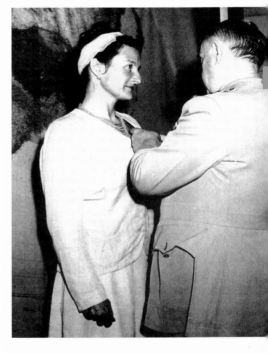

Major Ruby Bradley, who was an Army nurse in the Philippines and Korea, is the most highly decorated woman in the history of the American military. *The Office of Medical History, Office of the Surgeon General, United States Army*

The first woman and the first nurse promoted to general in the U.S. Army, Anna Mae Hays earned her star in 1970. She was Army Nurse Corps Chief from 1967–71. *The Office of Medical History, Office of the Surgeon General, United States Army*

Director of the Women's Army Corps from 1966–71, Elizabeth Hoisington (born 1918) was the first WAC promoted to general. *Courtesy of the Lake County Discovery Museum*

Jeanne M. Holm (born 1921) switched from the Army to the Air Force in 1952 and became its first woman general in 1971. *Department of Defense*

Dolley Madison (1768–1849) set the standards for entertaining and quiet diplomacy in the nation's capital that continue to be emulated today. *Courtesy of The University of Texas at Austin*

Eleanor Roosevelt 1884–1962) played an active political role throughout her life. President Harry Truman called her "First Lady to the World." *Library of Congress, LC-USZ62-25812*

As First Lady, Jacqueline Kennedy (1929–94) restored the White House and inspired interest in culture and the arts in the capital and beyond. *Library of Congress, LC-USZ62-21796*

Lady Bird Johnson (1912–2007) promoted beautification of the nation's cities and highways and the conservation of our natural resources. *Library of Congress, LC-USZ62-25816B*

Betty Ford (born 1918) raised awareness of women's health issues and set a new standard for openness in discussing them. *Library of Congress, LC-USZC4-2019*

A champion of literacy programs and advocate of volunteerism, Barbara Bush (born 1925) is the second woman to be both the wife and mother of American presidents. *Library of Congress, LC-USZ62-98303*

The first former president's wife elected to the U.S. Senate, in 2000, Hillary Clinton (born 1947) is now a serious contender for the Democratic presidential nomination.

As First Lady, Laura Bush (born 1946) continues to espouse the causes of literacy, reading, and early childhood education, and has taken active roles in health care and human rights.

Harriet Beecher Stowe (1811–96), author of *Uncle Tom's Cabin*, turned her opposition to slavery into an influential career as a novelist and essayist. *Library of Congress, LC-USZ62-11212*

Pearl S. Buck (1892–1973), prolific writer and the first American woman to win the Nobel Prize in Literature, opened the eyes of many westerners to life in China. *Courtesy of Pearl S. Buck International, pearl-s-buck.org*

Toni Morrison (born 1931) became the first African American woman awarded the Nobel Prize in Literature for her vivid portrayals of her characters' lives and society. *Portrait by Timothy Greenfield-Sanders*

Oprah Winfrey (born 1954), talk-show host, publisher, and actress, has been called the most influential woman in the world. *Copyright Lucy Nicholson/Reuters/ CORBIS*

Amy Tan (born 1952) drew on her own experiences in exploring the bonds between mothers and daughters and dramatizing the experience of first-generation Asian Americans. *Photo copyright Robert Foothorap*

Liz Balmaseda (born 1959) fled Cuba with her family and has won two Pulitzer Prizes for journalism, for her articles about Cuban and Haitian refugees and Elián González. *Photo Courtesy La Prensa San Diego*

Susan B. Anthony (1820–1906) spearheaded the struggle for women's suffrage during her six–decade career as a social activist. *Library of Congress, LC-USZ62-46713*

Elizabeth Cady Stanton (1815–1902) helped organize the first women's rights convention in 1848 and was the movement's strategist and author of its major documents. *The Schlesinger Library, Radcliffe Institute, Harvard University*

Lucretia Mott (1793–1880) was a Quaker minister, abolitionist, and one of the earliest advocates of political rights for women in the U.S. *Friends Historical Library of Swarthmore College*

Rosa Parks (1913–2005), who inspired the Montgomery Bus Boycott, in that city after the Supreme Court decision outlawing segregation on public transit. *Photo copyright UPI/Bettman/CORBIS*

Barbara Jordan (1936–96) delivering the keynote address at the 1976 Democratic National Convention in New York City. *U.S. News & World Report Magazine Photograph Collection. Library of Congress, LC-U9-32937-32A/33*

The first woman to graduate from medical school in the U.S., Elizabeth Blackwell (1821–1910) founded an infirmary and medical college for women in New York City. *The Schlesinger Library, Radcliffe Institute, Harvard University*

Physician Alice Hamilton (1869–1970) founded the field of occupational medicine and was the first woman appointed to a Harvard professorship. *Courtesy of the National Library of Medicine, Changing the Face of Medicine Exhibition*

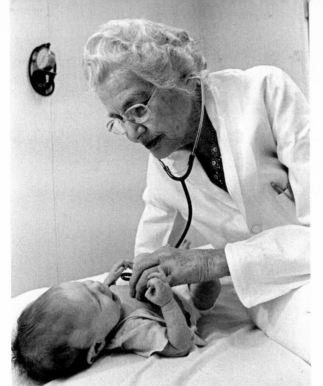

The founder of pediatric cardiology, Helen Taussig (1898–1986) diagnosed "blue baby" syndrome and helped develop the operation to correct the defect. *Photograph by permission of Tadder/ Baltimore*

Rachel Carson (1907–64), was a nature writer whose 1962 book *Silent Spring* helped to shape the new environmental consciousness. *Erich Hartmann, Magnum Photos*

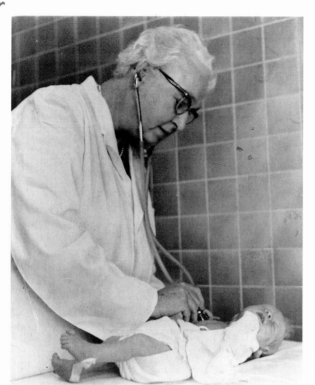

Pioneering anesthesiologist Virginia Apgar (1909–74) developed the Apgar Score, the first reliable test of the newborn's adaptation to life outside the womb. *Library of Congress, New York World–Telegram and the Sun Newspaper Photograph Collection, LC-USZ62-131540*

The first American woman to receive the Nobel Prize for Medicine or Physiology, Gerty Cori (1896–1957) explained how the body metabolizes glucose to produce energy. *Becker Medical Library, Washington University School of Medicine*

Maria Goeppert-Mayer (1906–72) won the 1963 Nobel Prize in Physics for her model of the nuclear shell structure of the atom. Only one other woman— Marie Curie—is a Nobel laureate in physics. *Photo courtesy of Argonne National Laboratory*

Rosalyn Yalow (born 1921) in her laboratory at the Bronx VA Hospital in 1977, after learning she had been awarded the Nobel Prize for Medicine for developing the technique of radioimmunoassay. *Copyright Bettmann/CORBIS*

In 1983, Barbara McClintock (1902–92) became the only woman to receive an unshared Nobel Prize in Physiology or Medicine for her work on the genetics of maize. *Courtesy of the Cold Spring Harbor Laboratory Archives*

Gertrude Elion (1918–99), who received a Nobel Prize in Physiology or Medicine in 1988 for her discoveries of how drugs work to suppress rejection of transplanted organs and treat diseases including childhood leukemia and AIDS. *Courtesy of GlaxoSmithKline Inc. Heritage Center*

Jane Addams (1860–1935) founded Hull House, the first American settlement house, and was the first American woman awarded the Nobel Peace Prize, in 1931. *Library of Congress, LC-USZ62-10598*

Emily Greene Balch (1867–1961), lifelong pacifist and Nobel Peace Prize recipient in 1946, nevertheless supported America's entry into World War Two. *Papers of Emily Greene Balch, Swarthmore College Peace Collection*

101

During 18 years in Congress, Lindy Boggs (born 1916) worked to end discrimination against women in credit and other critical areas. *Photo courtesy of Tulane University*

Dianne Feinstein (born 1933), the first woman senator from California, nearly left politics after serving as a member of the San Francisco Board of Supervisors.

Popular in Maine, Olympia Snowe (born 1946) has a reputation as an effective negotiator and consensus builder in the Senate.

Mary Bono (born 1961), who was elected to Congress after the death of her husband, Sonny, in 1998, has emerged as an effective representative.

As Secretary of Labor, Elaine Chao (born 1953) is the first Asian American woman to serve as a cabinet secretary. *Department of Labor cht. 5 > gres to ff. 254*

CHAPTER 5

Everything I Discovered Was New

Women in Medicine and Public Health

IF SOCIETY WILL NOT ADMIT OF WOMEN'S FREE DEVELOPMENT,
THEN SOCIETY MUST BE REMODELED.
–Elizabeth Blackwell

Women pioneers in medicine had to overcome the earliest obstacles, gaining access to the basic education that would allow them to contribute their talents. In the late nineteenth and early twentieth centuries, it was considered completely out of the question for a woman to study the human body in the presence of men. So medicine was one of the most difficult of all professions for women to enter. But the few hearty souls who had the stamina to persevere made huge discoveries that continue to be relevant today.

ELIZABETH BLACKWELL

Elizabeth Blackwell was born in Bristol, England, in 1821, where her father, Samuel, was a partner in a sugar refinery. She was the third of five surviving children of Samuel and Hannah Blackwell, who eventually had a total of nine children (four died in childhood). A deacon of the local Congregational Church, pious Samuel Blackwell espoused equal rights for women and was an outspoken opponent of slavery, despite the fact that he was painfully aware of the intimate link between sugar grown in the Americas and slave labor. The Blackwells lived in the fashionable new suburb of St. Paul's, and Samuel had his children taught at home by tutors, in part because as "dissenters," the Blackwell children weren't allowed to attend local schools, but also to give them a superior education. Samuel insisted that his five daughters receive the same education as their brothers. This upset Samuel's four unmarried sisters, who lived in their brother's large house; they thought the girls should be taught more "ladylike" subjects than arithmetic and history.

When Elizabeth looked back on her childhood in Bristol, she remembered the Blackwell household as a lively place. The children were included in the social evenings where Samuel and Hannah entertained visitors and discussed the issues of the day. Never mind that the guests might be missionaries; the food and conversation were abundant and lively, and Elizabeth relished the stories the missionaries told of their adventures in distant lands. Not all the children shared Elizabeth's enthusiasm for the religious atmosphere. For example, Anna, her oldest sister, described the family custom of prayers and Bible reading before breakfast as "horrid."

Several explanations have been given for why Samuel Blackwell decided to leave England for the United States in 1832: rioting in Bristol the previous year, brought on by economic hard times; problems in his sugar business stemming from the failure of Harwood and Blackwell's operations in Ireland and the bankruptcy of two sugar importers with whom the firm did business; and the religious tolerance that the United States offered. Whatever the reasons, the entire family—Samuel and Hannah, their eight children (the youngest, George Washington Blackwell, was born shortly after their arrival in the United States), the four unmarried sisters, and a governess–sailed for New York in August 1832. They landed in October and settled into a house near Washington Square. In partnership with a British firm, Samuel opened a new sugar refinery in Manhattan, sent his children to public schools, joined the abolition movement, and experimented with beet sugar as a possible substitute for cane sugar. After a disastrous fire in 1835 hobbled New York's already weakened economy, and his own refinery burned the following year, Samuel decided to start fresh in Cincinnati. He thought he could revive his fortunes by establishing the only sugar refinery in the west. But shortly after the Blackwells reached Ohio, Samuel, just forty-eight, died of a fever. His sudden death left his widow, Hannah, with nine children aged six through twenty, broke, and in debt in an unfamiliar city.

The three oldest Blackwell daughters–Anna, Marian, and Elizabeth–and Mary Blackwell, one of the aunts, did what educated American women often did in the nineteenth century: they started a school in their house. At first they accepted boys and girls, but they soon opted for an all-girls school, the Cincinnati English and French Academy for Young Ladies. The curriculum the four women offered included reading, writing, sketching, drawing, arithmetic, grammar, ancient and modern history, geography, natural and moral philosophy, botany, composition, French, and vocal music. They didn't enjoy teaching, but for four years the school provided a modest living for the Blackwell family. They closed it after most of their students withdrew during a downturn in the economy in 1841. Elizabeth did some tutoring, her mother and some of the younger girls opened a boardinghouse, and her brothers Henry and Sam sold hardware and did bookkeeping. When a letter arrived inviting any one of the three oldest Blackwell sisters to come to Henderson, Kentucky, to open a school, Elizabeth took the job. Marian wasn't willing to leave home, and Anna was in New York, teaching and making a start as a journalist.

Elizabeth lasted just one year in Kentucky. The townspeople were kind, and the school attracted so many students that she had to turn some away, but she felt out of place. In one letter home, despite her conviction that she would never marry, she joked that "I cannot find my other half here, but only about a sixth, which would not do." Twenty-three years old, she returned to Cincinnati, where she was invited by Harriet Beecher Stowe to join the Semi-Colon Club, the local literary society, but she still had no idea about what to do with her life.

Elizabeth spent time with Mary Donaldson, who was dying of uterine cancer. Like most proper Victorian women, the two friends had been conditioned to feeling, at best, embarrassment about their bodies. When a woman required medical attention, the doctor (a man) would examine his patient from behind a curtain. For most women, the experience of being touched by a man was humiliating, despite the fact that the physician could not actually see her. Mary told Elizabeth that she would have suffered less if a woman physician had been able to treat her, and she urged her friend—whose intellectual gifts and love of study were well known—to become a doctor.

The idea horrified Elizabeth. "The very thought of dwelling on the physical structure of the body and its various ailments filled me with disgust." Yet the more she thought about the idea—and the more her friends tried to discourage her from the futile attempt to become the first female physician in the United States—the more the challenge appealed to her. To learn the physiology and anatomy she would need for medical school, Elizabeth taught at the school run by physician and clergyman John Dickson in Asheville, North Carolina, where she had access to Dickson's medical books. A year later, she went to Charleston, South Carolina, to study with Dr. Samuel Dickson, John Dickson's brother and a medical professor. By 1847, Elizabeth was in Philadelphia, where she continued studying anatomy and solicited the support of two Quaker doctors, Joseph Warrington and William Elder, who agreed that women should be allowed to study medicine.

Her applications to numerous schools from Pennsylvania to

Maine were all rejected, but finally Geneva Medical College, a small
school in New York's Finger Lakes region, accepted her, possibly
out of respect for Dr. Warrington, who had recommended her, or
possibly because the faculty, suspecting that her application was
a prank perpetrated by a rival medical school, invited their own
students to vote on her application, and the students decided to go
along with the joke by accepting her.

When Elizabeth materialized in Geneva in November 1847, she
was permitted to stay. At first, many faculty members, students, and
townspeople were hostile, but she found an enthusiastic champion
in James Webster, the popular professor of anatomy, who even
learned to curtail his habitual vulgarity out of respect for his prim
protégée. Less than two years later, she graduated with honors, and
the audience applauded when she announced, prophetically, "It
shall be the effort of my life to shed honor on this diploma." But the
school didn't repeat its experiment with co-education again until
the mid-1860s, when the medical school was in desperate financial straits (it merged with Syracuse University's medical school in
1872).

Elizabeth's only hands-on experience with patients had been
during the summer of 1848, when she worked in the Philadelphia
Hospital, actually part of the city's Blocksley Almshouse. She wrote
her thesis (then a prerequisite for graduation from medical school)
on typhus, which she first observed and treated in her mostly Irish
immigrant patients in the almshouse. For further clinical training, she would have to go abroad, since American hospitals didn't
employ women doctors. In Paris she was limited to apprenticing
as a midwife at the public maternity hospital. There, while treating
an infant with purulent ophthalmia, she contracted the infection
herself and lost the sight of one eye. Thus ended her dream of a
surgical career.

James Paget, the first head of the medical school at London's
St. Bartholomew's Hospital and Queen Victoria's physician, invited
Elizabeth to study there. After a year of training, during which she

was allowed to study in every department except obstetrics (because the professor was opposed to women doctors) she returned to the United States, settling in New York City. She tried to open a practice, but had no luck in attracting patients. She likened her treatment to meeting a "blank wall of social and professional antagonism." So to make herself known to the public and to earn some money, Elizabeth lectured on health and exercise for young girls and women. Her lectures shocked most people, but a small group of Quaker women were drawn to her ideas and became her first patients. In addition, she published her lectures as *The Laws of Life, with Special Reference to the Physical Education of Girls* (1852).

With a growing practice, Elizabeth was also able to open a free clinic near Tompkins Square, one of New York's poorest neighborhoods. As its only physician, Elizabeth held clinic hours just three afternoons a week, but in the first year she treated over two hundred patients. When Emily Blackwell, her younger sister, and Marie Zakrzewska, who had both graduated from Western Reserve College's medical school in Cleveland, joined her in 1856, they opened the New York Infirmary for Women and Children. It was the first hospital staffed entirely by women.

Emily, five years younger than Elizabeth, had just as much difficulty as her sister in getting admitted to medical school and gaining acceptance. She was forced to leave Rush Medical College in Chicago after the Illinois Medical Society objected to a woman studying medicine, but she managed to complete her education at Western Reserve College in 1854. For the following two years, she studied in Europe, first under James Young Simpson, the professor of midwifery at the University of Edinburgh, one of the early innovators in obstetric medicine, and later in England, France, and Germany. Marie Zakrzewska, already head of midwifery at the Royal Charité Hospital in her native Berlin before she left to attend medical school in the United States, went directly to New York City following her graduation from Western Reserve.

Managing the infirmary quickly became Emily's responsibility. In

1858, barely two years after her younger sister joined the infirmary in New York, Elizabeth left to spend a year lecturing in England. When she returned, Marie Zakrzewska moved to Boston, where she was the professor of obstetrics at the New England Female Medical College. Meanwhile, Emily, who co-authored *Medicine as a Profession for Women* (1860) with Elizabeth, became an expert in administration. She secured state funding for the New York Infirmary, oversaw its growth into a full-fledged hospital that treated over seven thousand patients a year by the early 1870s, and was also the hospital's chief surgeon. Among the infirmary's many initiatives were a training program for nurses (1858) and the Out-Practice, or Tenement House Service, the first time doctors made house calls to charity patients, in 1866.

During the Civil War, the Blackwell sisters also helped train nurses who served in battle areas, and after 1865, they started planning a medical college associated with the New York Infirmary. The Women's Medical College opened in 1868, with a faculty of nine and fifteen students. Elizabeth was professor of hygiene, and Emily taught obstetrics and diseases of women. Elizabeth would have preferred to have women study medicine together with men, but in the face of continuing resistance to admitting women to the traditionally male medical schools she recognized that it was necessary to create separate schools for women. In some ways, however, the Women's Medical College was superior to the men's colleges: it required applicants to pass entrance examinations, something that few medical schools of the time demanded; the program lasted three years rather than two, and soon added a fourth year; and students spent more time training in the hospital than they did at other schools. Between 1868 and 1899, 364 women graduated as physicians at the Women's Medical College. It closed when the Cornell University medical school began accepting women.

Elizabeth suddenly moved to England in 1869. Her reasons for leaving the institution she had nurtured remain something of a mystery. Some scholars contend that she and Emily were at odds, but in her memoirs, written a quarter of a century later, Elizabeth wrote only that "the early pioneer work in America was ended" and suggested that there was more to be done in England. For several years, she lectured, helped to establish the National Health Society in 1871, treated patients in private practice, and campaigned for women's health and on other issues, such as repeal of the Contagious Diseases Act, which regulated prostitution as a way to control the spread of syphilis and other sexually transmitted diseases. As a Christian, Elizabeth opposed the law because she thought that focusing enforcement on women implicitly accepted the actions of men who hired prostitutes.

Ahead of her time in many ways, Elizabeth proclaimed that "prevention is better than cure" and incorporated improved public sanitation and hygiene into her medical outlook. She discerned the causal link between poverty and poor education and spoke out in favor of social cures to medical problems long before most others did. In books like *Counsel to Parents on the Moral Education of Children* (1876) and *The Human Element in Sex* (1884), she went against the grain of Victorian primness by openly discussing sex and other "forbidden" subjects. Her moral approach to medical as well as sexual issues, however, reveals her as very much a child of her age. And like almost all pioneers, she sometimes dismissed important new developments—vaccination and bacteriology are two examples—as scientific and medical dead ends.

Elizabeth and Emily lived out the last years of their lives on opposite sides of the Atlantic, but they died only three months apart, Elizabeth in Hastings, England, on May 31, 1910, and Emily in York Cliffs, Maine, on September 7. Other women—and men—were active in the struggle to open the medical profession to women, and the Women's Medical College in New York was not even the first institution of its kind. The Female Medical College of Pennsylvania was founded in 1850, and the New England Female Medical College, opened as a school for midwives in 1848, was expanded into a full medical school in 1856. But it is safe to say that no one played a more critical part in bringing women into medicine and improving medical care for women in the nineteenth century than the Blackwell sisters, especially our nation's first female medical school graduate, Elizabeth Blackwell.

ALICE HAMILTON ⌒

EVERYTHING I DISCOVERED WAS NEW AND
MOST OF IT WAS REALLY VALUABLE.

Alice Hamilton would certainly have disagreed with Elizabeth Blackwell about the value of bacteriology, but she was aware of how much she owed to the woman who made careers in medicine possible—and respectable—for American women. Born in New York City in February 1869, the same year Elizabeth Blackwell left the United States, Alice grew up in Fort Wayne, Indiana, where her grandfather, Allen Hamilton, had made his fortune earlier in the century in business, land speculation, finance, and railroads. The Hamilton family compound consisted of several large houses— known as the Homestead, the Red House, and the White House— that covered three city blocks in the middle of Fort Wayne. As many as twenty-five Hamilton descendants lived off the estate Allen had left, but since the fortune was in land, not liquid assets, they were often short of cash. The family possessed other forms of wealth, however. They were deeply religious: Allen was a founder of Fort Wayne's First Presbyterian Church and had arranged for a minister to come to the city. And they were Fort Wayne's most cultured family, in spite of an indifference to fashion and leisure that made them appear eccentric. Allen had helped his father and four siblings (three brothers, one sister) settle in Fort Wayne as well and paid for the educations of all his nieces and nephews. By the time Alice was born, all the children were expected to learn Greek, Latin, French, and German, which they often taught themselves, and it wasn't unusual for neighbors to find a group of young Hamiltons reading

Dante's *Divine Comedy* aloud in the original Italian. Seventeen cousins of Alice's generation formed the core of her social world; they often were not only childhood playmates but in many cases became lifelong companions. Still, the family had servants, and the children, girls included, attended private boarding schools and colleges and were encouraged to pursue their educations. Alice's grandmother, Emerine Hamilton, even created a free reading room for women, to encourage women without money and education to enjoy and profit from books. She also gave generously to the poor, supported the temperance movement, and contributed to the woman suffrage cause. Suffrage leaders stayed on the Hamilton estate when they came to Fort Wayne, and when Emerine died in 1889, she left $500 each to Susan B. Anthony and Lucy Stone to help them carry on their work. Andrew Hamilton, the oldest son of Allen and Emerine, owned the largest library in the city—six thousand volumes, including many rare books. The youngest child, Margaret, turned her carriage house into the Fort Wayne Art School.

Alice's father, Montgomery, the second of Allen and Emerine's five children, graduated from Harvard Law School but didn't enjoy much practical success. A wholesale grocery partnership, Heustis and Hamilton, failed after twenty years, and Montgomery increasingly retreated into a world populated by books and alcohol. Before his business failure, however, he devised for his four daughters (a son, Arthur, was born in 1886) a quirky but broad education. He thought the public schools spent too much time teaching arithmetic and American history, and their mother, Gertrude Pond Hamilton, objected to the long hours spent indoors. So Edith, Alice, Margaret, and Norah were educated at home. Montgomery taught them Latin, their mother introduced them to French, they learned German from the domestic help, and they were encouraged to read widely on their own. Fifteen-year-old Edith, who became one of the twentieth century's most renowned writers on classical literature and mythology, wrote to her cousin Jessie, "I hope you keep all my letters; some day, you know, they will be all treasured up as the works of 'Miss Hamilton, the American Addison, Scott & Shake-speare'!" Gertrude broadened her children's education by adding the novels of George Eliot to Montgomery's prescribed diet of British neoclassicism and history, and while their Presbyterian father insisted they learn the Westminster catechism, their Episcopalian mother read to them from the King James Bible.

From her daughters' perspective, Gertrude Hamilton's most extraordinary quality was her lack of possessiveness: she encouraged them to live for themselves and a larger world, not, as was common in Victorian America, to devote themselves to their husbands and children or care for their aging parents. Instead, she urged her children to take active roles in their lives, to look at the problems in the world and say, "Somebody must do something about it, then why not I?" As it turned out, the four Hamilton daughters never married. (Neither did all but one of their eight female cousins; when the youngest, Hildegarde Wagenhals, married, Alice declared, "The taboo is over at last.") Many years later, Alice credited her mother with teaching her that "personal liberty was the most precious thing in life."

The Hamilton women of Alice's generation most likely chose not to marry. Alice seems to have decided early on, perhaps while still in her teens, that she couldn't marry and have a career. At the time, the young men her own age didn't interest her; they were no match for her precocious siblings and cousins, and they didn't think of treating women as their intellectual equals—as Alice expected to be treated. Nevertheless, she enjoyed meeting new people, even those her cousins considered "stupid and silly," and didn't lack for suitors, although when she was twenty-two, she gravely pronounced, "I feel now as if the time for that sort of thing were over."

Alice set her sights on practicing medicine while still in high school and seems to have been undecided only about what sort of doctor she would be and where she would practice. In her memoirs, which she provocatively titled, *Exploring the Dangerous Trades*, she wrote, "As a doctor I could go anywhere I pleased—to far-off lands or to city slums—and be quite sure that I could be of use anywhere. I should meet all sorts and conditions of men, I should not be tied down to a school or a college as a teacher is, or have to work under a superior, as a nurse must do."

In 1890, the same year that Edith enrolled at Bryn Mawr College in the suburbs of Philadelphia, Alice started medical school at the Fort Wayne College of Medicine. It wasn't a highly regarded institution; she probably chose it in order to save money by being able to live at home. However, before she could matriculate, she had to study the sciences that she had ignored during her years of home schooling and even at Miss Porter's School for Young Ladies in Farmington, Connecticut, a boarding school that didn't impose required courses on its students, preferring to develop character, cultivation, and discipline in young women destined to become wives and mothers. Alice nevertheless valued her years at Miss Porter's, and she postponed her own entry into medical school so that there would be enough money for her youngest sister, Norah, to attend. Back in Fort Wayne, Alice studied chemistry, physics, and biology with a tutor and on her own, and then became one of six women at the local medical college. The program of study failed to impress her—she claimed it consisted mostly of anatomy—but her professors tried to make up for the lack of rigor by inviting her to assist at operations, letting her treat charity patients, and taking her to meetings of the medical society.

In 1892, Alice transferred to the medical school of the University of Michigan, one of the earliest institutions to switch from a purely lecture-based training to a rigorous four-year curriculum that emphasized clinical and laboratory work. Although she had difficulty getting used to a social world dramatically different from what she was accustomed to—the coarseness of many of her fellow students, Ann Arbor's generally casual attitude toward religion, and the fact that a number of her female patients were unmarried mothers—she liked the fact that the relationship between the sexes at medical school was relatively equal. She quickly overcame her habitual self-doubt and excelled in her work. She had difficulty getting used to having patients—"When it comes to living, feeling people, then I grow frightened," she wrote—but she came to empathize with the single mothers who bore the burden and onus of having had children while the "men have no more care of responsibility . . . than if they had never done it."

In Ann Arbor, Alice grew to be more independent and free-spirited. Although she continued to be a devout Christian, she became less severe about church attendance (one Sunday during her first year, she attended six services in a single day) and sometimes even worked in the laboratory on Sundays, something she had never done in Fort Wayne. Still, she taught Sunday school in a poor neighborhood of the city and lived at the home of one of her professors, Albert B. Prescott, who was an elder in the Presbyterian Church, and his wife, who befriended her genteel boarder. Dr. Prescott noted Alice's "severe distrust of her own abilities" but found that she possessed "incisive determination." In fact, she was allowed to graduate after just three semesters.

Her next step was more difficult. In the last decade of the nineteenth century, it was easier for a woman to find a medical school that would accept her as a student than a hospital where she could serve as an intern. She hoped to be invited by the New England Hospital for Women and Children, the outstanding hospital founded in 1862 by Marie Zakrzewska. When it seemed that there was no opening in Boston, Alice went to the Northwestern Hospital for Women and Children in Minneapolis. She left after three months, in September 1893, as soon as an offer came from the New England Hospital.

Alice was miserable at first, until she was assigned to work in the hospital's Pleasant Street Dispensary. To her delight, her new duties got her out of the hospital itself and into a number of the city's ethnic and immigrant neighborhoods. In a letter to her cousin Agnes, she called the Boston slums "not very bad slums, and very picturesque and interesting." Late one night she got lost trying to find her way home after attending to a patient in a saloon. She was afraid to ask directions of any of the men she passed, but she finally stopped a woman. "She was very kind. She led me back to my street and laughed at my fears. She was a chorus girl, she told me, and never had any trouble. 'Just walk along fast with your bag in your hand, not looking at anybody, and nobody will speak to you. Men don't want to be snubbed; they are looking for a woman who is willing.' It was good advice and it worked. I never had one unpleasant experience, though my night work took me into notoriously tough quarters of the city, and several times into houses of prostitution."

When her dispensary duties ended in March 1894, Alice was assigned to the medical ward, something she had dreaded. At the end of April, she cited "strong family demands" that made it necessary for her to return to Fort Wayne, asked to be released, and confided that she expected the hospital intended to reduce its intern staff soon anyway. The board allowed her to resign, though its minutes claimed that it was because "the best interests of the hospital will be served by her withdrawal."

Whether she found practicing medicine abhorrent or realized that she preferred science, she went back to Ann Arbor in February 1895. (In her memoirs, published in 1943, she wrote, "I soon decided that I would go into bacteriology and pathology instead of medical practice, but Dr. [George] Dock urged me to take a year in a hospital first, saying that my training would be too one-sided otherwise.") She landed a job as an assistant in bacteriology pioneer Frederick G. Novy's lab and hoped to get a Ph.D. from the University of Wisconsin or Johns Hopkins University. Johns Hopkins, the premier American medical institution, was her first choice, and since she had a medical degree, she would have been allowed to take courses. But she wouldn't have been eligible to receive a doctorate, because the university refused to grant degrees to women. So Alice and her sister Edith went to Germany, where they planned to study science (Alice) and classics (Edith) at the universities of Leipzig and Munich.

Two women—an American and an Englishwoman—had earned

Ph.D.s in Germany the previous year, but things weren't what the Hamilton sisters had hoped for there. Alice later claimed that she learned nothing new during an entire year in which she traveled from one German university to another. Attitudes toward them alternated between a patronizing protectiveness and scorn. In her memoirs, she recalled her reception in these words: "I had to accept the thinly veiled contempt of many of my teachers and fellow students because I was at once a woman and an American, therefore uneducated and incapable of real study."

Finally, in Frankfurt, she met Ludwig and Anna Edinger, who welcomed her and became lifelong friends. Ludwig, a pathologist, invited her to join his experiments on the olfactory system of fish, and she and Anna shared an interest in social reform. Despite her intellectual disappointments, she was pleased by the informality of relations between men and women in the lab and impressed by the quality of the science people did while maintaining what we would now call a laid-back attitude. Nevertheless, she was annoyed by the condescension of most of the male German doctors and scientists she encountered. They would ask, complacently, "But who will darn the stockings if women are going to be bacteriologists?" The devout Alice also found most people hypocritical in their religious beliefs and practices, and was shocked by the casual anti-Semitism and passivity of the Jews she met in response to it. "I am becoming an ardent champion of the Jews," she wrote, but she was perplexed that her Jewish friends (the Edingers, among others) seemed not to react to overt insults and tacit discrimination.

Alice and Edith returned from Europe in September 1896, to Baltimore, where Edith had been appointed headmistress of the Bryn Mawr School and Alice would work at the Johns Hopkins Medical School. There, with the help of Simon Flexner, a brilliant pathologist and later director of the Rockefeller Institute laboratory, she published her first scientific papers and also worked at the Johns Hopkins dispensary. She credited Dr. Flexner for teaching her to be fastidious in researching the scientific literature about one's experimental work, and she felt comfortable at Hopkins, where "the men I worked with accepted me without amusement or contempt or even wonder." She was excited by the possibility of examining the blood of malaria patients in the dispensary; Johns Hopkins treated patients from the Deep South and seamen who caught the disease in the tropics. In her memoirs, she wrote admiringly of the giants of turn-of-the-century medicine who taught at Johns Hopkins then— men like William Osler, whose clinic she sometimes visited "just for the pleasure of seeing how admirably he conducted it," and William Welch, whose devotion to efforts to eradicate contagious diseases like tuberculosis impressed her profoundly and quite likely inspired her own dedication.

Midway through her year at Johns Hopkins, Alice complained, "I am tired of being a failure." She feared that she wouldn't be able to find a job in her chosen field, but in the spring of 1897, the Woman's Medical School of Northwestern University invited her to teach pathology there. Members of the Johns Hopkins medical faculty had recommended her, and Osler advised her to accept. The position paid $1,000 annually for eight months' teaching, she would have time for research, and living in Chicago would mean that she could be associated with one of the settlement houses there. Initially, she was told that Hull-House, founded in 1889 by Jane Addams and Ellen Gates Starr, didn't have room for her, but shortly before the academic year began, Jane Addams invited Alice to join her. The association of these two visionary women—the social reformer and the scientist who wanted to help eradicate poverty as well as disease—turned into one of the most enduring of the settlement house movement. Alice ended up staying for twenty-two years and returned for part of the remaining sixteen years of Jane Addams's life.

Alice was familiar with the difficult lives of urban slum-dwellers from her internships in Minneapolis and Boston, but in Chicago she had the opportunity to observe its effects on the lives of the poor over long periods. She also discovered that the causes of diseases and the uneducated poor were often not ignorance but poverty and unhealthy working and living conditions. When she opened a well-baby clinic in the Hull-House basement, she realized that Italian immigrant women knew more about some aspects of nurturing infants than her medical school teachers had. For example, she counseled mothers to feed their babies only milk until they started teething, as she had learned to believe in medical school, but she soon realized that the infants were thriving on a much more varied diet than she had imagined. "So now when I see an Italian baby sucking a slice of salami I feel quite serene," she wrote. "Garlic, we are told, is full of most valuable vitamins and salami is full of garlic."

About other matters—hygiene and contagious disease—they were often less enlightened. The clinic, which soon started treating older children as well, was outfitted with a dozen bathtubs, and Alice spent much of her time convincing mothers to keep their infants clean, especially in the winter. Some Italian immigrants, fearing that Chicago's harsh winters would harm their children, sewed infants into their winter outfits. Birth control was something else many of her patients knew next to nothing about; Alice talked to one pregnant woman who had tried to induce a miscarriage by throwing herself down a flight of stairs. She believed that a family with more children than it could afford put the mother's health in jeopardy and trapped the entire family in the cycle of poverty that the settlement house movement was determined to break.

Listening closely to what her poor patients told her paid off when Alice turned to investigating the causes of occupational diseases and devising ways to combat them, because the workers' stories of exposure to industrial toxins was often different from—and more accurate than—the statements their employers made. By discovering the sources of contamination, Alice was sometimes able to find preventive measures that reduced or eliminated exposures and prevented diseases.

As long as Northwestern maintained its separate medical school for women, Alice had a job teaching pathology. After five years, however, the university merged its men's and women's medical schools into a single institution. For the female students, there were some positive results; from 1902 onward, they would share lectures, laboratories, and clinical work on an equal basis with their male counterparts. But the trend toward co-education in the early 1900s actually led to a drop in the number of women accepted by medical schools and the percentage of women entering the profession. Most medical schools continued to bar women as students well into the twentieth century, and most male doctors, including professors of medicine, persisted in thinking that women didn't belong in medicine.

For Alice Hamilton and other women like her, it meant that no matter how brilliant and accomplished they were, it would become next to impossible to find teaching positions in medical schools. As she wrote about Ruth Tunnicliffe, an outstanding researcher in bacteriology, "she could be a member of any scientific society she chose, could read papers and publish them, and win the respect of her colleagues quite as well as if she were a man, but she could not hope to gain a position of any importance in a medical school."

By a fortunate coincidence of timing, the McCormick Memorial Institute for Infectious Diseases was opening in Chicago just as the Women's Medical College was closing. Alice became a researcher in bacteriology there. Founded by Harold Fowler and Edith Rockefeller McCormick in memory of their young son, John Rockefeller McCormick, who died of scarlet fever in 1901, the institute was directed by Dr. Ludwig Hektoen, the first person to propose that matching blood types was the key to successful transfusions. Through five years as a teacher of pathology, Alice had kept up her scientific credentials by participating in research on the brain and nervous system at the University of Chicago. In her new research position, she began to publish widely, in the institute's own *Journal of Infectious Diseases* and elsewhere.

An outbreak of typhoid in Chicago that fall led to Alice's first major public health triumph. The city's Nineteenth Ward, the neighborhood where Hull-House was located, accounted for 14 percent of the cases in an area that had just 3 percent of the population. Alice suspected that the cause of the epidemic and its concentration in the slums could be traced to flies that fed on infected, exposed sewage in areas where plumbing was substandard and drainage poor. Alice and two of her Hull-House friends collected flies from places where there was standing water, determined that they were infected with the typhoid bacillus, and presented her findings to the Chicago Medical Society in January 1903. It was later discovered that the likely cause was a water main break that had allowed sewage to mix with the drinking water, and that the board of health had covered up the accident instead of taking immediate steps to address the threat. The scandal led to stricter enforcement of health regulations in Chicago's poor districts.

The typhoid study was the first of a series of efforts on Alice's part to employ science as a tool for bringing about changes in public policy. To combat tuberculosis among Chicago's working class, she undertook an ambitious study, hoping to demonstrate that exhaustion from overwork and unsanitary working conditions were factors that contributed to tuberculosis. Though her results were inconclusive, the study laid the groundwork for later, more exhaustive research that ultimately resulted in near elimination of the disease in the United States. She also explored the possibility that excessive childbearing led to higher infant mortality in working-class families, and she led a joint Hull-House–Chicago Medical Society campaign to improve the training and regulation of midwives.

To combat juvenile cocaine addiction, widespread in Chicago where druggists turned schoolboys into users by plying them with free samples, she enlisted the help of local police, who seized the "happy dust" from the boys and turned it over to Alice for testing. Pharmacists who refused to stop supplying happy dust to children voluntarily were prosecuted, and when lawyers for the druggists charged her with cruelty to animals because she was using laboratory rabbits to verify that the seized powder was cocaine, Alice tested it on her own eyes (cocaine causes the pupil to dilate). With her prodding, a state law prohibiting cocaine sales was passed, but the cases tried under it were dismissed on a technicality. The experience convinced Alice that "the American system which most needs reform is the system of criminal law."

Alice wasn't alone in searching for ways to improve the lives and health of the urban poor. As early as 1907, the state of Illinois appointed an Occupational Disease Commission to look for the causes of occupational diseases and propose remedies. Largely the brainchild of University of Chicago sociologist Charles Henderson, commission members looked at a broad sample of the "dusty trades" where workers in metal, glass, brick, stone, and similar materials daily produced and inhaled fine particles. Alice didn't immediately join the commission, but at about the same time she began working along similar lines. After a fire on a small island in Lake Michigan killed most of the workers trapped there and their employer did nothing for the families beyond paying for the dead men's funerals, she read *The Dangerous Trades*, by English physician Sir Thomas Oliver, and other reports on European progress in dealing with occupational hazards and diseases by introducing safeguards in the workplace and educating workers in proper procedures. Americans, by contrast, either claimed that occupational diseases weren't serious problems or that the American factory or workshop was so much safer than its European counterpart that the risks from dangerous materials were virtually eliminated. In fact, as Alice and her colleagues would demonstrate, the opposite was true, as she knew from experience it would be. "Living in a working-class quarter, coming in contact with laborers and their wives, I could not fail to hear tales of the dangers that working-men faced, of cases of carbon-monoxide gassing in the great steel mills, of painters disabled by lead palsy, of pneumonia and rheumatism among the men in the stockyards."

When the commission embarked on its second phase in 1909, Alice agreed to act as chief researcher. She oversaw investigations into a number of toxins used or produced in manufacturing–lead, arsenic, brass, carbon monoxide, the cyanides, and turpentine–and several afflictions of specific occupations: caisson disease (the bends), boilermaker's deafness, and nystagmus, a vision-impairing oscillation of the eyes that affected coal miners. Alice conducted the research on lead poisoning herself, and it was the jewel of the report that the commission submitted to the governor in 1911.

Because industrial processes weren't regulated and the means and materials of production weren't always well known, Alice deduced which industries employed lead by finding hospital patients who exhibited the symptoms of lead poisoning, talking to labor experts, and questioning doctors and pharmacists with patients and clients in working-class areas. She identified hundreds of cases of lead poisoning–in lead refineries; brass foundries; paint plants; factories making enameled plumbing fixtures, storage batteries, freight-car seals, coffin trim, and decals for decorating pottery; cut-glass work-shops, where lead was used in polishing; and even among cigar makers, who used lead "tinfoil" to wrap individual cigars. The commission's final report included a proposed occupational health bill, which failed to pass; but a less sweeping proposal did become the Illinois Occupational Disease Act of 1911.

In 1910, before the commission's report was published, Alice attended the Second International Congress on Occupational Accidents and Diseases in Brussels, where she presented a paper based on her research on lead. One of the few other Americans at the conference was the U.S. commissioner of labor, Charles P. Neill (Labor was still a Commerce Department bureau; it became a cabinet department on its own in 1912). Alice apparently impressed O'Neill profoundly, because shortly after she returned home to complete the commission report, he invited her to conduct a federal study along similar lines, starting with lead and extending into other dangerous trades at Alice's discretion. There would be no constraints on her work–Alice would be in charge of deciding which industries and plants to investigate and how to conduct her investigations–

and also no guarantees. She wouldn't receive a salary for her work, nor would the government pressure anyone to cooperate with her; it would be up to her to find the plants and persuade the owners to let her in. When she had completed her study, the bureau would negotiate with her to determine how much she would be paid.

Alice accepted immediately. In her memoirs, she wrote that she missed research but knew "that it was not in me to be anything more than a fourth-rate bacteriologist" and was cut out for work that balanced science and practical value. Despite her self-disparagement, she was no slouch at science. Between 1911 and 1914, with her new title of special investigator, she conducted nationwide studies of numerous lead-related industries. One smelting expert wrote of her, "Here is a woman writing on the metallurgy of lead who knows her job perfectly." She relied on persistence and politeness to gain entry into the plants, visited workers at home or in saloons when the managers tried to hide infected workers from "the lady from Washington," and assiduously documented her findings in order to compensate for the poor records kept by factories and hospitals. Then she cajoled and flattered foremen and owners in an effort to persuade them to clean up their factories and protect their workers. There were few government regulations to protect the health and safety of factory workers in those days, so Alice relied on moral suasion. "When I went into industrial medicine, I often felt that my sex was a help, not a handicap. Employers and doctors both appeared more willing to listen to me as I told them their duty towards their employees and patients than they would have if I had been a man. It seemed natural and right that a woman should put the care of the producing workman ahead of the value of the thing he was producing; in a man it would have been sentimentality or radicalism."

More often than not, especially in the early years, the owners, managers, and even the doctors who depended on the industries for their jobs denied the accuracy of her reports and obstructed her efforts. But her single-mindedness and the fact that her colleagues at the newly formed Bureau of Labor Statistics (a branch of the

Department of Labor) gave her their unqualified support brought results. Before World War I, Alice was one of the leading figures in the new field of industrial toxicology and the undisputed authority on lead in the American workplace.

Prior to the war, Germany supplied most of the explosives used in the United States and much of Europe, but by 1915 American plants had geared up to produce picric acid, TNT, fulminate of mercury, and other "wartime chemicals," many of which are actually by-products of converting bituminous coal into coke. Before the war, these gases were allowed to escape, but new plants were built that captured the gases to produce the explosive compounds for domestic use and to supply them to the Allies for military use. Nearly all of these compounds, as well as some chemicals used to make dyes and rubber that had also been imported from Germany, were toxic if inhaled or absorbed through the skin. When domestic manufacturing started, Alice added the plants that produced the chemicals to her list of places to be investigated.

The factory locations were secret, of course, so Alice visited plants she knew about, asked questions in bars and other workers' hangouts, looked for the telltale clouds of orange and yellow gases that were visible above the factory chimneys, and sometimes even followed "canaries," workers stained from contact with yellow picric acid. One worker Alice ran into actually referred to the plant where he helped manufacture picric for the French military as the "Canary Islands." As she had generally done, Alice conducted her investigations alone, but after the United States entered the war, a division of the National Research Council asked her advice in designing research they wanted to do in explosives and munitions plants. She recommended studies that combined laboratory experiments, monitoring infected workers, and in-plant testing. Alice herself supervised the testing–carried out by medical students–and believed that the attention the war brought to munitions and chemical substances conferred a new respectability on the field of industrial medicine.

Alice's prominence in the still young field of industrial toxicology persuaded the Harvard Medical School to offer her a faculty appointment–despite the fact that women were still barred as students. She accepted, even though the appointment was as an assistant professor, but only as a half-time commitment, to allow her time to continue the field work she loved. As the only woman on Harvard's faculty (her appointment shifted to the School of Public Health after its founding in 1922), Alice was denied certain traditional faculty perks–access to the Harvard Club, marching in faculty processions at commencements, or tickets to Harvard football games. On her side, she refused to back down from causes that she believed in, such as supporting a Quaker famine relief fund that aided postwar Germany, despite the objections of one of the university's major donors. She chided the university by announcing, "Yes, I am the first woman on the Harvard faculty–but not the first one who should have been appointed!" The university reciprocated by never promoting her. When she reached the mandatory retirement age of sixty-five in 1935, she still held the lowly rank of assistant professor.

Her 1925 textbook, *Industrial Poisons in the United States*, was the first such work published in the United States and raised the visibility of the field of industrial medicine. Both *Industrial Poisons* and her second book, *Industrial Toxicology* (1934), were aimed at helping physicians prevent industrial poisoning as well as treat its victims. She used her position and prominence as a bully pulpit to raise public awareness about hazardous materials. Even after her retirement, she continued to publish texts, reports, and articles into her nineties. She was a medical consultant for the Division of Labor Standards of the U.S. Department of Labor, appointed by Secretary Frances Perkins, the first woman cabinet secretary. In this capacity, she exposed the dangers of the viscous rayon industry, which she made the subject of her last investigation in 1937–1938, revealing that carbon disulfide, used in the manufacturing process, caused paralysis and mental problems. She also wrote magazine articles and published her autobiography, *Exploring the Dangerous Trades,* which was published in 1943.

Alice Evans

A Pennsylvania schoolteacher whose encounter with a free summer nature study course at Cornell University ignited a passion for science, Alice Evans initially seemed an unlikely heir to the legacy of Alice Hamilton. But after returning to school full-time at Cornell, where she earned a B.S. in bacteriology in 1909, she continued on to graduate work at the University of Wisconsin. Like upstate New York and her native Pennsylvania, Wisconsin was a major dairy farming region. After Alice received her master's degree in 1910, she found work with the U.S. Department of Agriculture's Bureau of Animal Industry, whose Dairy Division had a branch on the university campus in Madison where Alice had been studying. Her first assignment was to investigate better methods of making cheese. When a Department of Agriculture research facility opened in Washington, D.C., in 1913, Alice became the first woman with a permanent, full-time job in the Dairy Division.

At the time, uncontaminated milk–that is, milk free of bacteria that caused illness in human beings–was considered safe to drink. Alice discovered that two different types of bacteria found in milk were actually nearly identical. One, called *Bacillus abortus,* made pregnant cows miscarry but was thought to be harmless to people. *Micrococcus melitensis,* however, didn't harm the cows, but when people drank milk containing the bacteria, they contracted undulant fever (so called because one of the symptoms is a pattern of rising and falling body temperature that can spike as high as 104 degrees Fahrenheit). Undulant fever, which had first been observed in British soldiers who drank infected goat's milk on the island of Malta, is sometimes called Gibraltar or Malta fever.

Alice surmised that the bacteria that were often present in

"uncontaminated" cow's milk might be what caused human undulant fever. Her professional colleagues, doctors, and dairymen were skeptical when she first suggested her hypothesis in 1917 at a meeting of the Society of American Bacteriologists (forerunner to today's American Society of Microbiology). Alice's relatively modest academic credentials–she had an master's degree but not a Ph.D.–was one reason even a bacteriologist as eminent as Theobold Smith of the Rockefeller Institute (whose own work on *E. coli* dealt with diseases that can be spread through drinking bacteria-laden raw milk) dismissed her claim. Another was that she was a woman. As Alice wryly observed, "The Nineteenth Amendment was not a part of the Constitution of the United States when the controversy began, and he was not accustomed to considering a scientific idea proposed by a woman."

Three years later, however, other researchers replicated her findings, and this led to reclassification of the various bacterial strains–in cows, goats, and pigs (which Alice had also identified earlier)–as a new genus, *Brucella*, named for Sir David Bruce, a British military physician who traced the cause of the malady in soldiers stationed on Malta to the drinking of goat's milk. The disease was renamed brucellosis. Although pasteurization of milk was first demonstrated as early as 1886, Bruce and his colleagues didn't consider recommending it. Instead, they eliminated the threat of brucellosis by removing goat's milk from the British military diet on the island. In 1925, William Welch of Johns Hopkins, brokered a truce between Alice and Theobold, and three years later, Alice became the first woman elected president of the Society of American Bacteriologists.

Alice recommended that all milk be pasteurized, in order to eliminate the risk of getting the disease from drinking milk. The dairy industry opposed the remedy, however, because they would be required to install expensive pasteurizing machinery, but in the 1930s federal laws were enacted that required all American dairies to pasteurize the milk they sold. By then, Alice was demonstrating that many more cases of brucellosis existed than the medical profession suspected, and that infections lasted longer than had been thought. The reason for this was that brucellosis symptoms mimicked those of a number of other diseases and was often mistaken for one of them: influenza, typhoid fever, tuberculosis, malaria, or rheumatism. She herself was infected with brucellosis in 1922—human beings can get the disease through contact with infected animals as well as from drinking unpasteurized milk—and suffered intermittently for the next twenty-one years.

Alice's research included investigations of streptococci, the bacteria that cause pharyngitis (popularly called "strep throat"), rheumatic fever, scarlet fever, and other diseases, but her place in the history of microbiology and public health is assured primarily by her work on brucellosis. Her contribution has been called "one of the outstanding achievements in medical science in the first quarter of the 20th century."

MARTHA MAY ELIOT

In 1913, at about the time Alice Evans was beginning her groundbreaking research on bacteria in milk, another pioneer, Martha May Eliot, graduated from Radcliffe College. A brilliant student whose research on rickets helped define the protocols for preventing that childhood disease, she later headed the Children's Bureau from 1951 to 1956, and was the only woman signatory to the document establishing the World Health Organization. Martha completed her pre-med requirements as an undergraduate while earning a B.A. in classics. However, when she asked William Sedgwick, a pioneer in public health at MIT and Harvard, for advice, he discouraged her from applying to medical school. Instead, he recommended that she become a lab technician. Martha asked him, "Professor Sedgwick, suppose I was a man sitting here and asking you what my education should be were I to go into public health as a life interest?" He replied, "I would advise you to go to medical school and become a physician first, and then, when you have had some hospital work, to enroll in a school of public health." Martha shot back, "Well I believe you have answered my question very quickly and easily." On principle, Martha applied to Harvard Medical School, although Harvard didn't accept women at that time, but she was accepted at Johns Hopkins and received her M.D. with honors in 1918. She eventually returned to Harvard in 1957 to become a full professor in the School of Public Health. In a crowning irony, one year later she became the first woman to be awarded the American Public Health Association's Sedgwick Memorial Medal, named in honor of the man who had tried to talk her into a career as a lab technician.

HELEN TAUSSIG

A few years after Martha May Eliot left Cambridge, Massachusetts, with her Radcliffe College degree in search of a medical school that welcomed women students, Helen Taussig entered Radcliffe as a freshman. The youngest of four children of Frank Taussig, an eminent economist and Harvard professor (he was cofounder of the Harvard Business School), Helen's interest in medicine may have been inspired by her grandfather, William Taussig, a physician in Missouri. William specialized in treating visually impaired children and was one of the founders of a school for handicapped children in St. Louis. Helen's own early years were difficult. She suffered a partial loss of hearing as a child, had a mild case of TB herself, and was dyslexic. She had also lost her mother, Edith Brooke Taussig, to tuberculosis when she was just eleven years old. Her father, however, coached and encouraged her, and she was admitted to Radcliffe College in 1917.

After two years at Radcliffe and another two at the University of California, Berkeley, where she received her B.A., Helen then took courses at the medical schools of Harvard and Boston Universities. Because she was a woman, neither institution would accept her as a candidate for an M.D., but they allowed her to take classes. At Harvard, she wasn't even allowed to examine tissue samples under the microscope in the same laboratory as the male students, but had to work in a separate room.

At Boston University, Helen attended Alexander Begg's anatomy lectures. Begg, dean of the medical school and co-author of the standard anatomy text, got her interested in the workings of the heart and encouraged her to apply to Johns Hopkins. She entered the medical school at Johns Hopkins in the fall of 1923. By the time she completed medical school, she was deaf and thereafter depended on lip-reading and a bulky hearing aid. Nevertheless, she was elected to the honor society, was a fellow in cardiology at Johns Hopkins Hospital for one year, and followed that with a two-year internship in pediatrics.

One unusual component of the Johns Hopkins medical complex was the Harriet Lane Home for Invalid Children, the first children's hospital in the United States that was part of a university teaching hospital. Edwards A. Park, who was head of pediatrics at Johns Hopkins and director of Harriet Lane from 1927 to 1946, created the first clinics in a number of pediatric specialties—among them, cardiology, tuberculosis, endocrinology, seizure disorders, and psychiatry. The pediatric cardiology clinic opened in 1930 and Park asked Helen to be its director.

Helen compensated for her hearing loss with enhanced visual acuity and sense of touch. As a result, she developed an extraordinary ability to recognize abnormalities in the hearts of infants and children. Although she did use a specially amplified stethoscope to listen to patients' heartbeats, Helen relied more on her eyes and her hands. She used a fluoroscope, which projects images of the heart, lungs, and arteries onto a screen in real time, and she could feel changes in the shape and movement of the hearts and chests of children with congenital cardiac abnormalities when she examined them.

A number of Helen's young patients at Harriet Lane suffered from anoxemia (or cyanosis), more commonly called blue baby syndrome, because of the blue cast the infants' skin takes on as a result of low blood-oxygen levels. The symptoms are often barely discernible, with just a bluish pallor visible, and may not seem serious at first. Most "blue babies" appear to grow normally, with no other health or developmental problems. But these infants usually also had heart murmurs; their conditions deteriorate over time, and can even be fatal.

When Helen began to search for a way to treat anoxemia in the children she affectionately called her "little crossword puzzles," doctors had understood its causes for half a century. She surmised, however, that the reason the condition proved fatal wasn't that the children's hearts failed but that they were starved of oxygen because too little blood was reaching their lungs. But no one had found a way to correct the problem until Helen noticed something about infants born with another birth defect, called Patent Ductus Arteriosus.

The lungs of a fetus grow, but they don't function before birth. A developing child receives oxygen from its mother's blood, via the placenta. To bypass the fluid-filled lungs, the fetal circulatory system includes a small duct, called the ductus arteriosus, linking the pulmonary artery to the aorta. In most infants, the ductus arteriosus closes on its own soon after birth, usually in a day or less. Sometimes, closure takes longer, and in rare cases, it must be corrected by surgery or other means. Nearly all infants who had the operation recovered normally, but Helen saw that those with tetralogy of Fallot–blue babies–reacted differently. Whether the ductus arteriosus in those infants closed on its own or was closed surgically, they grew sicker, and some of them died.

Helen discovered that in blue babies, the ductus arteriosus actually helped to increase the amount of oxygen in their blood. After she heard Alfred Blalock, professor of surgery and surgeon-in-chief at Johns Hopkins, suggesting to Edwards Park that a shunt could be used to bypass an obstruction in the aorta, she speculated that infants with blue baby syndrome would improve if an artificial ductus arteriosus were created. Dr. Blalock believed that her idea would work, and he and surgical technician Vivien Thomas experimented from 1941 to 1944 to perfect the technique that came to be called the Blalock-Taussig operation.

The three of them performed their first operation on an infant with tetralogy of Fallot in November 1944 and repeated their success on two other cases before publishing an article about the Blalock-Taussig operation in the *Journal of the American Medical Association* the next year. Helen didn't directly participate in the surgeries themselves, but she observed all of them. After the third operation, in February 1945, "on a small, utterly miserable, six-year-old boy who ... was no longer able to walk," she described the dramatic changes in the young patient. "When the clamps were released [after Dr. Blalock had joined the blood vessels], the anesthesiologist said suddenly, 'He's a lovely color now!' I walked around to the head of the table and saw his normal, pink lips. From that moment the child was healthy, happy, and active."

The trio together performed over a thousand Blalock-Taussig operations by 1950, and the Blalock-Taussig shunt was quickly adopted worldwide as the standard treatment for blue baby syndrome. Denton Cooley, one of Dr. Blalock's surgical interns, who assisted at the operations in 1944 and 1945, credits Alfred Blalock with ushering in modern cardiovascular surgery and inspiring him to pursue a career in heart surgery. Dr. Cooley, of course, after moving to Houston, Texas, in 1951, introduced or perfected numerous revolutionary techniques in cardiovascular surgery, from treating aortic aneurysms to heart transplants. He is considered one of the premier pioneers in heart transplant operations.

Productive as it was, the Blalock-Taussig partnership included its share of tension, a common by-product of collaborations involving powerful personalities. Alfred Blalock, the confident surgeon, was often at odds with the protective physician, leading him to quip that if he made it into heaven it would be thanks to the fact that he'd managed to get along with Helen Taussig. The Blalock-Taussig operation remained the standard until advances in heart surgery made it possible to correct the leak in the heart wall and the defective pulmonary artery directly. When Helen published *Congenital Malformations of the Heart* in 1947, she was recognized as the leading figure in the new field of pediatric cardiology.

Young patients in search of the lifesaving operation flooded the hospital, and so did cardiologists and surgeons, who descended on Johns Hopkins from all over the world to learn diagnostic acumen from Helen and surgical techniques from Alfred Blalock. In 1959, her accomplishments were reflected in her rank and she was named professor of pediatrics.

More important from a medical perspective were the professional contacts she established with the doctors from other countries whom she met when they came to Johns Hopkins to observe the Blalock-Taussig operation. One of them was Alois Beuren, a West German physician, who told her early in 1962 "about all the limbless babies being born in Germany" and about the drug that was suspected of being the cause. The birth defect the infants suffered from was phocomelia (Greek for "seal limbs"). Their arms—in extreme cases, arms *and* legs—were severely deformed or missing; the hands and feet often resembled a seal's flippers.

Originally a rare condition, phocomelia suddenly became more common in Germany in 1959 and 1960, when 140 cases were observed—ten times as many as in the previous decade. Alois told Helen that doctors suspected that the cause was a sleeping pill, sold under the name Contergan, that had recently become popular as a way of controlling morning sickness in pregnant women. More than half the women whose babies had phocomelia had taken Contergan early in their pregnancies. Contergan was the brand name of thalidomide. No studies were done of the drug, but the pharmaceutical company that made Contergan voluntarily took it off the market in 1961.

On February 1, Helen arrived in Europe, where for six weeks she examined deformed infants in the two countries where the drug had been used, Britain and Germany, and consulted with the doctors who had raised the alarm about thalidomide. When she returned to the United States, she told Frances Kelsey, a physician at the Food and Drug Administration, what she had learned in Europe. Based on Helen's report, Dr. Kelsey ordered a stop to testing of thalidomide for potential sale in the United States. Even before the FDA announced that it would not approve the drug, Helen addressed a meeting of the American College of Physicians in April 1962, to let American doctors know what she had seen in Europe and to urge them to discontinue testing thalidomide on their patients.

Helen's immediate concern was the dangers of thalidomide, but she also saw a larger problem beyond the single tragedy. "All new drugs which circulate through the bloodstream should be screened for their effect on the offspring of pregnant animals," she wrote. Congress listened and passed legislation that tightened testing requirements for new drugs, effective February 1963, just one year after Helen went to Europe to see the damage from thalidomide at first hand.

Helen reached mandatory retirement age in 1963, but she never stopped working. For a number of years, she continued almost daily to visit the cardiology clinic she had helped to found. And she kept up her research. One of her studies involved following up with the early blue babies, children who had been operated on before 1950. Helen had kept in touch with so many of her former patients that contacting them didn't pose much of a challenge. In a paper she published in 1975, she confirmed that the blue babies hadn't suffered brain damage due to low oxygen supply to the brain before their operations. Most of these former patients had survived into adulthood, had completed educations, pursued successful careers, and had families.

Of the more than one hundred papers she published in her career (the first appeared in 1925), she wrote forty-one after she retired. Her last paper was written only a few days before she died in 1986, from injuries suffered in an automobile accident. It was vintage Helen. She had studied the hearts of five thousand birds at the Delaware Museum of Natural History over a period of three years, to test her hypothesis that congenital heart defects were genetic variants, not developmental mishaps. Her goal was to reassure the parents of children born with birth defects that they hadn't "caused" the problems by doing something wrong during pregnancy. It attested to the depth of her concern for people, not just patients. Over the course of her distinguished career, Helen received hundreds of awards and degrees, including the Albert Lasker Award in 1954 and the Medal of Freedom from President Lyndon Johnson in 1964. Her rare sensitivity was perhaps best captured in this simple statement that accompanied her honorary degree from Goucher College, in Towson, Maryland: "You have brought to medicine simplicity, kindness and compassion as only a complete woman can."

RACHEL CARSON

THE "CONTROL OF NATURE" IS A PHRASE CONCEIVED IN ARROGANCE, BORN OF THE NEANDERTHAL AGE OF BIOLOGY AND PHILOSOPHY, WHEN IT WAS SUPPOSED THAT NATURE EXISTS FOR THE CONVENIENCE OF MAN.

Alice Evans's methodology of killing brucellosis-causing bacteria by pasteurizing milk is a textbook example of one type of public health protocol: prevention by destroying the agent that causes the disease. In the case of brucellosis, pasteurization makes it possible to kill the bacteria while preserving the milk's nutritional value. But for other diseases, like malaria, which is caused by a parasite borne by anopheles mosquitoes, control efforts have focused on eliminating the insects that carry the parasite rather than the parasite itself.

At the midpoint of the twentieth century, the possibility of permanently eradicating malaria and other diseases carried by flies, mosquitoes, lice, and fleas seemed bright thanks to dichlorodiphenyltrichloroethane, commonly known as DDT. A Swiss chemist, Paul Müller, found that DDT promised to be an ideal insecticide, inexpensive to manufacture and use, and toxic to insects that prey on human beings and plants without harming either vegetation or people. First tested on the Colorado potato beetle in 1939, by 1944 it was employed to stop a typhus epidemic in Naples, Italy, and to prevent malaria outbreaks among American troops in the Pacific. Earlier in the war, malaria had hampered the military effort nearly as much as the Japanese.

During the two decades between 1945 and 1965, such dramatic progress was made against a number of epidemic diseases that scientists and public health officials predicted a future free of the threat of epidemics that had formerly decimated populations throughout the world. After all, it had been Louis Pasteur himself, who formulated the germ theory of disease and introduced the concept of vaccination to medicine, who declared, "It is within the power of man to rid himself of every parasitic disease." New vaccines were developed against polio, antibiotics were developed to treat a number of diseases, and insecticides–especially DDT–successfully eliminated diseases that depended on insects to spread infection. In every hemisphere, areas that had been plagued by malaria saw the disease eliminated or severely reduced. India, for example, saw deaths from malaria drop from as many as a million a year to zero. In 1948, long before DDT's full benefit could be measured, Paul Müller received the Nobel Prize in Physiology or Medicine for his work in proving the compound's effectiveness in combating disease.

Despite the remarkable inroads made against malaria, the dream of completely eliminating the disease was probably impossible to achieve. Some regions–such as the dense, but sparsely populated rain forest or sub-Saharan Africa–didn't lend themselves to programs in which 80 percent of the dwellings were sprayed over a short period. But even if every spot on the planet where malaria mosquitoes were found could have been treated with pesticides, not all the mosquitoes would have died. Unlike human beings, who produce only a few generations per century, insects have short life cycles and can produce many generations in the space of a few weeks, or even days. Some mosquitoes would be resistant or even immune to DDT, and as the "normal" mosquito population died off, a new population of DDT-resistant mosquitoes came into being.

Although Rachel Carson was recognized as a science writer of the first rank after the publication of her second book, *The Sea Around Us*, in 1951, she was no provocateur. The fame that came with writing a bestseller didn't make her any less publicity-shy than she had been during the previous fifteen years, when she worked as a biologist, writer, and editor for the government's Fish and Wildlife Service.

However, Rachel was the first major writer on science to oppose the accepted ideas about DDT. She grew up in the small southwestern Pennsylvania town of Springdale, where she was born in 1907, the youngest of three children. Her sister and brother were eight and ten years older than she; as a result Rachel spent much of her childhood alone, observing wildlife in the woods and writing. She published her first story in a children's magazine when she was ten years old.

At Pennsylvania College for Women (now Chatham College) in Pittsburgh, Rachel switched her major from English to biology after being fascinated by a required introductory course, but she didn't give up her literary ambitions. "I don't have much imagination," she told a friend. "Biology has given me something to write about." At the time, women were discouraged from going into the sciences, but she managed to get a scholarship to do graduate work at Johns Hopkins University, where she earned a master's degree in zoology in 1932. She spent her summers at the Marine Biological Laboratory in Woods Hole, Massachusetts, where in addition to doing research she discovered the ocean, which had enchanted Rachel from childhood but which she had never seen before her first summer at Woods Hole.

Two unexpected deaths—Rachel's father, Robert Carson, in 1935, and her married sister, Marian, one year later—left Rachel the chief financial support of the family, and she and her mother responsible for raising Marian's two young daughters, Virginia and Marjorie.

Rachel had to abandon hopes of earning a doctorate, but she found work with the Bureau of Fisheries that drew on her two loves: marine biology and writing. The bureau (which in 1939 merged with the Bureau of Biological Survey to make up the Department of the Interior's Fish and Wildlife Service) was creating a radio series on marine life, called *Romance Under the Water*, and Elmer Higgins, the biologist in charge of the project, hired Rachel to write the scripts. At the bureau, the broadcasts were humorously referred to as "seven-minute fish tales." Rachel was eventually made editor-in-chief of the Interior Department's service publications.

With the security of a civil service job in Washington, Rachel was able to settle into a house in Silver Spring, Maryland, with her mother and two nieces. She somehow managed to find time to write feature articles for the *Baltimore Sun*, and one essay that she began for the bureau eventually became her first national publication, "Undersea," an article that appeared in *The Atlantic Monthly* in September 1937. Urged to expand the piece into a book, she wrote *Under the Sea-Wind*, which was published in November 1941. The book, a natural history of oceans, was reviewed enthusiastically in both general and scholarly publications, but following the attack on Pearl Harbor and the U.S. entry into World War II a month later, it was largely ignored.

During the war years, Rachel wrote a series of booklets about the fauna and ecology of our national wildlife refuges under the general title *Conservation in Action*. Another series was devoted to food from the sea, to introduce the public to the benefits of a diet that included fish and shellfish and suggesting ways to prepare them. She was also involved in a study of underwater sounds, life, and terrain, part of an effort by the navy to develop systems to track submarine movements.

Rachel's next book, *The Sea Around Us* (1951), was the second in what became her trilogy about the world's oceans. Serialized in the *New Yorker* before publication in book form (the story was turned down by fifteen other magazines), it was an astonishing international success: it spent eighty-one weeks on the *New York Times* Best Seller list, won the National Book Award for nonfiction plus a host of other awards; and was translated into thirty-two foreign languages. By the time her third book, *The Edge of the Sea*, appeared in 1956, readers had begun to recognize Rachel's distinctive vision of marine life as an interconnected community of life forms, rather than independent elements that happened to share a common address. She was equally as curious about life along the seacoast and in the tidal pools formed by the ebb and flow of the sea against the shoreline. As she wrote, "To understand the shore, it is not enough to catalogue its life. Understanding comes only when, standing on a beach, we can sense the long rhythms of earth and sea that sculpted its land forms and produced the rock and sand of which it is composed. . . . It is not enough to pick up a shell and say 'This is a murex,' or 'That is an angel's wing.' True understanding demands intuitive comprehension of the whole life of the creature that once inhabited this empty shell: how it survived amid surf and storms, what were its enemies, how it found food and reproduced its kind, what were its relations to the particular sea world in which it lived."

The financial success of *The Sea Around Us* allowed Rachel to retire from the Fish and Wildlife Service and devote herself full-time to her writing and her family. She also acquired some land in Southport Island, Maine, and built a small house there. She and her mother had first visited the area around Boothbay Harbor in 1946, and now Rachel was free to spend more of her time close to her beloved ocean. Despite material security, however, life was far from serene for Rachel. In 1957, her niece Marjorie died, and one year later, her mother, aged eighty-nine, passed away as well. Rachel adopted Marjorie's young son, Roger, with whom she had enjoyed an especially close relationship, ever since he was born in 1952. Her last book, *The Sense of Wonder*, published the year after Rachel's own death from breast cancer in 1964, was based on "Help Your Child to Wonder," an article she wrote about exploring nature with her nephew (and adopted son), Roger.

Rachel's diagnosis of cancer came in 1960, after she had begun to work on what was to become *Silent Spring*. She was determined to complete the book, despite surgery and radiation therapy; she did some of the writing in bed, when she wasn't well enough to work at her desk. In many ways, the new book was a continuation of her earlier work, with its emphasis on the complex relationships between living creatures and their habitat. But *Silent Spring* also represented a major departure for Rachel. It was not about the sea, but about the ways in which human beings were altering the habitats of many creatures, possibly including themselves, through the massive use of synthetic insecticides.

Rachel had been concerned about the large-scale use of pesticides as a means of pest control for well over a decade. Her theories were consistent with her general view: that narrowly focused efforts to eliminate one predator were often blind to unintended damage caused to the total habitat. She was familiar with reports written by her Fish and Wildlife Service colleagues and other government scientists about experiments with DDT and other pesticides at the Patuxent Wildlife Research Center. In 1945, in fact, she offered to write an article for *Reader's Digest* about the experiments, in which she proposed looking at whether DDT "may upset the whole delicate balance of nature if unwisely used." She didn't write the article at the time, but she continued to follow the reports about DDT and other powerful pesticides.

The pesticide debate generated its share of headlines, especially in 1957, when the Department of Agriculture's use of highly toxic dieldrin and heptachlor to eliminate a nonnative pest, the fire ant, inspired protests from conservationists. Robert Cushman Murphy, one of the twentieth century's greatest ornithologists, went to court to stop the federal government from aerial pesticide spraying because of the risk to fish, birds, wild and domestic animals, and perhaps even people. What may have convinced Rachel that she should write her book was a letter from her friend Olga Owens Huckins, who maintained a private bird sanctuary in Massachusetts and reported that a large number of birds had died after aerial spraying of a mixture of fuel oil and DDT to control mosquitoes on the coast north of Boston. As she told a biographer, "Knowing the facts as I did, I could not rest until I had brought them to public attention."

The publication of *Silent Spring* provoked widespread controversy, as many—including the usually quiet Rachel—fully expected. The controversy arose not from the author's argument, however. Rachel favored using pesticides to prevent outbreaks of insect-borne diseases like malaria and to combat them when they occurred, and she also recognized that insecticides had legitimate agricultural applications. What she objected to was their indiscriminate use by large agricultural and agrichemical industries, and even in some public health efforts. In the book, she approvingly quoted a European scientist who counseled that the rule of thumb should be "Spray as little as you possibly can" rather than "Spray to the limit of your capacity."

She continued to strike the same measured note when she talked about the book after it was published. "It is not my contention that chemical pesticides must never be used," she said. "I do contend that we have allowed these chemicals to be used with little or no advance investigation of their effect on soil, water, and man himself." In *Silent Spring* itself, however, Rachel had been unsparing of those in industry and even in government agencies who failed to exercise caution, whether they were motivated by a desire for profit or a zeal to eliminate the last vestige of a deadly disease. She pointed to instances where even the best intentions might backfire, such as areas where spraying of insecticides wiped out not only the disease-carrying insects but all their natural predators as well. Later, if the disease bearers returned—not uncommon on islands that were part of a contiguous chain—their spread would be unchallenged, because the species that had kept their population in check no longer existed in that small island ecosystem. As she had said to Harvard entomologist E. O. Wilson when she was beginning to work on the book, "In my sincere opinion, the weight of evidence amounts to an overwhelming indictment of most of the present programs."

Therefore, although the press was enthusiastic, businesses and bureaucracies were up in arms. Reviewers compared the book to Upton Sinclair's book *The Jungle*, a fictional exposé of the meatpacking industry, and even to Harriet Beecher Stowe's *Uncle Tom's Cabin*. The *New York Times* wrote effusively in an editorial when portions of *Silent Spring* were serialized in the *New Yorker* during the summer of 1962, "If her series helps arouse enough public concern to immunize government agencies against the blandishments of hucksters and enforce adequate controls, the author will be as deserving of the Nobel Prize as was the inventor of DDT." Meanwhile, the secretary of agriculture who had served under President Dwight Eisenhower told her old boss that he suspected Rachel Carson of being a Communist; industry leaders accused her of hysteria and fanaticism; and chemical corporations threatened to sue the *New Yorker* and Houghton Mifflin, publishers of the book. In response, a *New Yorker* vice president shot back, "Everything in those articles has been checked and is true. Go ahead and sue." Instead, the chemical companies, through an industry trade group, spent $250,000 on ads and a parody of Rachel's style, called "The Desolate Year."

Shortly before the book was published, President John Kennedy announced that he would appoint a panel to investigate the pesticide use the *New Yorker* articles had discussed. Jerome Weisner, Kennedy's adviser for science policy who became president of MIT in the 1970s, was asked to staff the panel and direct its work. In September, when *Silent Spring* appeared, it became an instant bestseller, and CBS announced plans to produce a special report on the book in 1963. Despite efforts to discourage the network from broadcasting its TV special, the show aired in April. The effect, one of Rachel's biographers wrote, was the equivalent of reprinting the book.

The response in the nation's capital suggests how the pesticide controversy was taking center stage in the public consciousness. The morning after the telecast, Senator Abraham Ribicoff of Connecticut announced that the Senate Subcommittee on Reorganization and International Organization had scheduled hearings into environmental pollution and the federal roles in regulation and pest control. The hearings were to begin on May 16.

Not to be upstaged, the White House released the President's Science Advisory Committee report, endorsed by President Kennedy himself, on May 15, the day before the hearings were scheduled to start. *The Uses of Pesticides* recommended limiting pesticide residues "by orderly reductions of persistent pesticides" and proposed a complete ban on some chemicals, among them DDT and heptachlor, without suggesting how to accomplish the goal. The report endorsed two of *Silent Spring*'s central theses: that the current scientific paradigm of total pest eradication should be revised and that the public should be better informed about what pesticides are and how they are used. The report stated that before the book appeared, "people were generally unaware of the toxicity of pesticides." In response to that issue, the U.S. Department of Agriculture rapidly changed its regulations to shift the burden of proof from the public to the manufacturer. Previously, someone who believed that a chemical was harmful had to prove it, but now a new chemical couldn't be used until the manufacturer had documented that it was safe.

Despite the fact that her condition continued to worsen throughout 1963, Rachel never lost her perspective. When she accepted the National Book Award that year, she said, "It seems reasonable to believe—and I do believe—that the more clearly we can focus our attention on the wonders and realities of the universe about us the less taste we shall have for the destruction of our race. Wonder and humility are wholesome emotions, and they do not exist side by side with a lust for destruction."

Rachel has sometimes been called a founder of the modern environmental movement, but she was too modest to take credit for introducing consciousness of the relationship between individuals and their environment into the thinking of scientists and conservationists. She saw this consciousness as one of the distinctive features of modern biological thought. All of her writings were part of her effort to communicate a sense of wonder and humility about natural phenomena accurately in language that laypeople understood, but without oversimplifying the science. The popular success of *Silent Spring* in particular brought these ideas to people who would never see the inside of a scientific laboratory or a government office building. It also helped bring about the end of a paternalistic era in science policy; scientists—and especially those who formulated policy based on scientific evidence—were for the first time accountable to the public. She remained modest about claiming credit. In a letter, she wrote, "But now I can believe that I have at least helped a little. It would be unrealistic to believe one book could bring a complete change." Few books, however, have been such powerful catalysts.

Her work represents an effort to foster a climate hospitable to what she hoped would emerge as "the next major phase in the development of biology. Here and there awareness is growing that man, far from being the overlord of all creation, is himself part of nature, subject to the same cosmic forces that control all other life. Man's future welfare and probably even his survival depend upon his learning to live in harmony, rather than in combat, with these forces."

Rachel Carson died at her home in Silver Spring, Maryland, on April 14, 1964. The Coastal Maine National Wildlife Refuge was renamed in her memory in 1969, as the Rachel Carson National Wildlife Refuge. Opened in 1966, the refuge will ultimately comprise over nine thousand acres along fifty miles of the southern coast of Maine. With a varied topography that includes forested uplands, barrier beaches and dunes, coastal meadows, and salt marshes along the rocky shore that Rachel loved, the refuge offers protection to thousands of migratory birds each year.

Rachel summed up her vision of finding a happy medium between use and conservation in a letter she wrote to the *Washington Post* in 1953, not long after *The Sea Around Us*, her first major book, appeared. "The real wealth of the Nation lies in the resources of the earth—soil, water, forests, minerals, and wildlife. To utilize them for present needs while ensuring their preservation for future generations requires a delicately balanced and continuing program, based on the most extensive research. Their administration is not properly, and cannot be, a matter of politics."

The CBS television special that highlighted *Silent Spring* was screened at the 2007 Environmental Film Festival, along with a film, produced by the National Park Service, in which actress Meryl Streep read excerpts from Rachel's books. These remembrances commemorated the hundredth anniversary of her birth.

Virginia Apgar

A family that never sat down was one way Virginia Apgar described the household in which she grew up in suburban New Jersey. Born in 1909 to Charles Apgar and Helen Clarke, she was encouraged to pursue what interested her and ignore what didn't. Charles Apgar was an insurance executive whose avocations included science and music. Virginia emulated him in both areas, although she preferred biology and chemistry to the physical sciences that fascinated her father. When she wasn't studying or playing on school sports teams, she often joined her parents and brother to play music. One thing she didn't like doing was cooking. At a time when girls were expected to concentrate on the domestic sciences, she barely scraped through home economics.

At Mount Holyoke College, she worked at three part-time jobs to help pay her way, but still found time for seven varsity sports, writing for the college paper, acting in plays, and playing her violin in the school orchestra. When she graduated in 1929, with a B.A. in zoology, Virginia was one of four women accepted to the College of Physicians and Surgeons, Columbia University's medical school. She was fourth in the class of 1933 and began an internship in surgery at the university hospital, The Presbyterian Hospital, a specialty virtually closed to women at that time. As she later commented, "Even women won't go to a woman surgeon." Dr. Allen Whipple, chairman of the surgery department, suggested that Virginia explore anesthesiology, a medical specialty just then coming into its own.

Until the 1930s, anesthesia was generally performed by nurses, but as surgery itself got more complex, a demand emerged for more highly trained anesthesiologists. In addition, mortality rates for women giving birth in the United States were among the world's highest, and New York City was one of the areas spearheading efforts to improve the mother's chances of survival. Virginia began training under the nurse-anesthetists at Presbyterian, continued at the University of Wisconsin and New York's Bellevue Hospital, and became only the fiftieth doctor certified in anesthesiology in the United States.

When the Columbia-Presbyterian Medical Center formed its own department of anesthesiology in 1938, Virginia was appointed director. She was the first woman department head at the institution. Barely a decade later, she was named professor of anesthesiology at Columbia. The first woman with the rank of full professor, she had already formed a staff of physician-anesthesiologists, designed a training program for the hospital's residents, and introduced medical students to the new specialty of anesthesiology. As she did roughly every ten years throughout her career, Virginia also decided to shift gears; she handed her administrative responsibilities off to others in order to concentrate on clinical work. It's probably no coincidence that when she made the switch in 1949, anesthesia residents at Columbia also began doing a regular rotation in obstetrics.

Early in the 1950s, Virginia devised the deceptively simple test for evaluating newborn infants that is still used to measure the condition of the newborn immediately after birth and identify infants who need supplementary oxygen, resuscitation, or other forms of intervention. Called the Apgar score, after its inventor, a doctor or nurse checks the baby immediately after birth (in the first minute) and again after five minutes for the following: Appearance, Pulse, Grimace, Activity, and Respiration. Each criterion receives a score of 0 to 2. Total scores above 7 are satisfactory; babies who score between 4 and 7 require careful observation; and those whose scores are 3 or lower are in need of immediate intervention.

It's unlikely that the often-repeated anecdote about how the Apgar score came into being is true, but the story does reflect Virginia's legendary enthusiasm, energy, and responsiveness to people of whatever rank. As the tale is usually told, she was having a quick breakfast with a medical student one morning when the student asked how to assess the health of a newborn baby. "That's easy," Virginia is supposed to have replied, "You'd do it this way." Grabbing the proverbial napkin, she jotted down the five components of the Apgar score.

The inspiration, however, was probably Virginia's years of experience inside the delivery room, where in the course of assisting at more than seventeen thousand births, she found attention focused on the mother, to the potential detriment of the newborn. As she later wrote in *Is My Baby All Right?* (1972), "Birth is the most hazardous time of life. . . . It's urgently important to evaluate quickly the status of a just-born baby and to identify immediately those who need emergency care." Instead, infants who seemed healthy were quickly transferred to the hospital nursery, where no one looked for signs of conditions requiring urgent intervention. Too often, when it was realized that they needed help, it was already too late.

"I kept wondering who was really responsible for the newborn. I began putting down all the signs about the newborn babies that could be observed without special equipment and that helped spot the ones that needed emergency help." As an anesthesiologist, Virginia was more aware than most of the potentially adverse affects for newborn infants of anesthetics that didn't harm the mothers, but she believed that anyone—nurse or physician—could administer the test.

Virginia's goal in developing the Apgar score and encouraging its widespread adoption was to reverse a common practice in delivery rooms at the time: newborns who appeared to have severe problems at birth were often neglected. No attempt was made to rescue them, and they eventually stopped breathing on their own. In the official report, these infants were listed as "stillborn." Virginia's approach was to save as many infants as possible, whether by resuscitation or other means, and she promoted her point of view until it was adopted as standard practice. She studied the birth records of more than one thousand infants and reported on her new methodology in "A Proposal for a New Method of Evaluation of the Newborn Infant," in 1953. The Apgar score was quickly adopted in delivery rooms everywhere. The test wasn't designed to predict the long-term health of newborn infants; there are many latent conditions that cannot be detected in the first few minutes of life. What the Apgar score continues to do, however, is quickly measure the vital signs—skin color, heart rate, breathing, reflexes, and muscle tone—that offer clues to initial well-being or the need for immediate intervention.

Virginia's search for ways to improve neonatal health didn't end with the Apgar score and the more aggressive role it implied for those in the delivery room. She and her colleagues looked for ways to detect other problems of the newborn, as well as to adapt procedures in the delivery room so that they would favor better outcomes for mother and child. For example, she identified safer anesthetics and anesthesiological procedures and helped advance understanding of the best methods for administering transfusions and oxygen to newborns.

Unwilling to rest on her laurels, Virginia returned to school in the late 1950s, this time to earn a master's degree from the Johns

Hopkins School of Public Health in 1959. One year earlier, the March of Dimes had decided to broaden its focus to birth defects, and the organization offered Virginia the directorship of its new department. With characteristic self-deprecating humor, she said, "They said they were looking for someone with enthusiasm, who likes to travel and talk. I love to see new places, and I certainly can chatter." (She was famous as a rapid-fire, nonstop talker.)

In her role as the public face of the foundation, Virginia chose research grant recipients, raised money, and educated professional and lay audiences about efforts to combat birth defects around the world. She traveled constantly, played a crucial role in more than doubling the money available each year, and helped to establish birth defects as a medical subspecialty. In her eighth year at the foundation, she also took over as director of basic research. Virginia was credited with "doing more than any other physician to bring the problem of birth defects out of the back rooms."

The professional recognition and honors Virginia received would fill several pages, but her avocations revealed a remarkable versatility. Endlessly energetic, Virginia continued to be active in sports and to play music, as well as to build her own string instruments. There is still an annual string quartet played on instruments she made at New York Presbyterian Hospital in the Washington Heights section of Manhattan. Famous for carrying the equipment physicians need to perform emergency resuscitation with her at all times, the remark of Virginia's that is most often quoted is "Nobody, but nobody, is going to stop breathing on me." Unfortunately, her own life was cut short by chronic liver disease on August 7, 1974. Virginia Apgar was just sixty-five.

chpt. 6 — goes to pp. 292

CHAPTER 6

Lifting the Veil of Nature

The Nobel Prize in Science

FOR A RESEARCH WORKER, THE UNFORGOTTEN MOMENTS
OF HIS LIFE ARE THOSE RARE ONES, WHICH COME AFTER YEARS OF
PLODDING WORK, WHEN THE VEIL OVER NATURE'S SECRET SEEMS
SUDDENLY TO LIFT AND WHEN WHAT WAS DARK AND CHAOTIC
APPEARS IN A CLEAR AND BEAUTIFUL LIGHT AND PATTERN.
–Gerty Cori

The highest global recognition for research in physiology or medicine is the Nobel Prize, given each year in Stockholm, Sweden. In the United States, the Lasker Award is the most coveted. The few American women who have received one or both of these awards had to overcome the prejudice against women in scientific fields simply to get the positions in laboratories that made it possible for them to pursue their research interests. Some were even discouraged from attending college or university. The common denominator they all share is brilliance that ultimately made it impossible for their excellent work to be ignored.

GERTY CORI

It was the love of medicine that brought Gerty Radnitz and Carl Cori together, and devotion to scientific research and to each other that brought them the Nobel Prize in 1947. They were both born in Prague in 1896 and met when they entered medical school at the city's Carl Ferdinand University in 1914. Their backgrounds, however, were quite different. Prague was at the time part of Austria-Hungary, and Carl was descended from an old Austrian Catholic family whose members included many professors at the university. The bond was so strong that his parents chose to name him Carl Ferdinand. When he was two, his father, who had doctorates in medicine and zoology, became director of the Marine Biological Station in Trieste. Carl remembered the cosmopolitan port as "a fascinating city in which to grow up" and believed that attending school with German, Italian, and Yugoslav children who spoke several different languages made him immune to the racial prejudices that later swept through much of Europe. During vacations, Carl helped his father collect marine samples in the area around Trieste, absorbing scientific and historical lore as they traveled, visiting Roman archeological sites, and climbing in the Tyrolean Alps

Gerty's family had also lived in Prague for generations and were part of the circle of Jewish intellectuals and artists that included the writer Franz Kafka. Her father, Otto Radnitz, was a chemist who invented a method of refining sugar that led to a successful career in industry. Gerty and her two younger sisters were tutored at home before entering private school when they were ten. An uncle who was a professor of pediatrics encouraged her to study medicine. Few young women went to medical school in Austria-Hungary at the time, in part because only boys could attend a gymnasium, the only schools where the Latin, mathematics, and science courses that were indispensable for the rigorous medical school entrance examinations were offered. For two years after graduating from the girls' lyceum in Prague, Gerty studied privately for the medical school qualifying exams. In 1914, she took and passed them at a gymnasium in the Bohemian town of Tetschen (now Decin, in the Czech Republic).

Gerty and Carl hit it off immediately after meeting when they started their medical studies and spent as much time as possible together: studying, walking in the countryside, and taking ski trips. Their idyll was interrupted in 1916 or 1917, however, when Carl was drafted into the Austrian army and worked in several hospitals, including one in Slovenia that specialized in infectious diseases and another at a field hospital near the front in Italy. During this period, Gerty was in Prague, working in a military clinic for soldiers who had fallen ill or been wounded and at a clinic for refugees who had moved westward to escape the fighting.

When the war ended, Carl returned to Prague, where he and Gerty received their medical degrees and published the first results of their joint research in 1920. Prague had been relatively untouched by the war, and people had enough to eat there. But in Vienna, where Carl and Gerty went in 1920 to do postdoctoral work, there were food shortages, and many patients who were victims of the 1918 influenza pandemic died of pneumonia, often within twenty-four to forty-eight hours. Carl, who divided his time between internal medicine and the pharmacology institute at the Allgemeines Krankenhaus, Vienna's largest hospital, told an interviewer in the 1980s that "I never wanted to practice medicine, because as a doctor you were completely helpless. . . . I thought that one knew so little, that one should go to the laboratory to find out what was going on." Carl was one of the few doctors able to carry on some research at the time. Resources were scarce, but his father caught sixty frogs, which he shipped to Carl, who kept them locked up so that his hungry colleagues wouldn't eat them. He investigated the effect of nerve stimulation on the frogs' heartbeat.

Carl and Gerty married in August 1920, in Vienna. She converted to Catholicism before the wedding, probably to placate Carl's very traditional family. Gerty worked at Vienna's Carolinen Children's

Hospital and did research on the role of the thyroid in regulating body temperature. She had to leave the city after contracting xerophthalmia, a drying of the eye that was caused by a vitamin A deficiency. Her doctors at first thought that she was suffering from tuberculosis, but it cleared up as soon as Gerty returned to Prague, where vitamin-rich vegetables, meat, and dairy products were more widely available.

Carl and Gerty were gaining valuable experience in Vienna, but the economic situation continued to deteriorate in much of Europe during the early 1920s. Neither of their positions in Vienna paid a salary; they had staff titles, but the material benefits were limited to the right to take meals in the hospital cafeteria. Anti-Semitism was also on the rise, so it seemed likely that Gerty might never be appointed to a permanent, salaried position in a hospital. In 1921, the University of Graz agreed to hire Carl only after he provided proof of his Aryan ancestry. Not even a pharmacologist as eminent as Otto Loewi, with whom Carl worked briefly at the University of Graz, was secure. In 1936, Loewi was awarded the Nobel Prize in Physiology or Medicine; two years later he was compelled to transfer his prize money to a Nazi-controlled bank before he was allowed to leave Austria. .

Determined to leave Europe as soon as possible, Carl and Gerty even applied to work as doctors in the Dutch colony of Java. But when Carl was invited to join the staff of the State Institute for the Study of Malignant Disease (now Roswell Park Cancer Institute) in Buffalo, New York, he immediately left for the United States and Gerty joined him a few months later. As they had done from the time they were medical students, the Coris worked together, despite being told that their collaboration would be harmful to Carl's career. He was hired as head of the biochemistry department, while Gerty was offered a position as assistant pathologist and was later made an assistant biochemist. When they published the results of their research—they wrote fifty joint papers during their ten years in Buffalo alone—the lead author was always the one who had done more of the work on the topic they were addressing. Gerty published another eleven papers on work that she had conducted independently.

The Coris had begun inquiring into the way the body metabolizes sugar while they were still in Europe. In 1929, they published their first description of what came to be called the Cori cycle, the process by which energy is transported, transformed, and stored. The muscles store sugar as glycogen until energy is needed for physical activity, when it is converted into the form of sugar known as glucose. Some sugar is always retained in the muscles as lactic acid, however, which is sent to the liver to be resynthesized into glycogen and then returned to the muscles for storage. This inexhaustible loop, from the muscles to the liver and back to the muscles, which guarantees that the body always has a residue of lactic acid from which to manufacture new glycogen, is the Cori cycle. Their 1929 discovery and subsequent experimental results were the first full demonstration of how carbohydrates function in the body. It led to many further insights and applications, especially in the understanding and treatment of diabetes and the identification of other glycogen storage diseases.

The Coris made their first important discoveries about sugar metabolism in Buffalo, but it would be in Saint Louis that Gerty finally received the recognition her work deserved. At the Roswell Institute, the Coris were warned that their collaboration would imperil Carl's career, but they insisted on working together as they always had done. A number of universities—among them, Rochester, Cornell, and Toronto—made offers to Carl because of the research that he and Gerty had conducted together, but none of them was willing to offer her an appointment. Universities were often prohibited from employing a professor's spouse because of nepotism rules, but prejudice played a role as well. The offer from Rochester was contingent on Carl's agreeing to stop collaborating with Gerty in his research. When he refused, the Rochester administration tried to convince Gerty that it was "un-American" for a husband and wife to work together. The Coris, who had become naturalized American citizens in 1928, were not dissuaded.

Finally, the Washington University School of Medicine, in St. Louis, invited Carl to chair their pharmacology department and agreed to make Gerty a research fellow in the same department. Years later, when serious illness prevented Gerty from maintaining her customary grueling schedule, she quipped to her colleague Mildred Cohn, "I don't feel guilty about accepting my full salary [now] in spite of my frequent absence, because when Carl and I first came here, they paid me 10 percent of that they paid him."

Despite Gerty's lack of status at Washington University, while Carl was busy organizing and running his department, overseeing the research laboratory, and teaching medical students, she was free to focus on their joint research. They did not maintain the torrid pace of publication of their Buffalo years, but they continued to produce significant results. By 1936, the year their son, Carl Thomas, was born, they had successfully identified the steps in the conversion of glycogen to glucose, in particular the role of glucose-1-phosphate, a phosphoric acid compound named for its position on the glucose molecule. Their work showed how G-1-P–which became known as the Cori ester–was involved in initiating the conversion of glycogen into glucose and back again. Through their research they were also successful in identifying the enzyme–which they named phosphorylase–that acts as the catalyst for the body's production of usable energy (glucose) and storable energy (glycogen).

After a decade at Washington University, the importance of Gerty's contributions began to be acknowledged. When the Coris shifted from pharmacology to the Department of Biological Chemistry in 1943, Gerty was at last given a professorial title: associate professor of research in biological chemistry and pharmacology. In 1947, at about the same time as the Nobel Prize in Medicine or Physiology was being conferred on the Coris for their joint discoveries, Gerty was at last promoted to the rank of professor of biological chemistry. She was the first American woman–and only the third woman (after Marie Curie, in 1903 and 1911, and Irène Joliot-Curie, in 1935)–to receive a Nobel Prize in science.

The Coris' St. Louis laboratory was never very large, even by the standards of the time, although after the couple won the Nobel Prize and job offers began pouring in, Carl was able to pressure the university to enlarge the facilities for the preclinical departments. They never seriously considered leaving Washington University, and after 1947 large numbers of younger scientists applied to work with them. Over the years, six future Nobel Prize winners came to St. Louis to work with the Coris in their laboratory.

The year 1947 brought triumph to Gerty Cori, but also misfortune. That summer she was diagnosed with myelofibrosis, a rare bone marrow disease for which there is still no effective therapy. Despite pain and weakness (severe anemia is one of the effects of myelofibrosis), she continued to work and publish until just a few months before her death. There was some consolation in the recognition, however belated, that she and Carl enjoyed. Numerous awards from scientific organizations, honorary degrees (including one from the University of Rochester, which had tried to discourage her from continuing her research in 1931), and two terms on the board of the National Science Foundation, beginning in 1952. At a ceremony at Hobart and William Smith Colleges in Geneva, New York, in 1949, Gerti was one of twelve women in science honored on the centenary of the first medical degree bestowed on a woman, Elizabeth Blackwell. But the tribute that meant the most to Gerty was probably Carl's, when at the Nobel banquet in Stockholm, December 10, 1947, he spoke of his "deep satisfaction" that they had been awarded the prize together. "Our collaboration began thirty years ago when we were still medical students at the University of Prague and has continued ever since. Our efforts have been largely complementary, and one without the other would not have gone as far as in combination."

On October 26, 1957, Gerty died of complications of myelofibrosis. Carl remained at Washington University until 1966. In 1960, he married Anne Fitzgerald-Jones. After his retirement from Washington University, he and his wife moved to Cambridge, where Carl became a visiting professor at the Harvard Medical School. He died in 1984.

MARIA GOEPPERT-MAYER

In 1910, when Maria Goeppert was four years old, her family moved from Kattowitz (then part of Germany, now Katowice, Poland) to Göttingen, where her father, Friedrich Goeppert, had been named professor of pediatrics at Georgia Augusta University. The sixth generation in his family to hold a university appointment, Maria's father encouraged his only child to fulfill her intellectual promise as well. Her mother, also named Maria, had taught French and music before her marriage. At a very young age, excited by the intellectual ferment at Göttingen and surrounded by many of the giants of physics and mathematics, she later recalled deciding, "I wasn't going to be just a woman."

When it was time for Maria to start preparing for the *abitur* (a rigorous examination that functioned as both a prerequisite for high school graduation and entrance to university), she enrolled in the only girls' preparatory school in Göttingen. Due to financial difficulties, that school actually folded before Maria was able to take the examination, but she continued studying privately and passed the *abitur* in 1924. She initially studied mathematics, but switched to physics, thanks largely to the excitement created by Max Born, a pioneer of quantum mechanics, and other scientists who flocked to Göttingen largely because of his presence. Looking back at her decision to change fields, Maria later said, "Mathematics began to seem too much like puzzle solving. Physics is puzzle solving, too, but of puzzles created by nature, not by the mind of man."

Maria completed her doctorate in theoretical physics in 1930. Three Nobel Prize winners were members of her doctoral committee; in addition to Born, who would be recognized in physics in 1954, there was the physicist James Franck (1925) and Adolf Windaus, whose 1928 prize was for chemistry. Her dissertation was devoted to the question of whether an electron orbiting an atom's nucleus would emit two photons (quanta of light) when it leaps to a position closer to the nucleus. Her calculation—that it *would* emit two photons—was later proved experimentally, and her original work continues to be cited in the scientific literature.

Before she left Göttingen, Maria married Joseph Mayer, a young American physical chemist, who had come to Göttingen in 1929 on a Rockefeller International Education Board Fellowship to study with Franck. The couple moved to Baltimore, where Joseph had been hired as an associate professor of chemistry at Johns Hopkins University. There was no thought of offering Maria an appointment, but the physics department arranged for her to have the title of research assistant. The position paid no salary, but it gave Maria workspace in the Physics Building, recognition within the university's scientific community, and, periodically, a chance to lecture to graduate students.

Vienna-born Karl F. Herzfeld was the one physicist at Johns Hopkins when Maria arrived whose interests straddled both theoretical and chemical physics. This was also the area in which Joseph Mayer was working, and throughout the 1930s, Maria broadened her range to encompass this field as well. At the same time, she took advantage of her relatively unfettered situation to work with the Johns Hopkins experimentalists as well, and to revive her interest in mathematics through associations with several of the university's mathematicians. The bulk of her time, however, was spent with Joseph and Karl. She co-authored a number of papers with Karl Herzfeld and with her husband, and in 1940 she and Joseph published *Statistical Mechanics*, one of the first textbooks in the area of physics that deals with microscopic bodies. The collaboration with Dr. Herzfeld ended when he left Johns Hopkins to become chairman of the physics department at Catholic University in Washington, D.C., but the Mayers and the

Herzfelds remained lifelong friends even as their careers increased the physical distance between the two couples.

Despite Maria's marginal status at Johns Hopkins, she did teach occasional graduate courses, and her students later recalled that she could be intimidating. They found her familiarity with theoretical physics unnerving, and her lecturing style—highly technical, with little attention to background—could feel overwhelming. At the same time, the students appreciated the interest she took in their work, and they also cultivated affection for the young married science couple and their two young children, Maria Ann and Peter—a rarity at a time when few women made it into the elite ranks of physics. They were missed by their students when they left Baltimore for Columbia University, where Joseph Mayer had been offered an associate professorship in chemistry, in 1939.

For the first several years after they settled in the United States (1931–1933), Joe and Maria returned to Göttingen for the summers. There, Maria was able to continue working with Born, with whom she wrote "Dynamische Gittertheorie der Kristalle" (A Dynamic Latticework Theory of Crystals), which was published in *Handbuch der Physik* in 1931. Working on her own, she also published "Double beta-disintegration" in the journal *Physical Review* in 1935. Her paper predicted, accurately, that in some isotopes, two neutrons in the nucleus are transmuted into protons. The work, which employed the techniques she had developed in her doctoral thesis, helped advance understanding in the increasingly important area of nuclear physics.

Columbia proved even less hospitable to Maria than Johns Hopkins had been. She was given an office in the physics department, but no title, and, of course, no salary. At the end of 1941, however, nearby Sarah Lawrence College offered her a half-time teaching appointment, and she continued teaching there until the end of World War II. When Harold Urey started Columbia's Substitute Alloy Materials Project (SAM) in 1942, he hired Maria as a half-time researcher in the effort to separate uranium-235 from natural uranium to provide fuel for nuclear fission. At about the same time, Edward Teller recruited her to work on the Opacity Project, also based at Columbia, which was investigating matter and radiation at high temperatures, part of the effort to produce nuclear reactions and weapons. For several months of this research, in spring 1945, Maria, Edward, and other physicists–including Niels Bohr and Enrico Fermi–worked together at Los Alamos National Laboratory in New Mexico.

After the war, the Opacity Project moved to the University of Chicago, where Dr. Teller had joined the faculty. Maria and Joe also relocated to Chicago in 1946, he as a professor in the Department of Chemistry and the new Institute for Nuclear Studies, and she as an *unpaid* associate professor of physics at the institute. When the Argonne National Laboratory was founded, Maria was recruited to work there by Robert Sachs, one of her Johns Hopkins graduate students, and became a half-time senior physicist in the lab's Theoretical Physics Division. Argonne's mission included searching for peaceful applications of nuclear power. Maria was intimately involved in these efforts and did a great deal of her important work during her association with the laboratory. Among other things, she was the first person to solve the criticality problem–determining the mass of material needed to sustain nuclear fission–using a computer, the ENIAC, at Aberdeen Proving Ground in Maryland.

Maria's research during her association with the Argonne National Laboratory included her theory of the structure of atomic nuclei. She called it the "nuclear shell model" and described the electrons of the nucleus as orbiting in stable paths ("shells"). From this initial observation, she also inferred that some atoms are more stable than others, in particular those with 2, 8, 20, 28, 50, 82 and 126 protons or neutrons. She called these "magic numbers," because of their ability to stabilize atoms. Her theory went a long way toward explaining why some atomic nuclei are stable and why isotopes–atoms of an element containing differing numbers of protons–exist for some elements but not others. At about the same time, J. Hans D. Jensen, working independently of Maria, came to the same conclusions. They met in 1950 and one year later decided to pool their resources, develop the shell model together, and collaborate on a book about their discovery, which was published as *Elementary Theory of Nuclear Shell Structure* in 1955.

At Argonne, Maria learned most of her nuclear theory and set up a system of magic numbers to represent the numbers of protons and neutrons arranged in shells in the atom's nucleus. After developing her shell model of nuclear structure, she spent a long time looking for data to support it, especially since it did not conform to then-current ideas about quantum mechanics. She spent hours discussing the theory with her husband, whose knowledge of chemistry proved invaluable, and with Enrico Fermi, who had moved from Columbia to the University of Chicago at the same time as the Mayers. As often happened with this profoundly insightful thinker, it was Enrico who asked the question that led Maria to unlock the mystery. According to Joseph Mayer, Maria and Enrico were talking in her office when a telephone call for the Italian physicist interrupted them. As he left the room, Dr. Fermi offhandedly asked, "Is there any indication of spin-orbit coupling?"

Spin-orbit coupling describes a pair of motions that occur in tandem. One familiar example is the earth rotating on its axis as it concurrently orbits the sun. Like the earth, an electron spins as it orbits the nucleus. Maria immediately grasped the entire picture. "When he said it, it all fell into place. In ten minutes I knew . . . I finished my computations that night. Fermi taught it to his class the next week." Her theoretical and empirical results were published in a series of articles in the *Physical Review* between 1948 and 1950.

Joseph Mayer later remembered the conversation that followed Enrico's return from talking on the phone, and how surprised the physicist was at the swiftness with which Maria picked up on the implications of his question. Enrico "returned less than ten minutes later and Maria started to 'snow' him with the detailed explanation. . . . Maria, when excited, had a rapid-fire oral delivery, whereas

Enrico always wanted a slow detailed and methodical explanation. Enrico smiled and left: 'Tomorrow, when you are less excited, you can explain it to me.'"

One year following the publication of *Elementary Theory of Nuclear Shell Structure*, Maria was finally elected to the National Academy of Sciences. She had been publishing important scientific papers for a quarter century, including the one with Dr. Born (whose own Nobel Prize was belatedly conferred only in 1954). At last, the world seemed in a hurry to catch up with Maria's already distinguished career. When the University of California at San Diego opened in 1960, Maria was a professor of physics–her first full-time job–at the new campus. She was fifty-four years old.

Less than a year after the Mayers moved to San Diego, Maria suffered a stroke and struggled with health problems for the rest of her life. She continued to do research, to teach, and to publish, however. In 1963, Maria Goeppert-Mayer and Hans Jensen won the Nobel Prize for Physics for their description of the nuclear shell model. They shared the prize with Eugene Paul Wigner, whose work also dealt with quantum mechanics and who called Maria's doctoral thesis "a masterpiece of clarity and completeness." The second woman to win the Nobel Prize for Physics (Marie Curie was the first), Marie was the first woman to be recognized for work in the field of theoretical physics. She may well have smiled when she saw the headline in a San Diego newspaper: "S.D. Mother Wins Nobel Prize."

In 1971, a heart attack left Maria in a coma. She died on February 20, 1972. Two important awards were established in her memory, both of them earmarked for young women scientists. Argonne National Laboratory annually selects the Maria Goeppert-Mayer Distinguished Scholar from among woman scientists and engineers at early stages of their careers. Awardees conduct research at ANL and receive a salary and cash honorarium to enable the young scientist to conduct innovative research using Argonne's resources. Each year, the American Physical Society gives the Maria

Goeppert-Mayer Award, with a stipend and travel allowance, for outstanding achievement to a young woman physicist. The winner delivers a series of lectures on physics at four institutions and the society's annual meeting.

ROSALYN YALOW

Rosalyn Yalow was born in New York City in 1921, the second child of Simon and Clara Sussman. Her father was born on New York's Lower East Side to immigrants from eastern Europe, and her mother came to the United States from Germany when she was four. Neither of them completed high school, but they were eager for their son, Alexander, and their daughter to receive the best educations possible. Both of the children were early readers who started borrowing books from the public library in their Bronx neighborhood even before they entered primary school.

Rosalyn's parents were pleased that their daughter showed a gift for science, but when she entered Hunter College for Women (now part of the City University of New York) in 1937, they urged her to become an elementary school teacher and not set her sights on a career as a scientist. At the time, few women studied for advanced degrees, especially in the sciences, and even fewer were able to find employment in those fields. But Rosalyn, encouraged by two of her physics professors, tenaciously stuck with physics, inspired partly by Enrico Fermi's 1939 lecture at Columbia University about the newly discovered phenomenon of nuclear fission.

Rosalyn graduated from Hunter in 1941. She wasn't assured of being accepted into a Ph.D. program, so for a while she considered a compromise offer arranged by one of her Hunter professors: working part-time as a secretary to a biochemist at the Columbia University medical school while taking graduate courses in physics, as a way of cajoling her way to full-time status in Columbia's doctoral program. In March 1941, however, she jumped at an offer of a teaching assistantship in physics from the University of Illinois, to start in September.

Rosalyn arrived at the Champagne-Urbana campus several months before Pearl Harbor, but she quickly realized that one reason she'd been invited to Illinois was that the prewar draft had already reduced the pool of young men applying for advanced degrees. Some men were already in the military, and others had gone to work in defense industries to qualify for deferments that gave them at least a temporary reprieve from being called up. Nevertheless, Rosalyn was astonished to find that she was the only woman with faculty rank in the entire College of Engineering. In fact, the dean revealed, the last time the faculty had included a woman was in 1917, when the United States was also on the brink of war. For a young woman who, except for three undergraduate physics classes, had spent the previous ten years at a single-sex secondary school and college, being the only female was an uncomfortable novelty.

There were other adjustments for Rosalyn as well. Because Hunter had added the physics major when she was already a senior, her foundation in the subject was spotty. To compensate, in her first year at Illinois she audited undergraduate courses at the same time as she took her full complement of graduate physics and taught a freshman course. With no prior teaching experience, Rosalyn felt unprepared, so she attended the lectures of one of the young faculty members in order to pick up pedagogical pointers.

Instead of being praised for getting straight As in her courses while making the difficult adjustment to an alien world, Rosalyn had to suffer in silence when the department chairman, noticing the A minus she received in Optics lab, commented dismissively, "That A minus confirms that women do not do well at laboratory work." But she was doing what she had dreamed of doing and refused to allow long-held prejudice to discourage her.

Fortunately for Rosalyn, there were also people in the Illinois physics department who befriended and encouraged her, especially

Maurice and Gertrude Goldhaber, eminent husband-and-wife physicists who later moved to the Brookhaven National Laboratories. Maurice directed her doctoral dissertation, but Gertrude worked as an unsalaried scientist because the nepotism rules common at the time prohibited the hiring of spouses of faculty members. Another physics graduate student who arrived in Champagne-Urbana in September 1941 was Aaron Yalow, from Syracuse, New York. Rosalyn and Aaron married in 1943.

Shortly after the country entered the war in December 1941, the physics faculty at Illinois, like their colleagues at other institutions, often left to participate in defense-related work. Although Rosalyn's focus was on nuclear physics and she became an expert in the measurement of radioactive materials, she remained on campus and completed her Ph.D. in January 1945, barely three years after she had arrived in the Midwest. During that time, the campus was full of soldiers and sailors being trained in universities. Rather than remain in Illinois—where her department would never have considered hiring her as a regular faculty member—Rosalyn returned to New York and a research position at ITT. A year later, when the laboratory relocated, Rosalyn elected to take a job teaching physics at her alma mater; at this time, however, her students weren't undergraduate women but veterans enrolled in a pre-engineering program under the GI Bill.

By then, Aaron Yalow had rejoined Rosalyn in New York, where he took a position as a medical physicist at Montefiore Hospital in the Bronx. Rosalyn herself was interested in doing research in the medical uses of radioisotopes. Through professional acquaintances, she met Dr. Bernard Roswit, head of radiotherapy at the Bronx Veterans Administration Hospital, and started working part-time at the Bronx VA in 1947. In 1950, she resigned from Hunter College and moved to a full-time position developing the Radioisotope Service she had started three years earlier in a converted janitor's closet at the hospital. Rosalyn had conducted clinical investigations with Roswit and other VA physicians and published the results of eight of them. The collaborator with whom Rosalyn would carry out her most important work, however, was Solomon A. Berson, who completed his residency at the Bronx VA in spring 1950 and joined the Radioisotope Service in July. For twenty-two years, until Sol's death in 1972, the physicist and the physician worked together to produce the work that led in 1977 to Rosalyn becoming the first American-born woman to win a Nobel Prize in a science category.

Rosalyn traces her remarkable collaboration to the ease with which she and Sol learned from one another. Neither had made a formal study of investigative technique, but Rosalyn's doctoral research made her an expert in measuring radioactive substances, and working with Sol at the Bronx VA, she absorbed the art of medicine "directly from a master of physiology, anatomy and clinical medicine." Following a number of studies involving the measurement of radioisotopes in blood, the rate at which the thyroid and kidneys removed iodine from the blood, and analysis of serum proteins, in the mid–1950s Rosalyn and Sol turned their attention to hormones. The most accessible hormone–because highly purified samples were available–was insulin. They observed that patients–whether they were diabetics or not–developed antibodies to the insulin, and that by combining radioactive isotopes of insulin with the antibodies, it was possible to ascertain the amount of insulin in a sample of the patient's blood. Insulin, of course, is the hormone that controls blood-sugar levels. Prior to Rosalyn and Sol's study, it was believed that type 2 (adult-onset) diabetes occurred in patients whose bodies didn't produce insulin. They demonstrated, however, that diabetes results from the body's inability to use insulin *efficiently*.

This discovery was a major contribution to the understanding of the mechanism of diabetes, and the measuring process, which Rosalyn and Sol called radioimmunoassay (RIA), opened the door to many diagnostic, research, and therapeutic methods. Once it was refined, their technique was capable of measuring minuscule quantities–as little as a trillionth of a gram of a substance per milliliter of blood. Also known as the Yalow-Berson method, RIA allowed researchers and diagnosticians to identify all the hormones present in a blood sample, as well as the quantities of those hormones. It is no exaggeration to state, as the Nobel Committee did when Rosalyn was awarded the Nobel Prize for Physiology or Medicine, that RIA led to "the birth of a new era in endocrinology" that has altered the practice of many areas of medicine.

RIA and similar techniques that have been based on it are now able to measure many different molecules for a wide range of applications, from screening for illegal drugs, such as narcotics or performance-enhancing drugs, to detecting diseases such as hepatitis and some forms of cancer, calculating effective dosages for medicines, measuring growth-hormone levels to treat dwarfism, adjusting hormone levels of fertility patients, and conducting research into brain chemistry. Rosalyn, with Sol (who left the laboratory in 1968 and died in 1972) and other collaborators, played an important role in many of these discoveries.

The technique is highly sophisticated, but RIA can be employed in relatively simple medical laboratories. To make the process as widely available as possible, Rosalyn and Sol declined to patent their discovery, despite its commercial potential. "We never thought of patenting RIA," she said later. "Patents are about keeping things away from people for the purpose of making money. We wanted others to be able to use RIA."

The scientific and medical communities were initially skeptical, however. Rosalyn and Sol's scientific paper reporting their results was rejected for publication, largely because of their claim that the insulin had caused an immune reaction. At the time, the scientific community believed that these hormones were too small to stimulate an antibody reaction. Their paper was published in 1956, after the authors agreed to remove the word "antibody" from the title, and four years later they demonstrated that the human immune system did make antibodies in response to such small molecules and that their new methodology provided the technology that permitted them to prove it.

The second American woman (after Gerty Cori) to receive a Nobel Prize in Physiology or Medicine, Rosalyn had a year earlier (1976) become the first female winner of The Albert Lasker Award for Basic Medical Research. President Reagan bestowed the National Medal of Science on her in 1988, three years before she retired from the lab–renamed the Solomon A. Berson Research Laboratory in 1972, in memory of her collaborator, the lab that she had transformed from a janitor's closet to a world-class research facility.

BARBARA McCLINTOCK

As a very young child, Barbara (named Eleanor at birth) McClintock sometimes shuttled between her parents' home in Hartford, Connecticut, and an aunt and uncle in Massachusetts. According to some versions of her history, Barbara and her mother had a strained relationship, but at the time it wasn't unusual for extended family members to help with childrearing. In 1904, when Barbara, was two, Sara Handy McClintock gave birth to her fourth child and only son, Malcolm Rider. Despite their given names, her parents called their two youngest children Barbara and Tom. The two older children, both girls, were Marjorie and Mignon. It's likely that Barbara went to live for a while with her relatives in order to ease the burden on her mother, a part-time piano teacher who also wrote poetry and painted. Barbara's father, Thomas Henry McClintock, the son of British immigrants, was a homeopathic physician who often struggled financially to provide for his family.

Barbara had an unconventional childhood, especially for the early twentieth century. Sara McClintock, a Mayflower descendant, believed that her daughters should prepare for marriage, not careers, but Barbara's upbringing was anything but ladylike. In Campello, Massachusetts, she enjoyed accompanying her uncle, who sold fish, as he made his rounds in a horse-drawn wagon and, later, by truck. She traced her mechanical bent and her love of cars and nature to his influence. From her father she got a pair of boxing gloves when she was four years old, and her parents indulged her preference for outdoor activities—ice skating and roller skating, biking and ball games—over more feminine pursuits. From an early age, Barbara displayed a fierce independence, which her parents accepted and may have actively encouraged. When she took an extreme dislike to a teacher, her father arranged to have her study with a tutor, and when the weather was right, they saw nothing wrong with her playing hooky in order to spend the day ice skating. Once, when a neighbor told Barbara to act like a lady, Sara phoned the woman to ask her to stop meddling in her daughter's life.

The McClintocks moved to Brooklyn, New York, in 1908. Summers were spent in Long Beach, on Long Island's south shore, where Barbara remembered taking the family dog for solitary walks. "I used to love to be alone, just walking along the beach." By the time she entered Erasmus Hall High School in 1915, her family had gotten used to her habit of sitting quietly and thinking, and no longer wondered whether something was psychologically wrong with their daughter. In school, she loved problem solving so much that after sometimes finding her own original solution to a question, she would attack the same problem again, in order to find the "standard" answer as well.

Barbara was never antisocial, but during high school she didn't gravitate toward a group the way many adolescents do or feel a desire to conform socially. Sara worried that her daughter was turning into "a person who didn't belong to society," most likely because she wasn't maturing into the marriageable young lady she expected her daughters to become. Barbara, however, remembered feeling content, as long as she wasn't pressured "to conform in a group way."

Because of her family's financial circumstances and Sara McClintock's reservations about overeducated women, Barbara wasn't sure she would be able to attend Cornell University after graduating from Erasmus Hall in 1919. Shortly before the classes started in the fall, however, her father overruled his wife, and Barbara embarked for Ithaca, New York. She remained at Cornell until 1927, earning B.S., M.S., and Ph.D. degrees in botany in the course of eight years. She felt at home socially as well as intellectually, and was even elected president of the women's freshman class during her first year in college.

Cornell was already a prominent agriculture school in the 1920s, and the only undergraduate genetics course offered in Barbara's junior year was in the College of Agriculture's Department of Plant Breeding. At the time, genetics wasn't considered important to biologists. Most of the students in the course were agriculture majors with limited interest in the science for its own sake. For Barbara, however, it was a revelation. Professor C. B. Hutchison took note of her excitement, and when the course ended he invited her to register for a second, graduate-level genetics course that he was teaching in the spring semester of 1922. Of course, Barbara jumped at the invitation. As she recalled long afterward, "this telephone call cast the die for my future. I remained with genetics thereafter." By the end of the second semester, still an undergraduate, she was treated as a full-fledged member of the small coterie of Cornell graduate students studying maize cytogenetics, in Barbara's definition, "chromosomes and their genetic content and expressions" in corn—that is, how the plant reproduces and how it mutates.

While she was still a graduate student, Barbara applied the new staining techniques developed in the 1920s by John Belling to make her first major contribution to cytogenetics: the identification of the ten chromosomes of maize. This advance opened the door to a series of major discoveries made by the Cornell cytogenetics group by 1935, and Barbara played a major role in many of them. She would have been content to remain at Cornell for her entire career, but permanent appointments were scarce, especially for a woman. To make matters worse, mainstream biologists failed to appreciate the significance of early discoveries about genetics until much later. In Barbara's understated recollection, despite the conceptual framework provided by Gregor Mendel's principles of heredity, "there was reluctance on the part of some professional biologists to accept the revolutionary concepts that were surfacing."

From 1927, when she received her Ph.D., to 1931, Barbara was an instructor in botany at Cornell. She returned as a research associate in 1934, after three years on fellowships from the National Research Council and Guggenheim Foundation. Her Guggenheim Fellowship was intended to allow her to spend the 1933–1934 academic year at Kaiser-Wilhelm Institute in Berlin, working with Curt Stern, an eminent geneticist. By the time she left the United States, however, Stern was at the University of Rochester. He was one of the first German Jewish professors to leave his country because of the anti-Semitic policies that accompanied the rise of Nazism there. The head of the institute, Richard Goldschmidt, recommended that Barbara work at the Botanical Institute in Freiburg instead. Back at Cornell in late 1934, she wrote to Stern about her year in Germany. "I couldn't have picked a worse time. The general morale of the scientific worker was anything but encouraging. There were almost no students from other countries. The political situation and its devastating results were too prominent."

Lewis Stadler, of the University of Missouri, had shared his research on the effects of radiation on corn with Barbara and sent her strains of maize that he had irradiated. The X-rays caused some chromosomes to break, and Barbara began studying these processes. Most chromosomes did not break, and she attributed this to a structural feature of the chromosomal tip, which she called a telomere, that helps hold the chromosome together. Stadler arranged for Barbara to be hired as an assistant professor at Missouri in 1936. There, she discovered a breakage-fusion-bridge (bfb) cycle. Chromosomes would break, fuse at the point of rupture to form a bridge, and then break again at the same point when the cell divided.

By this time, Barbara's contributions to genetics were widely recognized in the scientific world. Nevertheless, her professional situation remained insecure. But after four years at the rank of assistant professor at Missouri, she decided that she would never be promoted or granted tenure at the university and decided to leave. She had clashed with Mary Guthrie, a biologist and protégée of the dean, Winterton C. Curtis, and feared that if Stadler left the university, as he had contemplated doing, her own position would be in jeopardy. Marcus Rhoades, a close friend and colleague from Cornell, offered to share his maize-growing plot at the Cold Spring Harbor Laboratory of the Carnegie Institution of Washington with Barbara during the summer of 1941 and arranged a visiting appointment for her at Columbia University, where he had recently joined the faculty. Before the fall semester began, Milislav Demerec, the new director of the Department of Genetics at Cold Spring Harbor, offered her a short-term appointment starting in September, which he pledged to convert to a full-time position as soon as he was able. In recommending her as a permanent scientist, Demerec praised Barbara for doing her work "so thoroughly and competently that there is no necessity for someone else to do additional work on the same problem." On April 1, 1942, her first day as a permanent staff member at Cold Spring Harbor, E. Carleton MacDowell, another geneticist at the laboratory, shouted, "We should mark today's date with red letters in the department calendar!"

Cold Spring Harbor turned out to be the perfect environment for Barbara. Although she wrote to a friend in St. Louis that the equipment in her new laboratory was inferior to Missouri's and she so jealously guarded her freedom that any job seemed to her a compromise, she was now free to pursue her own work in her own way. She wasn't expected to teach, something she despised doing, and she was less concerned about job discrimination because of her sex. As she wrote at the time, "I believe remaining here is the wisest thing to do–being a woman!" Barbara did remain until the end of her life. When she reached mandatory retirement age in 1967, she stayed on at Cold Spring Harbor as an emeritus scientist; her title was Distinguished Service Member. She also spent the decade from the mid-1960s to 1974 as Andrew D. White Professor-at-Large at

Cornell, an appointment that called for occasional public lectures and discussions with faculty and students, but no formal teaching. All this time, Cold Spring Harbor remained Barbara's home, and in 1980, as she neared her eightieth year, she bestowed on the Carnegie Institution, the laboratory's parent body, her most effusive praise, when she said, "That's what the Carnegie's for, to pick out the best people they can find and give them freedom."

Barbara had always preferred to follow her own insights with respect to the genetics of maize and not concern herself with the conventional wisdom. At times, she even refrained from publishing her results in order to avoid controversy, but when the thinking in molecular biology began to catch up with her ideas, recognition followed. As late as 1950, she explained that she hadn't "dared" to publish her observations of what she called "controlling elements" that regulated reproduction at the cellular level. "There is so much that is completely new and the implications are suggestive of an altered concept of gene mutation that I have not wanted to make any statements until the evidence was conclusive enough to make me confident" of its validity. In 1944, she was elected to the National Academy of Sciences—its third woman member—and the following year she was accepted into the Genetics Society of America, an organization she later headed. President Richard Nixon presented her with the National Medal of Science in 1971. Ten years later, she was the first person to receive a MacArthur Foundation "genius" grant, the same year she won the Lasker Award for basic medical research.

In 1983, her research into mobile genetic elements led to the Nobel Prize in Physiology or Medicine. She was the first woman—of any nationality—to receive an unshared Nobel Prize in Medicine. Her reaction revealed the same sense of wonder at nature and pleasure in research that characterized her entire career: "The prize is such an extraordinary honor. It might seem unfair, however, to reward a person for having so much pleasure over the years, asking the maize plant to solve specific problems and then watching its responses."

By the time of her Nobel, grants from the National Science

Foundation and the Rockefeller Foundation had allowed Barbara and a number of coscientists to carry out a quarter-century-long study of the varieties of maize in Central and South America. As Barbara explained in a letter to Curt Stern, the project to trace the origins of the various races of maize in the Americas began as a gesture of agricultural diplomacy with Latin America, "but it is proving to be quite interesting as a piece of research." Their analysis of the collection of maize samples, which demonstrated how varied the evolution of the species has been in the regions where it first grew, was published in 1981 as *The Chromosomal Constitution of Races of Maize.* It has been called a landmark study in evolutionary botany, ethnobotany, and paleobotany.

Barbara's revolutionary discoveries showed that genes weren't static elements, but could "move," and that the movement was connected to changes in corn from one generation to the next. By understanding the seemingly simple mechanisms that caused kernels of corn to change color, her work led the way to a deeper understanding of what genes do. Genetic mobility has now been shown to exist widely, in microorganisms such as bacteria, viruses, and yeast, and in insects, and animals, including human beings. In bacteria and viruses, mobile elements account for the ability of these microorganisms to transmit resistance to antibiotics. Some single-celled parasites use transposition to avoid their hosts' immune response; gene transposition also plays a role in turning normal cells into cancer cells, and it underlies the practice of genetic engineering. James Shapiro, a geneticist at the University of Chicago, called her the most important figure in biology in her time. At the end of the last century, scientists were still following the leads that Barbara had provided. Echoing one of Barbara's own statements–that "the real secret of all this is control. It is not transposition"–he observed, "The idea that the genome is capable of repairing itself, and that it is capable of reconstructing itself, that there are systems in the cell that can detect damage and do appropriate things to repair it, has tremendous implications for evolution as well as for genetics."

Barbara died at the age of ninety, of natural causes in a hospital near her home in Cold Spring Harbor, on September 2, 1992. Dr. James Watson, who shared the Nobel Prize in 1962 for his role in the discovery of the structure of DNA, was director of the Cold Spring Harbor Laboratory at the time of Barbara's death. He called her one of "the three Ms"–the three essential figures–in the history of the science of genetics. The other two are Gregor Mendel (1822–1884) and Thomas Hunt Morgan (1866–1945), who won the Nobel Prize in Medicine or Physiology–like Barbara's, unshared–in 1933.

RITA LEVI-MONTALCINI

In 1947, just about the time the Coris were informed of their Nobel Prize, Rita Levi-Montalcini, a young physician and neuroscientist, arrived in St. Louis from Turin, Italy. She had been invited by Viktor Hamburger, the illustrious embryologist at Washington University, to spend a semester or two in his laboratory. Seven years earlier, Rita had read Hamburger's 1934 article on nervous system development in chick embryos, repeated the original experiment, and published her different results in a Belgian journal. Hamburger proposed that they explore the issue together.

Rita's early life did not point toward a Nobel Prize. She was born in Turin in 1909, the youngest of Adamo Levi and Adele Montalcini's four children. Both families were members of Italy's old, distinguished community of Sephardic Jews. Her father, an electrical engineer and entrepreneur, was opposed to professional careers for his daughters; he believed that women were destined for marriage and refused to let Rita, Paola (her twin sister), or their older sister Anna attend university. Anna accepted the role of wife and mother, Paola became a painter, but Rita decided that "the subordinate role played by the female in a society run entirely by men made the status of a wife less than attractive," and she implored her father to permit her to attend medical school. At first he objected that "it was a long and difficult course of study, unsuitable for a woman," but he finally gave in to his daughter's persistent pleading. Joined by her cousin Eugenia, she spent eight months in 1930 intensively studying Latin, Greek, and mathematics in order to meet the high school graduation requirements. Rita's score on the medical school entrance examinations was the highest of that year's applicants. When she and Eugenia matriculated at the University of Turin's medical school, there were just five other young women in attendance.

Rita distinguished herself as a first-year medical student, but late in her second year, her father began to have symptoms of heart trouble. His businesses—an ice plant and a distillery in Bari— were doing poorly, and he compounded his difficulties by building new facilities in Turin despite the global economic depression. In 1932, after a series of heart attacks, Adamo Levi died.

Among the students at Turin were two friends of Rita's, Salvador Luria and Renato Dulbecco, who turned out to be future Nobel Prize winners in Physiology or Medicine as well. Their rigorous grounding in scientific method was largely due to Giuseppe Levi (no relation), a renowned histologist who terrified and inspired his students in equal measure. Levi was immensely popular at the university, not only because of his stature as a scientist but also for his outspoken antifascism. When Rita graduated in 1936, summa cum laude, she started a three-year training program in neurology and psychiatry, unsure whether she wanted to practice medicine full-time or devote at least part of her time to neurological research. That decision was made for her when Mussolini's Fascist government issued a series of declarations and laws that excluded Jews from the universities and the professions. She worked at a neurological institute in Brussels until just before the German army occupied Belgium in 1940. Her family decided to remain in Italy rather than emigrate, and Rita's brother Gino, an architect, helped her design and build a small table-top "laboratory" that she set up in her bedroom. For a short time, she also treated poor patients in

Turin at no charge, but the necessity of finding an "Aryan" physician to sign prescriptions made practicing too risky.

Rita's research project was the one she had seen described by Viktor Hamburger in the *Journal of Experimental Zoology*. Giuseppe Levi, who had also returned to Turin from Belgium when the Nazis invaded, helped her carry out her experiment. When the Allies began bombing Turin, a major industrial center, in 1941, the Levi-Montalcinis moved to a village about an hour away from the city. Rita took her mini laboratory with her, bought fertilized eggs from local farmers that she used to continue her experiments, and published the results in *Extrait des Archives de Biologie* in 1942. Contrary to the conventional wisdom of the time, that the nervous system was fixed, Rita began to see it as "plastic and malleable."

In her memoirs, Rita remembered the Italians as imbued with anti-Nazi feelings and sympathetic to persecuted people, and who "offered Jews protection at grave risk to themselves" throughout the land. But after Italy surrendered to the Allies in 1943 and the German army invaded the country, the Levi-Montalcinis attempted unsuccessfully to cross into Switzerland and then fled to Florence. Armed with false identity papers, they were able to rent a room in Florence from Consilia Leoncini, whom they contacted through a friend of Paola's. Consilia initially insisted that she would not offer shelter to Jews. They soon learned, however, that Consilia, an anti-fascist, had seen through their story immediately, and before long she invited them to join her in the evenings to listen to the BBC news broadcasts with her family. For a while, the city was relatively calm, and Rita was able to help Giuseppe Levi, who had reunited with his family in Florence, edit a new edition of his two-volume histology textbook.

In September 1944, after a tense month of fighting between German soldiers and Italian partisans, British troops reached Florence and the city was liberated. Rita offered her services as a doctor and was assigned to a makeshift hospital in a decaying barracks. Her patients were refugees who flooded the city from the area near

Bologna in the north, where fighting continued between German and Allied forces. Without a nurse to assist her, Rita treated infants and old people, many of them malnourished and dehydrated. The death toll was high and grew worse, as overcrowding and polluted water brought on an epidemic of typhoid. When the European war ended in May 1945, Rita's family was able to go home to Turin, and she returned to the university, where she resumed her work as an assistant lecturer in anatomy. Her experience among the refugees in Florence was so demoralizing that she decided never to practice medicine again.

When Viktor Hamburger's invitation to work in his laboratory at Washington University reached her, Rita accepted immediately. She intended to spend a year in St. Louis, but the results of her research were so encouraging that she ended up staying for thirty years. Together, she and Hamburger revisited the research each had originally done separately, into the effects of how amputation of the wings of chick embryos affects the development of their nervous systems. The results corroborated Rita's original findings. In 1956, she was made an associate professor at the university, and two years later she was promoted to full professor.

The most fruitful period of Rita's research occurred from 1953 to 1959, when Stanley Cohen, an American-born biochemist, joined the laboratory as a research associate. Each of them had an expertise in an area that the other knew relatively little about, and they educated one another. Rita, the neuroscientist, imparted her knowledge of the nervous system to Stanley, while he shared his knowledge of biochemistry with her. Rita discovered that minute quantities of a substance taken from tumors in mice stimulated the growth of nerve fibers within as little as thirty seconds. She noted that growth occurred even without direct contact between the tumor and in-vitro nerve cells, and she called the growth-causing substance nerve growth factor (NGF). In the course of several years, she and Stanley succeeded in isolating NGF, finding new sources of it, purifying it, and even developing antibodies to it, so that nerve growth could be accelerated or stopped. During this immensely fruitful period, Stanley effusively told her, "You and I are good, Rita, but together we are wonderful."

The discovery of NGF provided a glimpse into the mechanisms by which cells grow, differentiate, and survive—all of great interest to scientists in many fields. It also predicted the existence of other growth factors, and a number have been identified, including epidermal growth factor (EGF), which Stanley discovered in the course of his continuing research into NGF. EGF stimulates the growth of a variety of cells. Its medical potential appears virtually unlimited. For understanding cellular development and malfunction, it opens a window on birth defects and degenerative diseases like Alzheimer's, muscle-wasting diseases, the formation of tumors, and even the way wounds heal. Some of this new comprehension may lead to cures or prevention of some of the cruelest illnesses that afflict human beings, including cancer and senile dementia.

Rita has called the period from 1953 to 1959, when she and Stanley identified NGF, analyzed its composition, and learned to regulate it, "the six most intense and productive years of my life." However, they also put her in conflict with Hamburger, the head of the laboratory and Rita's original collaborator. In 1959, Stanley was forced out of Washington University and moved to Vanderbilt University, where he did most of the actual work on EGF. Rita never confronted Hamburger about Stanley's sudden departure, but hearing that Stanley was leaving the laboratory "sounded to her like the tolling of a funeral bell." Discreetly, however, in 1961 she created greater independence for herself by establishing a sister laboratory in Rome, with the help of a grant from the National Science Foundation. She holds dual citizenship in the United States and Italy, and until she retired from Washington University, she divided her year between the two countries. In Italy, she was director of the Institute of Cell Biology of the Italian National Council of Research. After her retirement, she and her twin sister, Paola, lived together in Rome until Paola's death in 2000.

In 1986, Rita Levi-Montalcini and Stanley Cohen received the Nobel Prize in Medicine or Physiology. The Nobel Committee praised Rita's accomplishment in discerning that nerve cell growth was fostered by a substance that traveled through bodily fluids as "a fascinating example of how a skilled observer can create a concept out of apparent chaos." That same year the two researchers were also the recipients of the Albert Lasker Award for Basic Medical Research. She was the fourth American woman to win a Nobel Prize in Medicine.

In the 1990s, Rita turned increasingly to humanitarian efforts, devoting particular attention to helping young women pursue their educations. With that goal in mind, she founded the Levi-Montalcini Foundation in 1992. In 1993, she was struck by words written by a young girl in a collection of letters by Bosnian children. Addressing the Serbs, the child wrote, "My angry people must forgive me if I cannot hate you, because I think that we twelve-year-olds have not yet fallen into the abyss of hatred." Through journalists working in Bosnia, Rita located the girl, Tomana Grubesic, by then a student at Zagreb University, invited her to Rome and gave her a Levi Montalcini Foundation scholarship to continue her studies. and to assist young people in the difficult choices regarding their fields of study. "I wanted her," she said, "to become an emblem of the new generations. Without hatred."

In 2001, the same year that she was made a senator for life in Italy, Rita shifted the focus of her foundation's work to educating women in Africa. Her small foundation, which has assisted hundreds of women, has also succeeded in attracting the attention of other organizations, including the American Jewish Joint Distribution Committee, which is collaborating with the Fondazione Levi-Montalcini in Ethiopia. A number of women have already graduated from Unity University in Addis Ababa, and others are continuing to study nursing, business, and law, among other fields. Most of the women are from villages; one of the tasks of the program is to help them adjust to city life. Manilo Dell'Ariccia, the country director for Ethiopia at the American Jewish Joint Distribution Committee, which provides on-site support, has said that it is impossible to calculate the impact of Rita's efforts. "In a country like Ethiopia, the possibility of female students coming from rural areas to study at the university level is almost zero."

Thanks to the support of other foundations and donors, the program to educate young women in Africa has been extended to ten countries on the continent. Rita sees her efforts as a small step toward African self-sufficiency and reversing the mass migrations that have exacerbated the problems these poor countries face. Ethiopia is one of the world's poorest countries, its literacy rate for teenaged girls is about 30 percent (and for boys less than 50 percent), and girls are often subjected to arranged marriages when they are as young as eight. As a result, girls are denied even basic education, health problems abound, and physical abuse is common.

Education offers the possibility of undoing the pattern. As Askale Sisay Ayele, one of Fondazione Levi-Montalcini's scholars, wrote, "Women's education is especially important." Ayele, one of six children from a poor rural family, studied marketing. "Because if one woman is educated, her whole family is educated, indirectly."

Study after study shows this insight is correct. Through the organization Vital Voices, which promotes women's education and rights throughout the world, I have seen the effects gender equality has on the quality of life in countries throughout the world. A World Bank study, "Engendering Development," released in 2000, found that countries with smaller gaps between women and men in areas such as education, employment, and property rights not only have lower childhood malnutrition and child mortality, they also have cleaner business and government and enjoy more rapid economic growth.

Rita started her foundation with her life savings. "I never cared about myself. I have a career I didn't expect. I have become a public person. I had never expected to become anything but a mild person." She saw similarities in the predicament African women face to those that confronted her under fascism during the 1930s and 1940s. She hopes that through scholarships and grants women will be able to have careers and roles in politics and "not only to be slaves of the time." Having solved intractable problems in science, Rita believes that with sufficient political commitment, Africa's problems can also be solved. "I would be very happy to die knowing that these women have a future."

There is nothing morbid in Rita's outlook. She continues to speak to young Italian students, exhorting them to be optimistic about other people and the future. Rather than falling into the contemporary trap of self-absorption, she tells them, they should take an interest in everything around them. "People, animals and the infinite variety of nature, from the blade of grass we tread on to the stars we marvel at in the heavens, may become—for those who have the necessary gifts—a subject for study at the highest level for a whole lifetime."

Rita's autobiography was published in English in 1988, as *In Praise of Imperfection: My Life and Work.* She has also written a book about the life and work of her twin sister Paola and published a collection of her own letters, both in Italian. Her scientific articles and essays about the social significance of science total more than two hundred publications. A number of her scientific articles have been collected as *The Saga of the Nerve Growth Factor: Preliminary Studies, Discovery, Further Development.*

On January 6, 2007, Rita turned ninety-eight, becoming the longest-living Nobel laureate in the history of the prize.

GERTRUDE ELION

Born in New York City in 1918 to Robert Elion and Bertha Cohen, immigrants from Lithuania and Poland, Gertrude Elion spent her childhood and college years in the Bronx, where she graduated with a bachelor's degree in chemistry from Hunter College for Women in 1937. Not yet twenty years old, Gertrude would have liked to go directly to graduate school, but her family (her father was a dentist) could not afford to send her. Instead, she looked for work in her field, but quickly discovered that there were no openings for a nineteen-year-old female chemist. "They wondered why in the world I wanted to be a chemist when no women were doing that."

Like many college freshman, Gertrude, who was only fifteen at the time, was interested in everything. But when her beloved grandfather died of stomach cancer in the summer of 1933, Gertrude resolved to study chemistry in order to help find a cure for cancer. Without either a research position or the means to continue her studies, however, her ambition seemed out of reach. Instead, she attended secretarial school for six weeks, but quit when she found a three-month job as a lab assistant in a nursing school. Out of work again, she talked her way into a position—at first unpaid, and later for a minuscule salary—in a one-man chemistry lab. As soon as she was able, she enrolled in the master's program at New York University and received her M.S. in chemistry in 1941. She supported herself as a substitute high school chemistry and physics teacher in the city public schools until she completed her degree.

Things changed for Gertrude once she had her master's, but not because of the degree. Like other women at the time the United States entered World War II, she benefited from the shortage of male employees in nonessential industries. Gertrude's first job was as a food chemist for A&P, testing the acidity of pickles, among other products. When Johnson & Johnson decided to open a chemistry lab, Gertrude was offered a staff job, but six months later the company had second thoughts about pharmaceutical research and Gertrude left. In 1944 she met George Hitchings, a biochemist at Burroughs Wellcome (now the pharmaceutical conglomerate GlaxoSmithKline) who was seeking cures for a number of diseases, including cancer, by developing antagonists to DNA synthesis. Gertrude knew very little about this area of biochemistry at the time, but it was exactly what she had promised herself she would pursue in 1933. George invited her to join his laboratory as a biochemist; she did, and she never left.

Not long after she started working at Burroughs Wellcome, Gertrude started taking courses toward a Ph.D. in chemistry at Brooklyn Polytechnic Institute (now Polytechnic University). Because she was working full-time, she took her courses at night, but after two years her department ask her to switch to full-time status, in order to demonstrate that she was serious about chemistry. Her work in the Burroughs Wellcome laboratory was so exciting, however, that she was reluctant to give it up. George reassured her that she wouldn't need a doctorate in order to continue their collaboration, so she withdrew from Polytechnic's Ph.D. program.

The approach that Gertrude and George Hitchings took from the first was to observe the effects of various compounds on the microorganisms—whether they encouraged growth or inhibited it, and why. At the time, no one knew the structure of deoxyribonucleic acid, or DNA. It was postulated by Oswald Avery of the Rockefeller Institute in 1944 that DNA played a role in the composition of genes. "So we were really starting at the very basic portion of the DNA and saying we don't know how it gets to be DNA, but let's find out how we can deal with it." One important goal was to discover compounds that were able to inhibit the growth of cancer cells or other harmful organisms without affecting healthy cells. In other words, instead of creating new drugs and then testing them to see which illnesses they were effective therapies for, Gertrude and George set out to understand what made a disease—specifically, a cancer—tick, and then designed drugs capable of interrupting the disease's progress.

Within a few years, Gertrude synthesized a purine (one of the building blocks of DNA and RNA) that arrested leukemia in mice. After some false starts with formulations that produced toxic side effects in patients, Joseph Burchenal, a specialist in the treatment of childhood leukemia at Sloan-Kettering Institute, used one of the new drugs, 6-mercaptopurine, to treat leukemia patients. A third of them went into complete remission. The results of the early trials were so promising for the treatment of leukemia in children that the Food and Drug Administration rushed to approve its use in 1953. Not only was it the first effective treatment for childhood leukemia, 6-MP is still prescribed today, for leukemia and a number of other diseases. The five-year survival rate (considered a "cure" for cancers of this type) for children under age five with leukemia, is now better than 80 percent.

Efforts to enhance 6-MP's effectiveness sometimes led to discoveries of wholly new applications. One of them, azathioprine (Imuran), developed by Gertrude and George in 1957, proved to be a powerful immune response suppressor. For years, it was the unique means to preventing rejection of transplanted organs, and it is also used to treat autoimmune diseases. Allopurinol, first produced in 1963, blocks uric acid formation. This property makes it valuable in the treatment of gout. Two other drugs, pyrimethamine and trimethoprim, also developed in the 1950s, are still used to treat malaria and bacterial infections. Very often, the new discoveries or applications were assisted by other scientists and physicians, who tested the Burroughs Wellcome compounds in different ways or wrote in to suggest new applications or directions of research.

Imuran was a notable success of this apparently serendipitous sort. Joseph Murray, who performed the first successful kidney transplants between twins at the Peter Bent Brigham Hospital, in Boston, was interested in preventing rejection in transplant recipients who weren't related to their donors. Gertrude and George were screening compounds in their lab using an immunological test they had devised. They began to work closely with Dr. Murray, who tested the compounds on dogs. Out of this collaboration came Imuran, first synthesized by Gertrude when she was searching for a better version of 6-MP. First employed to prevent organ rejection after a human kidney transplant in 1962, it was essential to successful transplants for twenty years. When Joseph Murray was awarded the Nobel Prize in 1990, he joked that Gertrude and George, who had preceded him by two years in being so honored, visited Brigham so often that they "knew most of our dogs by name." By then, over two hundred thousand kidneys had been successfully transplanted around the world. "Now, I didn't start to make a compound that would [suppress organ rejection]," Gertrude Elion told an interviewer, "but if you listen and keep your mind open, this is what can happen. This was the story of our lives."

The approach to researching new medicines that Gertrude and George first applied in the 1940s consistently bore fruit throughout their careers and has continued to do so. In 1977, Gertrude and colleagues developed acyclovir, an effective treatment for herpesvirus infections, which had been highly resistant to drugs until this discovery. Even after her retirement, researchers in her lab employed the approach to develop azidothymidine (AZT), to date the most successful drug in AIDS therapy. Despite the fact that the AZT researchers were the people who had worked with her to develop acyclovir and used the approach that she and Hitchings had developed, Gertrude refused to take any credit for the discovery. "All science is a continuation of science that went before," she said.

One of the researchers who worked on the development of AZT, Marty St. Clair, remembered things differently. A virologist who pioneered AZT as an AIDS treatment, she insisted that "Trudy had everything to do with AZT. Yes, officially she was retired, but she was there working with us and counseling us. She knew exactly what we were doing."

Gertrude never married. In 1941, she was engaged to a young man who died of bacterial endocarditis. Had penicillin been available at the time–it was widely produced only after World War II–he could have been cured. After this loss, Gertrude didn't seriously consider marrying, but she redoubled her commitment to applying her knowledge of chemistry to seeking cures for diseases. "My work became both my vocation and avocation," she recalled later. "Since I enjoyed it so much, I never felt a great need to go outside for relaxation."

In fact, Gertrude had many interests—among them, travel, photography, and music, especially opera. Unlike many scientists, she lacked musical talent, but she loved listening to music. She also had a close relationship to her younger brother, Herbert, and his six children. Eleven of her relatives accompanied her to Stockholm for the Nobel ceremonies.

Forty years would pass before Gertrude Elion and George Hitchings were named winners of the Nobel Prize in Medicine or Physiology for work that she began in 1945. That she took immense pleasure in the honor was obvious to anyone witnessing the ceremony. Her nephew, the physician Jon Elion, remembered watching his aunt on stage. The only woman in a crowd of men dressed in white tie and tails, Gertrude wore a blue chiffon dress and tapped her foot in time to the orchestra's rendition of an aria from Mozart's *Don Giovanni*, one of her favorite operas. But her goal had not been to gain recognition. "Nobody would aim for a Nobel Prize, because if you didn't get it, your whole life would be wasted. What we were aiming at was getting people well, and the satisfaction of that is much greater than any prize you can get."

By the time she retired in 1983, the laboratory had been in Research Triangle Park, in North Carolina, for thirteen years. Gertrude moved south with the company, and as she entered her ninth decade, she spent less time in the lab, but in a sense she was always present. In 1998, the year that George Hitchings died, the company opened its new research facility, the Elion-Hitchings Building. Gertrude maintained a lively interest in the ongoing work, until February 21, 1999, when she collapsed while on her daily walk. At midnight, she died at the University of North Carolina Hospital in Chapel Hill. Gertrude Elion was eighty-one.

Cpt. 7 > goes to pg 334.

CHAPTER 7

— Jane Addams —

Curing Social Misery

The Settlement House and Peace Movements

OF ALL THE ASPECTS OF SOCIAL MISERY NOTHING IS SO
HEARTBREAKING AS UNEMPLOYMENT.
—Jane Addams

Three American women have been awarded the Nobel Peace
Prize. One of them started out addressing the problems of
people in the poorest neighborhoods of Chicago. Another, the most
recent winner, raised awareness of the long-term harm caused by
landmines used in war that resulted in a universal effort to eliminate
their use. The third devoted much of her life to promoting peace
but supported the Allied effort in World War II as necessary to stop
the mass genocide from spreading.

JANE ADDAMS

Growing up in Cedarville, Illinois, a small town just south of the
Wisconsin border, Laura Jane Addams enjoyed the advantages of
being a member of a large, loving, prosperous, and politically influ-

ential family. Her father, John Huy Addams, was the wealthiest man in town. His prominence was due to his own industry, although he did get some help from his family and his wife's parents when he was starting out in business. At twenty-two years of age, John Addams had moved west from Pennsylvania in 1844, after a brief apprenticeship with a miller near Philadelphia and marriage to Sarah Weber, five years his senior and daughter of Colonel George Weber, a successful miller. He found adjoining flour and lumber mills on a beautiful site in Cedarville and settled with his new wife into the house across the road from the mills. Adjacent to the mills were 675 acres of forest land, which he planted in pine.

In the nearby large town of Freeport, John founded the Second National Bank and two insurance companies, and over time he invested in area real estate as well. He also rapidly became a force in local and state politics. Never one to socialize for its own sake, he spent his precious spare time improving the burgeoning local economy, in particular by promoting plans to create a railroad link to the large markets in Chicago and eastern cities. By persuading other local businessmen to invest in the Galena and Chicago Union Railroad, he became celebrated for his farsightedness when the railroad turned out to be a boon to local commerce and the most profitable line in the country throughout the 1850s.

That reputation for vision led to his election to eight terms in the Illinois Senate, from 1854 to 1870, and a close friendship and political alliance with Abraham Lincoln. John Addams was famously incorruptible: one of the future president's letters to his friend (whom he addressed as "My Dear Double D-'ed Addams") acknowledged that Lincoln knew that John would "vote according to your conscience, only it is matter of considerable importance to me to know how that conscience is pointing." John Addams could have won the governorship or a seat in the U.S. Senate had he sought either office. Instead, after eight terms as a state senator, he abruptly dropped out of electoral politics, never explaining his reasons.

Wealth, prominence, and privilege did not shield Jane's family from tragedy, however. By the time of her birth in 1860, the eighth of nine children, three of Jane's older siblings had died in infancy. Then, when Jane was two years old, her mother, Sara, died two weeks after giving birth to a stillborn baby girl. In 1867, another sister, sixteen-year-old Mary, fell victim to typhoid fever. Only four of the nine Addams children—Jane (called "Jennie), Mary Catherine, John Weber, and Sarah Alice—survived into adulthood. In addition, her brother, whom the family called Weber, spent long periods of his life in mental hospitals.

Despite a congenital curvature of the spine and her family's difficulties, Jane was a spirited girl. As the youngest child, she was also her father's darling. In turn, she idolized John Addams; she later wrote of her father that he "not only held fast my supreme affection, but also first drew me into the moral concerns of life." He was a profoundly serious man who, as his diary attests, considered dining in a fancy hotel frivolous even on his wedding trip. From him Jane early learned to distinguish between "the ruddy poverty of the country," where she grew up, and the squalid variety that "even a small city presents in its shabbiest streets." She made this discovery on a visit to Freeport with John Addams when she was six or seven. By the time she was eight, her strict Quaker father had persuaded his daughter not to wear her pretty new cloak to Sunday school, in order not to stand out from the less fortunate children. Although inequality "might never be righted so far as clothes went," she recalled John Addams telling her, people could "be equal in things that mattered much more than clothes," such as education and religion. Therefore, the clothes one wore to school and church should avoid calling attention to the material differences between rich and poor.

The closeness between father and daughter wasn't altered when John Addams remarried in 1868. His second wife was Anna Haldeman, an outgoing widow from nearby Freeport with two young sons of her own. From her father, Jane absorbed a variety of Christian faith that stressed good works in the service of others and avoided theological debate. A self-described Hicksite Quaker, after the prominent preacher and abolitionist Elias Hicks (1748–1830), John Addams taught Sunday school and attended several of the local Protestant churches but avoided getting entangled in doctrinal differences or disputes. Jane, though she was later in life baptized a Presbyterian, held fast to the Hicksite belief in an individual "inner light." She expressed this through actions that bespoke her personal integrity, commitment to the welfare of others, and a policy of tolerance and democracy in religion and political life.

Her father encouraged Jane's intellectual curiosity and rewarded her for reading, especially volumes of history and biography that he valued. Her childhood diary notes that she received five cents from her father whenever she completed one of the brief biographies of Alexander the Great, Solon, Julius Caesar, Cicero, and other ancient Greeks and Romans in *Plutarch's Lives* and twenty-five cents for each of the five volumes of Washington Irving's *Life of George Washington* she read. To collect her reward, Jane had to pass an oral examination to show that she had mastered the contents. The young girl also read translations of Homer, Virgil, and other classical poets, but her preferences were for works of history and novels by authors like Louisa May Alcott, especially *Little Women*, and Charles Dickens, whose entire body of work appealed to her.

The second Mrs. Addams added a note of liveliness to the household, tempering the mood of intense seriousness and Quaker sobriety that had reigned, especially in the five years following Sarah Addams's death. Anna played the guitar and the piano, skillfully enough to teach others. She read widely and organized family readings of Shakespeare's plays in which even John Addams sometimes took part. And she made sure that her stepdaughters started dressing in outfits "more tasteful in line and color" than they'd been accustomed to wearing. The cultural lessons left their mark on the young Jane. When she founded Hull-House twenty years later, among one of the very first cultural activities were the reading clubs for the community. Shakespeare was one of the favorite authors at the settlement.

Jane dreamt of attending Smith College, which opened in Northampton, Massachusetts, in 1875, one of the earliest women's colleges to grant bachelor's degrees. After college, she planned to go on to medical school. Her father and stepmother, however, insisted that she stay closer to home. In 1877, she entered Rockford Female Seminary, a small school about thirty miles from Cedarville, where three of her sisters had studied and John Addams was a member of the board of trustees. At Rockford, which was known as "The Mount Holyoke of the West," Jane quickly found herself at the center of the school's intellectual and social life, and she graduated as president and valedictorian of her seventeen-member class. She resisted the efforts of Anna P. Sill, Rockford's single-minded principal, to channel her energies into missionary work—in her diary, Jane dismissively wrote about Anna Sill, "She does everything for the love of God *alone*, and I do not like that"—without losing her enthusiasm for the institution or questioning her own religious convictions. By 1881, when Jane completed the four-year course of study at Rockford, the school didn't confer bachelor's degrees, but that changed one year later. At the 1882 commencement, Jane officially became the first Rockford graduate to receive a college degree.

Jane's relationship to her stepbrother George was always extremely close. Just six months apart in age, the two were constant companions from 1868, when John Addams and Anna Haldeman married, until 1877, when they left Cedarville to attend college at Rockford and Beloit. Throughout their undergraduate years, George visited Jane often at Rockford, and Jane and her Rockford friends made chaperoned trips to the Wisconsin campus. According to reliable accounts, for years Anna was after her son and stepdaughter to marry. It isn't known whether the two young people seriously considered the possibility, but like his stepsister, George never married. After graduating from Beloit, he did research in biology at Johns Hopkins University in Baltimore. While there, he suffered a nervous breakdown from which he never fully recovered.

Two of the close friendships Jane formed at Rockford were with

Ellen Gates Starr and Catherine Waugh. Catherine went on to attend Northwestern University's law school, start a law firm with her husband, Frank McCulloch, and become a leader in women's efforts to gain the rights to vote and to serve as judges and jurors in Illinois. Ellen, forced to leave Rockford after one year because of financial reversals in her family, nevertheless became one of Jane's closest lifelong friends.

There is little doubt that Jane had the makings of an excellent physician. She combined the concern for others that would later make her famous with a rigorous, analytic mind that took naturally to the scientific method. She also believed, from her undergraduate days onward, that every woman should master at least one of the natural sciences, "for only with eyes thus accustomed to the search for truth can she detect all self-deceit and dogmatism." Undeterred by the fundamentalist bent of most of the Rockford faculty, Jane found her way to the writings of Charles Darwin, whose *Origin of Species* (1859) had introduced the concept of evolution to the biological sciences two decades earlier. Darwin's ideas about biological change attracted Jane, but she rejected their use to lend a veneer of scientific validity to the arguments of what came to be called "social Darwinism."

Borrowing the phrase "survival of the fittest" from the English philosopher Herbert Spencer (1820–1903), social Darwinists claimed that just as certain members of species developed adaptations that increased their chances of survival in a particular environment, some human individuals or groups were better equipped than others to succeed in life. Therefore, social Darwinists argued, private and public programs aimed at curing social, political, and economic ills were a waste of time and resources. Jane, who would soon lead the way in demonstrating the practical value of social reforms, saw no scientific basis for applying Darwin's ideas about biological organisms to social phenomena.

Flush with her academic successes at Rockford and planning to start medical school in the fall of 1881, Jane should have enjoyed a summer of triumph, but unexpected events transformed those months into a period of personal tragedy. On July 2, Charles Julius Guiteau, a mentally unstable attorney, shot and wounded President James A. Garfield in Washington, D.C. Guiteau, who believed that Garfield's narrow defeat of Democratic candidate General Winfield Scott Hancock had cost him a government appointment, described the assassination as "a political necessity." Charles Guiteau's father, Luther, was cashier of John Addams' bank in Freeport, and his half-sister Flora was one of Jane's close friends. President Garfield, mortally wounded, died in September. Despite considerable evidence that Charles Guiteau's insanity was largely responsible for his actions, he was convicted of murder after a lengthy trial and hanged in June 1882.

Not long after the assassination, John Addams took his family on vacation to Wisconsin, hoping to get them away for a while from the disturbing reminders of the Garfield assassination at home. Near Green Bay, his appendix ruptured, and on August 17, he died in a Green Bay hospital. After returning to Cedarville for the funeral, Jane went ahead with her plans to enroll in the Women's Medical College of Philadelphia that fall, but she dropped out of school for health reasons at the end of her first year and had surgery to correct the curvature of her spine. This period marked the beginning of nearly a decade of what Jane later called the "snare of preparation" (a phrase she had read in Leo Tolstoy), during which she searched in vain for her life's calling.

Jane found inspiration in the uncompromising ideals she had absorbed from her father's counsel and example, but the high standards also left her feeling inadequate to the challenge. John Addams taught his daughter to listen to her conscience and to act in ways intended to benefit others as well as being true to her convictions. Jane's beliefs ran deep, but she couldn't find a way out of her confusion about what to do with her life. She wasn't searching for what we commonly think of as a career, but for a vocation, and not one considered suitable for women, such as teaching or missionary work. Not long after John Addams' death, she had written in her diary about her anguished search and self-doubt: "The difficulty is not in bearing our ills, but in knowing what ills are necessary, not in doing what is right but in knowing what is right to do. I suppose to say that I do not know just what I believe is a form of cowardice, just going on trying to think things out instead of making up my mind, but then why am I happier when I am learning than when I am trying to decide? For I do not think there could be any happiness in being a coward."

Harry Haldeman, the older of Jane's two stepbrothers, performed the successful operation on her spine. Eleven years older than Jane, he had become "a clever and daring surgeon" in Iowa, where he and Jane's sister Alice had settled after marrying in 1876 (John and Anna had both objected strenuously to this marriage, but it turned out well). While Jane was still in Philadelphia, Harry consulted an eminent orthopedic surgeon, who after examining her, predicted "She'll not live a year." Harry's reply: "You don't know her. She'll outlive us all."

After convalescing for many months, all the while strapped into an uncomfortable back brace, Jane was well enough to travel to Europe with Anna. From 1883 to 1885, she made the grand tour that was fashionable for young women from good families. When she returned, she and her stepmother alternated between winters in Baltimore, where George Haldeman was studying, and summers in Illinois. Jane continued struggling to figure out what to do with her life. Despite the intellectual excitement of lectures and informal reading courses at Johns Hopkins, Jane considered her two winters in Baltimore "the nadir of my nervous depression and sense of maladjustment."

In 1887, no closer to an idea for her future, Jane returned to Europe, traveling much of the time with her friends Ellen Gates Starr, then a teacher in Chicago, and Sarah Anderson. Sarah, one of Jane's instructors at Rockford, would later become principal of the school. It was with Sarah that Jane visited Toynbee Hall, the original settlement house, which opened in 1884 in the East

End of London, a working-class neighborhood of Irish and Jewish immigrants. In her memoirs Jane insisted that she'd begun to think about opening a settlement house before her second trip to Europe. Very possibly she had, but there's no question that she had heard and read about Toynbee Hall and that her visit and meeting with Canon Samuel Barnett, who created this first university settlement together with his wife, Henrietta, strongly influenced Jane's decision to pattern her institution on the English model. After observing the activities at the London settlement, for the first time since her father's death she ceased to feel "absolutely at sea so far as any moral purpose was concerned." She grasped that by founding her own settlement house she could fulfill her "desire to live in a really living world" and not merely in "a shadowy intellectual or aesthetic reflection of it."

Named in memory of Arnold Toynbee (1852–1883), the Oxford economic historian who popularized the term "industrial revolution," Toynbee Hall introduced programs of education, housing, health care, and job and vocational training that later inspired the public and private reform and social welfare initiatives of the twentieth century. Before Canon Barnett founded the settlement house, where he was "warden" for over twenty years, he was Vicar of St. Judes, Whitechapel, a parish surrounded by slums. There he introduced a number of educational and recreational programs for the poor. Oxford University students often visited St. Judes and volunteered there in the activities that Canon Barnett had already started. Those young men began to discuss how it might be possible to bring about broader social reforms. One of the first volunteers was Arnold Toynbee, whose study of history convinced him that it was urgently important to narrow the gap between rich and poor that industrialization had already begun to widen.

When Jane and Ellen returned from Europe in 1889, they wasted no time in putting their plans into action. In Chicago, Jane noticed a mansion at the corner of Halsted and Polk Streets, built in 1856 by real estate developer Charles J. Hull, that she decided would be ideal for their settlement. She described it as "a fine old house standing well back from the street, surrounded on three sides by a broad piazza, which was supported by wooden pillars of exceptionally pure Corinthian design and proportion." The once-fashionable neighborhood was now a seedy commercial zone crowded with sweatshops and surrounded by poor immigrant enclaves from a host of European countries: Italians, Germans, Polish and Russian Jews, French Canadians, and Bohemians. Charles Hull had recently died, but Helen Culver, Hull's cousin and business partner, quickly overcame her initial skepticism and agreed to a long-term, rent-free lease to the settlement house founders. Later, she went even further and donated the buildings and land outright to Hull-House. The two young women moved in, furnished the house with family heirlooms, souvenirs of their European travels, and some new purchases, and set out, as Jane wrote a few years after Hull-House opened, to create an environment "pledged to the unity of life, to gather to itself the sense of righteousness to be found in its neighborhood, and as far as possible in its city; to work towards the betterment not of one kind of people or class of people, but for the common good."

Their bold experiment was an immediate success. By the end of its first year, Hull-House was overflowing, with two thousand people a week: children filling its kindergarten, people of all ages pursuing cultural activities at club meetings, and adult students, many of whom had never been to school, flocking to classrooms after work to learn English or other skills. The curious and the culture-starved attended exhibitions in the art gallery, eager readers borrowed books from the library, those with legal questions sought advice, and the jobless hunted for work through the employment bureau. Jane and Ellen raised money for Hull-House's programs and upkeep, lobbied politicians in their neighbors' behalf, and recruited educated volunteers to teach, care for children and the sick, and respond to individual and community needs.

As the programs outgrew the available space in the original

building, where the residents lived and which housed the offices, an art gallery, kitchen, and a number of the early activities, Hull-House spread out into nearby properties that were home to its coffee house, a gymnasium, a swimming pool, a book bindery, spaces for art, music, and drama, a library, a cooperative boarding house for young women, and a labor museum. Some forty separate programs were available at Hull-House by 1893. Some of its innovations were firsts not merely for poor neighborhoods but for any neighborhood. For example, Hull-House boasted the first community arts school in the country, where classes included not only drawing and painting but practical arts like bookbinding, in which Ellen took particular interest. Besides benefiting the local residents, mostly immigrants and their children, Hull-House constituted a training ground of unprecedented richness for social workers and others interested in observing social reform in action and testing new approaches. The settlement ultimately spread out over thirteen buildings and a playground in Chicago, and maintained a camp near Lake Geneva, Wisconsin.

Jane and her colleagues didn't just offer the educational, social, and cultural programs they decided the community needed most. Early on, the settlement's activities were as likely to spring from what the people proposed. And their tastes and interests proved surprisingly wide. The classes designed to help the adult immigrants learn to read, speak, and write English were popular, of course, but so were the lectures and discussions of classics of English and European literature and philosophy, subjects that were unlikely to have much practical impact on the lives of factory and sweatshop laborers or mothers busy raising large families of young children. One perennial favorite was Shakespeare's plays, which were not only read and studied but performed by enthusiastic amateur players, along with classical dramatists like Sophocles. Ellen Starr, whose interests ranged over literature and the visual arts, taught Dante and Robert Browning as well as lecturing on Renaissance art. Rockford native Julia Lathrop, who moved into Hull-House the year after its founding, led the Plato

Club, which held weekly discussions ranging widely over philosophical and religious topics.

There was nothing dilettantish, however, about Hull-House's educational effort. There were courses aimed at the very young as well as the old, with subjects that ran the gamut from industrial arts, for boys who hoped to find work as skilled laborers, to the sciences and fine arts. For the industrial arts classes, Jane sought out not professional teachers but "intelligent workingmen," who were employed in the trades whose skills they taught and who were better able to introduce their charges to the vocations than trained instructors could. For the college extension courses, in contrast, qualified university graduates and professors were the faculty.

The Hull-House educational program actually predated the University of Chicago's own college extension courses, and the standards were from the start as rigorous as those of university offerings for adults. Many of the instructors were drawn from the university's staff. Within a few years, Hull-House had upwards of 150 students studying the history of art, mathematics, classical and modern languages, literature, history, drawing and painting, natural sciences, and bookkeeping. Some participants were seeking only personal enrichment and never completed the full course requirements or took the examinations, but others were as disciplined as the most ambitious college students. In fact, Hull-House helped a number of them qualify for full-fledged university educations, but the real goal at the settlement was to give working people access to the world of knowledge, without cutting them off from their national and ethnic traditions.

Hull-House's successes as a social experiment established it as the cultural center of its neighborhood, and also a magnet for distinguished visitors from other places. Numerous lectures were given there by scholars from the University of Chicago, though Jane allowed that the audiences were sometimes bored by the dry academic manner of older professors accustomed to the formal atmosphere of the classroom. According to her, the most popular

Hull-House lectures were a series on evolution delivered by a young scientist from the university who was still consumed with an infectious enthusiasm for his subject. "It's not that simple people like to hear about little things," she observed, "they want to hear about great things simply told." Over the years, a few of the dozens of celebrated visiting speakers at Hull-House were the lawyer Clarence Darrow, suffragist Susan B. Anthony, modern architect Frank Lloyd Wright, investigative journalist Henry Demarest Lloyd, and African American leader W. E. B. Du Bois.

John Dewey had a special relationship both to Hull-House and Jane Addams. He visited the settlement several years before he joined the University of Chicago's faculty in 1894, returned often to lecture, and was on the organization's board. Professor Dewey acknowledged the influence that Jane's work and ideas had on his own philosophy and theories of education, and often assigned her writings as texts in his university courses. Through the Extension Division of the University of Chicago, Jane herself taught many college courses, though she refused repeated invitations to accept a formal academic appointment at the institution. John Dewey delivered a popular series of lectures, under the title "Social Psychology," at Hull-House. He fully agreed with Jane's insistence on putting ideas to work to effect social and political reforms, and in fact he resigned from Chicago in 1904 because of a dispute about the laboratory school he had started on the university campus in order to test and refine his ideas about pedagogy in actual classroom settings.

Alice Hamilton, the founder of industrial medicine, was a Hull-House resident for over twenty years, until she left Chicago in 1919 to become Harvard University's first female professor. With Jane and Emily Greene Balch, Alice attended the International Peace Congress at The Hague in 1915, an experience that led to their book *Women at the Hague: The International Congress of Women and Its Results*. Other people were influenced by Jane's work but didn't take to the Hull-House atmosphere. Charlotte Perkins Gilman, prolific writer of fiction ("The Yellow Wallpaper," *Herland*,) and essays

(*Women and Economics*) was one person who felt uneasy living in such close proximity to the poor and oppressed. Following a meeting with Jane at a women's political conference in 1895, she moved into Hull-House, but left a few months later.

Many women and a number of men (Hull-House was a coeducational enterprise, though most of the best known of the residents were women) felt immediately at home at Hull-House. Florence Kelley (1859–1932) was one of them. A child of privilege, she grew up on a large estate in the Philadelphia suburbs, the third of eight children, and was educated at home and at Quaker schools before becoming one of the first women to matriculate at Cornell University. Her father, William Darrah "Pig-Iron" Kelley, was a wealthy businessman who advocated workers' rights and a Jacksonian Democrat who switched to the Republican Party in the 1850s over the issue of slavery. From 1859 until his death in 1890, he represented a Pennsylvania district in the U.S. Congress.

It was Florence who was behind the Hull-House employment bureau. While she helped people from the area find work, she also investigated conditions in the garment industry's sweatshops for the Illinois Bureau of Labor Statistics and conducted a survey of Chicago's Nineteenth Ward (where Hull-House was located) for the federal commissioner of labor. Her parallel investigations, into sweatshops and the slum areas where they were located, were the basis for much of *Hull-House Maps and Papers*, published in 1895. These provided a detailed, graphic representation of the area that for the first time, employed statistical methods to analyze economic and social problems. Her results led to the passage of an Illinois law prohibiting child labor, requiring a shorter workweek for women, and implementing state oversight of sweatshops. When reform-minded John Peter Altgeld was elected governor of Illinois in 1892, he asked Florence to take the position of chief factory inspector.

By the mid-1890s, Hull-House residents were working closely with the Juvenile Protective Association, a civic group dedicated to improving the prospects of Chicago's youth in the city's poorer areas. The association persuaded businesses to stop selling alcohol and cigarettes to minors, campaigned to dissuade young people from committing the petty crimes that often got them into trouble, and convinced the police to turn young miscreants over to the care of the association rather than arresting them. The city's first juvenile probation officer was Hull-House resident Alzina Stevens. Born in Maine in 1849, Alzina went to work in that state's textile factories when she was just thirteen. Not long afterward, she caught her hand in a machine and lost her right index finger. Alzina's disability didn't prevent her from becoming a crack typesetter when she moved to Chicago, however, where she became active on behalf of workers.

When Florence became chief factory inspector, she recruited Alzina as her assistant. Alzina soon began acting as a juvenile probation officer, even though no such job existed at the time. Thanks largely to her efforts, the city soon responded to pleas from concerned citizens to create a separate system of justice for children. "We make criminals out of children who are not criminals by treating them as if they were criminals," asserted Frederick Wines, who was head of the Illinois Board of Charities. Instead of imprisoning children with adult criminals, he called for a juvenile court, presided over by its own judges, and whose goal was to create an environment for rehabilitation rather than incarceration.

Florence's association with Jane and Hull-House continued until 1899, when she left Chicago for New York City, where the newly formed National Consumers League appointed her its executive director. She remained in the position until her death in 1932. In New York, she made the Henry Street Settlement her new base of operations and inaugurated campaigns for reforms at the national level. The six-year-old settlement, founded by Lillian Wald in 1893, was one of about a hundred settlement houses established in the ten years after Jane Addams and Ellen Starr opened the doors of Hull-House to Chicago's poor.

If Hull-House began primarily as an effort to enrich the educational, social, and recreational lives of people living in the vicinity, it quickly became a center of an even more important kind as well. By getting to know their neighbors, Jane and the other residents learned crucial lessons about the exploitation of workers, the corruption of much urban politics, and the price that women were paying because they lacked the right to vote. The more popular Hull-House became as a gathering place through its network of clubs, classes, and services, the more people revealed to Jane about their lives away from the settlement. The coffeehouse attracted many of the locals, despite the absence of alcohol. "This would be a nice place to sit in all day if one could only have beer," one man confided to Jane. She never considered adding a saloon to Hull-House, but Jane was constantly looking for new ways the settlement could be useful to its constituents.

Some of Hull-House's most constructive programs, like the day nursery and social clubs, often revealed the suffering that lay just beneath the surface in many of the immigrant families. Jane later recalled devoted mothers who dropped their young children off at the Children's House, as the day nursery was called, before going to work to support them, because their husbands had abandoned them. Because the immigrants' sons and daughters spoke English and had some education, they were often more employable than their parents, so many families plucked them out of school and sent them to work as soon as they could, even when they themselves were young and healthy enough to continue working. Sometimes, the responsibility was too much for the young people to bear. Jane recalled one thirteen-year-old girl whose family depended on her wages. Once she borrowed $3 from a friend, as much as the girl earned in a week, but couldn't repay it unless she refused to hand her wages over to her parents. Unable to withhold the money or even to tell her parents what had happened, she committed suicide.

When Canon Barnett embarked on his experiment at London's Toynbee Hall, he believed that three broad justifications existed for initiatives like settlement houses. First, he didn't believe that governments would be able to give sufficient help to the poor through public agencies. Next, he thought that the more fully the public and private sectors understood what kinds of assistance were needed, the more effective their programs would be. Finally, he believed in the existence of a humanitarian impulse to aid the less fortunate. In the main, Jane agreed with Barnett's perspective, but she gave her project a more American—and perhaps Quaker-inspired—flavor. "The American Settlement," she wrote, "perhaps has not so much a sense of duty of the privileged toward the unprivileged, of the 'haves' to the 'have nots,' to borrow Canon Barnett's phrase, as a desire to equalize through social effort those results which superior opportunity may have given the possessor." In other words, where Barnett had seen class and privilege, Jane found only good fortune and the possibility of equalizing opportunity for all.

The ambitiousness of Jane's vision, and the impact she had on politics and society in Chicago, touched nearly every area that affected the lives of people in cities at the turn of the twentieth century. She took part in local investigations of midwifery practices, drug abuse, milk quality, garbage collection, the health of the poor, and juvenile delinquency. Many of her initiatives had the goal of reducing the high incidence of infant mortality. One result of Jane's efforts to improve hygiene in her neighborhood was the only salaried position she ever held: garbage inspector for the Nineteenth Ward. Her responsibilities included making sure the contractor actually collected the garbage on schedule and hauled it to the dump, seeing that landlords equipped their buildings with bins for refuse, pressuring the firm responsible for removing dead animals to do its job, and even introducing a modest recycling program for tin cans and other metal. Jane took particular pride in one civic victory that resulted directly from her efforts to raise the standards of municipal sanitation. A filthy side street not far from Hull-House turned out to have a paved surface hidden under eighteen inches of garbage that had been piling up for years. After she talked the mayor into visiting the place, he agreed to restore the stretch of pavement to its original pristine state.

Because public programs to address poverty and health care didn't yet exist, Jane encouraged private efforts and philanthropy to fill the vacuum. She also set an example for local residents by acting as a citizen-gadfly, pressuring the local alderman, John Powers, and other notoriously corrupt municipal officials to deliver the services already mandated by law and to serve notice that the citizens expected more of their elected representatives. By getting to know their community intimately, Hull-House volunteers could sometimes overcome the skepticism of municipal officials. For example, to improve health and hygiene in the Nineteenth Ward, the settlement house volunteers lobbied for the area's first public bathhouse. Even after being told that residents wouldn't use public baths, they persevered—and were proven right. The bathhouse was popular, and it contributed to boosting health as well as hygiene in the neighborhood. In the wake of the 1893 depression, Jane and her supporters actually succeeded in persuading the city council to take steps to do something about the widespread joblessness, after it first claimed that unemployment wasn't the government's problem.

On the economic front, the settlement house assumed a supporting role for some of the city's most exploited workers, in particular women who worked in the garment industry. In 1891, one large shirt-maker cut already low wages in half, and the next year the cloakmakers started hiring cheaper female pieceworkers instead of the more skilled male tailors they had formerly employed. Jane compared the American labor movement of the late nineteenth and early twentieth century to the mass movement a century earlier for universal franchise, which overturned a system where only property owners had the right to vote. The unions run by men often denied equal representation to women, or effectively barred them because they held their meetings in the only places large enough to accommodate their numbers and cheap enough for them to afford: the social halls on the second floors of neighborhood saloons. When Hull-House was made available to the workers, male and female, the women were able to join the men or, failing that, free to organize on their own.

The women of the Nineteenth Ward had usually gone to work in order to help their families get by, but Jane insisted that it was essential for them to take a broader view of economic life. She praised their ties to family and stressed that when a woman "enters industrial life, that is not enough. She must supplement her family conscience with a social conscience. She must widen her family affection to embrace the children of the community."

Over time, the efforts centered around Hull-House succeeded in making it possible for workers to join forces based upon their common economic needs, rather than remain at odds because of social differences. Similarly, Jane encouraged employers and workers to adopt a cooperative stance wherever possible, based on her belief that disputes between labor and management were better settled through a search for common ground than through confrontations and strikes.

No matter how large Hull-House or Jane's reputation grew, she never lost sight of the people the settlement house was designed to serve. The world might identify Hull-House exclusively with Jane, but she knew that its success depended on its ties to its community. A popular writer and speaker who used her frequent public appearances to solicit financial and moral support for her project, she tried to bring the neighborhood with her. "I never addressed a Chicago audience on the subject of the Settlement and its vicinity without inviting a neighbor to go with me," she wrote in her autobiography, "that I might curb my hasty generalization by the consciousness that I had an auditor who knew the conditions more intimately than I could hope to do." Still, she couldn't avoid the administrative responsibilities that came with Hull-House's dozens of programs nor the demands on her time taken by fundraising, public relations, and her increasing involvement with causes that grew out of settlement work.

Jane's conflict over her role led to a somewhat comic confrontation with Leo Tolstoy, whom she met in 1896, when Jane took a trip to Europe to recuperate from typhoid fever. She admired

Tolstoy's writings, as well as his public identification with laborers, with whom he daily went to work at Yasnaya Polyana, his family's four-thousand-acre estate south of Moscow. Tolstoy lived at Yasnaya Polyana most of his life, and founded a school for the workers' children there, where he also taught at the same time as he wrote *War and Peace*, *Anna Karenina*, and many of his other works of fiction and essays. As soon as Jane and her colleague Mary Rozet Smith were introduced to the author, who always wore a peasant worker's outfit, he criticized Jane's luxurious clothes and questioned whether her wealth didn't isolate her from the poor people she professed to help. He was particularly acerbic when she told him that part of Hull-House's operating expenses came from farm property she owned. "So you are an absentee landlord?" she remembered his saying. "Do you think you will help the people more by adding yourself to the crowded city than you would by tilling your own soil?"

Jane recognized that there was an element of posturing in Tolstoy's chastisement, but she took his words to heart, and when she returned to Chicago, she started working in the new Hull-House bakery two hours a day. Before long, however, she realized that what might work for Tolstoy at Yasnaya Polyana wasn't practical in the middle of Chicago. "The half dozen people invariably waiting to see me after breakfast, the piles of letters to be opened and answered, the demand of actual and pressing human wants—were these all to be pushed aside and asked to wait while I saved my soul by two hours' work at baking bread?" She quit the bakery and found other ways to achieve unity with her working-class neighbors.

Like other women active in social reform at the end of the nineteenth century, Jane toiled without the benefit of one of the political arena's most powerful weapons: the right to vote. As she did with other causes, Jane's approach to the suffrage question was grounded in common sense. In an 1897 speech she said, "I am not one of those who believe—broadly speaking—that women are better than men. We have not wrecked railroads, nor corrupted legislatures, nor done many unholy things that men have done; but then we must remember that we have not had the chance."

Because many of the issues to which Jane was committed affected women, directly or indirectly, and required legislative remedies, her female allies came from nearly all of the city's ethnic groups and social strata: Lutherans from Scandinavia, where women had been voting for two hundred years; workers seeking better conditions in their factories; mothers' groups lobbying for clean food and all-day kindergartens; poor immigrants from eastern and southern Europe desperate for cleaner outdoor markets. In Chicago, she campaigned for municipal suffrage, and on the national stage, she was elected first vice president of the National American Women Suffrage Association in 1911. Jane noted the "complete absence of traditional women's rights clamor, but much impressive testimony from busy and useful women that they had reached the place where they needed the franchise in order to carry on their own affairs."

Simultaneously, she recognized the claims of other disenfranchised groups, and enlisted as a charter member of the NAACP at its founding in 1909. In one important area, however, Jane parted company with many of her fellow supporters of women's suffrage. In her work on behalf of workers, she had campaigned for laws that protected workers, especially women and children. Jane actively campaigned for passage and ratification of the Nineteenth Amendment, guaranteeing women the right to vote, but she refused to endorse the equal rights amendment that was proposed not long afterwards. Jane had worked hard to bring about legislation designed to safeguard women in industry, and she believed that equal legal rights for women would make the protective legislation unconstitutional.

As the new century dawned, Jane's achievements at Hull-House seemed secure. But in the period before public funding was available for the settlement house's programs, Hull-House depended almost entirely on private philanthropy. Jane's outspokenness about economic and workplace issues, however, started to alienate a number of the wealthy people who had been benefactors. Fortunately, she was gaining in public stature more quickly than she was losing support, so Jane compensated for the diminished donor support by going on lecture tours and publishing books. A prolific and compelling writer even as a college student, Jane could bring life even to dry topics by her habit of linking them to her personal experiences. *Democracy and Social Ethics* (1902), the first of her dozen books, has been called "as interesting as a novel." Eight years later, her memoir of her role in the American settlement movement, *Twenty Years at Hull-House* (1910), was a bestseller that turned Jane into a national celebrity.

Jane was fifty years old in 1910, but she showed no signs of consolidating her reputation by avoiding controversy. Even as Yale University awarded her the first honorary degree it had ever granted to a woman, she was helping to found the American Civil Liberties Union and the NAACP. These political stances, her continuing advocacy of women's suffrage, and her vocal opposition to the United States' entry into World War I made her an ever-more controversial figure. Her popularity remained so high, however, that when Theodore Roosevelt sought the presidency in 1912 as the Progressive Party's candidate, he asked Jane to second his nomination. She was the first woman to take part in the presidential nominating process.

Even prior to the U.S. entry into the war in 1917, Jane began to come under attack for her pacifism. Her views about war, though, had been evolving for a decade. In lectures and articles that date from the early 1900s, Jane had spelled out a general opposition to war. As early as 1907, her series of lectures at the University of Wisconsin were published as *Newer Ideals of Peace*. Nor was she alone in speaking out. Other prominent Americans advocated peaceful solutions to conflict at the time, notably Andrew Carnegie, who in 1910 established the Carnegie Endowment for International Peace. Its first president was Elihu Root, secretary of war under Presidents McKinley and Theodore Roosevelt, and later Roosevelt's secretary of state. Root was awarded the Nobel Peace Prize in 1912, the second American so honored. The first had been President Roosevelt himself, in 1906, who was recognized by the Nobel Committee for his efforts to promote international mediation of differences as an alternative to armed conflict.

When the Peace Palace at The Hague, which Carnegie underwrote, was dedicated in 1913, Jane spoke at the ceremony. She chaired the Women's Peace Party, which was founded in 1915, and was president of the International Congress of Women, which met at The Hague that same year. The congress chose Jane as the founding president of the Women's International League for Peace and Freedom (WILPF), a position she held until 1929.

In 1915, she broke with most of her friends—including, and with particular bitterness, John Dewey—to oppose World War I, and later the American entry into the war. In 1931, during economically difficult but politically calmer times, Jane was named the first American woman to receive the Nobel Peace Prize. She shared the prize with Nicholas Murray Butler, who as president of Columbia University had earlier fired several of his own professors for opposing World War I, but who in 1925 assumed the presidency of the Carnegie Endowment for International Peace.

Because she spoke so boldly against U.S. entry into World War I, she paid the consequences. The press pilloried her, and the Daughters of the American Revolution withdrew her membership in their patriotic organization. It is even rumored that she was referred to as "the most dangerous woman in America." Undeterred, Jane worked with Herbert Hoover, head of the wartime Food Administration and the American Relief Administration after the armistice, to send food to hungry citizens all over Europe.

The last decade of Jane's life was plagued by declining health. She suffered a heart attack in 1926, and afterward was never entirely well. She was hospitalized in December 1931 and could not travel to Oslo to receive her Nobel Prize in person, and she never delivered the Nobel lecture that is a traditional part of the ceremony. In its presentation speech, however, the Nobel Committee called Jane's movement from social work to her espousal of the cause of peace "only a natural step." In Chicago, the committee found, her goal was to assist everyone who sought help, whether the search was for education, a job, or any other service Hull-House offered. Furthermore, Jane's goodwill extended to people of every nationality. "She became the leading woman in the nation, one might almost say its leading citizen. Consequently, the fact that she took a stand for the ideal of peace was of special significance; since millions of men and women looked up to her, she could give a new strength to that ideal among the American people."

Jane was not only the first American woman to be honored with a Nobel Peace Prize, she and cowinner Nicholas Murray Butler were the first two Americans who hadn't been a president, vice president, or cabinet secretary. When her health permitted, Jane continued to work until her death, from cancer, in 1935. Her funeral was held at Hull-House, and she was buried in Cedarville, her birthplace. The Hull-House campus that Jane founded continued to operate at its original location until 1962, when the original building was converted into a museum under the aegis of the College of Architecture and the Arts at the University of Illinois at Chicago. The work of the original Hull-House continues at a number of centers in the city of Chicago and its suburbs, collectively known as the Hull-House Association. On May 21, 2006, seventy-one years after Jane's death, the state of Illinois declared December 10, the anniversary of her receipt of the Nobel Peace Prize, Jane Addams Day.

In a talk Jane delivered in 1892 that she later included in her memoir *Twenty Years at Hull-House,* Jane summed up her reasons for devoting so much of her life to the settlement movement and to the causes of equality and peace that she considered parts of the same fabric of values and beliefs: "The best speculative philosophy sets forth the solidarity of the human race. . . . Without the advance and improvement of the whole, no man can hope for any lasting improvement in his own moral or material individual condition;

and that the subjective necessity for Social Settlements is therefore identical with that necessity, which urges us on toward social and individual salvation."

EMILY GREENE BALCH

Emily Greene Balch was destined to become one of Jane Addams's closest comrades in arms in social reform and the movement to persuade the world's nations to reject war as an acceptable means to political ends. She was born on January 8, 1867, barely a year after the end of the Civil War, the third of her parents' six children to live past infancy (two babies died). Her parents, Francis V. and Ellen (Noyes) Balch, were first cousins. During the Civil War, her father was released from military duty for health reasons and became secretary to Senator Charles Sumner of Massachusetts. Although they started out poles apart in politics, the two men formed a close friendship, and Francis was influenced by the more progressive views expressed in works like *The True Grandeur of Nations*, a reflection on war based on Senator Sumner's 1845 Independence Day address. Francis remembered that "again and again I found myself pulling up my conservative stakes and planting them nearer to his position until it was only a matter of time when I should be brought into entire agreement with him."

Francis's ideas played an important role in shaping Emily's values. Like John Huy Addams, he recognized his precocious daughter's intellectual promise early on and spurred her to make the most of it. Francis himself had been a brilliant student at Harvard, but so modest that he took pains to avoid taking all the top academic prizes when he graduated. He was proud of Emily and the close bond between father and daughter intensified after Ellen Balch died in 1884. In one of his letters to her, he wrote, "I believe you can do a great deal of good. You have a very sound mind on all social questions, a high order of ability and a kindly and equable spirit. I believe that you will always have many loving friends and be a strong influence." Francis took an active interest in his daughter's intellectual growth. He read widely in areas that interested her, recommended books, and discussed economic and political issues with her. For a while, he hoped that Emily might join his law practice, but he subsequently decided that she was destined for other things. For her part, Emily considered her father "the most selfless man I have ever known."

At the time, a college-educated woman was still such an oddity that Emily expected "to be constantly met with the would-be amusing protest that people were afraid to talk with me, I was so learned." Francis would have liked Emily to do her college studies at the Harvard Annex, the university's school for women that was finally chartered as Radcliffe College in 1894. Instead, Emily decided to attend Bryn Mawr College to give moral support to her high school friend Alice Bache Gould. Alice's father, the eminent astronomer Benjamin Apthorp Gould, was horrified at the idea of his daughter attending college, especially in Cambridge. Gould eventually relented, provided Alice study out of town, so she and Emily entered the newly established Bryn Mawr College in 1886. Emily completed her degree requirements in three years, in time to graduate as a member of Bryn Mawr's first graduating class. She later described her decision to take her degree early as "a disadvantage to everything but my vanity," since she had to separate prematurely from her college friends and lost what she considered the critical year of undergraduate work. Nevertheless, the faculty thought highly enough of her accomplishments to award her the college's first European Fellowship, which provided for a year of graduate study in France.

After a year of preparatory study in Cambridge, Emily attended economics and history lectures at the Sorbonne in 1890–1891; she did research on the French working class and relief programs, which became the basis for her first book, *Public Assistance of the Poor in France* (1893). Over the next several years, she took courses at Harvard and the University of Chicago and then spent the

1895–1896 academic year studying economics at the University of Berlin.

Equally important was a summer seminar she attended in Plymouth, Massachusetts, in 1892, where she met Jane Addams and Katherine Coman, professor of history and economics at Wellesley College. Inspired by Jane's example, Emily and other like-minded women founded Denison House that fall, on Tyler Street, in a mixed Greek, Italian, and Syrian immigrant neighborhood in Boston whose residents worked in local laundries, tobacco factories, and garment workshops. Denison House was the first settlement in Boston. Its residents and volunteers included many well-known people. Amelia Earhart was a social worker there for two years before her 1928 transatlantic flight, and before one Denison House benefit, she flew over Boston to drop leaflets advertising the event. It continues to operate today as part of a local federation of settlement houses.

When Emily had completed her year of study in Berlin, Katherine Coman asked her to join the Wellesley faculty. She accepted, thinking that teaching would offer her the chance to encourage more women students to work for social betterment, and soon established herself as a dynamic, popular instructor. She distinguished herself by her sense of concern about the impact of her disciplines—economics and sociology—on the lives of ordinary people and insisted that to learn about a subject students should engage in field observation as well as library research. In her own work, Emily applied the same freshness of approach and rigorous methodology, notably when she published *Our Slavic Fellow-Citizens* (1910), a study of the immigrant communities of Slavs in the United States, which in the early twentieth century numbered about eight hundred thousand people. In the course of her research, she spent extended periods in the American cities where these immigrants had congregated, and in 1904–1905 took an unpaid leave of absence from Wellesley to travel to the areas of Austria-Hungary where the immigrants had lived before coming to the United States. Emily's approach lent unprecedented richness to her portrait of an ethnic group in the United States and helped convince her that an open-door policy on immigration would, at that period, benefit the country. The study was described as "a landmark in the scientific analysis of immigration," as well as a spirited defense of its benefits.

By 1913, Emily had risen to professor of economics and sociology at Wellesley. Throughout this period, in addition to teaching, research, and publishing, she kept up a busy schedule of involvement in local, statewide, and national affairs. She served on municipal boards for children and urban planning and state commissions on industrial education and immigration. She played active roles in efforts to enact a women's suffrage amendment, achieve racial justice, improve child labor laws, raise workers' wages, and guarantee them decent working conditions. One state committee she chaired was responsible for the first minimum-wage law passed in the United States. All of these efforts were logical extensions of her teaching and scholarly interests, and vice versa.

The prospects for world peace preoccupied Emily even before the outbreak of World War I, but 1914 turned out to be a major turning point. She had kept abreast of the activities of the earlier peace conferences at The Hague (in 1899 and 1907), but she hadn't participated directly in either one. But as a delegate to the International Congress of Women at The Hague in 1915, she was one of the founders of the Women's International Committee for Permanent Peace, and from that point on her efforts focused mainly on the group's work and similar efforts by other organizations. During the war and in the years following the armistice, she helped draw up proposals for peace that were presented to the belligerent nations; she was a member of an informal commission (it had support from the U.S. Congress) that met with high officials in Scandinavia and Russia to promote mediation as an alternative to war; and she wrote, jointly with Jane Addams and Alice Hamilton, *Women at The Hague: The International Congress of Women and Its Results* (1915). While the war was still going on, she also stepped in to replace the ailing Jane Addams as a delegate to the Neutral Conference for Continuous Mediation. Based in Stockholm and conceived by Henry Ford, who was strongly antiwar, this was one of several groups that advocated alternative political means to settling international differences. Among Emily's important contributions was "International Colonial Administration," a paper that outlined a system similar to the mandate concept that the League of Nations eventually established in the Middle East and elsewhere.

In order to avoid the suggestion that Wellesley College agreed with her antiwar views, Emily took a leave of absence from her faculty position. In 1917, when she asked to extend her leave, the college trustees refused and instead voted to fire her. Rather than continue teaching elsewhere, Emily concentrated on her efforts to eliminate war, took up journalism, and continued to publish political and social analyses. *Approaches to the Great Settlement*, which appeared in 1918, considered a number of topics pertaining to the end of World War I and the Russian Revolution of 1917. A year later, she returned to Europe for the second convention of the International Congress of Women held in Zurich in 1919, where she agreed to serve as secretary of the organization's newly founded arm, the Women's International League for Peace and Freedom (WILPF), based in Geneva. She made major contributions to WILPF's peace proposal, which was published while war continued. President Woodrow Wilson said, "I think the proposal is without any doubt the best which has so far been put forward," and he included some of those principles in his famous "Fourteen Points" speech to Congress in 1918 and in the covenant that established the League of Nations. Emily remained active in WILPF for the rest of her life but ceased to be secretary in 1922, except for a period of eighteen months starting in 1934, when the organization was in financial straits and Emily resumed the role of secretary without accepting a salary.

During the 1920s and 1930s, Emily often assisted the League of Nations in its efforts to bring about disarmament, create an

international system for aviation, eliminate drug trafficking, safeguard the rights of minorities and stateless persons, and address the
world economic crisis. She also lobbied the government, in an effort
to get the United States to cooperate more closely with the League's
initiatives. Rather than confronting large abstract issues head-on,
Emily preferred to tackle problems on which agreement was more
likely—for example, health or medical assistance. She also advocated
keeping Antarctica an international zone, an ideal that was formally
adopted only in 1959, almost at the end of her long life.

With the rise of Nazism in the 1930s, Emily actively worked
to aid those people, Jews and others, whom the Nazis persecuted
and helped many of them resettle in the United States. In *Refugees
as Assets* (1930), she made the case that in addition to humanitarian reasons, there are economic and cultural benefits for a liberal
policy toward refugee immigration. As World War II drew closer,
she made a bold move, putting herself at odds with her pacifist
friends. Because of her experience with the refugees she began to
believe that sometimes war is the only alternative to stop mass per-
secution and genocide. "A small barking dog cannot stop a dashing
train," she wrote, recognizing that Germany and its allies were bent
on military conquest. "Fascism and national socialism today can
be destroyed only through means which are capable of impressing
the brutal men of fascism and national socialism." She supported
American participation in the war, saying,

> About my attitude toward the war, it is chiefly that on the
> political plane a state may have to choose between alterna-
> tive evil possibilities—making war or acquiescing in the prog-
> ress of the conqueror toward extinguishing liberty every-
> where and setting up the policies exemplified in the German
> treatment of the Jews and in the Gestapo, etc. After Pearl
> Harbor, I think the USA had no other practicable course
> open to her other than that she has chosen, and I can only
> hope that her joining the UN [a WWII term referring to the

Allies] may effectively hasten victory. I am grateful to the
COs [conscientious objectors]; I think they bear useful witness to the supremacy of conscience and the hidden wrong
of war. But I am glad that there are not enough of them, in
the peace-loving countries only, to impede the war.

Around that time, in a letter to Rabbi Stephen Wise, president of
the World Jewish Congress, about the horrors of genocide and war
in Europe, she wrote that the people in the free nations bore some
of the blame for the "slaughter and destruction. We were not ready
in time with any other method than this slow and cruel one."

At home, Emily condemned American suspicion and mistreatment of foreign-born citizens and residents that were common
during the war. Just as she strove to aid persecuted minorities in
Europe, she assisted Japanese Americans who had been wrongly
interned at home.

By the end of World War II, Emily was seventy-eight years old
and no longer widely known to the general public, but knowledgeable people in education and public policy knew about her contributions. They applauded the Nobel Committee's decision to award
the Peace Prize to her in 1946. (She shared the prize with John
R. Mott, president of the World Alliance of the YMCA.) Vladimir
Simkhovitch, professor of economic history at Columbia University, praised her unceasing devotion: "I have never met anyone who
has, as she has done, for decade after decade given every minute of
her life to the work for peace between nations." In presenting the
prize, the committee paid homage to her policy of seeking practical,
incremental progress rather than making grand but empty statements, and her inclusion of moral concerns in the political sphere.
As Emily herself wrote, "International unity is not in itself a solution. Unless this international unity has a moral quality, accepts the
discipline of moral standards, and possesses the quality of humanity, it will not be the unity we are interested in."

She was too ill to attend the Nobel ceremony in person, so her acceptance was read in Oslo by Gunnar Jahn, chairman of the Nobel Committee. In it, she modestly insisted that the "true recipient" was the Women's International League for Peace and Freedom, with herself as symbol or figurehead, and she donated her half of the prize to WILPF, just as Jane Addams had done in 1931. Two years later, she was in Europe to deliver her Nobel Lecture, entitled "Toward Human Unity or Beyond Nationalism." Emily's speech didn't predict "a perfect world just around the comer," it prescribed a patient, gradual international effort by people dedicated to a future of liberty, democracy and humanity.

Even in old age Emily continued to work for the causes to which she had devoted her life. In 1959, when she was in her nineties, Emily cochaired the committee for the centennial celebration of Jane Addams' birth. Jane had been her inspiration and colleague, and the only other American woman to receive a Nobel Peace Prize at that time. Six months after the centenary, Emily Balch died in Cambridge, at the age of ninety-four.

Jody Williams

When Jody Williams first became involved in the effort to ban landmines, in 1991, it was not an issue that attracted support from many quarters. Throughout the late 1970s, the International Committee for the Red Cross led a few other nongovernmental organizations (NGOs) in an attempt to pressure governments to restrict the use of "indiscriminate" weapons like landmines or ban them altogether. This resulted in the Convention on Conventional Weapons (CCW), Protocol II of which regulated the use of landmines in warfare, but didn't provide for their removal or elimination. And in the more than ten years since the CCW was adopted, little had changed.

Jody's childhood in Brattleboro, Vermont, where she was born in 1950, was different from most children's in one important respect: her older brother was born deaf. At the time, the emphasis in education of the deaf was to have them adapt to the hearing world, but her brother's profound deafness made that impossible. Unable to communicate, he was subjected to cruelty and ridicule by other children. Jody did her best to defend him, to serve as "the voice he didn't have," but he eventually fell victim to schizophrenia and she realized that she couldn't protect him. Ultimately, this led her to try to help people "who had less emotional impact on me personally. You know, if you start defending and speaking for one vulnerable person, why would you not want to speak for other vulnerable people?"

In Jody's account, the decade after her graduation from the University of Vermont, with a bachelor's degree in psychology and "no marketable skills," was a period of "floundering." But she was far from idle. After earning a master's degree in Spanish and English as a Second Language in 1976, she taught in Mexico for two years, as well as in the UK and Washington, D.C. Living in Mexico gave Jody her first close look at dire poverty and the desire to do more than teach language classes or work in an office, as she had been doing. She took a second master's degree in 1984, this one in international relations from the Johns Hopkins School of Advanced International Studies (SAIS), but she had no ideas for putting her new degree to vocational use.

Through most of the 1980s, Jody worked for two organizations whose focus was on Central America: the Nicaragua-Honduras Education Project and Medical Aid for El Salvador, in Los Angeles, where for six years she was deputy director in charge of humanitarian relief. She was teaching English as a Second Language in Washington, D.C., when a volunteer at a Metro station handed her a leaflet from an organization concerned about human rights violations in El Salvador. She went to a meeting, started volunteering while still teaching during the day, and "it touched me and changed my life." The more involved she became, the better she felt "about myself as a citizen of this country."

Jody's predicament during this period was reminiscent of the years Jane Addams called her "snare of preparation" a century earlier, and her way out was as unexpected as Jane's 1888 visit to Toynbee Hall had been. For Jody, it was the leaflet inviting her to a meeting about El Salvador. But six years later, when the political situation in Central America stabilized for reasons that had little to do with Jody's humanitarian efforts, she found herself once again without a sense of direction. She decided to get out of political work and consulted with a career counselor, until late in 1991, when the Vietnam Veterans of America Foundation and the German aid organization Medico International asked her to put together an international effort to eliminate anti-personnel landmines from the arsenal of war. "I had never thought about landmines in my life."

Undaunted by predictions that it would take thirty years before landmines could be eliminated, if then, Jody accepted the challenge. She has said that "we started it because we knew that it was the right thing to do," with no assurance that the campaign would succeed and never dreaming that its impact would be so rapid and dramatic. Jody served as founding coordinator, and less than a year later, she had enlisted four more NGOs to join the International Campaign to Ban Landmines. The six organizations that comprised the ICBL steering committee were Handicap International, Human Rights Watch, Medico International, the Mines Advisory Group, Physicians for Human Rights, and the Vietnam Veterans of America Foundation. Their initial appeal made to all countries was to stop using, manufacturing, buying, selling, or stockpiling anti-personnel landmines. In addition, the ICBL requested governments to fund programs to remove existing mines and aid people who have been wounded by them.

The modern landmine–an explosive device planted on or just below the ground and detonated when a person or vehicle comes into contact with it or trips a wire–has existed since the early eighteenth century. During the Civil War, Brigadier General Gabriel J. Rains, a West Point graduate from North Carolina, developed the first reliable anti-personnel mines; they were designed to explode when a person walking over one applied just seven pounds of pressure. While building his prototypes, Rains lost two fingers on his right hand, but for the last two years of the war, many of the mines were effectively deployed. An unknown number of unexploded mines remained in the ground after the war ended. When five of them were found in 1960, their powder charges were still live.

But landmines were not widely used until World War I, when they were deployed as antitank weapons. During World War II, large minefields were sown in North Africa to prevent opposing troops from encroaching on military positions. In the last year of the war, both sides increasingly deployed anti-personnel mines in western Europe as well, where a relatively small number still remain, especially in France and the Netherlands. It is estimated that since 1939, over 400 million anti-personnel mines have been laid around the world, and over 100 million of them remain in the ground, in more than eighty countries spread across every inhabited landmass except North America and most of western Europe. In addition, it is reported that up to 5 million new mines a year are added to the stockpile, and that more new mines are buried every day than current demining operations remove.

Once the campaign was launched, Jody started soliciting support of ICBL from leaders of NGOs concerned about arms reduction, human rights, and economic growth in the third world. Developing countries are the most threatened by landmines, and their presence impedes nearly every constructive activity of the NGOs working in those areas, from children and education to economic development, aid to refugees, and medical services. The campaign issued a series of papers that documented the extent of the harm caused by landmines in the worst-affected regions, especially Africa, Asia, the Middle East, and Latin America. The details in these reports were used to publicize the problem and especially to raise awareness in the media, so that print and television would increase their coverage of the topic.

Through the ICBL, Jody engaged the interest of prominent figures in and out of government and secured the cooperation of

UN agencies and the International Committee of the Red Cross, the organization that had spearheaded the first efforts to eliminate landmines. Whenever possible, she took advantage of platforms like the European Parliament, the United Nations, and the Organization of African Unity to raise the visibility of the campaign. People of international stature, among them Nobel Peace laureates Archbishop Desmond Tutu and Nelson Mandela, embraced the cause, and within four years the coalition that ICBL represented had swelled to 1,300 NGOs in eighty-five countries (it has since added another one hundred-plus organizations and has a presence in ninety countries). To draw the world's governments into participation, the parliaments in countries all over the world were flooded with petitions signed by hundreds of thousands of their citizens.

The greatest boost to the campaign came in early 1997, when Diana, Princess of Wales, visited victims of landmines in Angola—where there are probably more mines in the ground than in any other country—and Bosnia and began to promote the idea of banning and removing landmines. Wherever Diana went, the media followed. As a result, people around the world took in the powerful images of "what it is like for the poorest of the poor to live in the middle of a mine field." In the wake of Diana's involvement came a series of documentaries and interviews that kept the issue in the public eye. Since then, other admired personages, including Queen Noor of Jordan, have lent their prestige and influence to the campaign.

However useful landmines may be as instruments of war, they pose unique problems after a conflict has been settled, because once they have been sown, they remain hidden and potentially lethal just below the ground's surface. When a war has ended, there is often no record of exactly where landmines were placed. Most of the wars of the past half century have been internal conflicts fought in poor countries. The landmine, which costs only a few dollars to construct, became the weapon of choice in these conflicts. Removing a single mine, however, can cost several hundred dollars or more and is a risky business that many governments had neither the will

329

Leading Ladies

nor the means to attempt. Jody has used the example of Cambodia, where between 4 and 6 million mines are hidden over half the land area. When its long civil war finally ended in 1991, the plans to establish a democracy in Cambodia included bringing its hundreds of thousands of refugees back to the country and giving each family enough farmland to allow it to become self-sufficient. But because the land intended for distribution was so heavily mined, it couldn't be farmed. Instead of becoming independent farmers contributing to economic growth, the returning refugee families received the equivalent of $50 and a year's supply of rice.

Jody has spoken and written extensively about how the lingering presence of landmines cripple economies as well as people, especially in the developing world. In 1995, she and Shawn Roberts published *After the Guns Fall Silent: The Enduring Legacy of Landmines.* The book traces the social and economic drain of medical treatment for mine victims, as well as the costs in lost employment, arable land, pasture, and trade in four countries with high concentrations of land compromised by the widespread presence of landmines. Mines aren't laid in isolated zones surrounded by barbed wire, Jody told one interviewer. "They put them where people go. They put them next to watering holes, along the banks of the river, in the fields." Landmines don't discriminate between civilians and combatants. After the war has ended, the danger of undetected mines robs people "of the opportunity to use the land to build their own societies."

The ICBL's original strategy was to try to work through the review process that was built into the Convention on Conventional Weapons, hoping to add a ban to the controls and restrictions that already existed. That approach didn't yield results, but it succeeded in increasing awareness among the signatories to the CCW. Several of them began to take steps on their own. The first to act was the United States, where a moratorium on exports of landmines was enacted in 1992. Not long afterward, in 1995, Belgium announced that it was ending the use, production, trade, and stockpiling of the weapons, and several other European countries followed the Belgian precedent.

As more countries came forward on their own to express interest in exploring the possibilities for banning landmines, Jody and the
ICBL decided to try to channel that movement in a novel direction.
As the expiration of the CCW review approached, they invited the
nations that publicly endorsed the concept of a ban to send representatives to a meeting with members of the NGOs that were
under the ICBL's umbrella. Starting with a group of seven or eight,
there were seventeen governments with official presences by the
third meeting in 1996. Canada, which had by this point taken the
lead in working toward a full landmine ban, offered to play host to
a meeting of pro-ban countries just five months later. The proposed
agenda was as simple as it was bold: to figure out how to bring a
total landmine ban into existence.

When the meeting convened in Ottawa in early October 1996,
fifty governments sent representatives as full participants and
another twenty-four nations were present as observers. The goals
were to formulate an Ottawa Declaration that states would sign
to indicate their intention to ban landmines in the future, and to
develop an Agenda for Action, listing concrete steps to be taken in
the announced direction. At the closing ceremony, however, Lloyd
Axworthy, Canada's foreign minister, shocked the participants by
challenging them to meet again one year later with a completed
treaty draft ready for signature and to sign it at that time. Even the
states most disposed to enacting a ban were stunned.

Jody calls what happened during the next year historic. "For the
first time," she has said, "smaller and middle-sized powers had come
together, to work in close cooperation with the nongovernmental
organizations of the International Campaign to Ban Landmines, to
negotiate a treaty which would remove from the world's arsenals a
weapon in widespread use." In its scope and its results, it truly was
unprecedented. This was the type of citizen movement, growing
from the grass roots, that influenced the actions of governments.

There is an echo of Jane Addams in a remark made by the
French ambassador to Oslo when the treaty was in the final stages

of negotiation and drafting. "This is historic not just because of the treaty," she said. This is historic because, for the first time, the leaders of states have come together to answer the will of civil society." A century earlier Jane transformed the relationship between Chicago's poor immigrant communities and their local government by showing them "how to use the political system that was wasting city taxes on the friends of the local politicians, and to make the city do something for them." Thus the three American women who have received the Nobel Peace Prize are linked through their ideas, their tactics, and—most important—their commitment to improving people's lives throughout the world.

As soon as the Ottawa participants recovered from their initial shock, they got to work. A draft, prepared by the Austrian contingent early in 1997, was fleshed out in a series of meetings held in several European capitals. During three weeks of negotiations in Oslo in September, eighty-nine nations contributed to putting into final form what became known as the Ottawa Landmine Treaty (its formal title is unwieldy: the Convention on the Prohibition of the Use, Stockpiling, Production and Transfer of Anti-Personnel Mines and on Their Destruction). Its main provisions outlaw using, producing, acquiring, stockpiling, or transferring anti-personnel landmines. It requires stockpiles to be destroyed within four years and emplaced mines to be removed within ten years, and mandates increased assistance for the process of removing mines and to aiding victims.

When the participating countries met again in Ottawa one month after the Oslo sessions, 121 countries signed the landmine treaty, and 3—Canada, Mauritius, and Ireland—ratified it on the spot. Its goals, as expressed in the preamble, are "to put an end to the suffering and casualties caused by anti-personnel mines, that kill or maim hundreds of people every week, mostly innocent and defenseless civilians and especially children, obstruct economic development and reconstruction, inhibit the repatriation of refugees and internally displaced persons, and have other severe consequences for years after emplacement." Before it went into force on March 1, 1999, 155 countries had either signed and ratified the treaty or declared their commitment to be bound by it after that date, through a single-step process known as accession. The Ottawa Landmine Treaty was intentionally designed to send a clear message, instead of being undercut with exceptions added in order to induce reluctant governments to add their signatures. It permits states to keep or transfer as many anti-personnel mines as necessary for training in mine detection, clearance, and destruction techniques. Mines may also be transferred in order to have them destroyed, and antitank and antivehicle mines equipped with anti-handling devices that prevent them from being tampered with are not prohibited by this treaty.

The United States has not signed the Ottawa Landmine Treaty, mainly because the landmines in the demilitarized zone (DMZ) of Korea still protect South Korea. However, the United States supports efforts to rid the world of the threat landmines represent and is taking steps of its own toward that goal. The United States has adopted a policy that

- Eliminates persistent (permanent) landmines from the U.S. arsenal and ends their use by 2010
- Continues development of nonpersistent ("smart") mines that will deactivate within a certain time period and pose no humanitarian threat after war
- Seeks a worldwide ban on sales of all persistent landmines

This policy will go far toward eliminating danger to civilians after the mines' military purpose no longer exists. To facilitate demining, it is U.S. policy to deploy only mines that can be easily detected, using standard devices like metal detectors. The United States has also increased its funding of humanitarian mine action, which surveys and marks areas that have been mined, removes mines, and informs the populations in affected areas of the best methods for avoiding injury or loss of life.

Ten years have passed since the efforts of Jody Williams and the International Campaign to Ban Landmines resulted in the Ottawa Landmine Treaty and the awarding of the Nobel Peace Prize to the ICBL and to Jody, its founding coordinator. Only thirteen countries have continued to produce landmines since the treaty went into effect, despite the many countries that have not accepted its provisions as binding. Nonstate actors, however, continue to employ landmines as weapons; one of the ICBL's chief initiatives today is to bring about universal agreement not to use anti-personnel mines in hostilities of any kind.

The work of removing landmines has begun, but most of that work remains to be done. Jody has often spoken about "kids all over the world who every single day of their life have to worry about getting their leg blown off when they walk out their front door" because of the millions of landmines remaining in the ground, in locations for which records are poor or nonexistent. According to some estimates, seventy people around the world are struck by landmines every day. Half of them are killed immediately or die soon afterward from loss of blood and exposure.

The Nobel Committee praised Jody and the ICBL for two unprecedented achievements. The first was its success in moving public opinion in record time–a little more than five years–from indifference and passivity about landmines to determination to eliminate them. The second was in setting a precedent for collaboration between governments and the civil society to achieve political ends. Before the landmine campaign, the committee noted, there was no global civil society that was international in scope. Today it exists. Other coalitions have begun to adapt the model of collaboration between governments and NGOs to address other problems of similar scope and seriousness. Jody was an adviser to a study of the impact of armed conflict on children led by Grace Machel, the former First Lady of Mozambique. She believes that the ICBL's approach is well suited to other issues like the use of child soldiers.

Jody continues to speak and write about landmines and the ongoing work of ICBL. After sharing the Nobel Prize with the organization, however, she shifted roles to become ambassador for the campaign and a member of the ICBL advisory board. For five years, beginning in 1999, she was senior editor of the annual *Landmine Monitor Report*, an exhaustive record of how the Landmine Treaty is being implemented and complied with around the world. She is also a Distinguished Visiting Professor of Social Work and Global Justice in the Graduate School of Social Work at the University of Houston.

One of Jody's messages, especially when she speaks to young people, is refreshingly simple and encouraging: by working together, ordinary people can bring about profound changes in their world. In her view, that was the most valuable lesson that she learned from the ICBL's astonishing achievement: "the power of individuals to work with governments in a different way." She tells people, "If you care enough to complain, volunteer for one hour a week. If that doesn't fit into your schedule, one hour a month." Of course, Jody's efforts on behalf of the ICBL consumed her round the clock for five years, and they continue to occupy her. But tens of thousands of volunteers, investing varying amounts of their time, accomplished what the Nobel Committee compared to the signal humanitarian achievements of the last century. "It is a hand outstretched to the victims, both those who have been maimed and those in danger. It is a demonstration of care and compassion that transcends all national boundaries."

Clpt. 8 > gres to 365

CHAPTER 8

Commitment
Overcomes Adversity

"opposition"

The Making of Leaders

I AM NOT A QUITTER. I DON'T QUIT.
–Dianne Feinstein

Most women in public life today, especially those elected to office, have overcome obstacles. We have had to prove that we can be effective and that we are strong–and resilient–enough to withstand the knocks of political campaigns.

Some women, however, have been tested in ways that go far beyond having to prove themselves just because they are women. These are women who have risen from tragedy to become leaders, showing an extra measure of calm under fire and grace under pressure in personal or public crises.

I have profiled a few of these remarkable women. They are people I know personally, who have succeeded despite the extraordinary calamities that befell them. They were not prepared for the new roles thrust upon them, but met the challenges through natural talent and strength of character.

LINDY BOGGS

If ever an American deserved to be called a born politician, Lindy Boggs does. Yet no one, least of all Lindy herself, ever expected that she would be a candidate for political office. Born into a long line of southern planters who had sent one of their sons into public life in every generation, Marie Corinne Morrison Claiborne (nicknamed "Lindy," from her father Roland Claiborne's name) was born in the house her great-grandfather had built on his sugar plantation in Pointe Coupee Parish, Louisiana. It was a privileged world, but by the time she was six, that world—and the protection and privilege it conferred—had begun to shrink. In 1918, when Lindy was just two, her father died in the worldwide influenza epidemic, and she and her mother, Corinne Morrison Claiborne, went to live with Lindy's grandparents on Brunswick Plantation. Four years later, however, her grandfather Claiborne died and the life of privilege ended. His widow was forced to sell the heavily mortgaged property to make sure there would be enough money to pay for her sons' educations.

At Tulane University, where Lindy attended the women's college, Sophie Newcomb, she danced at a "strictly chaperoned" party with a young man whom she had just met. Before anyone had a chance to cut in on the pair, he told her, "I'm going to marry you someday." Afterward, she asked one of her friends, "Who was that crazy fellow?" It was Hale Boggs, and he did marry her, in 1938. It wasn't love at first sight on Lindy's part, but they got acquainted while working on the campus newspaper, the *Hullabaloo* (her first ambition was to follow in the footsteps of photojournalist Margaret Bourke-White). Hale impressed Lindy with his brilliance and grasp of politics. All the time she was in college, however, she had numerous beaux, including a medical student she saw regularly. Hale Boggs got into the habit of leaving an apple on her desk at the *Hullabaloo* office each day, "to keep the doctor away," he said.

Even before their marriage in 1938, Lindy and Hale were

involved in local reform politics while she taught high school and he completed law school. When Hale ran successfully for Congress in 1940, he was just twenty-six years old, the youngest congressman at the time and one of the youngest in American history. From the first campaign, Lindy was a full partner in Hale's congressional career, which stretched (with just one interruption, from 1942 to 1946) over three decades, until his disappearance in 1972. With characteristic understatement, Lindy described herself as "one of thousands of wives who had come to Washington at the insistence of her husband's ambition. In a city that lacked any strong personal constituency, these women became its backbone, running the charitable organizations, working very hard to relieve some of the social problems, and helping to build many an edifice . . . We became a major resource not only to the city but also to our husbands."

Lindy understood how crucial this supporting role was to Hale's political career and relished the prospect of sticking to it. When Lindy and Hale Boggs arrived in Washington at the beginning of Franklin Roosevelt's third term, Lindy regarded the First Lady as "an integral part of the presidency" who acted as analyst and trend-spotter for the president. Of course, Eleanor Roosevelt was also a standard-bearer for civil, and women's, and human rights. Lindy has called her "the woman for whom I've had the most admiration throughout the years–my heroine, a great political activist."

At the time, Louisiana was still a strictly segregated state, but as Lindy has noted, "there is a bond among Southern women" formed after the Civil War, "when everybody was impoverished together and the women, black and white of all generations, borned one another's babies, nursed one another's sick, and buried one another's dead." In her own family, that bond was forged even earlier and went deeper. Lindy's great-grandparents reunited as many of the families of the slaves on their plantation as they could find. The two women who were part of the Claiborne household in New Orleans were descended from those families.

Lindy acknowledges that in her youth "segregation was the law of the land, and few people, black or white, publicly questioned it." That changed, especially after World War II, and she realized that without equality of opportunity and the ability to participate in government, "there is no true democracy." She credited "the love I felt from the African American women who raised me" for influencing her perceptions and inspiring her to work for equality. Other experiences made a difference, too, especially driving back and forth between New Orleans and Washington when the congressional sessions began and ended in January and June.

Writing about the late 1940s, Lindy said, "If anyone ever needed persuading to be an integrationist, a long automobile trip with children and a black housekeeper would do it." Their housekeeper, former schoolteacher Emma Cyprian, couldn't join the Boggs family in restaurants, motels or gas station restrooms along their route. In some places, they got around Jim Crow policies by staying with friends or at old-fashioned southern resorts that allowed the nannies of white families to share their employers' accommodations.

By the time the Voting Rights Act came up for debate years later (1965), four generations of the family were deeply interested in politics, and all the family's women "pushed [Hale] hard on civil rights. "He led us, and then we pushed him: Cokie and Barbara [Hale and Lindy's two daughters] and me . . . Hale's Mamma and my Mamma and Grandmother Rets." In particular, Lindy remembered "Bessie Rogers, Emma Cyprian, Aunt Hannah Hall–black women who had raised me and helped me raise my children, women who had been prevented from voting because of their color." Cokie reminded her father that she had to take a literacy test before she could register to vote, a test that could have disqualified anyone the registrars wanted to reject. Hale Boggs promised to vote for the bill, but he didn't intend to speak in favor of it during the debate; he feared that the backlash against him might cost him his congressional seat the next year. In fact, some of his black supporters in Louisiana were worried about the same thing and wanted him to make a show of opposition in order to keep his white constituents' loyalty.

As often happens in politics, things didn't turn out as planned when the bill was debated on the floor of the House. When Joe Waggoner, a Shreveport congressman and friend of the Boggs family, argued that the Voting Rights Act wasn't needed, that anyone who wanted to vote in Louisiana was able to register and to vote, Hale felt he had to speak. He opened by acknowledging that many "good, sincere people" were afraid that "if we made suffrage universal, as it most properly should be, there would be a decline in the caliber of our government." But that hadn't happened, he said, in counties throughout the South where universal suffrage had been introduced. He declared that he was going to vote for the bill "because I believe the fundamental right to vote must be part of the great experiment in human progress under freedom which America is." The bill passed, 333 to 85, so Hale could have safely avoided putting his political future in jeopardy. But prodded, perhaps, by the women closest to him, he not only became one of only twenty-two southern congressmen to vote for it but one of its most eloquent advocates.

By 1972, Hale was the House majority leader, unopposed for reelection to his congressional seat and in line to become Speaker of the House when Carl Albert retired in 1978. With no need to worry about his own campaign, he threw himself into helping friends and colleagues in tight races. One of them was Congressman Nick Begich from Alaska. The two of them went to Alaska to campaign on the weekend of October 14. On Sunday, October 15, Hale spoke on Nick's behalf at a dinner in Anchorage, and the next day, the two of them and a Begich aide, Russell Brown, headed to another fundraiser in Juneau in a small plane piloted by an experienced pilot named Don Jonz. Somewhere between the Chugach Mountains and Juneau, the plane went down and was never found.

Lindy and her family returned home from Alaska after a few

days, while the search for the plane and its passengers continued for another five weeks. The day after Thanksgiving, the official search was suspended until the following spring. Almost as soon as Lindy got home to New Orleans, political friends and allies started urging her to run for Hale's seat. In shock and torn because Hale had not been found, she has said she never actually decided to run but suddenly she was running. Against numerous primary opponents, Lindy received 75 percent of the votes cast, and in the general election she did even better, outpolling her opponent by more than four to one.

Lindy had been campaigning for her husband since he entered politics more than thirty years earlier, so she knew all about running for office. But she was unprepared for the difficult choices every officeholder has to make. As her older daughter Barbara, who would make her own mark in New Jersey politics, warned, when it comes to voting, "There's no 'Maybe' button, Mamma." Every decision meant hurting or disappointing the people on the other side, and Lindy was an artful—and natural—appeaser. In politics as the Boggses and their colleagues practiced it, it was often the wife's task to comfort constituents who were unhappy with the way their representative had voted. This was so integral a part of political fence-mending that Lindy's close friend, Lady Bird Johnson, who had encouraged her to run for Congress, asked, "Do you suppose you can do the job without a wife?"

Lindy had one advantage that few first-term members of Congress enjoy—knowing everyone who was anyone in the House, Republican as well as Democrat. She wasn't sworn in until two months after the opening of the congressional term, but she nevertheless managed to get appointed to the Banking and Currency Committee, her first choice of assignments, because Speaker Carl Albert persuaded Tip O'Neill, the new majority leader, and Gerald Ford, minority leader and close friend of the Boggses, to agree to add a member to that committee.

As a recently widowed woman (in fact, before Lindy could make a declaration of death in Louisiana, Congress first had to declare Hale's seat vacant when it convened in January), Lindy became acquainted with being a political candidate, a congresswoman, and a woman "discriminated against in matters of credit" at more or less the same time. Men usually got mortgages, but women were usually turned down. Many women worked to support families because their husbands were staying in school. Still, the wife's income wasn't considered "stable." "What if she gets pregnant and has to quit her job?" was the stereotypical bank officer's question. So when Lindy's Banking and Currency Committee wrote an amendment to a lending bill to prohibit discrimination on the basis of age, race, or veteran status, Lindy penciled "or sex or marital status" into her copy and coyly said to her colleagues, "I'm sure it was just an oversight that we didn't have 'sex' or 'marital status' included. I've taken care of that, and I trust it meets with the committee's approval." It did.

In fact, this issue was beginning to gain state attention as well. In 1973, I entered the Texas State Legislature, when for the first time in our state's history, five women were elected to the House of Representatives in a single election. The five of us–four Democrats and me–joined forces to secure equal credit rights for women in Texas. Women who were single, as I was at the time, had a very hard time establishing credit.

Lindy and the sixteen other women in Congress (fifteen in the House plus Kansas Senator Nancy Kassebaum) "each became a surrogate congresswoman for the thousands of women who had no female representation and felt more comfortable making their suggestions for legislative or administrative proposals to other women. They created the Congresswomen's Caucus." To research critical issues and propose legislative programs to address them, they formed what soon became the Women's Research and Education Institute (WREI).

One of Lindy's earliest initiatives was an effort to secure equal credit from lenders for women in business; this led to broader legislation reforming credit for women, the elderly, and minorities in the Equal Credit Opportunity Act. The legislation's intended thrust was partially reversed by industry objections that is was too complicated. It wasn't until the year before Lindy retired from Congress that the full panoply of equal credit protections became law.

Sometimes, even after legislation becomes law, failure to apply it can undermine its effectiveness. When Lindy later sold the family house in suburban Bethesda, Maryland, to her daughter and son-in-law, Cokie and Steve Roberts, planning to move into a condominium on Connecticut Avenue in Washington, she applied for a mortgage. It was her first time doing something that is commonplace now but was then still a rarity: applying for a mortgage without a husband's income to rely on. Her congressional salary was sufficient to qualify her for the mortgage, but the bank officer, a woman, asked for detailed financial statements and insurance policies. Lindy objected that she had a "financial statement right here that's adequate for the coverage of this mortgage." "It's a federal requirement," the officer replied, apparently unaware of who her applicant was. She soon found out. "My dear," Lindy said, "I am the author of the law that forbids this type of requirement for female persons and the elderly. You are not complying with the federal regulation, you are in defiance of it. There can be no discrimination because of race, veteran status, age, sex, or marital status." The loan officer excused herself to confer with her supervisor, came back a few minutes later, and granted the loan.

Lindy's focus was much like mine; she believes, as I do, that "women's issues" are overwhelmingly economic issues. She would say, "Women vote their pocketbooks even more than do men, unless there is an urgent overriding question of war and peace." As illustration, she recites the areas she focused on during her two decades in Congress: "equal rights for women in business, banking and home ownership; the promotion of women in the workplace; better jobs in government and equal opportunities in government contracts; and equal opportunity for higher education, especially in science

and medicine." I have followed a similar path, building on her successes. Because of our personal experience, we knew the necessity
of winning women's retirement opportunities. I have passed laws
to assure more secure retirements for women through homemaker
IRAs and pension makeup for women over fifty, because women
move in and out of the workplace more than men do and thus lose
the compound interest that creates a nest egg for later years. Senator Barbara Mikulski of Maryland has been my Democratic cospon-
sor in pushing for retirement security for women.

How successfully Lindy managed to balance her public commit-
ments and her devotion to her three children—Barbara Sigmund,
whose own political career was cut short when she succumbed to
cancer in 1990; Cokie Roberts, the political journalist; and Thomas
Hale Boggs Jr., a respected Washington attorney and lobbyist—as
well as her grandchildren and great-grandchildren—may have been
summed up best in a toast Tommy made at a Boggs celebration in
the 1990s: "Mother, campaign manager, mother, consummate hostess, mother, civil rights advocate, mother, congresswoman, grandmother, conventions chairman, mother, author, great grandmother,
ambassador, mother."

One pivotal moment in Lindy's balancing act came in 1982.
That was the year when Barbara Boggs Sigmund, having already
served as a Princeton, New Jersey, borough council member and
Mercer County freeholder, decided to run for Congress—initially
for the House, but she switched to the Senate race when Harrison
Williams's seat became vacant. Had she been elected, Lindy and
Barbara would have been the first mother-daughter pair in congressional history. But Barbara, whose cancer was diagnosed at just
about the time she declared her candidacy, lost in the Democratic
primary to Frank Lautenberg, the eventual victor. Irrepressible Barbara rebounded to become the first female mayor of Princeton a
year later.

Nineteen eighty-two was also the first year more women than

men voted in elections for Senate and House seats–by a margin of 2 million. The political world noticed the demographic shift, and "many male members of Congress suddenly 'discovered' the Congresswomen's Caucus." The women who had struggled to make the caucus effective were aware that although large numbers of women were voting, there were still only twenty-three women in Congress. So they not only welcomed the interest the men expressed in women's issues, they decided to dissolve the Congresswomen's Caucus and reform as a co-ed entity, the Congressional Caucus on Women's Issues. Within a decade, they had attracted about 125 male members. "Our expansion gave us new clout," Lindy says. The reinvention of the Congresswomen's Caucus was vintage Lindy–savvy politics combined with openness to other constituencies.

Lindy retired from Congress at the end of her ninth term, in 1990. She hadn't wearied of public service, but she wanted to spend more time with her daughter Barbara, whose cancer had returned after having been in remission for seven years. She now spends most of her time in New Orleans, in a three-story house on Bourbon Street that was built in 1795 for an official of the Spanish king. She inherited the house from her Aunt Frosty (Maybart Morrison), who died in late 1972, just a month after Hale Boggs' plane disappeared. The house suffered moderate damage in Hurricane Katrina, but it is intact. "I adore living on Bourbon Street, although it is not a suitable residential area in the opinion of some of my friends and relatives," Lindy slyly commented. In 2005 she came to Texas to meet me for a celebration of the designation of the El Camino Real de los Tejas as a national historic trail. It starts in Louisiana and runs all the way across Texas to the Mexican border. There she was at the age of eighty-nine, looking great, making a speech on behalf of her beloved Louisiana. Her ties to Louisiana haven't kept her from remaining involved in the larger world. Between 1997 and 2001, for example, Lindy, a devout Roman Catholic, was the United States ambassador to the Vatican–another first for a woman.

DIANNE FEINSTEIN

At first glance, it may appear that Dianne Feinstein's early life was a privileged one. The eldest of three daughters of Leon Goldman, a brilliant, successful San Francisco surgeon and professor, she was born in 1933 but was spared the experience of deprivation that afflicted many Americans during the Depression. She attended exclusive private schools and then went on to Stanford University, where she discovered a talent and taste for politics and earned her B.A. in history in 1955. While in college, she modeled clothes for the company owned by her uncle, Morris Goldman. Dianne absorbed Morris Goldman's liberal, populist politics, which contrasted with her father's conservative ideas, and attended her first San Francisco Board of Supervisors meetings under her uncle's tutelage.

Beneath the surface, however, the Goldman household was anything but serene. Diane's mother, Betty, suffered from an undiagnosed brain disorder that resulted from a bout of childhood encephalitis. She was also an alcoholic who abused her children and attempted suicide. As the oldest child, Dianne often succeeded in shielding her sisters Lynne and Yvonne from their mother's physical and emotional abuse, by confronting Betty herself or getting the younger ones out of harm's way. Despite Betty Goldman's volatile behavior, Dianne insists that her childhood wasn't unhappy. She was close to her father, who also tried to maintain stability in the home. At times her mother doted on Dianne, whose blue-green eyes, pale complexion, and striking features resembled her own. But there was also a tension between them. "Some terrible things happened, but I did not have a terrible childhood," is what Dianne said later. Eventually, in the mid–1970s, her mother's behavior grew so erratic that she had to be committed to a mental institution.

During Dianne's childhood, even the exclusive schools were a mixed blessing. Her father, a Jew, at first enrolled her in a Jewish primary school, but by the time she started high school, Dianne had switched to the Roman Catholic Convent of the Sacred Heart High

School, either in an effort to please Betty Goldman or because one of the girl's teachers had recommended the school for her gifted student. Leon Goldman had apparently married his wife, whose family name was Rosenburg, believing that she was also Jewish, but Betty, born in Russia, claimed to have been Russian Orthodox. Before she enrolled at Sacred Heart, Dianne attended public schools and the Temple Emanuel Sunday School. At the convent of the Sacred Heart, she was the only Jewish student.

Dianne calls her uncle, successful and savvy, her political mentor: "Everything I know about politics I learned from my Uncle Morris. He's the one who taught me that people will talk to you if you will listen." She honed her skills as a campaigner as an undergraduate at Stanford. Before declaring her candidacy for a student government office in her junior year, she talked to students on campus and "found out that they would rather elect a monkey, a giraffe or an ant before they would elect a woman." Already the practical politician—she has said that "winning may not be everything, but losing has little to recommend it"—Dianne decided that instead of running for student-body president and losing to a giraffe, she would try for the vice presidency. She won.

After college, Dianne didn't apply to law school, the traditional stepping-stone to political life, but she won a fellowship from the Coro Foundation on Criminal Justice, followed it with an internship at the Industrial Welfare Commission, and then went to work in the San Francisco District Attorney's office. There she met Jack Berman, a prosecutor, whom she married in 1956. Their daughter, Katherine Anne, now a California judge, was born the following year, but in 1959 the couple divorced.

Through Governor Edmund G. "Pat" Brown, who was Leon Goldman's patient and the father of one of Dianne's high school classmates, she secured an appointment to the California Women's Board of Terms and Parole. Brown was interested in reforming the sentencing and parole process for women convicted of crimes; Dianne was one of several younger women he appointed. Over five years, Dianne participated in more than five thousand parole hearings. Later, she served on the San Francisco Mayor's Committee on crime, a position that gave her entrée into local San Francisco politics. She also remarried in 1962, to Bertram Feinstein, a surgeon who was twenty years older than her. Dianne's second marriage help her to harmonize her personal and political lives; Bert Feinstein adopted Katherine Anne and supported his wife's interest in public service.

Dianne waited until 1969 before standing as a candidate in a citywide election. She ran for the San Francisco Board of Supervisors and surprised even herself by finishing ahead of all seventeen other candidates, including five incumbents, all of whom were running for reelection. Her victory made her the first woman supervisor elected in her own right—without first having been appointed by the mayor—since a suffragette named Margaret Mary Morgan served a single two-year term from 1921 to 1923.

For a political unknown and first-time candidate like Dianne, her election was certainly an upset. But it had been no fluke and contained hints of her later electoral triumphs. She ran a professional campaign, aided by Sandy Weiner, a resourceful campaign manager. Backed by money raised through her family's broad political, professional, and social connections, the election effort was able to blanket the city with posters, with one word, "Dianne," boldly displayed in red. She attracted support from virtually every important constituency in San Francisco: party regulars and business interests, civil rights and labor leaders, and the city's nascent environmental and gay rights movements. In addition, she ran a number of television ads shot throughout the city, which portrayed her as articulate, engaging, and approachable.

From the beginning, Dianne had her sights set on higher office. The Board of Supervisors is responsible for maintaining basic services, essential but unexciting; true power in San Francisco resides with the mayor. Twice during her first five years as supervisor, in 1971 and 1975, Dianne ran for mayor, first against Joseph Alioto and then George Moscone, both powerful, popular incumbents. She lost both times. About the 1975 contest, she observed, "I'm a centrist, basically. And what happened was, I got squeezed very clearly between the left and right" in a three-way race with Moscone and a conservative supervisor who played the role of spoiler. For four of her eight years on the board she was also its president, a position traditionally awarded to the candidate who garners the largest popular vote. But even as president, the limitations of the Board of Supervisors frustrated her.

Dianne was also going through a difficult period in her personal life. In 1978, Bertram Feinstein died of cancer. Following two dispiriting years of searching for a cure for her husband's condition when none existed, and just three years after her beloved father succumbed to the same disease, Dianne resolved to leave public service and announced her decision to reporters on the morning of November 27.

Unforeseen events about two hours later changed her plans and the future of California politics. Dan White, an unbalanced former supervisor who had resigned and then tried, unsuccessfully, to get Mayor George Moscone to reappoint him, shot and killed the mayor and Harvey Milk, the city's first openly gay supervisor, who had lobbied against a White reappointment, in their city hall offices. Dianne, the board's president, whose office was next door to Harvey's, heard gunshots and even caught a glimpse of Dan White running past her open door, but did not immediately realize what had happened. As White fled the building, she rushed to Harvey's office and futilely tried to save his life. A few minutes later, still wearing the dress stained with blood from Harvey's wounds, she made her first public appearance as acting mayor of San Francisco at a press conference called to inform San Franciscans of the double murder.

News of the violent deaths of two popular political figures spread through a city still in shock following the assassination of Congressman Leo J. Ryan and the mass murder–suicide of 913 members of Jim Jones's People's Temple in Jonestown, Guyana. That tragedy had occurred barely a week earlier, on November 18. The cult's headquarters were in San Francisco, and Congressman Ryan had gone to Jonestown to investigate reports that members were being mistreated and held against their will. The crisis seemed to galvanize Dianne, who promised her fellow citizens that "as we reconstructed the city after the damage done by the earthquake and fire, so, too, can we rebuild from the spiritual damage caused to the body politic." She was formally named mayor by her fellow supervisors a week later and wasted no time in delivering on her promise by calmly making sure that the city continued to function, reassuring San Franciscans that Harvey Milk had not been singled out because of his sexual orientation, and guaranteeing that the investigation of the murders was being conducted in a spirit of thoroughness and fairness.

By all accounts, Dianne proved herself an extraordinarily effective mayor, over an eleven-year period, until 1989. Difficult to classify as either liberal in the classic San Francisco mold or conservative, she managed to combine tough anticrime policies and a pro-business posture with a strong commitment to social programs. As mayor, she balanced the city's budget while improving services, promoted economic growth but protected the historic character of San Francisco's downtown, added public housing and lowered unemployment, opposed discrimination in employment and other areas, and increased spending on social programs, among them, efforts to combat homelessness and AIDS. Her advocacy of gun control legislation spurred an effort to recall her in 1983, but she turned it back handily (by a better than four-to-one margin) and was elected to her second full term as mayor, again with more than 80 percent of the votes cast. She also attracted the 1984 Democratic Convention to her city and cultivated a national reputation for herself as mayor. When Walter Mondale was looking for a qualified woman as his running mate, Dianne was one of the names on the short list. She would have relished running for vice president, but when Mondale's choice was announced in July, she graciously told the press, "With Geraldine Ferraro go my hopes and the hopes of all the women of this nation." In the 2000 presidential race, when Dianne had served in the Senate for eight years, Al Gore weighed the possibility of asking her to join his ticket as well, before choosing Senator Joe Lieberman.

After she left office as San Francisco's mayor, Dianne lost narrowly in the 1990 race for governor against Senator Pete Wilson. Richard Blum, an investment banker whom she married in 1980, helped Dianne, who lacked a statewide organization or political base, finance her campaign. One of her most daring initiatives in that campaign was her pledge that if she was elected half the jobs in her administration would go to women. She then won the special election in 1992 to choose the successor to Governor Wilson in the Senate and has been reelected three times, in 1994, 2000 and 2006. During the 1992 campaign, she frequently appeared in public together with Barbara Boxer, running for California's other Senate seat. Dianne and Barbara both won convincing victories in the primary and general elections, the first time that two women from a single state had been elected to the Senate simultaneously. There are now three states in which both U.S. senators are women; Maine and Washington have joined California.

As a senator, Dianne refined her philosophy of governing "from the center" and emerged as an effective moderate on many issues. Since then, she has risen to positions of influence on key Senate committees: Judiciary, Appropriations, and Intelligence. She and I have led the appropriations committee on Veterans' Affairs and Military Construction. When Republicans have been in the majority, I have chaired; when Democrats were the majority, she was chair. There has never been a time when we couldn't work out all the issues, and we've had very few differences in this area. Dianne and I cosponsored the Hutchison-Feinstein Overseas Basing Act, legislation to create a commission that studied the efficiency of U.S. bases overseas. We had visited installations in foreign countries that were inefficient and constrained training opportunities because of limited ground or air space. The commission's work resulted in a restructuring of bases in Germany and Korea, downsizing some and closing others, and a plan to bring seventy thousand troops home to the United States, where they will be able to train more effectively.

Dianne's legislative interests extend to technology, crucial in California's high-tech industries; crime and the rights of crime victims, especially as they affect the well-being of American youth, families, and urban areas; and women's issues, notably cancer treatment and research. Dianne chairs the Senate Cancer Coalition and was lead sponsor of the Feinstein-Hutchison Breast Cancer Research Stamp, which to date has raised more than $40 million for breast cancer research.

The women of the Senate (there are sixteen of us now) have dinner together once a month, to relax and get to know each other better. Dianne and I try to meet for dinner as often as we can. We have much in common, though our states are very different. A little-known talent of Dianne's, which we do not share, is that she is an artist. She relaxes by painting flowers in watercolor. I love her work and have two of her prints in my home in Dallas, a constant reminder of a special friendship.

Olympia Snowe

Olympia Snowe has never lost an election, but in her early life she endured many disappointments. Born in Augusta, Maine, in 1947, Olympia Jean Bouchles was the daughter of George and Georgia Goranites Bouchles. George, who had immigrated from Greece, and Georgia, the daughter of Greek immigrants, both died before Olympia was ten. Her mother succumbed to breast cancer when Olympia was eight. Her father did not feel that he could take proper care of her and her brother, so he sent Olympia away to school at St. Basil's Academy, a Greek Orthodox school in Garrison, New York. She told me that she remembers the day she was put in the car to drive to Garrison as if it were yesterday. She knew her father was doing what was best for her, but she still chokes up when she recalls the moment of departure.

Olympia wrote to her father every day from St. Basil's, until he died later that year, of a heart condition. She was ten years old. She then returned to Auburn, Maine, to live with her aunt and uncle, Mary and James Goranites, who had five children of their own. Her brother, John, was raised by other relatives. Her uncle also died while Olympia was a student at Saint Basil's, but she remained close to her Aunt Mary throughout her life. She graduated from Auburn's Edward Little High School in 1965 and went on to the University of Maine, where she received a bachelor's degree in political science in 1969.

Not long after finishing college, Olympia married Peter Snowe, a member of the Maine State Legislature, switched her party affiliation to Republican, and managed then U.S. Congressman William S. Cohen's district office from 1971 to 1973. That year sorrow entered her life again, when Peter was killed in an automobile accident. Urged by friends and political colleagues to run in the special election for her late husband's seat as Auburn's representative, she was elected a month later with 60 percent of the votes and won a full term in 1974.

Olympia has said that the deaths of both her parents, her uncle, and her husband by the time she was twenty-six have given her insight into the other people's suffering. "I've lost a lot of close members of my family over time, and I've learned that it can happen to anybody. People may not suffer the same misfortune, but it can be misfortune of another kind, and it can have an impact. It gives me the ability to identify with people. It's made me empathetic, sympathetic, because unfortunately I've had enough tragedies to appreciate how things can change in one's life. It gives you a better understanding of what people have gone through."

Empathy and effectiveness proved to be a winning combination with Maine voters, and Olympia quickly made her way up the state's legislative ladder. In 1976, she moved to the Maine Senate, where she represented Androscoggin County, and two years later, she ran successfully for the U.S. House of Representatives from Maine's Second District when William Cohen gave up his House seat to enter the race for the Senate. When George Mitchell retired as Maine's senior senator in 1994, Olympia scored a solid victory over Democratic congressman Tom Andrews. Her 1989 marriage to Governor John R. McKernan Jr. gave Olympia the distinction of being the only First Lady of a state who was also a member of Congress. Since her initial Senate election, she has been reelected twice, in 2000 and 2006, each time by increasingly large margins. In fact, she boasts the best electoral record of any Maine politician since World War II, with eleven victories in as many tries for major office.

Olympia pays tribute to her illustrious predecessor, Margaret Chase Smith, for striking a balance between national and international issues, on the one hand, and the local concerns of Maine's residents, on the other. Calling the state's first woman representative and senator a great role model, she points to her combination of political and personal virtues: "Her independence was legendary, and she certainly paved a path of integrity and honesty." People in Maine know that what's on their minds matters to their senator, the first woman to represent them in the House or Senate since Margaret Chase Smith.

She spends nearly every weekend in the state, making "Main Street tours" where she visits a town (Portland, the largest city in the state, has barely sixty-five thousand inhabitants) and talks to people on the street and in the shops about their lives and their concerns. She calls her tours "better than any poll I can think of." Back in Washington, she works on the problems she's uncovered at home, and often gets results. She and her colleague, Senator Susan Collins, also an effective grassroots, hands-on senator, worked tirelessly to turn back plans to close military bases in Maine, thereby saving local jobs. They also worked successfully on legislation to provide relief for low-income residents with high heating costs in one of the country's coldest states. In fact, in the monthly polls taken state by state to gauge job approval of each state's senators, Olympia and Susan are always at the top. Maine likes the two women who represent them very much.

Ever since her earliest days as a member of Congress, Olympia has been especially sensitive to the need to reshape health policy to benefit men and women equally. As a member of the Women's Caucus, she was instrumental in ordering a study that revealed inequities in medical research conducted under the aegis of the National Institutes of Health. The results led to the Women's Health Equity Act, which changed national health policy so that women were included in trials of drugs and medical procedures involving diseases that affected them as well as men, and mandated more research into diseases that had been ignored, among them breast cancer (which was responsible for the early death of Olympia's mother, Georgia Bouchles), osteoporosis, and ovarian and cervical cancer. She supports initiatives like National Breast Cancer Awareness Month, because "when it comes to breast cancer, the difference between life and death for many women can be measured in a commitment to mammograms, self-exams, and regular doctor visits."

As a senator, Olympia is known as a moderate. She has also demonstrated a willingness to take positions even in the face of opposition from her own party. This quality plays well with Maine's voters. A member of the Senate Finance Committee since 2001, she has a major voice in federal bills affecting taxes, international trade, health care and health insurance, social welfare, and Social Security. She was instrumental in efforts to add prescription drug coverage to Medicare. Her constituents benefit from improvements to Medicare, of course, but Olympia was motivated by her concern for all beneficiaries of the Medicare system, "It is time that we provide clarity for our seniors, informing them of the services available that will lower the costs of their prescription drugs and strengthen the overall integrity of the Medicare entitlement."

Through all of the losses she suffered early in her life, what sustained her, Olympia says, was knowing that she was loved and cared for, by her parents, her uncle, and ultimately by her aunt. The nurturing of family and extended family was her anchor.

ILEANA ROS-LEHTINEN

Many Cubans who flocked to the United States in the wake of Fidel Castro's 1959 revolution weren't expecting to settle permanently in this country. But after the Bay of Pigs invasion in 1961 failed to launch a popular uprising against the Communist regime, the Cuban refugee communities in South Florida began to swell.

Amanda Adato Ros and her two children, Henry and Ileana, boarded one of the last commercial flights from Havana in 1960. Ileana recalls how excited she was, at the age of eight, to be riding in an airplane. She noted, however, that her mother did not share her happy mood, and it soon became clear that the round-trip ticket was really one-way (Ileana now has the return ticket to Havana framed in her Florida office).

Her father, Enrique Emilio Ros, joined his family a few months later. The family moved into Little Cuba, a section of Miami where the refugees helped each other cope. Ileana remembers that no one had money, but they didn't feel poor. The community was very close-knit and supportive. Enrique and Amanda worked at menial jobs, her father as a delivery truck driver for a dry cleaner and her mother in the kitchen of a Miami hotel. Despite a degree from the University of Havana, Enrique spoke no English, and neither did any of the other family members. While working, he started taking courses at Miami-Dade County Community College and ultimately graduated from the University of Miami.

Ileana's father instilled a sense of patriotism for their new country in his children, and a sense of gratitude to the American people for their generosity and the opportunities the Cuban refugees enjoyed in the United States. At first, luxuries were rare, however. Ileana remembers the used bicycle her parents bought for her and her brother Henry to ride to school. They couldn't afford two bikes, so

Ileana rode on the handlebars, while Henry, one year older, pedaled. She attended public elementary and high schools in Miami, and earned an associate's degree from Miami-Dade County Community College. In 1975, she earned a B.A. in higher education and in 1987 an M.S. in educational leadership from Florida International University..

After college, Ileana taught school, and in 1978 she founded Eastern Academy, a bilingual elementary school in Hialeah, where she taught for nine years. The school's bilingual focus signaled a trademark theme of Ileana's political career, dual loyalty to American democratic values and her Cuban linguistic and cultural origins. During her time at Eastern Academy, Ileana was a volunteer in the political campaign of a friend, Demetrio Perez. "I enjoyed the campaigning and developed a strong interest in politics," she told an interviewer, and started thinking about running herself, for a seat on the Miami-Dade School Board. "It seemed like a natural extension of my interests in education and politics."

When she made her own try for political office, in 1982, it was for the Florida State Legislature. Ileana was elected, served for four years, and then ran successfully for the state Senate. Credit for helping to shape Ileana's mainly conservative political philosophy and guiding her career in electoral politics is given to her father. Despite the encouragement and support of family and friends, however, getting a foothold in Florida politics wasn't easy for an outsider. "In the beginning, I had to run against the political establishment of the time, and it was vicious," she recalled. "But I knew what it was going to be like, so I did not let it get to me. I concentrated on my mission and my objectives, and I didn't worry about the rest of it. It's the same sort of opposition that anyone who doesn't fit the established culture would receive."

Ileana credits her persistence and toughness for finally wearing down her opponents' resistance. Gradually, she says, a more tolerant mood took over. "Today, that culture of hostility is not in evidence, and there are many more minorities and women in public office." In fact, since Ileana broke through the invisible barrier, other Latina women have followed her into Congress.

Shortly after she entered the Florida legislature, she met a fellow representative, Dexter Lehtinen. They married and have two children of their own, Amanda and Patricia, as well as Dexter's son and daughter, Douglas and Katherine, from his previous marriage. Dexter Lehtinen later served as the U.S. attorney in Miami, appointed by President George H. W. Bush, and is now in private practice in that city.

When long-time Florida congressman Claude Pepper died in 1989, Ileana entered the special primary election to choose candidates for the position of U.S. representative from Florida's Eighteenth Congressional District. All told, eleven aspirants entered the primaries, five Republicans and seven Democrats. One of them was Jo Ann Pepper, the late congressman's niece, but political insiders predicted that Rosario Kennedy would emerge as the Democratic winner, thus setting up the first head-to-head contest for a House seat between two Cuban American women. As expected, Ileana won the Republican primary, but her Democratic opponent was Gerald Richman, not Kennedy.

In the November showdown, when Ileana polled 53 percent of the vote, the results were regarded as marking the emergence of Cuban Americans as a force in Florida politics. Her victory made her the first Cuban American and the first Latina woman of any national origin to serve in Congress. The singer Celia Cruz, who fled Cuba at the same time as the Roses and rallied support for Ileana, exclaimed, "Los Cubanos han ganado!" (The Cubans have won!) In the eight ensuing elections, she has been returned to office by wider margins—and in four of them (1994–2000) was unopposed. In 2002, her district was redrawn to include the environmentally sensitive Florida Keys. The themes of her campaigns and legislative agenda have remained remarkably consistent: opposition to Castro's Communist rule in Cuba; broad support for antidiscrimination policies, in particular with regard to immigrants and gays; advocacy of bilingual education; a strong environmental stance, especially where south Florida's natural resources are concerned; and a pro-family tax policy.

As a member of the House Committee on International Relations, Ileana has won praise for her focus on human rights issues on a broad front that begins, naturally, with her native Cuba but also encompasses Northern Ireland, Lebanon, Syria, Iran, Saudi Arabia, Afghanistan, Pakistan, the Congo, and China. She has chaired the Subcommittee on Middle East and Central Asia and is now its ranking Republican member. Her outspoken support of Israel stresses its right to enjoy peace and security. To encourage the return of democracy to Cuba, Ileana advocates three main thrusts: trade restrictions and other economic sanctions to pressure Cuba to change its policies; free elections, ideally without Fidel Castro as a candidate; and the requirement that any visitor to Cuba who confers with Castro should also meet with his political opponents and demand free elections in the island nation. Her goal, she says, is to "make the dream of freedom a reality for the enslaved people of Cuba."

At home as well as abroad, she emphasizes legislation and policies that improve education, safeguard children's welfare, protect senior citizens, promote women's rights and health, and guarantee the rights of crime victims, especially with regard to crimes of violence. There is no doubt that Ileana's outlook has broadened considerably since she was first elected to Congress, but she never loses sight of the causes that impelled her toward politics more than twenty-five years ago. To maintain her close ties to the people she represents and to keep abreast of their concerns, she spends as much time as she can in her district and insists on making her home in south Florida, not Washington. "I don't want to lose touch with the people and issues that are closest to my heart. Many of the issues that I have become involved with have been brought to my attention by my constituents." By remaining a familiar, accessible presence in south Florida, Ileana is able to keep up her contacts with her young constituents and to encourage them, especially the young women, to make a contribution to their communities. She has even fulfilled a lifelong dream of earning a doctorate; it was conferred in 2004 by the University of Miami.

Staying close to her family is important to Ileana as well. She gives them much of the credit for her political success. Ileana's father continues to serve as her campaign manager. "He's very low-key and likes to stay out of the public eye, but he's an integral part of every campaign. My mom is also a wonderful organizer and a great people person." Her brother isn't directly involved in political life, but he keeps the family business going, "which makes it possible for the rest of us to do what we do." Ileana's parents live across the street from the Lehtinens, so her children can go back and forth to their grandparents' house at will. It is that close-knit extended family that allows her to work in Washington during the week and know her children are surrounded with love.

ELAINE CHAO

Elaine Chao was born in 1953 in Taiwan, halfway across the globe from where she now lives. Her parents had fled there in 1950 with other Chinese Nationalists who left the mainland after the civil war ended in a Communist victory. In 1961, Elaine's mother, Ruth, Elaine, and her two sisters joined their husband and father in New York. James S. C. Chao had left Taiwan three years earlier, initially settling in New York City. Ruth and her children didn't have an easy voyage; it took them a month to cross the Pacific from Hong Kong by freighter. After the family was reunited in New York, the Chaos had three more daughters.

When Elaine started school, there was no bilingual education, and she didn't know any English. Not understanding everything her teachers said to the students, she wrote down everything she heard, and when her father returned from his grueling fourteen-hour days at work, the two of them would review her copious notes and lessons for that day. Patiently, he deciphered her misspelled words and made sure she understood everything. Before long, Elaine had mastered the language and was excelling in school unaided by her father.

By the time Elaine reached high school, the Chaos had moved to Long Island. Elaine, the eldest of six daughters, graduated from Syosset High School in 1971, then majored in economics at Mount Holyoke College, where she received a B.A. in economics before going on to Harvard Business School for an M.B.A. In the mid–1960s, James Chao had started a shipping company that concentrated on traffic between the United States and Taiwan, where he had maintained business contacts. One of Elaine's first jobs after Harvard was at Citibank, where she was a loan officer whose specialty was ship financing. She moved to California with Bank America and began to play an active part in Republican politics.

Elaine's first contact with official Washington came in 1983, when she was named a White House Fellow and worked in the Office of Policy Development. Three years later, she put her experience in shipping to work as deputy administrator in the Department of Transportation Maritime Administration. In 1988 she was appointed chairwoman of the Federal Maritime Commission and the next year she was named deputy secretary of transportation.

Elaine's first high-visibility role in public service began in 1991, when she was appointed director of the Peace Corps. She brought to the position an innovative approach geared to promoting economic development and focused on expanding into the former Soviet republics in eastern Europe and Central Asia, as well as the Baltic states: Estonia, Latvia, and Lithuania. To attract volunteers with business backgrounds to Russia and neighboring countries, the Peace Corps added small-business development to traditional assignments like teaching and health care. Elaine expanded the Corps' geographic reach as well; in addition to former Soviet countries, Peace Corps volunteers could also choose postings to the People's Republic of China. She saw benefits accruing to both the host countries and the volunteers: "Memories of living in a developing nation are part of who I am today and give me a profound understanding of the challenges of economic development."

After a year heading the Peace Corps, Elaine was invited to become president and chief executive officer of the United Way, which was recovering from a period of financial mismanagement. Between 1992 and 1996, she restored public confidence and credibility to the organization that supports a host of vital education, health, and social service programs in American communities. She then spent four years as a Distinguished Fellow at the Heritage Foundation, a Washington think tank, before being nominated by President George W. Bush as his secretary of labor, a cabinet position she still holds. She is the first Asian American woman to serve as a cabinet member.

As labor secretary, Elaine has been instrumental in developing new regulations that increase overtime protection by raising overtime eligibility minimums for low-wage workers, the first change in overtime rules since the mid-1970s. She has required trade unions to disclose more fully to the rank and file how membership dues are spent. She has overseen Department of Labor efforts to improve employer accountability, steps that have resulted, for example, in retroactive payments to immigrant workers who had received illegally low wages. To help unemployed and laid-off workers find new jobs, Elaine has focused Labor Department efforts on reforming training programs.

Another of Elaine's innovations as labor secretary has been to encourage small businesses, especially those owned by women. Among the features on the department's user-friendly website are topics covering compliance regulations and filings in clear language geared toward owners of businesses, not bureaucrats. Elaine has participated personally in a series of "summit meetings" held throughout the country and tailored for aspiring women entrepreneurs. The Women's Entrepreneurship in the 21st Century summits run the gamut of topics from securing start-up financing to doing business overseas. As one business association official remarked, "She's certainly reaching out to working women generally and women business owners in particular, even though that's technically not within her portfolio."

Elaine is married to Senator Mitch McConnell of Kentucky, Republican leader of the U.S. Senate. The Chaos are among Washington's top "power couples."

MARY BONO

In the language of show business, Mary Bono had not one but two hard acts to follow: first as Sonny Bono's second wife, after Cher, the female half of one of the most popular husband-and-wife singing duos in the country; and then as Sonny's successor in Congress after his tragic fatal accident in 1998. Neither was on her mind while she was growing up in southern California in the 1960s and 1970s. Her family had moved from Cleveland, Ohio, to south Pasadena when Mary was a year old. "I never in my wildest dreams, when I was young, imagined a career in politics," she told one interviewer. As a child, Mary had dreamed of enjoying a very different sort of limelight, that of world-class gymnast. She discovered gymnastics when she was ten, while watching the 1972 Munich Olympics on television. Mary, together with millions of other viewers, was mesmerized by the diminutive seventeen-year-old Soviet star Olga Korbut, who won three gold medals. "I looked up to Olga Korbut [who returned to win a fourth gold medal in Montreal in 1976] as a role model, and that's what I wanted to be. If there were a wall I would do a cartwheel on it; if there were a lawn I would tumble on it."

Mary continued to train with the team Gymnastics Olympica through high school, and she remains a devotee of physical fitness. But by the time she entered the University of Southern California in 1980, gymnastics was a hobby. At USC, she majored in art history, graduating in 1984. Her father, Clay Whitaker, is a surgeon and her mother holds a B.S. in chemistry, but Mary worked her way through college. She met Sonny during a college graduation party that was held at a restaurant the singer owned, not long after his high-profile marriage to Cher ended. Sonny and Mary married in 1986, and had two children—a son, Chesare Elan, born in 1988, and Chianna Marie, a daughter, born 1991. The Bonos lived in Palm Springs, California, which is part of the district that Sonny represented in Congress from 1995 until January 5, 1998, when Mary's world changed abruptly. She and Sonny were skiing together at Lake Tahoe when he hit a tree and died almost instantly.

Sonny's funeral was carried live on national television, and I admired Mary for asking Cher to deliver a eulogy. Mary and Cher had been close from the time Mary and Sonny started dating. The day he died, Mary contacted Cher, who was overseas but immediately returned to California. She stayed at the Bono home until after the funeral. Mary wanted a public reconciliation between Sonny and Cher; Cher's moving eulogy fulfilled Mary's magnanimous wish, and the two women remain close to this day.

Following the funeral, and still grieving, Mary was besieged by people advising her to run for Sonny's congressional seat. One of the most persuasive arguments was made by her mother. Karen Whittaker, with four children, had never fulfilled her own professional dreams. She had graduated from Berea College in Kentucky, hoping for a scientific career, but instead she stayed home to raise her children. Now she encouraged her daughter to go for it, to live her life. She assured Mary that she was strong enough to stand for office and serve her country.

It was a tough campaign. Mary had to face personal opposition from Sonny's mother, who publicly opposed her election. Mary didn't respond to the personal attacks. She kept her focus on her children and the campaign, won the special primary election to become the Republican candidate and went on to win her the seat in Congress as well. On April 7, 1998, she was sworn in as a U.S. representative and has been reelected by large margins in her four subsequent biennial elections.

Like her late husband, Mary has a generally conservative outlook, but she has emerged as somewhat of an independent in her thinking about issues. Her first desire was to see as many of her husband's legislative initiatives through as possible, but to play a constructive political role, as well. "I needed to have my own agenda," she says.

Among the interests that Mary has made her own in Congress are health care, the environment, the economy, and Native American rights. In 2000, for example, she introduced legislation to create the Santa Rosa and San Jacinto National Monument near Palm Springs. She also helped broker an agreement to compensate the Torres Martinez Desert Cahuilla Indians for land seized from the tribe in 1908.

That Mary doesn't quite fit the stereotypical image of politician may, in fact, be one of the reasons for her success. In an interview, she commented, "I see myself as such a citizen politician. I don't see myself as the career, helmet-haired politician, and that might cost me one day." But, she says, she loves her district and its people, and "I hope to continue to represent them in a good way as long as they'll have me."

Most women who serve in Congress have compelling stories, because they have overcome obstacles to win. There are still only 74 women in the House, out of a total of 435 seats, and 16 women senators out of 100, less than 20 percent of the total. The women I have profiled here faced extraordinary challenges that changed the direction of their lives in dramatic ways. Others I admire, who rose from suffering to lead, are former Senator Paula Hawkins, a Florida Republican who served from 1981 to 1986. After she retired from public life, Paula revealed that she had been sexually abused as a child and published the book, *Children at Risk: My Fight Against Child Abuse*, which she described as "a personal story and a public plea." Congresswoman Carolyn McCarthy, a Democrat from New York, ran for Congress on a gun control platform after her husband was murdered and her son severely injured by a random shooting on a Long Island Rail Road commuter train in 1993. Though I differ with Carolyn on the gun issue, I admire her commitment and strength.

All the women I have known in Congress have special qualities, a strong work ethic, perseverance, and spirit. They have brought a different experience to the table, assuring that legislation is more representative of all views and needs, and adding a distinctive voice to the national debate.

End of chpt, 8

The End!

366

goes to pg (only) pg. 367... (handwritten)

Acknowledgments

I appreciate the HarperCollins team in so many ways.

    Howard Cohn, the research and draft writer, is a gem. His research skills are phenomenal. When we were crashing on a very short deadline, both drafting and editing on four hours of sleep in the last month, he never lost his good nature.

It was editor Claire Wachtel's idea to write the book, expanding on the women trailblazers we profiled in *American Heroines: The Spirited Women Who Shaped Our Country*. We both believe that their stories need to be told so that future generations have the full picture of American history.

My husband, Ray, is a gifted writer with invaluable suggestions.

There are several people who, through friendship, helped me juggle this book with my other responsibilities to my constituents and my family. Peggy Carr, Trisha Wilson, Lindsey Parham, Gail Thomas, Shannon Callewart, Mary Jarratt, Bari Levingston, James Christoferson, Jason Fuller, John Etue, Bethany Smith, Jan Benson, Doug Goff, Carl Holshouser, Russell Bailey, Marc Short, Father Larry Smith, and Father Steve Swann have all contributed in invaluable ways.

Finally, Jo Brim has been part of our extended family for fifteen years. Without her loyalty and support, and the help of Pauline Suell, the book couldn't have been finished.

gres to pg. 378... = 10??

Suggestions for Further Reading

CHAPTER 1: THE GOOD FIGHT: WOMEN IN THE MILITARY

Sybil Ludington and Deborah Sampson

Melissa Lukeman Bohrer, *Glory, Passion, and Principle: The Story of Eight Remarkable Women at the Core of the American Revolution* (New York: Atria Books, 2003).

Alfred Fabian Young, *Masquerade: The Life and Times of Deborah Sampson, Continental Soldier* (New York: Knopf, 2004).

Sarah Emma Edmonds

Laura Leedy Gansler, *The Mysterious Private Thompson: The Double Life of Sarah Emma Edmonds, Civil War Soldier* (New York: Free Press, 2005).

Sara Emma Edmonds, *Memoirs of a Soldier, Nurse, and Spy: A Woman's Adventures in the Union Army*; introduction and annotations by Elizabeth D. Leonard (Dekalb: Northern Illinois University Press, 1999). This is a new edition of *Nurse and Spy in the Union Army* (1865).

Rose Greenhow

Ann Blackman, *Wild Rose: Rose O'Neale Greenhow, Civil War Spy* (New York: Random House, 2005).

Doris Faber, *Rose Greenhow, Spy for the Confederacy* (New York: Putnam, 1968).

Ishbel Ross, *Rebel Rose; Life of Rose O'Neal Greenhow, Confederate Spy* (New York: Harper, 1954).

Elizabeth Van Lew

Elizabeth R. Varon, *Southern Lady, Yankee Spy: The True Story of Elizabeth Van Lew, a Union Agent in the Heart of the Confederacy* (New York: Oxford University Press, 2003).

Mary Edwards Walker

Dale L. Walker, *Mary Edwards Walker: Above and Beyond* (New York: Forge, 2005).

Virginia Hall

Judith Pearson, *The Wolves at the Door: The True Story of America's Greatest Female Spy* (Guilford, CT: Lyons Press, 2005).

CHAPTER 2: FIRST LADIES: THE HARDEST UNPAID JOB IN THE WORLD

Dolley Madison

Catherine Allgor, *A Perfect Union: Dolley Madison and the Creation of the American Nation* (New York: Henry Holt, 2006).

Richard N. Cote, *Strength and Honor: The Life of Dolley Madison* (Mt. Pleasant, SC: Corinthian Books, 2005).

The Selected Letters of Dolley Payne Madison, David B. Mattern and Holly C. Shulman, eds. (Charlottesville, VA: University of Virginia Press, 2003).

Helen Taft

Carl Sferrazza Anthony, *Nellie Taft: The Unconventional First Lady of the Ragtime Era* (New York: Morrow, 2005).

Helen Herron Taft, *Recollections of Full Years* (New York: Dodd, Mead, 1914).

Edith Wilson

Phyllis Lee Levin, *Edith and Woodrow: The Wilson White House* (New York: Scribner, 2001).

Edwin Tribble, ed., *A President in Love: The Courtship Letters of Woodrow Wilson and Edith Bolling Galt* (Boston: Houghton Mifflin, 1981).

Ishbel Ross, *Power with Grace: The Life Story of Mrs. Woodrow Wilson* (New York: Putnam, 1975).

Edith Bolling Wilson, *My Memoir* (Indianapolis and New York: Bobbs-Merrill, 1939).

Eleanor Roosevelt

Blanche Wiesen Cook, *Eleanor Roosevelt: Volume One: 1884–1933* (New York: Viking Press, 1992).

371.

_____, *Eleanor Roosevelt: Volume Two: 1933–1938: The Defining Years* (New York: Penguin Books, 1999).

Joseph P. Lash, *Eleanor and Franklin* (New York: W. W. Norton, 1971).

_____, *Eleanor: The Years Alone* (New York: W. W. Norton, 1972).

Eleanor Roosevelt, *This Is My Story* (New York: Harper, 1937).

_____, *This I Remember* (New York: Harper, 1949).

_____, *On My Own* (New York: Harper, 1958).

_____, *Autobiography* (New York: Harper, 1961).

_____, *It Seems to Me: Selected Letters of Eleanor Roosevelt*, Leonard C. Schlup and Donald W. Whisenhunt, eds. (Lexington: University Press of Kentucky, 2001).

_____, *My Day: The Best of Eleanor Roosevelt's Acclaimed Newspaper Columns, 1936–1962*; David Emblidge and Marcy Ross, eds.; introduction by Blanche Wiesen Cook (New York: Da Capo Press, 2001).

Bess Truman

Margaret Truman, *Bess W. Truman* (New York: Macmillan, 1986).

Robert H. Ferrell, editor, *Dear Bess: The Letters from Harry to Bess Truman, 1910–1959* (New York: W. W. Norton, 1983; reprinted, Columbia, MO: University of Missouri Press, 1998).

Margaret Truman, *Harry S. Truman* (New York: William Morrow, 1973).

_____, *Souvenir: Margaret Truman's Own Story* (New York: McGraw-Hill, 1956).

Harry S. Truman, *Memoirs.* 2 volumes (New York: Doubleday, 1955–1956).

Mamie Eisenhower

Susan Eisenhower, *Mrs. Ike: Memories and Reflections on the Life of Mamie Eisenhower* (New York: Farrar, Straus & Giroux, 1996).

Lester and Irene David, *Ike and Mamie: The Story of the General and His Lady* (New York: Putnam, 1981).

Dwight D. Eisenhower, *Letters to Mamie,* John S. D. Eisenhower, ed. (Garden City, NJ: Doubleday, 1978).

Julie Nixon Eisenhower, *Special People* (New York: Simon & Schuster, 1977).

Dorothy Brandon, *Mamie Doud Eisenhower: A Portrait of a First Lady* (New York: Scribner, 1954).

Jacqueline Kennedy

Barbara A. Perry, *Jacqueline Kennedy: First Lady of the New Frontier* (Lawrence: University Press of Kansas, 2004).

Donald Spoto, *Jacqueline Bouvier Kennedy Onassis: A Life* (New York: St. Martin's Press, 2000).

Sarah Bradford, *America's Queen: The Life of Jacqueline Kennedy Onassis* (New York: Viking, 2000).

Mary Van Renssalaer Thayer, *Jacqueline Kennedy: The White House Years* (Boston: Little, Brown, 1971).

Lady Bird Johnson

Lewis L. Gould, *Lady Bird Johnson: Our Environmental First Lady* (Lawrence: University Press of Kansas, 1999).

Lady Bird Johnson, *A White House Diary* (New York: Holt, Rinehart and Winston, 1970).

Pat Nixon

Julie Nixon Eisenhower, *Pat Nixon: The Untold Story* (New York: Simon & Schuster, 1986)

Betty Ford

John Robert Greene, *Betty Ford: Candor and Courage in the White House* (Lawrence: University Press of Kansas, 2004).

Betty Ford, with Chris Chase, *The Times of My Life* (New York: Harper & Row, 1978).

Betty Ford, with Chris Chase, *Betty, a Glad Awakening* (Garden City, NY: Doubleday, 1987).

Rosalynn Carter

Rosalynn Carter, *First Lady from Plains* (Boston: Houghton Mifflin, 1984).

Dawn Langley Simmons, *Rosalynn Carter: Her Life Story* (New York: F. Fell Publishers, 1979).

Nancy Reagan

James G. Benze Jr., *Nancy Reagan: On the White House Stage* (Lawrence: University Press of Kansas, 2005).

Bob Colacello, *Ronnie and Nancy: Their Path to the White House* (New York: Warner Books, 2004).

Michael Deaver, *Nancy: A Portrait of My Years with Nancy Reagan* (New York: Morrow, 2004).

Nancy Reagan, with Bill Libby, *Nancy* (New York: Morrow, 1980).

Nancy Reagan, with William Novak, *My Turn: The Memoirs of Nancy Reagan* (New York: Random House, 1989).

Barbara Bush

Pamela Kilian, *Barbara Bush: Matriarch of a Dynasty* (New York: St. Martin's Press, 2002).

_____, *Barbara Bush: A Biography* (New York, St. Martin's Press, 1992).

Barbara Bush, Reflections: *Life After the White House* (New York: Scribner, 2004).

_____, *Barbara Bush: A Memoir* (New York: Scribner, 1994).

Hillary Clinton

Hillary Clinton, *Living History* (New York: Simon & Schuster, 2003).

Laura Bush

Ronald Kessler, *Laura Bush: An Intimate Portrait of the First Lady* (New York: Doubleday, 2006).

Chapter 3: If There's a Book You Want to Read: Novelists and Journalists

Harriet Beecher Stowe

Joan D. Hedrick, *Harriet Beecher Stowe: A Life* (New York: Oxford University Press, 1994).

Charles Edward Stowe and Lyman Beecher Stowe, *Harriet Beecher Stowe: The Story of Her Life* (Whitefish, MT: Kessinger Publishing, 2005); reprint of the 1911 biography by her son and grandson.

Charles Edward Stowe, *Life of Harriet Beecher Stowe: Compiled from Her Letters and Journals* (Honolulu: University Press of the Pacific, 2004); reprint of the 1889 edition.

Barbara A. White, *The Beecher Sisters* (New Haven: Yale University Press, 2003).

Eliza Jane Poitevent

James Henry Harrison, *Pearl Rivers, Publisher of the Picayune* (New Orleans: Dept. of Journalism, Tulane University, 1932).

Pearl Buck

Peter J. Conn, *Pearl S. Buck: A Cultural Biography* (Cambridge and New York: Cambridge Press, 1996).

Theodore F. Harris, *Pearl S. Buck: A Biography*, 2 vols. (New York: John Day, 1969–1971), written in consultation with Pearl Buck.

Pearl Buck, *The Exile* (New York: Reynal & Hitchcock, 1936).

_____, *Fighting Angel; Portrait of a Soul* (New York: Reynal & Hitchcock, 1936).

_____, *The Child Who Never Grew*, with a foreword by James Michener (Rockville, MD: Woodbine House, 1992); reprint of the 1950 edition.

_____, *My Several Worlds, a Personal Record* (New York: Day, 1954).

Toni Morrison
Wilfred D. Samuels and Clenora Hudson-Weems, *Toni Morrison* (Boston: Twayne, 1990).
Danille Taylor-Guthrie and Toni Morrison. *Conversations with Toni Morrison* (Jackson: University Press of Mississippi, 1994).

Amy Tan
Amy Tan, *The Opposite of Fate: A Book of Musings* (New York: G. P. Putnam, 2003).

María Elena Salinas
María Elena Salinas, *I Am My Father's Daughter: Living a Life Without Secrets* (New York: Rayo, 2006).

CHAPTER 4: A DREAM OF THE FUTURE: WOMEN'S SUFFRAGE AND CIVIL RIGHTS

Susan B. Anthony
Geoffrey C. Ward and Kenneth Burns, *Not for Ourselves Alone: The Story of Elizabeth Cady Stanton and Susan B. Anthony* (New York: Alfred A. Knopf, 1999).
Alma Lutz, *Susan B. Anthony: Rebel, Crusader, Humanitarian* (Boston: Beacon Press, 1959).
Jean H. Baker, *Sisters: The Lives of America's Suffragists* (New York: Hill & Wang, 2005).
Susan B. Anthony, *Failure Is Impossible: Susan B. Anthony in Her Own Words*, ed. Lynn Sherr (New York: Times Books, 1996).

Elizabeth Cady Stanton
Judith Wellman, *The Road to Seneca Falls: Elizabeth Cady Stanton and the First Woman's Rights Convention* (Urbana: University of Illinois Press, 2004).
Elisabeth Griffith, *In Her Own Right: The Life of Elizabeth Cady Stanton* (New York: Oxford University Press, 1984).
Elizabeth Cady Stanton, *Eighty Years and More: Reminiscences, 1815–1897*, introduction by Ellen Carol DuBois; afterword by Ann D. Gordon (Boston: Northeastern University Press, 1993).
Ellen Carol DuBois, ed., *The Elizabeth Cady Stanton–Susan B. Anthony Reader: Correspondence, Writings, Speeches*; foreword by Gerda Lerner (Boston: Northeastern University Press, 1992).
Mary Jo Buhle and Paul Buhle, eds., *The Concise History of Woman Suffrage: Selections from History of Woman Suffrage, by Elizabeth Cady Stanton, Susan B. Anthony, Matilda Joslyn Gage, and the National American Woman Suffrage Association* (Urbana: University of Illinois Press, 2005).

315.

Lucretia Mott

Dorothy Sterling, *Lucretia Mott* (New York: Feminist Press at CUNY, 1999).

Otelia Cromwell, *Lucretia Mott* (Cambridge, MA: Harvard University Press, 1958).

Lucretia Mott, *Selected Letters of Lucretia Coffin Mott*, Beverly Wilson Palmer, ed. (Urbana: University of Illinois Press, 2002).

Rosa Parks

Douglas Brinkley, *Rosa Parks* (New York: Viking, 2000).

Virginia Durr

Virginia Foster Durr, *Freedom Writer: Virginia Foster Durr, Letters from the Civil Rights Years,* ed. Patricia Sullivan (New York: Routledge, 2003).

_____, *Outside the Magic Circle: The Autobiograhy of Virginia Foster Durr*, ed. Hollinger F. Barnard (Tuscaloosa: University of Alabama Press, 1985).

Barbara Jordan

Mary Beth Rogers, *Barbara Jordan: American Hero.* (New York: Bantam, 1998).

Austin Teutsch, *Barbara Jordan: The Biography* (Cedar Park, TX: Golden Touch Press, 1997).

Barbara Jordan, with Shelby Hearon. *Barbara Jordan: A Self-Portrait* (Garden City, NY: Doubleday, 1979).

_____, *Barbara C. Jordan: Selected Speeches*, Sandra Parham, ed. (Washington, D.C.: Howard University Press, 1999).

Chapter 5: Everything I Learned Was New: Women in Medicine and Public Health

Elizabeth and Emily Blackwell

Dorothy Clarke Wilson, *Lone Woman: The Story of Elizabeth Blackwell, the First Woman Doctor* (Boston: Little, Brown, 1970).

Elinor Rice Hays, *Those Extraordinary Blackwells* (New York: Harcourt, Brace, & World, 1967).

Ishbel Ross, *Child of Destiny: The Life Story of the First Woman Doctor* (New York: Harper, 1949).

Alice Hamilton

Barbara Sicherman, *Alice Hamilton: A Life in Letters* (Cambridge, MA: Harvard University Press, 1984).

Madeline Grant, *Alice Hamilton: Pioneer Doctor in Industrial Medicine* (New York: Abelard-Schuman, 1967).

Alice Hamilton, *Exploring the Dangerous Trades* (Boston, MA: Northeastern University Press, 1985); reprint of the 1943 edition.

Alice Evans
Virginia L. Burns, *Gentle Hunter: Biography of Alice Evans, Bacteriologist* (Laingsburg, MI: Enterprise Press, 1993).

Rachel Carson
Mark Hamilton Lytle, *The Gentle Subversive: Rachel Carson, Silent Spring, and the Rise of the Environmental Movement* (New York: Oxford University Press, 2007).
Linda J. Lear, *Rachel Carson: Witness for Nature* (New York: Henry Holt, 1997).
Rachel Carson, *Always, Rachel: The Letters of Rachel Carson and Dorothy Freeman, 1952–1964: The Story of a Remarkable Friendship* (Boston: Beacon Press, 1996).

Helen Taussig
Sherwin B. Nuland, *Doctors: The Biography of Medicine* (New York: Random House, 1989).

CHAPTER 6: LIFTING THE VEIL OF NATURE: THE NOBEL PRIZE IN SCIENCE

Maria Goeppert-Mayer
Ioan James, *Remarkable Physicists: From Galileo to Yukawa* (Cambridge, England: Cambridge University Press, 2004).
Andrea Gabor, *Einstein's Wife* (New York: Viking, 1995).
Joan Dash, *A Life of One's Own* (New York: Harper & Row, 1973).

Rosalyn Yalow
Eugene Straus, *Rosalyn Yalow, Nobel Laureate: Her Life and Work in Medicine* (New York: Plenum Trade, 1998).
Remarkable Physicists: From Galileo to Yukawa (Cambridge, England: Cambridge University Press, 2004).
Andrea Gabor, *Einstein's Wife,* (New York: Viking, 1995).

Barbara McClintock
Nathaniel C. Comfort, *The Tangled Field: Barbara McClintock's Search for the Patterns of Genetic Control.* (Cambridge, MA: Harvard University Press, 2001).
Evelyn Fox Keller, *A Feeling for the Organism* (San Francisco: W. H. Freeman, 1983).

Rita Levi-Montalcini

Rita Levi-Montalcini, *In Praise of Imperfection: My Life and Work*; Luigi Attardi, trans. (New York: Basic Books, 1988).

Gertrude Elion

Mary Ellen Bowden, Amy Beth Crow, and Tracy Sullivan, *Pharmaceutical Achievers* (Philadelphia: Chemical Heritage Foundation, 2001).

Chapter 7: Curing Social Misery: The Settlement House and Peace Movements

Jane Addams

Louise Knight, *Citizen: Jane Addams and the Struggle for Democracy* (Chicago: University of Chicago Press, 2005).

Victoria Bissell Brown, *The Education of Jane Addams* (Philadelphia: University of Pennsylvania Press, 2004).

Katherine Joslin, *Jane Addams: A Writer's Life* (Urbana: University of Illinois Press, 2004).

Jean Bethke Elshtain, *Jane Addams and the Dream of American Democracy: A Life* (New York: Basic Books, 2002).

James Weber Linn, *Jane Addams: A Biography*; introduction by Ann Firor Scott (Urbana: University of Illinois Press, 2004).

Gioia Diliberto, *A Useful Woman: The Early Life of Jane Addams* (New York: Scribner, 1999). Reprint of 1910 edition.

Allen F. Davis, *American Heroine: The Life and Legend of Jane Addams* (London: Oxford University Press, 1973).

Jane Addams, *Twenty Years at Hull-House*; edited with and introduction by Victoria Bissell Brown (New York: Bedford/St. Martin's, 1999); originally published in 1910.

_____, *The Jane Addams Reader*, Jean Bethke Elshtain, ed. (New York: Basic Books, 2002).

Florence Kelley

Kathryn Kish Sklar, *Florence Kelley and the Nation's Work* (New Haven, CT: Yale University Press, 1995).

Emily Greene Balch

Mercedes M. Randall, *Improper Bostonian: Emily Greene Balch, Nobel Peace Laureate, 1946* (New York: Twayne, 1964).

CHAPTER 8: COMMITMENT OVERCOMES ADVERSITY

Lindy Boggs

Lindy Boggs, with Katherine Hatch. *Washington Through a Purple Veil: Memoirs of a Southern Woman* (New York: Harcourt Brace, 1994).

Dianne Feinstein

Jerry Roberts, *Dianne Feinstein: Never Let Them See You Cry* (San Francisco: Harper, 1995).

Celia Morris, *Storming the Statehouse: Running for Governor with Ann Richards and Dianne Feinstein* (New York: Scribner's, 1992).

Catherine Whitney, *Nine and Counting: The Women of the Senate* (New York: Morrow, 2000).

Olympia Snowe

Catherine Whitney, *Nine and Counting: The Women of the Senate* (New York: Morrow, 2000).

Paula Hawkins

Paula Hawkins, *Children at Risk: My Fight Against Child Abuse* (Bethesda, MD: Adler & Adler, 1986).

End of Suggestions for further reading.

Copyright 2007

pg. 379

INDEX

Index) goes to pg. 396...

-A-

abolitionist movement, xiv, 127–33,
168, 170, 171, 177–78, 180, 181, 208,
209, 296
abortion issue, 95, 101
acyclovir, 291
Adams, Abigail, 42, 51, 109, 114, 174
Adams, John, 42
Adams, Sherman, 75
Addams, Jane, 222, 293–317, 319,
320–21, 330–31
childhood reading of, 296
European travel of, 300–301,
311–312
family of, 293–98, 300
father-daughter relationship of,
295–96, 299
Garfield assassination and, 299
at 1915 Hague congress, 305, 320
Nobel Peace Prize of, 315–16,
324
in peace movement, 314–316
publications of, 314, 316–17
public health reforms of, 309–310
Tolstoy's encounter with, 311–312

-A-

vocational search of, 299–301,
325–26
women's suffrage and, 312–13, 314
see also Hull-House
Addams, John Huy, 294–96, 299, 317
Adoption and Safe Families Act (1997),
119–20
African Americans, 49, 50, 63, 73, 75,
117, 132
enfranchisement of, 171–72, 181,
338–39
political activists, 145–46
Scottsboro boys, 187
Southern racist attitudes toward,
185–86
African American women, 144–53,
184–206
authors, 144–48
college presidents, 205–6
television journalists, 149–53
*After the Guns Fall Silent: The Enduring
Legacy of Landmines* (Williams and
Roberts), 329
Air Force, U.S., 34–38

-A-

Air Force Nurse Corps, U.S., 35
Albert, Carl, 339, 340
Alcott, Louisa May, 20, 296
Alioto, Joseph, 347–48
Allén, Sture, 148
Altgeld, John Peter, 306
Alzheimer's disease, 112–14, 284
American Equal Rights Association,
  171–72, 181
American Jewish Joint Distribution
  Committee, 285–86
American Public Health Association,
  234
American Revolution, 2–10, 11
  heroic ride in, 3–4
  spying in, 4–5
  volunteers in, 5, 11
  wives accompanying husbands in,
    8–10
  women enlisting in, 2, 5–8
American Woman Suffrage Association
  (AWSA), 173
Anderson, Jennie Herron, 48
Anderson, Marian, 63, 69, 73
Anderson, Sarah, 300–301
Andrews, Tom, 353
Anthony, Susan B., 166–77, 216, 305
  as abolitionist, 168, 170, 171
  appearance of, 169, 170
  arrest of, for voting in 1872 election,
    173–74
  biography of, 175–76
  colleagues of, 170, 171–72, 174–75
  credo of, 176
  Declaration of Rights for Women
    publicly read by, 174
  later years of, 175–76
  marriage renounced by, 170–71
  nickname bestowed on, 175
  Nineteenth Amendment and, 175,
    176, 177, 183
  NWSA founded by, 173–75, 176, 181

  personality of, 169–170, 171, 175
  Stanton's collaboration with,
    169–170, 171, 172, 174–75,
    181–82, 183
  Train and, 172–73, 176
  Washington memorials to, 183–84
  women's suffrage movement
    history compiled by, 174–175
Anti-Slavery Convention of American
  Women, 180
Apgar, Virginia, 250–54
Argonne National Laboratory, 265,
  267
Army Nurse Corps (ANC), 21–24,
  30–33
army nurses, 20–24
  at Anzio, 23–24
  as casualties, 23, 24
  in Civil War, 14, 15, 20–21, 213
  in Korean War, 23, 24, 31
  medals awarded to, 21, 22, 24
  in Philippines, 21–23
  star ranks achieved by, 30–33
  in Vietnam War, 32
  in World War I, 21
  in World War II, 21–24, 31
Arnold, Benedict, 3
Aung San Suu Kyi, 124–25
authors, xiv–xv, 127–65
  abolitionist, xiv, 127–33
  African American, 144–48
  China as subject of, 137–44, 153–57
  see also journalists
Avery, Oswald, 289
Axworthy, Lloyd, 330
azathioprine (Imuran), 290–91
azidothymidine (AZT), 291

-B-

Babbitt, Bruce, 90
bacteriology, 220, 224, 228, 231–33,
  240
Bailey, Ann, 8

Baker, Josephine, 26
Baker, Kristin, 37
Balch, Emily Greene, 305, 317–24
    Denison House founded by, among
        others, 319
    immigrant Slavs studied by, 319–20
    Nobel Peace Prize of, 323–24
    in peace movement, 320–24
    publications of, 318, 319, 321, 322
    refugee immigration supported by,
        322
    on Wellesley faculty, 319–21
    World War II supported by, 322–23
Bales, Susan Ford, 103
Balmaseda, Liz, xiv, 157–60
Baraka, Amiri, 146
Barbara Jordan: A Self Portrait (Jordan),
    204
Barker, Jacob, 44
Barnett, Samuel and Henrietta, 301
Barry, Dave, 157
Bass, Ronald, 156
Bay of Pigs invasion, 82, 355
Beard, Margaret, 186
Beecher, Catharine, xiii, 128–29, 130
Beecher, Henry Ward, 128, 132
Beecher, Lyman, 128, 129, 132
Begg, Alexander, 235
Begich, Nick, 339
Beloved (Morrison), 148, 151
Benjamin, Judah, 11
Berson, Solomon H., 271–72, 273
Bess W. Truman (Daniel), 67
Betty: A Glad Awakening (Betty Ford),
    102
Betty Ford Center, 102–103
Beuren, Alois, 238
Binney, Barnabas, 8
birth defects, 235–40, 254, 284
    thalidomide as cause in, 238–39
Blackwell, Elizabeth, xiii, 207–15, 261
    clinical training of, 211–12

at Geneva Medical College, xiii,
    210–11
girls physical education lectures of,
    212
colleagues of, 212–14
publications of, 213–14
Blackwell, Emily, 212–15
Blackwell, Henry, 170, 176
Blake, James, 190
Blalock, Alfred, 236–37, 238
Blalock-Taussig operation, 236–38
Bloomer, Amelia, 169
blue baby syndrome, 235–38, 239–40
Bluest Eye, The (Morrison), 146–47
Boggs, Hale, 336–41, 344
Boggs, Lindy Claiborne, 336–44
Bohr, Niels, 265
boilermaker's deafness, 227
Bolling, William Holcombe, 52
Bones, Helen Woodrow, 52
Bonesetter's Daughter, The (Tan), 157
Bono, Mary Whitaker, 362–64
Born, Max, 262–63, 264, 267
Bowser, Mary Elizabeth, 19
Boxer, Barbara, 350
Bradford, William, 6
Bradley, Ruby, 21–23
Breckenridge, Lucy, 11
Brewer, Margaret A., 35
Brezhnev, Victoria, 96
Brinkley, Douglas, 187–88
Brown, Claude, 146
Brown, Edmund G. "Pat," 346
Bruce, Sir David, 232
brucellosis (undulant fever), 231–33,
    240
Buck, John Lossing, 138–40, 141
Buck, Pearl, xiv, 137–44, 145
    adopted children of, 139, 143
    marriages of, 138–40, 143
    Nobel Prize of, 142–43, 148
    novels of, 138–39, 140–43, 144, 151

Buck, Pearl (*cont.*)
    Pulitzer Prize of, 142
    retarded child of, 139, 141, 143
    as women's rights advocate, 143–44
Burbank, Nathaniel, 136
Burchenal, Joseph, 289–90
Burma, 31, 124–25
Burn, Harry, 177
Burr, Aaron, 40, 128
Bush, Barbara Pierce, 39–40, 114–17
Bush, George H. W., 114–17, 123, 352, 361
Bush, George W., 114–15, 123–26
Bush, Laura Welch, 122–26
Butler, Josephine, 178
Butler, Nicholas Murray, 315, 316

caisson disease, 227
Califano, Joseph, 105
Carmichael, Stokely, 146
Carnegie Endowment for International Peace, 314, 315
Carson, Claiborne, 194
Carson, Rachel, 240–50
    with Fish and Wildlife Service, 242, 243, 244, 245
    national wildlife refuge named for, 249–50
    pesticide warning of, 245–50
    trilogy about oceans published by, 243–44, 250
Carter, Jimmy, 103–8, 116, 119, 147
Carter, Rosalynn Smith, 103–8
Catling, Lorna, 30
Catt, Carrie Chapman, 175
Chao, Elaine, 359–62
Cher, 362, 363
Chiang Kai-shek, 139
Chiang Kai-shek, Madame, 63
Child, Julia, 26
Children at Risk: My Fight Against Child Abuse (Hawkins), 364

Child Who Never Grew, The (Buck), 139
China, xiv, 137–44, 153–57
China, People's Republic of, 96, 99, 143, 155
Chirac, Jacques, 30
Churchill, Winston, 63
Civil Rights Act (1964), 86
civil rights movement, 62, 184–206
    activists in, 145–46, 189
    bus desegregation in, 184–97; *see also* Parks, Rosa
Civil War, 129, 132, 171, 337
    landmines in, 326–27
Civil War, women in, 10–21
    enlistments of, 10–18
    male comrades of, 13–14, 16
    memoirs of, 15–16, 17–18
    need for medical attention by, 12–13, 14
    as nurses, 14, 15, 20–21, 213
    pregnant, 14
    romantic attractions of, 14–15
    spying by, 15, 17, 18–20
    as wives accompanying husbands, 11, 14
Clark, Mark, 24
Clark, Mildred Irene, 32
Clarke, Amy, 11
Clay, Henry, 45
Clemens, Samuel (Mark Twain), 132, 142
Cleveland, Frances, 79
Cleveland, Grover, 53
Clinton, Bill, 118, 119, 120, 196, 204
Clinton, Hillary Rodham, 95, 118–22
cocaine addition, juvenile, 225–26
Cohen, Stanley, 283–85
Cohen, William S., 352, 353
Collins, Susan, 121, 353–54
Coman, Katherine, 319
Commission on Immigration Reform, U.S., 204

Committee for a More Beautiful
    Capital, 88–89
Committee for the Preservation of the
    White House, 84
Congress, U.S., 21, 48, 75, 85, 89, 113,
    120, 152, 175, 176, 177, 320, 321
    drug testing legislation of, 239
    First Lady's staff funded by, 105
    keeping one's word in, 201–2
    military rank restrictions lifted by,
        25, 32
    Parks honored by, 197
    senior citizen legislation of, 106–7
    Stanton's 1866 campaign for
        election to, 183
    White House improvements funded
        by, 42–43, 68–69
    women in, 64, 201, 202–3, 336–59,
        362–65
    women's military pensions awarded
        by, 9–10
    see also Senate, U.S.
Congressional Medal of Honor, 21
Congresswomen's Caucus, 341, 344
Constitution, U.S., 106, 202–3
    Fourteenth Amendment, 171, 173
    Nineteenth Amendment, xiv, 175,
        176, 177, 183, 232, 313
Convention on Conventional Weapons
    (CCW), 324, 329, 330
Conyers, John, 195
Cooley, Denton, 237
Coolidge, Calvin, 60
Coolidge, Grace, 57
Corbin, Margaret, 8–10
Cori, Gerty Radnitz, xiv, 255, 256–62,
    273
    Nobel Prize of, 260–61
    sugar metabolism research of,
        259–60
Cox, James M., 56, 60
Cruz, Celia, 357

Cuban émigrés, xiv, 82, 157–60,
    355–59
Curie, Marie, 261, 267
Curtis, Winterton C., 277
Cutts, Anna Payne, 43, 45
Cyprian, Emma, 338

- D -

Dangerous Trades, The (Oliver), 226
Daniel, Margaret Truman, 66, 67–68,
    69, 70
Darragh, Lydia, 4–5
Darrow, Clarence, 305
Darwin, Charles, 298
Daughters of the American Revolution
    (DAR), 6, 10, 63, 69, 315
Davis, Jefferson, 19, 21
DDT, see
    dichlorodiphenyltrichloroethane
Declaration of Rights for Women, 174
Declaration of Sentiments, 169, 178–79,
    180, 181, 183
de Gaulle, Charles, 29
Dell'Ariccia, Manilo, 285–86
De Mattei, Louis, 154, 156–57
Demerec, Milislav, 277
Denison House, 319
DePauw, Linda, 6
DePeyster, Robert, 44
Desjardins, Susan Y., 37
Dewey, John, 305, 315
Diana, Princess of Wales, 328
dichlorodiphenyltrichloroethane
    (DDT), 240–42, 245, 246, 248
Dickerman, Marion, 61
Dickson, John and Samuel, 210
Distinguished Service Cross, 29
Dix, Dorothea, 15, 20
Dix, Dorothy (pseud.), 136–37
Donaldson, Mary, 210
Donovan, William J. "Wild Bill," 28, 29
Dorothy Dix Talks (Gilmer), 136–137
Douglass, Frederick, 168, 177

Dred: A Tale of the Great Dismal Swamp (Stowe), 132
Dreiser, Theodore, 142
Du Bois, W. E. B., 305
Duerk, Alene B., 35
Dulbecco, Renato, 281
Durr, Virginia and Clifford, 189, 191

Earhart, Amelia, 63, 319
Early, Jubal, 17
East Wind, West Wind (Buck), 140
Edinger, Ludwig and Anna, 221
Edmonds, Sarah Emma, 12–17
Edward R. Murrow Award, 164
Eisenhower, Dwight D., 32, 70, 71–77, 93, 99, 110, 247
Eisenhower, John Sheldon, 71, 72
Eisenhower, Mamie Doud, 57, 70–77, 93, 94, 99
Elder, William, 210
Elion, Gertrude, 287–92
    Nobel Prize of, 290–91, 292
Elion, Jon, 292
Eliot, George, 131, 217
Eliot, Martha May, 233–34
"Endgame" (Tan), 155
Environmental Film Festival, 250
Environmental Protection Agency, 97
epidermal growth factor (EGF), 284
Equal Credit Opportunity Act, 341–42
equal rights amendment, 95, 105, 202, 313
Erskine, David Montagu, 42
Evans, Alice, 231–33, 240
Exploring the Dangerous Trades (Hamilton), 217–18, 231
explosives factories, 229

Fall, Albert, 56
Farley, James, 61
Feinstein, Dianne Goldman, 124–25, 335, 345–51

Feinstein-Hutchison Breast Cancer Research Stamp, 351
Fermi, Enrico, 265, 266–67, 268
Fields, Annie, 133
Filipino Constabulary Band, 49
Firestone, Harvey, 102
First Ladies, xiv, 39–126
    Arlington National Cemetery burials of, 51, 83
    beautification projects of, 39, 48–49, 88–89, 90
    as both mother and wife of presidents, 51, 114, 117
    causes supported by, 39–40, 49–50, 51, 57–58, 61, 62–63, 64–65, 68, 72, 76, 77, 84–85, 88, 96–99, 104, 105–8, 110–12, 116–17, 118, 119–21
    congressional testimony of, 106
    cultural projects of, 47, 49, 76, 82–83, 89
    historic preservation projects of, 39, 80–81, 83, 120–21, 126
    as hostesses, 41–42, 43, 44, 45, 48, 63, 68, 73–74, 81, 107
    inaugural precedents set by, 41–42, 47, 73, 87, 104, 109, 116
    journalism of, 61, 62, 65, 78, 83
    at national party conventions, 51, 57, 94, 113, 115, 124, 126
    as presidential widows, 76–77, 82–83
    publications of, 51, 62, 64, 65, 90, 102, 103, 108, 112, 121
    White House improvement projects of, 42–43, 68–69, 79–80, 83, 84, 89, 98, 111, 114, 120–21
    as women's rights advocates, 61, 62, 64, 75, 95, 96, 105–6, 119, 120, 124–25
Fitzgerald, Geraldine, 57
Flexner, Simon, 221–22

Floyd, Catherine "Kitty," 41
Fondazione Levi-Montalcini, 285–87
Food and Drug Administration (FDA), U.S., 239, 290
Forces Françaises de l'Interieur, 29
Ford, Elizabeth "Betty" Bloomer, 39, 85, 99–103, 105, 113
Ford, Gerald, 36, 100, 340
Ford, Henry, 321
Foster Grandparent Program, 111
Fourteenth Amendment, 171, 173
France, 21, 25–30, 54–55, 66, 81, 318
Franck, James, 263
Freedmen's Aid Society, 16
Freeman, Tom, 198, 199
Fugitive Slave Law (1850), 130, 148

Gage, Matilda Joslyn, 174–75
Galt, Gertrude Bolling, 52
Garambouville, Louis-Marie Turreau de, 42
Garfield, James H., 299
Garner, Margaret, 148
Garrison, William Lloyd, 168, 180
Gates, George Porterfield, 70
genetics, 273–80
    DNA in, 280, 288–90
Geneva Medical College, xiii, 210–11
George VI, King of England, 28, 63
Gilman, Charlotte Perkins, 305–6
Gilmer, Elizabeth M., 136–37
Ginsberg, Ruth Bader, 184
Goeppert-Mayer, Maria, 262–68
    awards established in memory of, 267–68
    dissertation of, 263, 267
    Nobel Prize of, 267
    publications of, 263, 264, 266, 267
Goillot, Paul, 29–30
Goldhaber, Maurice and Gertrude, 269–70
Goldschmidt, Richard, 276

González, Elián, 159–60
Good Earth, The (Buck), 138–39, 140–43, 144, 145, 151
Gorbachev, Mikhail, 112
Gorbachev, Raisa, 117
Gore, Al, 350
Gould, Alice Bache, 318
Graham, Martha, 100
Grant, Ulysses S., 19
Gray, Ed, 192
Grayson, Cary T., 55, 56
Great Britain, 27–29, 30, 211–12, 213–14, 231, 232, 300–301
Greenback Party, 172
Green Door, 106
Greene, John Robert, 102
Greenhow, Rose O'Neal, 18
Groening, Matt, 157
Grubesic, Tomana, 285
Guiteau, Charles Julius, 299
gun control legislation, 349, 364–65
Guthrie, Mary, 277

Hagerty, James, 75
Hagidorn, Mary, 1
Haldeman, George, 297, 300
Haldeman, Harry, 300
Hall, Edwin Lee, 26
Hall, Mary Livingston Ludlow, 58
Hall, Virginia, 25–29
Hallström, Per, 142–43
Hamburger, Viktor, 280, 282, 283, 284
Hamilton, Alexander, 4, 128, 202
Hamilton, Alice, 215–31, 320
    at German universities, 220–21
    at Hull-House, 222–23, 224–26, 305
    as industrial toxicologist, 223, 226–31
    marriage renounced by, 217
    on medical school faculties, 222, 229–30

Hamilton, Alice (*cont.*)
  memoirs of, 217–18, 220, 221, 222, 228, 231
  scientific publications of, 221, 224, 230
Hamilton, Edith, 216–17, 218, 220–21
Hance, Kent, 123
Hancock, Winfield Scott, 299
Hardeman, Dorsey, 200–201
Harding, Warren G., 56–57, 60
Harper, Ida Husted, 175, 176
Harper, Margaret, 32
Harriet Lane Home for Invalid Children, 235, 38
Harris, Ellen, 75
Harris, Patricia, 105
Harrison, Benjamin, 46
Hate Crimes Statistics Act, 117
Hawkins, Paula, 364
Hayes, Rutherford B., 46, 80
Hays, Anna Mae, 30–33, 37–38
Head Start program, 88
Healing and Hope (Betty Ford), 103
Hearst, William Randolph, 136
Hektoen, Ludwig, 224
Henderson, Charles, 226
Henry Street Settlement, 307
Heritage Foundation, 361
Herzfeld, Karl F., 263–64
Heston, Charlton, 112
Hicks, Elias, 296
Higgins, Elmer, 243
Highway Beautification Act, 89
Hinojosa, María, 163
History of Woman Suffrage (Anthony), 174–75
Hitchings, George, 288–92
Hobby, Bill, 204
Hoefly, E. Ann, 35
Hoisington, Elizabeth P., 33–34, 37–38
Holbrook, Alva Morris, 134

Holm, Jeanne, 34–38
Holmes, Oliver Wendell, 131
Hooker, Isabelle Beecher, 128
Hoover, Herbert, 315
Hospital Sketches (Alcott), 20
Howe, Louis, 60, 61
Howe, William, 2–3, 4–5
Huckins, Olga Owens, 246
Hughes, Charles Evans, 54
Hughes, Sarah T., 87
Hull, Charles J., 301–2
Hull-House, 222, 296, 301–16
  children's clinic of, 222–23
  day nursery of, 308
  educational programs of, 302–5
  employment bureau of, 306
  funding of, 313–14
  residents of, 222–23, 224–26, 303–4, 305–7
  social reform pursued by, 309–11
  Toynbee Hall as model for, 300–301
Hull-House Maps and Papers, 306
Hundred Secret Senses, The (Tan), 157
Hurricane Katrina, 137, 344
Hutchison, C. B., 275
Hutchison-Feinstein Overseas Basing Act, 350–51

I Am My Father's Daughter (Salinas), 160, 165
Imuran (azathioprine), 290–91
India, 31, 241
industrial toxicology (occupational diseases), 223, 226–31, 305
  explosives factories in, 229
  lead poisoning in, 227–29
  viscous rayon industry in, 230
In Praise of Imperfection: My Life and Work (Levi-Montalcini), 287
Institute of Museum and Library Services, 125

Intermediate-Range Nuclear Forces (INF) Treaty (1987), 112

International Campaign to Ban Landmines (ICBL), 326–30, 333–34

International Congresses of Women, 305, 315, 320, 321

International Woman Suffrage Association, 176

Is My Baby All Right? (Apgar), 252

Israel, 64, 358

It Takes a Village (Clinton), 121

J

Jacobson, Eddie, 66

Jahn, Gunnar, 324

Japan, 48–49, 68

Jefferson, Thomas, 41, 42, 43, 44, 104

Jennings, Hal B., 33

Jensen, J. Hans D., 266, 267

John Day Company, 140

John Paul II, Pope, 163

Johnson, Andrew, 83

Johnson, Eliza, 83

Johnson, Lady Bird Taylor, 76–77, 83–90, 105, 125, 340
  beautification projects of, 39, 88–89, 90
  job description given by, 87
  media business owned by, 84, 85–86

Johnson, Lyndon B., 30, 77, 82, 83–90, 199–200, 240

Joliot-Curie, Irène, 261

Jones, Jim, 348–49

Jones, Leroi, 146

Jordan, Barbara, 197–206
  as college professor, 203–4
  oratorical skills of, 198–99, 200, 202–3, 204–5
  political career of, 200–203, 204
  as role model, 205–6
  as women's rights advocate, 204–5

journalists, 61, 62, 65, 78, 83, 84, 108, 133–37
  African American, 149–53
  Hispanic American, 157–65
  television, 149–53, 160–65

Joy Luck Club, The (Tan), 155–56

K

Kassebaum, Nancy, 341

Keep America Beautiful campaign, 89

Kelley, Florence, 306–7

Kelsey, Frances, 239

Kennedy, Caroline Bouvier, 79, 82

Kennedy, Jacqueline Bouvier, *see* Onassis, Jacqueline Bouvier Kennedy

Kennedy, John F., 76, 78–83, 94, 199–200
  assassination of, 82, 83, 84, 86–87
  foreign travel of, 81
  inauguration of, 57, 65
  1963 Nuclear Test Ban Treaty signed by, 62
  pesticides investigation ordered by, 247, 248

Kennedy, John Fitzgerald, Jr., 79

Kennedy, Rosario, 357

Khrushchev, Nikita, 82

King, Martin Luther King, Jr., 146, 192–93, 194

King, Stephen, 157

Kitchen God's Wife, The (Tan), 156, 157

Kleberg, Richard, 84

Klein, Margaret "Peg," 37

Knollwood retirement home, 76

Knox, Alexander, 57

Knox, Henry, 8

Korean War, 23, 24, 31

Ku Klux Klan, 185–86

L

Labor Department, U.S. 227, 228–29, 230, 359–62

Lady Bird Johnson Wildflower Center, 90

landmines, banning of, 324–34
   Ottawa Landmine Treaty, 330–33,
      334
   U.S. policy on, 332
Lansing, Robert, 55–56
Lasker Award, 240, 255, 273, 278, 285
Lathrop, Julia, 303–4
Lautenberg, Frank, 343
*Laws of Life, with Special Reference to
   the Physical Education of Girls, The*
   (Blackwell), 212
LBJ Foundation, 90
lead poisoning, 227–29
League of Nations, 51, 55, 60, 321–22
League of Women Voters, 61, 64
Lees, Carlton, 90
Legacy of the Parks program, 97
Lehman, Herbert H., 62
Leoncini, Consilia, 282
Levi, Giuseppe, 281, 282
Levi-Montalcini, Rita, 280–87
   nerve growth factor (NGF) isolated
      by, 283–84, 285, 287
   Nobel Prize of, 280, 285, 287
   publications of, 282, 287
   women's education foundation of,
      285–87
   in World War II, 281–83
Life of Susan B. Anthony, The (Harper),
   176
Light in the Piazza (Spencer), 125
Lincoln, Abraham, 17, 80, 83, 131, 294
Lloyd, Henry Demarest, 305
Loewi, Otto, 258
Loving, Walter, 49
Luce, Clare Boothe, 69
Ludington, Sybil, 2–4, 5
Luria, Salvador, 281
Lusitania, 53

MacArthur Foundation, 278
McCarthy, Carolyn, 364–65

McCarthy, Joseph, 74
McClintock, Barbara, 273–80
   awards of, 278
   at Cold Spring Harbor Laboratory,
      277–78, 280
   genetic mobility discovered by,
      279–80
   genetics training of, 274–76
   maize research of, 275, 276, 278–79
   Nobel Prize of, 278–79
McConnell, Mitch, 362
MacDowell, Carleton, 277
McKee, Fran, 35
McKernan, John R., Jr., 353
McKinley, William, 97, 314
Madison, Dolley Payne, 18, 40–45, 68,
   109
Madison, James, 18, 40–45, 80, 202
Malraux, André, 81
Mandela, Nelson, 196–97, 328
Marine Corps, U.S., 35, 37
Marshall, Thomas Riley, 55–56
Martin, Hattie, 11
Mayer, Joseph, 263–67
medicine, 207–54
   anesthesiology in, 250–54
   Apgar score in, 251–53
   biochemistry in, 256–62, 280–92
   first woman qualified in, xiii,
      207–15
   genetics in, 273–80
   neurological research in, 280–87
   Nobel laureates of, 241, 255,
      256–62, 268–92
   pediatric cardiology in, 234–40
   pharmaceutical research in, 287–92
   physics in, 270–73
   see also public health
Medicine as a Profession for Women
   (Blackwell and Blackwell), 213
Medico International, 326
Mellon, Rachel "Bunny," 80

Memoirs of a Soldier, Nurse and Spy
(Edmonds), 15–16
Mendel, Gregor, 276, 280
Mental Health Systems Act (1980),
106
Mexican-American War, xv, 10
Michel, Grace, 333
Mikulski, Barbara, 121, 184
military, U.S., 121–22, 125–26
integration of, 73, 187–88
military, women in, 1–38, 105
combat duty of, 2, 24, 25, 34–35, 37
issues of concern to, 2
medals awarded to, 28, 29
military occupational specialties
(MOS) of, 25
recruitment of, 25
star ranks achieved by, 1–2, 25,
30–38
"unisex weapons" and, 35
see also army nurses; *specific wars*
military academies, 1, 2, 37
military pensions, 9–10, 13, 15, 16
spousal benefits of, 50, 76, 122
milk, bacteria in, 231–33, 240
Milk, Harvey, 348–49
Miller, Merle, 69
Mitchell, George, 353
Mona Lisa (Leonardo), 81
Moncure, Henry, 45
Mondale, Walter, 349–50
Monroe, Elizabeth, 68
Monroe, James, 44
Montgomery Improvement
Association (MIA), 192–94
More, Eleanor Herron, 48
Morgan, Frances Tracy, 10
Morgan, J. P., Sr., 10
Morgan, Margaret Mary, 347
Morgan, Thomas Hund, 280
Morrison, Toni, 127, 144–48
awards of, 147

children's books of, 148
Nobel Prize of, 148
novels of, 146–48
Moscone, George, 347–49
Mott, James, 179, 180
Mott, John R., 323
Mott, Lucretia Coffin, 171, 177–81
as abolitionist, 180, 181
Seneca Falls Convention organized
by, 178–79, 180–81, 182
speeches of, 179–80, 181
Washington memorials to, 183–84
Moulson, Deborah, 167–68
Müller, Paul, 240–41
Murphy, Robert Cushman, 245–46
Murray, Joseph, 290–91
My Turn (Reagan), 112

— N —

Nacogdoches, Tex., xv
Nancy Reagan Afterschool Program,
112
Nast, Thomas, 135
Nation, Carry, 136
National Academy of Sciences, 267,
278
National American Woman Suffrage
Association, 173, 313
National Association for the
Advancement of Colored People
(NAACP), 64, 187, 189, 195, 313,
314
antisegregation lawsuit of, 190–94
National Book Award, 147, 248
National Book Festival, 125
National Book Foundation, 151
National Center for Voluntary Action,
96
National Child Protection Act (1993),
152
National Civic Federation, 50
National Consumers League, 307
National Council on the Arts, 147

National Cultural Center, 76
National Endowment for the Humanities and the Arts, 81
National League of Families of American POW-MIA, 111
National Literacy Act, 116
National Medal of Science, 273, 278
National Science Foundation, 261, 279, 284
National Woman Suffrage Association (NWSA), 173–75, 176, 181
Native American Rights, 364
Navy, U.S., 35, 36–37
Navy Nurse Corps, U.S., 35
Neall, Daniel, 180
Neill, Charles P., 227
nerve growth factor (NGF), 283–84, 285, 287
Neutral Conference for Continuous Mediation, 321
New England Female Medical College, 213, 214
New Orleans Times-Picayune, 134–37
    Pulitzer Prizes awarded to, 137
    women writers on, 135, 136–37
New York Infirmary for Women and Children, 212–13
Nicholson, George, 134, 135, 136, 137
Nineteenth Amendment, xiv, 175, 176, 177, 183, 232, 313
Nixon, Edgar Daniel "E.D.," 187, 190–91, 193, 194
Nixon, Pat Ryan, 77, 78, 85, 91–99, 105
Nixon, Richard M., 77, 92–99, 100, 110, 115, 278
Nobel Prize, xiv, 255–92
    for Literature, 142–43, 148
    for Peace, 142, 293, 334
    for Physics, 262–68
    for Physiology or Medicine, 241, 255, 256–62, 268–92
Noor, Queen of Jordan, 328

Novy, Frederick G., 220
Nuclear Test Ban Treaty (1963), 62
nystagmus, 227

O

O'Connor, Sandra Day, 95, 184
Office of Strategic Services (OSS), 28–29
Of Plymouth Plantation (Bradford), 6
Oliver, Sir Thomas, 226
Onassis, Jacqueline Bouvier Kennedy, 40, 51, 77–84, 89
    cultural projects of, 76, 82–83
    foreign travel of, 81, 82
    historic preservation projects of, 39, 80–81, 83
    journalism career of, 78, 83
    as presidential widow, 77, 82–83
    second marriage of, 83
    White House restoration project of, 79–80, 83, 84, 98
O'Neill, Tip, 340
Opacity Project, 265
Oprah Book Club, 151–52
Order of the British Empire (OBE), 28, 30
organ transplants, 237, 290–91
Osler, William, 222
Ottawa Landmine Treaty, 330–33, 334

P

Paget, James, 211
Paige, Rod, 121
Palmetto-Leaves (Stowe)
Parish, Susan "Susie" Ludlow, 60
Park, Edwards A., 235, 236
Parks, Raymond, 187, 195–96
Parks, Rosa, 184–97
    airbase job of, 187–88
    arrest of, 190–91
    awards of, 196
    bus boycott and, 191–92, 193–95
    institute established by, 196
    Ku Klux Klan threat and, 185–86

Mandela's tribute to, 196–97
memorials to, 197
Montgomery bus segregation defied by, 187–90, 196
in NAACP, 187, 189, 190–94, 195
public role of, 195–97
threats against, 195
trial and conviction of, 192, 195
Pasteur, Louis, 241
Paterson, John, 7–8
Patten, John Ed, 197
Patuxent Wildlife Research Center, 245
Peace Corps, 360–61
peace movement, 314–34
Pearl S. Buck Foundation, 143
Pearson, Judith, 30
pediatric cardiology, 234–40
Pendergast, Tom, 66
Pepper, Claude, 357
Perez, Carlos Andres, 95–96
Perkins, Frances, 230
Perkins, Mary, 167
Persian Gulf War, 35
pesticides, 240–50
DDT, 240–42, 245, 246, 248
pharmaceutical research, 287–92
Philippines, 47, 48, 49
Santo Tomas Interment Camp in, 21–23
Phillips, Susan, 32
Phillips, Wendell, 168, 181
phocomelia, 238–39
physics, 262–72
nuclear, 264–68, 270–73
Pocahontas, 52
Poitevent, Eliza Jane, 133–37
Picayune transformed by, 135–37
poems of, 133–34
Por, Orlando, 12
Prescott, Albert B., 219
Preserve America, 126

Presidential Medal of Freedom, 100, 196, 240
President's Commission on Mental Health, 106
Progressive Party, 176, 314
Prosser, Ichabod, 3
public health, 215–34, 309–10
bacteriology in, 220, 224, 228, 231–33, 240
juvenile cocaine addiction and, 225–26
occupational diseases in, *see* industrial toxicology
pesticides and, 240–50
prevention in, 240
tuberculosis and, 225
typhoid epidemics and, 224–25
public office, xiv, 64, 75, 96, 335–65
Pulitzer Prize, 137, 142, 158, 159–60
Purple Heart medal, 24

Quakers, 4–5, 40, 41, 166–68, 178–80, 181, 212, 230, 306, 309
equal status of women among, 166, 178–79, 210
Hicksite, 295–96
Quevedo, José, 158
Quintero, José Agustín, 134–35

radioimmunoassay (RIA) technique, 271–73
Radziwill, Lee, 79
Rains, Gabriel J., 326–27
Rake, Denis, 30
Randolph, James Madison, 41
Randolph, Martha, 41
Rayburn, Sam, 85
Reagan, Nancy Davis, 39, 40, 109–14
Reagan, Ronald, 95, 109–14, 115, 123, 273
Recollection of Full Years (Taft), 51
Refugees as Assets (Balch), 322

Reid, James 14–15
Reno, Janet, 119
Revere, Paul, 4, 8
Revere, Major Paul, 19
Revere family, 19–20
Rhoades, Marcus, 277
Ribicoff, Abraham, 248
Richards, Ann, 123, 204
Richman, Gerald, 357
Robbins, Jerome John, 14
Roberts, Cokie Boggs, 338, 342, 343
Roberts, Shawn, 329
Robinson, Jo Ann, 191
Rodriguez, Elliott, 165
Roe v. Wade, 95, 101
Rolfe, John, 52
Roosevelt, Alice Longworth, 60
Roosevelt, Eleanor, 57–65, 67, 68, 72,
    85, 109, 113, 337
    at Allenswood Academy, 58–59
    causes supported by, 57–58, 61,
        62–63, 64–65
    congressional testimony of, 106
    DAR membership resigned by, 63,
        69
    publications of, 62, 64, 65
    at United Nations, 64, 65, 112
Roosevelt, Franklin Delano, 51, 59–64,
    67, 337
Roosevelt, Sara Delano, 59, 60
Roosevelt, Theodore, 46–47, 50–51,
    60, 176, 314–15
Root, Elihu, 314–15
Rosa Parks Freedom Award, 196
Ros-Lehtinen, Ileana, 355–59
Roswit, Bernard, 270
Rusk, Thomas J., xv
Ryan, Leo J., 348
Ryan, William, Sr. 91

Sachs, Robert, 265
Salinas, María Elena, 160–65

Sampson, Deborah, 5–8
Saving Fish from Drowning (Tan), 157
Schlesinger, Arthur, 81
Sea Around Us, The (Carson), 242,
    243–44, 250
Sedgwick, William, 233–34
Sedgwick Memorial Medal, 234
Seelye, Linus H., 16–17
Selden, Henry, 173
Senate, U.S., 1, 55, 56, 66–67, 74, 86,
    152, 343
    pesticide hearings of, 248
    women in, 118, 121–22, 124–25,
        184, 341, 345–55, 364
Seneca Falls Convention, 169, 178–79,
    180–81, 182
Sense of Wonder, The (Carson), 244–45
settlement houses, 222, 293–324
    Denison House, 319
    Henry Street Settlement, 307
    justifications for, 308–9
    Toynbee Hall, 300–301, 308–9, 326
    see also Hull-House
Seward, William, 45
Shapiro, James, 279–80
shark repellant, 26
Shaw, Anna Howard, 176
Sher, Richard, 150
Sigman, Blanche F., 24
Sigmund, Barbara Boggs, 338, 340,
    343, 344
Silent Spring (Carson), 245–50
Sill, Anna P., 297
Silliman, Gold Selleck, 3
Silver Stars awards, 24
Simkhovitch, Valdimir, 323
Simmons, Ruth, 205–6
Simpson, James, Young, 212
6–mercaptopurine (6–MP), 289–90
Smith, Gerrit, 177
Smith, Margaret Chase, 353
Smith, Theobold, 232

Snowe, Olympia Bouchles, 351–55
social Darwinism, 298
Society of American Bacteriologists, 232
Song of Solomon (Morrison), 151
Souvestre, Marie, 58–59
Spanish-American War, 21
Spencer, Elizabeth, 125
Spencer, Herbert, 298
Stadler, Lewis, 276, 277
Stanton, Elizabeth Cady, 106, 143–44, 166, 177–84
    as abolitionist, 177–78
    Anthony's collaboration with, 169–70, 171, 172, 174–75, 181–82, 183
    Declaration of Sentiments of, 169, 178–79, 180, 181, 183
    1866 congressional campaign of, 183
    male relatives' disapproval of, 182
    marriage of, 170, 178, 182
    as married women's rights advocate, 182
    Mott's collaboration with, *see* Mott, Lucretia Coffin
    personality of, 169, 170–71, 183
    publications of, 182–83
    Seneca Falls Convention organized by, 169, 178–79, 180–81, 182
    Washington memorials to, 183–84
Stanton, Henry Brewster, 170, 177–78, 182
Starr, Ellen Gates, 222, 298, 300–302, 307
St. Clair, Marty, 291
Steele, Elaine Eason, 196
stem cell research, 113–14
Stern, Curt, 276, 279
Stevens, Alzina, 307
Stone, Lucy, 170, 173, 176, 216
Storrs, Anthony, 173
Stowe, Calvin Ellis, 129, 130, 132

Stowe, Charles Edward, 129, 130, 131, 133
Stowe, Harriet Beecher, 127–33, 210, 247
    biographers of, 133
    in Civil War years, 132
    Florida estate of, 132–33
    foreign travel of, 131–32
    novels of, xiv, 127, 130–31, 132
    siblings of, 128
Stride Toward Freedom (King), 194
Stuart, Gilbert, 43–44
Sula (Morrison), 147
Sumner, Charles, 317
Supreme Court, U.S., 46, 47, 51, 173, 174
    civil rights decisions of, 191, 192, 195
    women on, 95, 105, 184
sweatshops, 306

— T —

Taft, Charlie, 47, 51
Taft, Helen "Nellie" Herron, 46–51, 83, 89, 116
Taft, Robert, 51
Taft, William Howard, 46–51
Tan, Amy, xiv, 153–57
    children's books of, 157
    as "literary garage band" member, 157
    novels of, 155–56, 157
    stories of, 155
Task Force on National Health Care Reform, 120
Taussig, Helen, 234–40
    awards of, 240
    blue baby syndrome discovered by, 235–38, 239–40
    publications of, 237, 238, 239–40
    thalidomide warning of, 238–39
Taylor, Anna Mary, xv
Taylor, Zachary, 45

Teller, Edward, 265
temperance movement, 168, 169, 170, 177, 216
Texas, Republic of, xv
Texas Book Festival, 124, 125
thalidomide, 238–39
Thomas, Vivien, 236–37
Tilghman, Tench, 10
Todd, John Payne, 40, 45
Tolstoy, Leo, 145, 311–12
Tompkins, Sally, 21
Torres Martinez Desert Cahuilla Indians, 364
Toynbee, Arnold, 301
Toynbee Hall, 300–301, 308–9, 326
Train, George Francis, 172–73, 176
Truman, Elizabeth "Bess" Wallace, 65–70, 73
Truman, Harry S., 29, 65–70, 73, 76
Truman, Margaret, *see* Daniel, Margaret Truman
Tryon, William, 3–4
Tunnicliffe, Ruth, 224
Turow, Scott, 157
Tutu, Desmond, 328
Twain, Mark (Samuel Clemens), 132, 142
Tyler, John, 53

U

Udall, Stewart, 88
Uncle Tom's Cabin (Stowe), xiv, 127, 130–31, 132, 247
undulant fever (brucellosis), 231–33
United Nations, 64, 65, 76, 107, 115, 327–28
United Way, 361
Urey, Harold, 264–65

V

Van Lew, Elizabeth, 19–20
Vatican, 344
Vaught, Wilma L., 36
Velasquez, Loreta Janeta, 17–18

Verne, Jules, 172
Victoria, Queen of England, 80, 211
Vietnam Veterans of America Foundation, 326
Vietnam War, 32, 34, 90, 98, 100, 110–11
Vindication of the Rights of Woman, A (Wollstonecraft), 181
viscous rayon industry, 230
Vital Voices, 286
Voorhis, Jerry, 93
Voting Rights Act (1965) 338–39

W

"Waiting Between the Trees" (Tan), 155
Wald, Lillian, 307
Walker, Mary Edwards, 21
Wallace, Margaret Gates, 65, 70
Walsh, Richard, 140, 143
War of 1812, 10, 43–44
Warrington, Joseph, 210, 211
Washington, George, 4–5, 7, 39, 40, 41, 45, 58, 80
Stuart portrait of, 43–44
Washington, Martha, 42
Watson, James, 280
Waugh, Catherine, 298
Webster, Daniel, 45
Webster, James, 211
Weiner, Sandy, 347
Weisner, Jerome, 247
Welch, William, 222, 232
Welcome Home Adoption Program, 143
Welty, Eudora, 125
Western Female Institute, 129, 130
Westmoreland, William C., 33
Whipple, Allen, 251
White, Alice, 186
White, Dan, 348–49
White House, 32, 41–44, 46, 116, 131
children born in, 79

domestic management of, 62, 73, 74, 77

Easter egg rolls at, 75

first families' furnishings in, 42, 79–80

First Ladies' improvement of, 42–43, 68–69, 79–80, 83, 84, 89, 98, 111, 114, 120–21

honor guard of, 105

220th anniversary celebration of, 120–21

visitors to, 97–98

War of 1812 destruction of, 43–44

White House Conference on Aging, 107

White House Conference on Natural Beauty, 89

White House Diary, A (Lady Bird Johnson), 90

White House Fine Arts Committee, 79–80

White House Historical Association, 80

White House Salute to American Authors series, 125

Whiting, Leonard, 5

Wigner, Eugene Paul, 267

Wildflowers Across America (Johnson and Lees), 90

Willard, Emma, xiii, 167, 177

Williams, Jody, 324–34

    ICBL organized by, 326–30, 333–34

    Nobel Peace Prize of, 331, 333, 334

    publications of, 329, 334

Williams, Laura, 17

Wilson, Edith Bolling Galt, 52–57, 65

Wilson, E. O., 247

Wilson, Pete, 350

Wilson, Woodrow, 51, 52–57, 60, 321

Windaus, Adolf, 263

Winder, W. H., 43

Wines, Frederick, 307

Winfrey, Oprah, 149–53

Wise, Rabbi Stephen, 323

Wollstonecraft, Mary, 181

Wolves at the Door, The (Pearson), 30

Woman in Battle, The (Velasquez), 17

Woman's Loyal National League, 171

Woman's State Temperance Society, 169

women:

    Afghan, 124

    African, 152, 285–87

    African American, *see* African American women

    alcoholic, 102

    bravery of, 1

    Chinese, 138, 140–41, 142–43

    Chinese American, 153–57, 359–62

    discrimination against, 11, 18, 169, 178, 180, 201, 242, 255, 259–60, 268, 269, 277

    education for, xiii-xiv, 11, 84–85, 121, 128, 152, 177, 209, 285–87

    "masterless," 6

    in nineteenth-century teaching profession, 167

    as presidential candidates, 117, 118, 122, 173, 205

    Quaker, equal status of, 166, 178–79, 210

    restricted education of, 167, 177, 181, 207, 208, 256

    retirement security for, 343

    as single parents, 147, 219

    writing as career for, 133

"Women and the Constitution" conference, 105–6

Women at the Hague: The International Congress of Women and Its Results (Addams, Balch, and Hamilton), 305, 320

Women's Armed Services Act, 29

Women's Army Corps (WAC), 25, 33–34, 36

Women's Auxiliary Army Corps (WAAC), 33, 35
Women's Entrepreneurship in the 21st Century, 361–62
Women's Health Equity Act, 354
Women's International Committee for Permanent Peace, 320
Women's International League for Peace and Freedom (WILPF), 315, 321, 324
Women's Medical College, 213, 214, 299
Women's Peace Party, 315
Women's Research and Education Institute (WREI), 341
women's rights, 46, 168, 169, 172, 173, 182–83, 208, 298, 310–11, 313
    Buck's advocacy of, 143–44
    as economic issues, 341–43
    equal credit in, 341–42
    equal pay in, 168, 173, 179, 181, 260
    First Ladies' advocacy of, 61, 62, 64, 75, 95, 96, 105–6, 119, 120, 124–25
    Jordan's advocacy of, 204–5
    of married women, 170, 182
    to property, 169, 170, 182
women's rights conferences and conventions, 173, 176, 305, 315, 320, 321
    in Beijing, 120
    First Ladies at, 105–6, 120
    in Seneca Falls, 169, 178–79, 180–81, 182
    women's suffrage, 46, 51, 106, 128, 166–84, 216, 298, 308
    Addams' advocacy of, 312–13, 314
    black enfranchisement linked to, 171–72, 181
    Fourteenth Amendment vs., 171, 173

Sewell-Belmont House archives on, 183–84
state laws on, 175
    see also Anthony, Susan B.; Stanton, Elizabeth Cady
Woodhull, Victoria, 173
Wooster, David, 3, 4
World Anti-Slavery Convention (1840), 178
World Conference on Women (Beijing, 1995), 120
World Health Organization, 233
World War I, 21, 25, 60, 66, 257, 320–21
    landmines in, 327
    U.S. entry into, 54, 229, 314, 315
    Wilson and, 53–55
World War II, 21–30, 33–34, 35–36, 67, 68, 72, 85, 92–93, 243, 270
    army nurses in, 21–24, 31
    Balch's support of, 322–23
    Eleanor Roosevelt in, 63–64
    espionage in, 25–30
    Italy in, 281–83
    landmines in, 327
    women's employment opportunities in, 269, 288
Wright, Frank Lloyd, 305
Wright, Martha Coffin, 180

—X—

X Corps, U.S., 31

—Y—

Yalow, Rosalyn Sussman, 268–73
    marriage of, 270
    Nobel Prize of, 271, 272, 273
    physics training of, 268–70
    radioimmunoassay (RIA) technique of, 271–73
Young, Andrew, 146, 202

—Z—

Zakrewska, Marie, 212, 213, 219
Zhou Enlai, 96, 144